Tax and Financial Planning
for Professional Partnerships

Tax and Financial Planning for Professional Partnerships

THIRD EDITION

Nigel Eastaway
and
Brian Gilligan
*Partners in Moores Rowland,
Chartered Accountants*

Butterworths
London, Edinburgh and Dublin
1996

United Kingdom	Butterworths, a Division of Reed Elsevier (UK) Ltd, Halsbury House, 35 Chancery Lane, LONDON WC2A 1EL and 4 Hill Street, EDINBURGH EH2 3JZ
Australia	Butterworths Pty Ltd, SYDNEY, MELBOURNE, BRISBANE, ADELAIDE, PERTH, CANBERRA and HOBART
Canada	Butterworth Canada Ltd, TORONTO and VANCOUVER
Ireland	Butterworth (Ireland) Ltd, DUBLIN
Malaysia	Malayan Law Journal Sdn Bhd, KUALA LUMPUR
New Zealand	Butterworths of New Zealand Ltd, WELLINGTON and AUCKLAND
Singapore	Malayan Law Journal Pte Ltd, SINGAPORE
South Africa	Butterworth Publishers (PTY) Ltd, DURBAN
USA	Michie Butterworth, CHARLOTTESVILLE, Virginia

All rights reserved. No part of this publication may be reproduced in any material form (including photocopying or storing it in any medium by electronic means and whether or not transiently or incidentally to some other use of this publication) without the written permission of the copyright owner except in accordance with the provisions of the Copyright, Designs and Patents Act 1988 or under the terms of a licence issued by the Copyright Licensing Agency Ltd, 90 Tottenham Court Road, London, England W1P 9HE. Applications for the copyright owner's written permission to reproduce any part of this publication should be addressed to the publisher.

Warning: The doing of an unauthorised act in relation to a copyright work may result in both a civil claim for damages and criminal prosecution.

© Nigel Eastaway and Brian Gilligan 1996

A CIP Catalogue record for this book is available from the British Library

ISBN 0 406 02303 4

Typeset by Poole Typesetting, Bournemouth, Dorset
Printed and bound in Great Britain by Antony Rowe, Chippenham, Wiltshire

Preface

The purpose of this book is to explain a number of ways in which the tax liability of professional partnerships might be reduced to a minimum with effective planning and to suggest ways in which the financial and fiscal control of the partnership might be improved. It is not intended as a general textbook on partnership taxation. There is a concentration on the problems of medium-sized and small partnerships as large international practices have specialised problems of their own, which are outside the scope of this book.

Special attention has been given to the particular problems and advantages of partnerships and service companies in the main professions.

This third edition leads with the changes brought about by the Finance Acts 1994 and 1995, introducing self-assessment and the current year basis of assessment. These radical alterations represent the most fundamental change to partnership taxation for more than seventy years and are dealt with in some detail. The rules regarding basis periods and years of assessment under the old "previous year basis" are now contained in Appendix I.

We would like to thank our colleagues in Moores Rowland for their encouragement and assistance, and in particular to Nick Jenkins, Malcolm High and Clive Weeks for their assistance on Chapters 8, 10 and 13 respectively and to Edward Magrin and David Trill for their helpful and constructive comments to the text. We would also like to thank Ralph Ray BSc (Econ), FTII, Solicitor for his assistance in drafting the precedent Partnership Agreement and agreement for the transfer of a business to a company, Paul Gauntlett of Moores Marr Bradley Ltd for his contribution to Chapters 12 and 14, and Leslie Livens who made the original suggestion of expanding the New Law Cassette, "Tax Planning for Solicitors and Barristers", into the present work. We also wish to thank Mrs Celia Duncan and Mrs Debbie Thorne for typing and re-typing the manuscript until it eventually reached the final form.

The law is as stated at 1 September 1996.

Nigel Eastaway
Brian Gilligan
Clifford's Inn
London EC4

Contents

Preface		v
Table of Statutes		ix
Table of Cases		xv
Chapter 1	The nature of partnership	1
Chapter 2	The current year basis of assessment	5
Chapter 3	Taxable income and allowable expenditure	57
Chapter 4	The sole proprietor	69
Chapter 5	Cash basis	73
Chapter 6	Capital taxes	79
Chapter 7	Overseas activities	125
Chapter 8	Miscellaneous taxes	133
Chapter 9	The partnership agreement	135
Chapter 10	Service and associated trading companies	157
Chapter 11	Provision for retirement	181
Chapter 12	Financial control of partnerships	197
Chapter 13	Partnership insurance	217
Appendix I	The preceding year basis	231
Appendix II	Partnership changes under the preceding year basis	267
Index		277

Table of statutes

References in this Table to *Statutes* are to Halsbury's Statutes of England (Fourth Edition) showing the volume and page at which the annotated text of an Act may be found. Page references printed in **bold** type indicate where the Act is set out in part or in full.

Business Names Act 1985	143
s 4	135
(1)(a)(i)	2
(b)	2
(3)	2
Capital Allowances Act 1990 (43 *Statutes* 1115)	
s 3	252
22	66
24	66, 252
25	66
26(1)(b)	66, 165
34	66
35(2), (3)	66
37	253
39-41	66
51	67
60	66
67A	67
68-71	67
75	66, 82, 165, 253
76(5)	66
77	82, 141, 261
140(2)	23
(3)	23, 252
141	253
152	82, 253
(1)	82
154	253
157	253
(4)	261
158	82, 253, 261
(i)	253
Capital Allowances Act 1990—*contd.*	
s 160	246, 251
(5)	26
(6)	25
Sch AA1	67
para 4	67
Capital Gains Tax Act 1979	
s 59(a), (b)	120
123	178
Companies Act 1985 (8 *Statutes* 104)	169
s 88	170
Dentists Act 1957 (28 *Statutes* 251)	
s 38, 39	157
Employers' Liability (Compulsory Insurance) Act 1969 (16 *Statutes* 70)	219
Finance Act 1927	
s 55	170
Finance Act 1950 (42 *Statutes* 51)	
s 46	145
Finance Act 1958 (41 *Statutes* 273)	
s 34(4)	170, 170
Finance Act 1965 (42 *Statutes* 77)	
s 22(4)	121
Finance Act 1971 (13 *Statutes* 182)	
s 17	79
Finance Act 1985 (41 *Statutes* 369)	
s 47	241
82	134
85 (1)	134
Finance Act 1989	192
Finance Act 1991	
s 72	76
Finance Act 1993	
s 115	66

Table of statutes

Finance Act 1993—*contd.*
  Sch 13 66
Finance Act 1994................ 5
  s 93 98
    200 .... 28, 40
    205 13
    209(4), (5).................. 19
    211(2) 23, 70
    213(3)-(10) 25
  Sch 1
    para 2(4) 45
  Sch 12 115
  Sch 20
    para 1(2)(a), (b) 27, 28
      2(2) 27, 28, 29, 30, 31
        33, 39, 40, 41, 42, 47
        (a) 33
        (b) 27, 29, 30, 31, 33,
          39, 40, 41, 42, 47
        (4) 28, 29, 30, 31, 33,
          40, 42, 47, 51
        (4A), (4B) 31
        (5) 27, 28, 29, 30, 31, 32,
          33, 39, 40, 41, 42, 47, 50
      3(1) 26, 239
        (2) 31, 32
        (3), (4) 33
      4(2) 56
Finance Act 1995 (41 *Statutes* 484): 5
  s 33, 34 52
    39(2), (4).................. 52
    41 53
    58 183
    90 76
    117 .... 18, 38
    121 236
    126(7) 127
    140 76
  Sch 6..................... 52
    para 13, 19............... 53
  Sch 11..................... 183
  Sch 22.................... 38, 51
    para 1 38
      (2)(a) 40, 41, 50
      (b).............. 40, 41
      (3)................. 39
      (4)................ 40, 50
      (2)................. 50
      (4)(a), (b) 50
      3..................... 45
      (1)(b) 45, 47
      4................. 45, 46, 47
      5 .... 45, 51
      (2)................. 51

Finance Act 1995—*contd.*
  Sch 22–*contd.*
    para 6-8 50
      9..................... 54
      (1)(b) 55
      (2)................. 55
        (a) 54
      (3)................. 54
      10 54
      (3) 54
      13 38
      (2)................. 54
      14.................... 42
      (1)(a) 39
      15-17................. 44
      18.................... 54
      (1) 54
      19 55
      (2)(a), (b) 54
      20 .... 54, 55
Finance (No 2) Act 1992
  s 71........................ 163
Friendly Societies Act 1974
  (19 *Statutes* 49)............. 185
Income and Corporation Taxes
  Act 1988 (44 *Statutes* 1) 6
  s 5 .... 263, 264
    10(1) 163
    Schedule A 34, 38, 51, 52, 53,
      58, 59, 164, 259
  s 18 126
    Schedule D 2, 3, 4, 65, 128,
      186, 189, 234, 260, 264
    Case 1: 1, 3, 5, 34, 50, 52, 53, 57,
      59, 76, 125, 126, 144, 149,
      174, 179, 180, 185, 206,
      231, 233, 252, 257, 263
    Case II: 1, 3, 5, 34, 50, 52, 53, 57,
      58, 59, 76, 125, 126, 128,
      144, 149, 206, 231, 233,
      252, 257, 263
    Case III: 51, 54, 55, 58, 59, 126,
      144, 206, 259, 263
    Case IV: 34, 51, 54, 55, 259, 263
    Case V: 34, 50, 51, 53, 54, 55, 59,
      126, 127, 259, 263
    Case VI: 3, 34, 51, 52, 53, 59, 60
      76, 77, 174, 175, 180,
      259, 263
  s 19 130
    Schedule E 2, 3, 4, 58, 61, 66,
      130, 146, 162, 163, 186,
      189, 193, 234, 252
    Case I, II, III 130

Table of statutes

Income and Corporation Taxes Act
1988—*contd.*
s 21(2)	52
25	52
34	65, 259
35	259
36	259
60	231, 233, 247
(1)	10
(3)	11, 27, 28, 30, 31, 32, 33, 39, 40, 41, 42, 47, 247
(a)	7, 8, 9, 10, 11, 12, 14, 5, 17, 20, 21, 24, 38
(b)	7, 8, 9, 10, 11, 12, 14, 15, 16, 17, 18, 20, 21, 27, 28, 29, 30, 31, 33, 39, 40, 41, 42, 47, 84
(4)	35, 236, 245, 247, 248, 249, 250
(5)	7, 16, 20, 247, 248, 249, 250, 251
(6), (7)	235
61	11, 79, 233, 241
(1)	6, 7, 8, 9, 10, 11, 12, 14, 15, 16, 17, 18, 20, 21, 24, 37, 48
(2)	7, 8, 9, 11, 20, 21
(a)	9, 10, 11, 21, 37
(b)	16
(3)(a)	9, 10, 12, 15, 17
(b)	15, 18
62	12, 79, 84, 233, 236, 239, 241, 251
(2)	28, 84
(a)	13, 15, 29
(b)	14, 16
(3)(b)	18
(4)	28, 244
(5)	13, 14, 15, 16, 29
62A	12, 13, 14, 15, 20
63	31, 32, 80, 239, 241, 251
(1)(a)	32
(b)	18, 32
63A	8, 9, 10, 11, 13, 14, 15, 16, 17, 18, 21, 29, 30, 37, 38
(1)	13
(3)	32
64	55
65	53
(4)	127, 128
(5)-(9)	127
65A	53
67	236

Income and Corporation Taxes Act
1988 —*contd.*
s 72(2)	7
74	44, 50, 61, 69, 185, 219, 229
(a)	58
(g)	229
82	53, 63
83	65
84	63
87	64, 65
90	62
100	44, 75
(1)(b)	75
(1A)	75
(1C)-(1F)	76
101	44
(1)	175
(a), (b)	75, 174, 175
(2)	76, 174
102(2)	174
103	75, 76
104	74, 75, 76, 175
(1), (2),	175
(6)	174
105	76, 77
106	77
(2)	77, 175
107	76
108, 109	77
109A	76
(3), (5)	76
110	74
(2)	76
110A	126
111	1, 37, 125
(2)	34
(3)	34
(a)	47
(4)	34
(5)	18
(6)	34
(7)	34, 52, 59
(8)	34, 36, 37, 52
(9), (13)	38
112 (1)	127
(1A), (1B)	126
(5)	127
113	1, 74, 79, 127, 257, 258
(1)	80, 180, 257
(2)	47, 79, 80, 82, 84, 141, 234, 239, 241, 253, 258
114	179, 180
(3)	31

Table of statutes

Income and Corporation Taxes Act
1988—*contd.*
s 114(3)(b)	80, 180
115(5)	127
116	179
(2)(a)	180
117	258
125	178
132(2)	131
148	58
157	163, 229
162	162, 176
188(4), (5)	58
192	130
193	130, 131
(1)	130
194	131
198	65
239(6)	161
257BA, 257BB	257
288	258
294	115
338	178
348	262
349	63, 258, 262
350	63, 262
353	50, 51, 52, 63
359	207, 263
361	176
362	50, 64, 144, 147, 206
363	50, 64, 147, 206
379A	53
380	19, 76, 255, 257, 258, 259
(1)	19, 21, 257
(a)	20, 21
(b)	20, 21, 23
(2)	257
381	20, 21, 22, 60, 61, 70, 127, 259, 260
382(4)	22
383	70, 257, 259
384	257
385	20, 21, 257, 258
(1)	19
386	258, 261
387	258, 263
388	22, 259
390	261
392	19, 259
401	65
414	161, 176
(1)	176
416	45, 161
417	176
(3)	161

Income and Corporation Taxes Act
1988—*contd.*
s 417(3)(b)	176
520(4)(a)(ii)	26
577	65, 167
589A, 589B	65
590	190
601, 612	192
Pt XIV Ch III (ss 618-629)	140
s 619-622	183
623(2)	3, 59
(3)	182
625(3)	188
(b)	188
628	71, 90, 148, 185, 186
(2)	90, 186
Pt XIV Ch IV (ss 630-655)	140
s 630	181
631-636	181
637	181, 225
638 (2)	181, 189
639	181
640	181, 183
(3)	182
641	181
642	181
(4)	188
643	181
644	3, 181
(2)	59
645-653	181
656(1)	228
683	71, 186
703, 707	195
739, 740	129, 130
745	129
747	130
(4)	130
748-756, 765	130
770	219
779, 780	144
788(1)	125
786	59
790	125
824(1)	264
833(4)-(6)	3, 90
839	44, 55
840	45
Sch 6	163
Sch 12	
para 6	130
Sch 14	221
Sch 15	221
Sch 19	64

Table of statutes

Inheritance Tax Act 1984—*contd.*
  Sch 25 130
  Sch 26 130
Inheritance Tax Act 1984 (42 *Statutes* 603)
  s 10 . . . . 145, 223, 228
    (1) 89
  18 . . . . 142, 191
  19, 21 189
  43(2) 228
  56(4) 65, 92
  64, 65 . . . . 221, 223
  104(1)(a) 91, 92, 161
    (b) 92, 162
  105 . . . . 91, 92
    (1)(a) 91, 92, 161
    (c) 162
    (d) 92
    (2)(1)(a) 161
    (3)(1)(a) 161
  110(b), (c) **92**
  112(2) 93
  113 222
  151 . . . . 189, 190
  160 94
  161 193
  211 144
  227 94
    (7) 94
  234 94
  237(3) 144
  267 128
  270 . . . . 89, 142, 145
Limited Partnership Act 1907 (32 *Statutes* 662)
  s 6 3
Mental Health Act 1959 (28 *Statutes* 616) 140
Partnership Act 1890 (32 *Statutes* 635) 92, 141
  s 1 . . . . 1, 89
  2(1) 2
  4 89
    (2) 125, 143
  19 122
  20 89
  22 144
  24 89
    (1) 89, 149
  26 143
  27 3
  32-35 143

Partnership Act 1890—*contd.*
  39 2
  44 143
    (3)(b) 89
Social Security Contributions and Benefits Act 1992
  s 2 3
Social Security Pensions Act 1975 (40 *Statutes* 134)
  Sch 1A 189
  Sch 13 189
Stamp Act 1891 (41 *Statutes* 188)
  s 1 134
  54-61 170
  Sch 1 . . . . 134, 170
Taxation and Chargeable Gains Act 1992 (43 *Statutes* 1439) . . . 97, 98
  s 3 162
  12 128
  13 130
  18 103
  24(2) **116**, 119, 120, 121, 122, 145, 164
  35 . . . . 101, 103, 107
    (3)(d) 102
  36 101
  37(3) 105, 118, 145, 187
  38(1)(a), (b) 115
  42 100
  44 108
  53 115
  55(5) 102
  58 142
  59 . . . . **96**, 97, 121, 122
  80, 83, 85, 87, 91 130
  116 114
  152 . . . . 69, 105, 106, 107, 177, 178
  153 . . . . 105, 106, 107
    (1) 105
  154 . . . . 106, 107, 108, 164
  155-158 . . . . . 105, 106, 107, 164
  162 . . . . 109, 168, 170, 172, 173, 177, 178
    (1) 171, 178
    (3) 171
    (4) 177
  163, 164 . . . . . 69, 110, 143, 177
  164A-164N 69, 114
  165 . . . . 165, 172, 177, 178
  210 . . . . 221, 223, 225
  224 69
  253 62
  286 . . . . 89, 145
    (3) 100
    (4) **96**, 100, 103

Table of statutes

Taxation and Chargeable Gains Act
1992—*contd.*
Sch 2 107
   para 4, 18 107
Sch 3 101
   para 1 102
Sch 4 102
Sch 6 .... 69, 110, 143
   para 1 (2) 111
        10(3) 111
Sch 8 164
Sch 12 98
Taxes Management Act 1970
(42 *Statutes* 124) 5
s 12AA (2)-(5) 56
  12AB (1) 56
  42 .... 23, 252, 253
    (3) 117

Taxes Management Act 1970—*contd.*
s 55 264
   (3A) 264
  56 264
  86 264
   (3)(a), (aa) 264
   (b) 264
  118(3) 1
Value Added Tax Act 1994
(48 *Statutes* 669)
s 8 134
  45 134
Sch 5 134
Sch 8
  Group 7
    para 2(c) 134

Table of cases

Allied Newspapers Ltd v Hindsley (Inspector of Taxes) [1937] 2 All ER 663,
  21 TC 422, 81 Sol Jo 569; affd [1937] 4 All ER 677n, 21 TC 422, CA 64
Anderton (Inspector of Taxes) v Lamb [1981] STC 43, 55 TC 1, [1980] TR 393,
  124 Sol Jo 884; on appeal (1982) Times, 28 April, CA 107
Anderton and Halstead Ltd v Birrell (Inspector of Taxes) [1932] 1 KB 271,
  16 TC 200, 101 LJKB 219, [1931] All ER Rep 796, 146 LT 139 62
Anglo-French Exploration Co Ltd v Clayson (Inspector of Taxes) [1955]
  3 All ER 779, [1956] 1 WLR 1314, 36 TC 545, 34 ATC 298, 49 R & IT 73,
  [1955] TR 291, 99 Sol Jo 912, L(TC) 1753; affd [1956] 1 All ER 762,
  [1956] 1 WLR 325, 36 TC 545, 35 ATC 36, 49 R & IT 317, [1956] TR 37,
  100 Sol Jo 226, CA 57
Associated Restaurants Ltd v Warland (Inspector of Taxes)
  [1989] STC 273, 61 TC 51, CA 67
Atherton (Inspector of Taxes) v British Insulated and Helsby Cables Ltd
  [1925] 1 KB 421, 10 TC 155, 94 LJKB 319, 69 Sol Jo 103, 132 LT 288,
  41 TLR 55, CA; affd sub nom British Insulated and Helsby Cables Ltd
  v Atherton (Inspector of Taxes) [1926] AC 205, 10 TC 155, 4 ATC 47,
  95 LJKB 336, [1925] All ER Rep 623, 134 LT 289, 42 TLR 187, HL 63
Atkinson v Dancer [1988] STC 758, 61 TC 598, [1988] 34 LS Gaz R 50 110
A-G v Boden [1912] 1 KB 539, 81 LJKB 704, 105 LT 247 .... 90, 145,
                                                                        147
Ayrshire Pullman Motor Services and D M Ritchie v IRC (1929) 14 TC 754 .. 2

Back (Inspector of Taxes) v Whitlock [1932] 1 KB 747, 16 TC 723, 101 LJKB
  698, [1932] All ER Rep 241, 76 Sol Jo 272, 147 LT 172, 48 TLR 289 127
Barr, Crombie & Co v IRC (1945) 26 TC 406, 1945 SC 271 58
Benson (Inspector of Taxes) v Yard Arm Club Ltd [1979] 2 All ER 336,
  [1979] 1 WLR 347, [1979] STC 266, 53 TC 67, [1979] TR 1, 123 Sol Jo
  98, CA 66
Bentleys, Stokes and Lowless v Beeson (Inspector of Taxes) [1952] 2 All ER
  82, 33 TC 491, 31 ATC 229, 45 R & IT 461, [1952] TR 239, 96 Sol Jo 345,
  [1952] TLR 1529, CA 61
Berry (L G) Investments Ltd v Attwooll (Inspector of Taxes) [1964] 2 All ER
  126, [1964] 1 WLR 693, 41 TC 547, 43 ATC 61, [1964] TR 67, 108 Sol
  Jo 318 62
Blackburn (Inspector of Taxes) v Close Bros Ltd (1960) 39 TC 164, 39 ATC
  274, 53 R & IT 430, [1960] TR 161 58
Bond v Pittard (1838) 7 LJ Ex 78, 1 Horn & H 82, 2 Jur 183, 3 M & W 357 .. 2

Table of cases

Bowden (Inspector of Taxes) v Russell and Russell [1965] 2 All ER 258,[1965] 1 WLR 711, 42 TC 301, 44 ATC 74, [1965] TR 89, 109 Sol Jo 254 61
Bowie (Inspector of Taxes) v Reg Dunn (Builders) Ltd [1974] STC 234, 49 TC 469, 53 ATC 74, [1974] TR 77 57
Bristow (Inspector of Taxes) v William Dickinson & Co Ltd [1946] KB 321, 27 TC 157, 174 LT 310, 62 TLR 252, sub nom Dickinson (William) & Co Ltd v Bristow (Inspector of Taxes) [1946] 1 All ER 448, 25 ATC 43, 115 LJKB 296, CA 62
British-Borneo Petroleum Syndicate Ltd v Cropper (Inspector of Taxes) [1969] 1 All ER 104, [1968] 1 WLR 1701, 45 TC 201, 47 ATC 266, [1968] TR 255, 112 Sol Jo 804 57
Brown v IRC [1965] AC 244, [1964] 3 All ER 119, [1964] 3 WLR 511, 42 TC 42, 43 ATC 244, [1964] TR 269, 108 Sol Jo 636, 192 Estates Gazette 457, 1964 SC (HL) 180, 1964 SLT 302, HL 59
Brown v Tapscott (1840) 9 LJ Ex 139, 6 M & W 119 2
Bucks v Bowers (Inspector of Taxes) [1970] Ch 431, [1970] 2 All ER 202, [1970] 2 WLR 676, 46 TC 267, 48 ATC 588, [1969] TR 559, 114 Sol Jo 15: 142
Bulloch (Alexander) & Co v IRC [1976] STC 514, 51 TC 563, [1976] TR 201: 2, 142

Caillebotte (Inspector of Taxes) v Quinn [1975] 2 All ER 412, [1975] 1 WLR 731, [1975] STC 265, 50 TC 222, 54 ATC 61, [1975] TR 55, 119 Sol Jo 356 61
Calder v Allanson (1935) 19 TC 293 2
Californian Copper Syndicate Ltd v Inland Revenue (Harris, Surveyor of Taxes) (1904) 5 TC 159, 6 F 894 57
Campbell Connelly & Co Ltd v Barnett (Inspector of Taxes) [1994] STC 50, 66 TC 380, CA 107
Carr (Inspector of Taxes) v Sayer [1992] STC 396, 65 TC 15 66
Carson (Inspector of Taxes) v Cheyney's Executor [1959] AC 412, [1958] 3 All ER 573, [1958] 3 WLR 740, 38 TC 240, 37 ATC 347, 51 R & IT 824, [1958] TR 349, 102 Sol Jo 955, HL 75
Carter (Inspector of Taxes) v Sharon [1936] 1 All ER 720, 20 TC 229, 80 Sol Jo 511 127
Chancery Lane Safe Deposit and Offices Co Ltd v IRC [1966] AC 85, [1966] 1 All ER 1, [1966] 2 WLR 251, 43 TC 83, 44 ATC 450, [1965] TR 433, 110 Sol Jo 35, 197 Estates Gazette 13, L(TC) 2172, HL ... 61
Chetwode (Lord) v IRC [1977] 1 All ER 638, [1977] 1 WLR 248, [1977] STC 64, 51 TC 647, [1977] TR 11, 121 Sol Jo 172, L(TC) 2632, HL 129
Chibbett v Joseph Robinson & Sons (1924) 9 TC 48, [1924] All ER Rep 684, 132 LT 26 58
Clarke (J H) & Co Ltd v Musker (Inspector of Taxes) (1956) 37 TC 1, 35 ATC 297, 49 R & IT 574, [1956] TR 261, L(TC) 1796 63
Clinch v IRC [1974] QB 76, [1973] 1 All ER 977, [1973] 2 WLR 862, [1973] STC 155, 49 TC 52, 52 ATC 201, [1973] TR 157, 117 Sol Jo 342 ... 129
Cole Bros Ltd v Phillips (Inspector of Taxes) [1982] 2 All ER 247, [1982] 1 WLR 1450, [1982] STC 307, 55 TC 188, 126 Sol Jo 709, HL 67
Colquhoun v Brooks (1889) 14 App Cas 493, 2 TC 490, 54 JP 277, 59 LJQB 53, 38 WR 289, [1886-90] All ER Rep 1063, 61 LT 518, 5 TLR 728, HL 125
Connelly (C) & Co v Wilbey (Inspector of Taxes) [1992] STC 783, 65 TC 208: 272

Table of cases

Cooke (Inspector of Taxes) v Beach Station Caravans Ltd [1974] 3 All ER 159, [1974] 1 WLR 1398, [1974] STC 402, 49 TC 514, 53 ATC 216, [1975] RA 360, [1974] TR 213, 118 Sol Jo 777, L(TC) 2524 66

Cooper (Inspector of Taxes) v Stubbs [1925] 2 KB 753, 10 TC 29, 94 LJKB 903, [1925] All ER Rep 643, 69 Sol Jo 743, 133 LT 582, 41 TLR 614, CA 60

Copeman (Inspector of Taxes) v William Flood & Sons Ltd [1941] 1 KB 202, 24 TC 53, 19 ATC 521, 110 LJKB 215 .... 62, 69

Cottingham's Executors v IRC [1938] 2 KB 689, [1938] 3 All ER 560, 22 TC 344, 10 LJKB 623, 82 Sol Jo 761, 159 LT 519; affd [1939] 1 KB 250, [1938] 4 All ER 663n, 22 TC 344, 108 LJKB 223, 83 Sol Jo 14, 160 LT 7, CA 129

Cowcher (Inspector of Taxes) v Mills & Co Ltd (1927) 13 TC 216 64

Customs & Excise Comrs v Exeter Golf and Country Club Ltd [1980] STC 162; affd sub nom Exeter Golf and Country Club Ltd v Customs and Excise Comrs [1981] STC 211, CA 60

Customs and Excise Comrs v Glassborow (t/a Bertram & Co) [1975] QB 465, [1974] 2 WLR 851, sub nom Customs and Excise Comrs v Glassborow [1974] 1 All ER 1041, [1974] STC 142, [1974] TR 161, 118 Sol Jo 170 ... 133, 143

Davies (Inspector of Taxes) v Braithwaite [1931] 2 KB 628, 18 TC 198, 10 ATC 286, 100 LJKB 619, [1931] All ER Rep 792, 75 Sol Jo 526, 145 LT 693, 47 TLR 479 .... 57, 125

Devon Mutual SS Insurance Association v Ogg (Inspector of Taxes) (1927) 13 TC 184 62

de Walden (Lord Howard) v IRC [1942] 1 KB 389, [1942] 1 All ER 287, 25 TC 121, 111 LJKB 273, CA 129

Dickenson v Gross (Inspector of Taxes) (1927) 11 TC 614, 137 LT 351 2

Dixon (Inspector of Taxes) v Fitch's Garage Ltd [1975] 3 All ER 455, [1976] 1 WLR 215, [1975] STC 480, 50 TC 509, 54 ATC 151, [1975] TR 123, 119 Sol Jo 628, L(TC) 2569 66

Dodd and Tanfield v Haddock (Inspector of Taxes) (1964) 42 TC 229, 42 ATC 130, [1963] TR 117 2

Dollar (t/a I J Dollar) v Lyon (Inspector of Taxes) [1981] STC 333, 54 TC 459: 69

Dreyfus v IRC (1929) 14 TC 560, CA 92

Earlspring Properties Ltd v Guest (Inspector of Taxes) [1993] STC 473; affd [1995] STC 479, CA 62, 69

Edwards (Inspector of Taxes) v Bairstow and Harrison [1956] AC 14, [1955] 3 All ER 48, [1955] 3 WLR 410, 36 TC 207, 34 ATC 198, 48 R & IT 534, [1955] TR 209, 99 Sol Jo 558, L(TC) 1742, HL 57

Edwards (Inspector of Taxes) v Warmsley Henshall & Co [1968] 1 All ER 1089, 44 TC 431, 46 ATC 431, [1967] TR 409 65

Ellis (Inspector of Taxes) v Lucas [1967] Ch 858, [1966] 2 All ER 935, [1966] 3 WLR 382, 43 TC 276, 45 ATC 90, [1966] TR 87, 110 Sol Jo 605 58

English Crown Spelter Co Ltd v Baker (Surveyor of Taxes) (1908) 5 TC 327, 99 LT 353 62

Erichsen v Last (1881) 1 TC 351; affd (1881) 8 QBD 414, 4 TC 422, 46 JP 357, 51 LJQB 86, 30 WR 301, 45 LT 703, CA 126

Farmer (Surveyor of Taxes) v Scottish North American Trust Ltd [1912] AC 118, 5 TC 693, 81 LJPC 81, 105 LT 833, 28 TLR 142, HL 63

Table of cases

Farrell (Surveyor of Taxes) v Sunderland SS Co Ltd (1903) 4 TC 605, 67 JP 209, 9 Asp MLC 416, 88 LT 741	2
Fenston v Johnstone (1940) 23 TC 29, 84 Sol Jo 305	2, 3
Ferguson's Trustees v Donovan [1929] IR 489, SC	125
Findlay's Trustees v IRC (1938) 22 ATC 437	94
Firestone Tyre and Rubber Co Ltd v Llewellin (Inspector of Taxes) [1957] 1 All ER 561, [1957] 1 WLR 464, 37 TC 111, 50 R & IT 172, 101 Sol Jo 228, HL	126
Furniss (Inspector of Taxes) v Dawson [1984] AC 474, [1984] 1 All ER 530, [1984] 2 WLR 226, [1984] STC 153, 55 TC 324, 128 Sol Jo 132, HL	219
Gallagher v Jones (Inspector of Taxes) [1994] Ch 107, [1994] 2 WLR 160, [1993] STC 537, 66 TC 77, [1993] 32 LS Gaz R 40, CA	61, 62
Gardner (John) & Bowring, Hardy & Co Ltd v IRC (1930) 15 TC 602	1, 2
Gaunt v IRC [1913] 3 KB 395, 7 TC 219, 82 LJKB 1131, 109 LT 555	231
Glasgow Heritable Trust Ltd v IRC (1954) 35 TC 196, 33 ATC 145, 47 R & IT 127, L(TC) 1688, 1954 SC 266, 1954 SLT 97	57
Glenboig Union Fireclay Co Ltd v IRC (1922) 12 TC 427, 1 ATC 142, 59 SLR 162, 1922 SC (HL) 112	58
Gordon v IRC [1991] STC 174, 64 TC 173	108, 109
Gray (Inspector of Taxes) v Seymours Garden Centre (Horticulture) (a firm) [1993] 2 All ER 809, [1993] STC 354; affd [1995] STC 706, [1995] 30 LS Gaz R 35, CA	66
Gray & Co Ltd v Murphy (Inspector of Taxes) (1940) 23 TC 225	228
Gubay v Kington (Inspector of Taxes) [1984] 1 All ER 513, [1984] 1 WLR 163, [1984] STC 99, 57 TC 601, 128 Sol Jo 100, [1984] LS Gaz R 900, HL	126
Hale v Shea (Inspector of Taxes) [1965] 1 All ER 155, [1965] 1 WLR 290, 42 TC 260, 43 ATC 448, [1964] TR 413, 109 Sol Jo 12	185
Hall (Inspector of Taxes) v Lorimer [1994] 1 All ER 250, [1994] 1 WLR 209, [1994] STC 23, 66 TC 349, [1994] ICR 218, [1994] IRLR 171, [1993] 45 LS Gaz R 45, 137 Sol Jo LB 256, CA	3
Hall (George) & Sons v Platt (Inspector of Taxes) (1954) 35 TC 440, 33 ATC 340, 47 R & IT 713, [1954] TR 331, 164 Estates Gazette 497, L(TC) 1711	2
Hampton (Inspector of Taxes) v Fortes Autogrill Ltd [1980] STC 80, 53 TC 691, [1979] TR 377	66
Harmel v Wright (Inspector of Taxes) [1974] 1 All ER 945, [1974] 1 WLR 325, [1974] STC 88, 49 TC 149, 52 ATC 335, 118 Sol Jo 170, L(TC) 2504	127
Harrison (Inspector of Taxes) v Willis Bros (Willis and Executors of Willis) [1966] Ch 619, [1965] 3 All ER 753, [1966] 2 WLR 183, 43 TC 61, 109 Sol Jo 875, sub nom Willis and Willis Executors v Harrison 44 ATC 343, [1965] TR 345, CA	1
Hart (Inspector of Taxes) v Sangster [1957] Ch 329, [1957] 2 All ER 208, [1957] 2 WLR 812, 37 TC 231, 36 ATC 63, 50 R & IT 349, [1957] TR 73, 101 Sol Jo 356, CA	54
Hawker v Compton (1922) 8 TC 306	2
Hinton (Inspector of Taxes) v Maden and Ireland Ltd [1959] 3 All ER 356, [1959] 1 WLR 875, 38 TC 391, 38 ATC 231, 52 R & IT 688, [1959] TR 233, 103 Sol Jo 812, L(TC) 1913, HL	66

Table of cases

Horton v Young (Inspector of Taxes) [1972] Ch 157, [1971] 3 All ER 412, [1971] 3 WLR 348, 47 TC 60, 50 ATC 207, [1971] TR 181, 115 Sol Jo 388, CA	65
Hoye (Inspector of Taxes) v Forsdyke [1981] 1 WLR 1442, [1981] STC 711, 55 TC 281, 125 Sol Jo 514	131
Hugh v Rogers (Inspector of Taxes) (1958) 38 TC 270, 37 ATC 412, 52 R & IT 140, [1958] TR 369	60
Hume (Inspector of Taxes) v Asquith [1969] 2 Ch 58, [1969] 1 All ER 868, 45 TC 251, 47 ATC 377, [1968] TR 369, 112 Sol Jo 947, sub nom Home (Inspector of Taxes) v Asquith [1969] 2 WLR 225	75
Humphries & Co v Cook (Inspector of Taxes) (1934) 19 TC 121	271
Hunt (Inspector of Taxes) v Henry Quick Ltd [1992] STC 633, 65 TC 108, [1992] 31 LS Gaz R 39	66, 67
Income Tax General Purposes Comrs for City of London v Gibbs [1942] AC 402, [1942] 1 All ER 415, 24 TC 221, 111 LJKB 301, 86 Sol Jo 147, sub nom IRC v Gibbs 166 LT 345, HL	1
IRC v Barclay Curle & Co Ltd [1969] 1 All ER 732, [1969] 1 WLR 675, [1969] 1 Lloyd's Rep 169, 45 TC 221, 48 ATC 17, [1969] TR 21, 113 Sol Jo 244, [1969] RVR 102, 1969 SC (HL) 30, 1969 SLT 122, HL	66
IRC v Brander and Cruickshank [1971] 1 All ER 36, [1971] 1 WLR 212, 46 TC 574, 49 ATC 374, [1970] TR 353, 115 Sol Jo 79, 1971 SC (HL) 30, 1971 SLT 53	58
IRC v D Devine & Sons Ltd (1963) 41 TC 210, 42 ATC 358, [1963] TR 381, CA	110
IRC v David C MacDonald (1955) 36 TC 388, 34 ATC 340, 49 R & IT 152, [1955] TR 331, L(TC) 1757	57
IRC v Falkirk Iron Co Ltd (1933) 17 TC 625, 1933 SC 546, 1933 SLT 283	64
IRC v Graham's Trustees [1970] TR 343, [1971] RVR 303, 1971 SC 1, 1971 SLT 46, HL	1
IRC v Helical Bar Ltd [1972] AC 773, [1972] 1 All ER 1205, [1972] 2 WLR 880, 48 TC 221, 51 ATC 1, [1972] TR 1, 116 Sol Jo 276, HL	245
IRC v Land Securities Investment Trust Ltd [1969] 2 All ER 430, [1969] 1 WLR 604, 45 TC 495, 48 ATC 185, [1969] TR 173, 113 Sol Jo 407, 211 Estates Gazette 405, HL	64
IRC v Morrison (1932) 17 TC 325, 1932 SC 638, 1932 SLT 441	74
IRC v Scott Adamson (1932) 17 TC 679, 11 ATC 481, 1933 SC 23, 1933 SLT 33	254
IRC v Scottish and Newcastle Breweries Ltd [1982] 2 All ER 230, [1982] 1 WLR 322, [1982] STC 296, 55 TC 252, 126 Sol Jo 189, 1982 SLT 407, HL	67
IRC v Toll Property Co Ltd (1952) 34 TC 13, 31 ATC 322, 45 R & IT 574, [1952] TR 303, L(TC) 1608, 1952 SC 387, 1952 SLT 371	57
IRC v William Sharp & Son (1959) 38 TC 341, 38 ATC 18, 52 R & IT 534, [1959] TR 21, 1959 SLT 78	64
IRC v Williamson (1928) 14 TC 335	1
Jackson (Inspector of Taxes) v Laskers Home Furnishers Ltd [1956] 3 All ER 891, [1957] 1 WLR 69, 37 TC 69, 35 ATC 469, 50 R & IT 48, [1956] TR 391, 101 Sol Jo 44, 168 Estates Gazette 584, L(TC) 1805	64

Table of cases

Jarrold (Inspector of Taxes) v John Good & Sons Ltd [1962] 2 All ER 971, [1962] 1 WLR 1101, 40 TC 681, 41 ATC 170, [1962] RA 273, 9 RRC 188, [1962] TR 181, 106 Sol Jo 688, [1962] RVR 653; affd [1963] 1 All ER 141, [1963] 1 WLR 214, 40 TC 681, 41 ATC 335, [1962] RA 681, 9 RRC 270, [1962] TR 371, 107 Sol Jo 153, [1963] RVR 25, CA	66
Johnson Bros & Co v IRC [1919] 2 KB 717, 12 TC 147, 89 LJKB 94, 121 LT 643	69
Johnston (Inspector of Taxes) v Britannia Airways Ltd [1994] STC 763	61, 64
Jones (Samuel) & Co (Devonvale) Ltd v IRC (1951) 32 TC 513, 30 ATC 412, [1951] TR 411, L(TC) 1569, 1952 SC 94, 1952 SLT 144	64
Keir & Cawder Ltd v IRC (1958) 38 TC 23, 37 ATC 17, 51 R & IT 367, [1958] TR 13, L(TC) 1858, 1958 SC 189, 1958 SLT 86	228
Kirkham v Williams (Inspector of Taxes) [1991] 1 WLR 863, [1991] STC 342, CA	57
Kneen (Inspector of Taxes) v Martin [1935] 1 KB 499, 19 TC 33, 13 ATC 454, 104 LJKB 361, [1934] All ER Rep 595, 79 Sol Jo 31, 152 LT 337, CA	126, 127
Law Shipping Co Ltd v IRC (1923) 12 TC 621, 3 ATC 110, 1924 SC 74	64
Lawrence (Inspector of Taxes) v Ridsdale [1976] STC 227, 51 TC 376, [1976] TR 45, 120 Sol Jo 302, L(TC) 2580	121
Leeds Pemanent Building Society v Procter (Inspector of Taxes) [1982] 3 All ER 925, [1982] STC 821, 56 TC 293	67
Lewis v IRC [1933] 2 KB 557, 18 TC 174, 103 LJKB 689, 149 LT 511, CA	231
Lingen v Simpson (1824) 1 Sim & St 600	89, 92
London Bank of Mexico and South America v Apthorpe (Surveyor of Taxes) [1891] 2 QB 378, 3 TC 143, 56 JP 86, 60 LJQB 653, 39 WR 564, 65 LT 601, 7 TLR 567, CA	125
Lyons (J) & Co Ltd v A-G [1944] Ch 281, [1944] 1 All ER 477, 113 LJ Ch 196, 88 Sol Jo 161, 170 LT 348, 60 TLR 313	67
McCash and Hunter v IRC (1955) 36 TC 170, 34 ATC 113, 48 R & IT 366, [1955] TR 117, L(TC) 1728	73
McGowan (Inspector of Taxes) v Brown and Cousins (trading as Stuart Edwards) [1977] 3 All ER 844, [1977] 1 WLR 1403, [1977] STC 342, 52 TC 8, [1977] TR 183, 121 Sol Jo 645, 244 Estates Gazette 133, L(TC) 2650	58
McGregor (Inspector of Taxes) v Adcock [1977] 3 All ER 65, [1977] 1 WLR 864, [1977] STC 206, 51 TC 692, [1977] TR 23, 121 Sol Jo 240, 242 Estates Gazette 289, L(TC) 2633	110
McKie v Luck (1925) 9 TC 511	2
MacKinlay (Inspector of Taxes) v Arthur Young McClelland Moores & Co [1990] 2 AC 239, [1990] 1 All ER 45, [1989] 3 WLR 1245, [1989] STC 898, 134 Sol Jo 22, HL	61
Mallalieu v Drummond (Inspector of Taxes) [1983] 2 AC 861, [1983] 2 All ER 1095, [1983] 3 WLR 409, [1983] STC 665, 57 TC 330, 127 Sol Jo 538, HL	61
Mannion (Inspector of Taxes) v Johnston [1988] STC 758, 61 TC 598	110
Marshall Hus & Partners Ltd v Bolton (Inspector of Taxes) [1981] STC 18, 55 TC 539, [1980] TR 371, L(TC) 2804	7

Table of cases

Marson (Inspector of Taxes) v Morton [1986] 1 WLR 1343, [1986] STC 463,
59 TC 381, 130 Sol Jo 731, [1986] LS Gaz R 3161 57
Mason v Tyson (Inspector of Taxes) [1980] STC 284, 53 TC 333, [1980] TR 23,
124 Sol Jo 206 61
Mason (Inspector of Taxes) v Innes [1967] Ch 1079, [1967] 2 All ER 926,
[1967] 3 WLR 816, 44 TC 326, 46 ATC 143, [1967] TR 135, 111 Sol Jo 376,
CA 58, 59
Meyer & Co v Faber (No 2) [1923] 2 Ch 421, 93 LJ Ch 17, 67 Sol Jo 576,
129 LT 490, 39 TLR 550, CA 89
Minister of National Revenue v Anaconda American Brass Ltd [1956] AC 85,
[1956] 1 All ER 20, [1956] 2 WLR 31, 34 ATC 330, 49 R & IT 333, [1955]
TR 339, 100 Sol Jo 10, 2 DLR (2d) 1, PC 61
Mitchell (Inspector of Taxes) v B W Noble Ltd [1927] 1 KB 719, 96 LJKB 484,
[1927] All ER Rep 717, 71 Sol Jo 175, 137 LT 33, 43 TLR 245, sub nom
B W Noble Ltd v Mitchell (Inspector of Taxes) 11 TC 372, 43 TLR 102,
CA 62
Morden Rigg & Co and R B Eskrigge & Co v Monks (Inspector of Taxes)
(1923) 8 TC 450, CA 2
Munby v Furlong (Inspector of Taxes) [1977] Ch 359, [1977] 2 All ER 953,
[1977] 3 WLR 270, [1977] STC 232, 50 TC 491, [1977] TR 121, 141 JP 518,
121 Sol Jo 87, L(TC) 2643, CA 66
Murgatroyd (Inspector of Taxes) v Evans-Jackson [1967] 1 All ER 881, [1967]
1 WLR 423, 43 TC 581, 45 ATC 419, [1966] TR 341, 110 Sol Jo 926 ..... 61, 229
Murray (Inspector of Taxes) v Goodhews [1978] 2 All ER 40, [1978] 1 WLR 499,
[1978] STC 207, 52 TC 86, [1977] TR 255, 121 Sol Jo 832, L(TC) 2665,
CA 58

Neubergh v IRC [1978] STC 181, [1977] TR 263, L(TC) 2655 126
Newsom v Robertson (Inspector of Taxes) [1953] Ch 7, [1952] 2 All ER 728,
33 TC 452, 31 ATC 429, 45 R & IT 679, [1952] TR 401, 96 Sol Jo 696,
[1952] 2 TLR 636, L(TC) 1622, CA 65
Newstead (Inspector of Taxes) v Frost [1980] 1 All ER 363, [1980] 1 WLR 135,
[1980] STC 123, 53 TC 525, [1980] TR 1, 124 Sol Jo 116, L(TC) 2774, 130
NLJ 136, HL 128
Nolder (Inspector of Taxes) v Walters (1930) 15 TC 380, 9 ATC 251, 47 Sol
Jo 337, 46 TLR 397 .... 61, 69
Norman v Golder (Inspector of Taxes) [1945] 1 All ER 352, 26 TC 293,
114 LJKB 108, 171 LT 369, CA 61, 229
Northend (Inspector of Taxes) v White & Leonard and Corbin Greener (a firm)
[1975] 2 All ER 481, [1975] 1 WLR 1037, [1975] STC 317, 50 TC 121, 119
Sol Jo 188, L(TC) 2552, sub nom Northend (Inspector of Taxes) v Beveridge's
Executors 54 ATC 66, [1975] TR 65 59

O'Brien (Inspector of Taxes) v Benson's Hosiery (Holdings) Ltd [1977]
Ch 348, [1977] 3 All ER 352, [1977] 3 WLR 206, [1977] STC 262,
53 TC 241, [1977] TR 111, 121 Sol Jo 376; on appeal [1979] Ch 152,
[1978] 3 All ER 1057, [1978] 3 WLR 609, [1978] STC 549, 53 TC 241,
[1978] TR 147, 122 Sol Jo 439, CA; revsd [1980] AC 562, [1979] 3 All
ER 652, [1979] 3 WLR 572, [1979] STC 735, 53 TC 241, [1979] TR 335,
123 Sol Jo 752, HL 121

Table of cases

O'Culachain v McMullan Bros [1990] 1 IR 363	66
Odeon Associated Theatres Ltd v Jones (Inspector of Taxes) [1971] 2 All ER 407, [1971] 1 WLR 442, 48 TC 257, 49 ATC 315, [1970] TR 299, 115 Sol Jo 224, 218 Estates Gazette 1005; affd [1973] Ch 288, [1972] 1 All ER 681, [1972] 2 WLR 331, 48 TC 257, 50 ATC 398, [1971] TR 373, 115 Sol Jo 850, 221 Estates Gazette 1270, CA	61, 64
Ogilvie v Kitton (Surveyor of Taxes) (1908) 5 TC 338, 1908 SC 1003	125
O'Grady (Inspector of Taxes) v Bullcroft Main Collieries Ltd (1932) 17 TC 93	64
Ostime (Inspector of Taxes) v Australian Mutual Provident Society [1960] AC 459, [1959] 3 All ER 245, [1959] 3 WLR 410, 38 TC 492, 38 ATC 219, 52 R & IT 673, [1959] TR 211, 103 Sol Jo 811, HL	125
Owen v Southern Rly Co of Peru Ltd (1954) 36 TC 602; on appeal (1955) 36 TC 602, CA; on appeal sub nom Southern Rly of Peru Ltd v Owen (Inspector of Taxes) [1957] AC 334, [1956] 2 All ER 728, [1956] 3 WLR 389, 36 TC 602, 32 ATC 147, 49 R & IT 468, [1956] TR 197, 100 Sol Jo 527, L(TC) 1778, HL	61, 64
Patrick (Inspector of Taxes) v Broadstone Mills Ltd [1954] 1 All ER 163, [1954] 1 WLR 158, 35 TC 44, 32 ATC 464, 47 R & IT 41, [1953] TR 441, 98 Sol Jo 43, L(TC) 1675, CA	61
Pegler v Abell (Inspector of Taxes) [1973] 1 All ER 52, [1973] 1 WLR 155, [1973] STC 23, 48 TC 564, [1972] TR 261, 116 Sol Jo 192	71
Pepper (Inspector of Taxes) v Daffurn [1993] STC 466, 66 TC 68, [1993] 2 EGLR 199, [1993] 32 LS Gaz R 40, [1993] 41 EG 184	110
Petrotim Securities Ltd (formerly Gresham Trust Ltd) v Ayres (Inspector of Taxes) [1964] 1 All ER 269, [1964] 1 WLR 190, 41 TC 389, 42 ATC 421, [1963] TR 397, 107 Sol Jo 908, CA	58, 160
Philippi v IRC [1971] 3 All ER 61, [1971] 1 WLR 684, 47 TC 75, 50 ATC 16, [1971] TR 17, 115 Sol Jo 189, L(TC) 2381; affd [1971] 3 All ER 61, [1971] 1 WLR 1272, 47 TC 75, 50 ATC 37, [1971] TR 167, 115 Sol Jo 427, L(TC) 2404, CA	129
Pommery and Greno v Apthorpe (Surveyor of Taxes) (1886) 2 TC 182, 56 LJQB 155, 35 WR 307, 56 LT 24, 3 TLR 242	126
Pratt v Strick (Inspector of Taxes) (1932) 17 TC 459	2
Prince v Mapp (Inspector of Taxes) [1970] 1 All ER 519, [1970] 2 WLR 260, 46 TC 169, 48 ATC 449, [1969] TR 443, 114 Sol Jo 110	61, 229
Prior (Inspector of Taxes) v Saunders [1993] STC 562, 66 TC 210	61
Purchase v Stainer's Executors. See Stainer's Executors v Purchase (Inspector of Taxes)	
R v City of London Income Tax Comrs. See Income Tax General Purpose Comrs for City of London v Gibbs	
R v Holden [1912] 1 KB 483, 7 Cr App Rep 93, 76 JP 143, 81 LJKB 327, 22 Cox CC 727, 56 Sol Jo 188, 106 LT 305, 28 TLR 173, CCA	89
Rankine (D and G R) v IRC (1952) 32 TC 520, 31 ATC 20, 45 R & IT 506, [1952] TR 1, 1952 SC 177, 1952 SLT 153	73
Reed (Inspector of Taxes) v Young [1985] STC 25, 59 TC 196, 129 Sol Jo 68, [1984] LS Gaz R 3595, CA; affd [1986] 1 WLR 649, [1986] STC 285, 59 TC 196, 130 Sol Jo 410, [1986] LS Gaz R 2002, HL	258

Table of cases

Richart (Inspector of Taxes) v J Lyons & Co Ltd [1989] STC 665, 62 TC 261, CA	108
Robson v Dixon (Inspector of Taxes) [1972] 3 All ER 671, [1972] 1 WLR 1493, 48 TC 527, 51 ATC 179, [1972] TR 163, 116 Sol Jo 863	131
Rodriguez v Speyer Bros [1919] AC 59, 88 LJKB 147, [1918-19] All ER Rep 884, 62 Sol Jo 765, 119 LT 409, 34 TLR 628, HL	89
Rolls-Royce Motors Ltd v Bamford (Inspector of Taxes) [1976] STC 162, 51 TC 319, [1976] TR 21	272
Royal Bank of Canada v IRC [1972] Ch 665, [1972] 1 All ER 225, [1972] 2 WLR 106, 47 TC 565, 51 ATC 233, [1972] TR 197, 115 Sol Jo 968, L(TC) 2429	129
Royal Mutual Benefit Building Society v Walker (1968) 45 TC 171, 47 ATC 145, [1968] TR 129, 206 Estates Gazette 1195	57
Rutherford v IRC (1926) 10 TC 683, 1926 SC 689	231
Sabine (Inspector of Taxes) v Lookers Ltd (1958) 38 TC 120, 37 ATC 227, [1958] TR 213, CA	57
St John's School v Ward (Inspector of Taxes) [1974] STC 69, 49 TC 524, 52 ATC 326, [1974] RA 49, [1973] TR 267; affd (1975) 49 TC 524, 53 ATC 279, [1975] RA 481, [1974] TR 273, L(TC) 2531, [1975] STC 7n, CA	66
Salt v Chamberlain (Inspector of Taxes) [1979] STC 750, 53 TC 143, [1979] TR 203, 123 Sol Jo 490	57
Sargent (Inspector of Taxes) v Barnes [1978] 2 All ER 737, [1978] 1 WLR 823, [1978] STC 322, 52 TC 335, [1978] TR 93, 122 Sol Jo 299, L(TC) 2683	65
Saywell v Pope (Inspector of Taxes) [1979] STC 824, 53 TC 40, [1979] TR 361	2
Schofield (Inspector of Taxes) v R & H Hall Ltd [1975] STC 353, 49 TC 538, L(TC) 2536, CA	66
Scottish Northern American Trust Ltd v Farmer. See Farmer v Scottish Northern American Trust Ltd	
Sharkey (Inspector of Taxes) v Wernher [1956] AC 58, [1955] 3 All ER 493, [1955] 3 WLR 671, 36 TC 275, 34 ATC 263, 48 R & IT 739, [1955] TR 277, 99 Sol Jo 793, L(TC) 1748, HL	58, 160
Shop Investments Ltd v Sweet [1940] 1 All ER 533, 23 TC 39, 84 Sol Jo 290, 163 LT 92, 56 TLR 482	60
Simmons v IRC [1980] 2 All ER 798, [1980] 1 WLR 1196, [1980] STC 350, 53 TC 461, 124 Sol Jo 630, HL	57
Smith (Surveyor of Taxes) v Incorporated Council of Law Reporting for England and Wales [1914] 3 KB 674, 6 TC 477, 83 LJKB 1721, 111 LT 848, 30 TLR 588	62
Snook (James) & Co Ltd v Blasdale (Inspector of Taxes) (1952) 33 TC 244, 31 ATC 268, [1952] TR 233, L(TC) 1598, CA	62
Southern (Inspector of Taxes) v Borax Consolidated Ltd [1941] 1 KB 111, [1940] 4 All ER 412, 23 TC 597, 19 ATC 435, 110 LJKB 705, 85 Sol Jo 94	64
Spencer (James) & Co v IRC (1950) 32 TC 111, 29 ATC 245, 43 R & IT 644, [1950] TR 153, 1950 SC 345, 1950 SLT 266, L (EPT) 97	64
Spiers v Mackinnon (Inspector of Taxes) (1929) 14 TC 386, 8 ATC 197	125

Table of cases

Stainer's Executors v Purchase (Inspector of Taxes) [1952] AC 280, 32 TC 367, 30 ATC 291, [1951] TR 353, sub nom Gospel v Purchase (Inspector of Taxes) [1951] 2 All ER 1071, 45 R & IT 14, 95 Sol Jo 801, [1951] 2 TLR 1112, HL	75
Stekel v Ellice [1973] 1 All ER 465, [1973] 1 WLR 191, 117 Sol Jo 126	2
Stephenson (Inspector of Taxes) v Payne, Stone, Fraser & Co (a firm) [1968] 1 All ER 524, [1968] 1 WLR 858, 44 TC 507, 46 ATC 348, [1967] TR 335, 112 Sol Jo 443	160
Stott and Ingham v Trehearne (Inspector of Taxes) (1924) 9 TC 69	69
Taylor v Chalklin (1945) 26 TC 463	2
Taylor v Good (Inspector of Taxes) [1974] 1 All ER 1137, [1974] 1 WLR 556, [1974] STC 148, 49 TC 277, 53 ATC 14, [1974] TR 15, 118 Sol Jo 422, CA	57
Temperley (Inspector of Taxes) v Visibell [1974] STC 64, 49 TC 129, 52 ATC 308, 118 Sol Jo 169, 231 Estates Gazette 111, L(TC) 2501	107
Texas Land and Mortgage Co Ltd v Holtham (Surveyor of Taxes) (1894) 3 TC 255, 63 LJQB 496, 1 Mans 429, 10 R 398, 10 TLR 337, DC	64
Thomson (Inspector of Taxes) v Moyse [1961] AC 967, [1960] 3 All ER 684, [1960] 3 WLR 929, 39 TC 291, 39 ATC 322, [1960] TR 309, 104 Sol Jo 1032, HL	127
Tod (Inspector of Taxes) v Mudd [1987] STC 141, 60 TC 237	108
Turner v Last (Inspector of Taxes) (1965) 42 TC 517, 44 ATC 234, [1965] TR 249	57
Van den Berghs Ltd v Clark (Inspector of Taxes) [1935] AC 431, 19 TC 390, 14 ATC 62, 104 LJKB 345, [1935] All ER Rep 874, 153 LT 171, 51 TLR 393, HL	57
Vestey v IRC [1980] AC 1148, [1979] 3 All ER 976, [1979] 3 WLR 915, [1980] STC 10, [1979] TR 381, 123 Sol Jo 826, HL	129
Vestey v IRC (No 2) [1980] AC 1148, [1979] 3 All ER 976, [1979] 3 WLR 915, [1980] STC 10, [1979] TR 381, 123 Sol Jo 826, HL	129
Waddington v O'Callaghan (Surveyor of Taxes) (1931) 16 TC 187	2
Walker (Inspector of Taxes) v Carnaby, Harrower, Barham and Pykett [1970] 1 All ER 502, [1970] 1 WLR 276, 46 TC 561, 48 ATC 439, [1969] TR 435, 114 Sol Jo 35, L(TC) 2346	58
Walsh v Randall (Inspector of Taxes) (1940) 23 TC 55, 84 Sol Jo 305	127
Watkins (Inspector of Taxes) v Ashford Sparkes & Harward [1985] 2 All ER 916, [1985] 1 WLR 994, [1985] STC 451, 58 TC 468, 129 Sol Jo 350, [1985] LS Gaz R 2169	61
Werle & Co v Colquhoun (1888) 20 QBD 753, 2 TC 402, 52 JP 644, 57 LJQB 323, 36 WR 613, 58 LT 756, 4 TLR 396, CA	126
Westward Television Ltd v Hart (Inspector of Taxes) [1969] 1 Ch 201, [1968] 3 All ER 91, [1968] 3 WLR 480, 45 TC 1, 47 ATC 200, [1968] TR 181, 112 Sol Jo 484, L(TC) 2280, CA	254
Wetton, Page & Co v Attwooll (Inspector of Taxes) [1963] 1 All ER 166, [1963] 1 WLR 114, 40 TC 619, 41 ATC 324, [1962] TR 301, 106 Sol Jo 959	73

Table of cases

Whiteman v Sadler [1910] AC 514, 79 LJKB 1050, 17 Mans 296, 54 Sol Jo 718, 103 LT 296, 26 TLR 655, HL	89
Wickwar (Inspector of Taxes) v Berry [1963] 2 All ER 1058, [1963] 1 WLR 1026, 41 TC 33, 42 ATC 181, [1963] TR 205, 107 Sol Jo 493, CA	63
Wilcock (Inspector of Taxes) v Frigate Investments Ltd [1982] STC 198, 55 TC 530, [1981] TR 471	64
Williams v Evans (Inspector of Taxes) [1982] 1 WLR 972, [1982] STC 498, 59 TC 509, 126 Sol Jo 346	108
Willingale (Inspector of Taxes) v International Commercial Bank Ltd [1978] AC 834, [1978] 1 All ER 754, [1978] 2 WLR 452, [1978] STC 75, 52 TC 242, [1978] TR 5, 122 Sol Jo 129, L(TC) 2672, HL	61
Wimpey International Ltd v Warland (Inspector of Taxes) [1989] STC 273, 61 TC 51, CA	67
Wisdom v Chamberlain (Inspector of Taxes) [1968] 2 All ER 714, [1968] 1 WLR 1230, 45 TC 92, 47 ATC 60, [1968] TR 49, 112 Sol Jo 314, L(TC) 2267; revsd [1969] 1 All ER 332, [1969] 1 WLR 275, 45 TC 92, 112 Sol Jo 946, L(TC) 2292, sub nom Chamberlain (Inspector of Taxes) v Wisdom 47 ATC 358, [1968] TR 345, CA	57
Yarmouth v France (1887) 19 QBD 647, 57 LJQB 7, 36 WR 281, 4 TLR 1	66

Chapter 1

The nature of partnerships

GENERAL

The introduction of self-assessment in 1996–97 has necessitated a complete change in the basis of assessment for the taxation of trades, professions or vocations carried on either alone or in partnership. The new current year basis of assessment applies from 1997–98 to businesses which commenced prior to 6 April 1994. The preceding year basis of assessment continues to apply up to and including 1995–96 for such businesses and 1996–97 is a transitional year.

The current year basis also applies to new businesses set up on or after 6 April 1994 and, in the case of partnerships, to a business where there has been a cessation on a change of partners after 6 April 1994 where there has been no election for continuation under TA 1988 s 113(2). This chapter describes various aspects common to all partnerships.

The old "previous year" rules are likely to be around for a little while as clients and advisers agree past years with the Inland Revenue. These rules can be found at Appendix I.

Partnership is defined in the Partnership Act 1890, s 1 as the relation which subsists between persons carrying on business in common with a view of profit. TA 1988, s 111 draws a wider net in that it provides that where a trade or profession is carried out by two or more persons jointly, income tax in respect thereof shall be computed in one sum, and shall be separate and distinct from any other tax chargeable on those persons or any of them and joint assessments shall be made in the partnership name. This also applies in Scotland notwithstanding that a Scottish partnership is a separate legal entity, TMA 1970, s 118(3); *Harrison v Willy Bros* (1965) 43 TC 61; *R v City of London Comrs (ex p Gibbs)* (1942) 24 TC 22; *IRC v Graham's Trustees* (1970) TR 343. The wording of this section does suggest that a joint venture, that is a business operation between two or more parties, not constituting a full partnership, might be assessed for taxation purposes as a partnership and this view is supported by the decision in *John Gardner and Bowring Hardy & Co Ltd v IRC* (1930) 15 TC 602, where a coal importer and a coal merchant entered into an informal arrangement during a coal strike which was taxed as a partnership. A partnership is assessed to tax on its trading profits under Schedule D Cases I and II and the tax liability is the aggregate of the partners' individual liabilities on their share of the combined assessment.

Whether or not a partnership exists for tax purposes has been considered in a number of cases. It is primarily a question of fact (*IRC v Williamson* (1928) 14 TC

335; *Calder v Allanson* (1935) 19 TC 293 and the existence or otherwise of a partnership agreement is not conclusive (*Hawker v Compton* (1922) 8 TC 306; *Dickenson v Gross* (1927) 11 TC 614; *Fenston v Johnstone* (1940) 23 TC 29).

A partnership agreement might confirm the existence of a partnership already in being but cannot retrospectively produce a partnership which did not exist at the time (*Ayrshire Pullman Motor Services and Ritchie v IRC* (1929) 14 TC 754; *Waddington v O'Callaghan* (1931) 16 TC 187; *Taylor v Chalklin* (1944) 26 TC 463; *Saywell and Others v Pope* (1979) STC 824).

There is no specific age below which it is impossible to be a partner but it might be difficult in practice to show that minor children were effective partners in a business (*Alexander Bulloch & Co v IRC* [1976] STC 514).

Whereas the sharing of profits implies partnership *Fenston v Johnstone* (1940) 23 TC 29; *Morden Rigg & Co and RB Eskrigge & Co v Monks* (1923) 8 TC 450; *George Hall & Son v Platt* (1954) 35 TC 440; *John Gardner and Bowring Hardy & Co Ltd v IRC* (1930) 15 TC 602), it is not itself conclusive (*Pratt v Strick* (1932) 17 TC 459; *Dodd & Tanfield v Haddock* (1964) 42 TC 229).

The sharing of losses is highly indicative of a partnership although not conclusive (*Brown & Tapscott* (1840) 6 M & W 119; *Bond v Pittard* (1838) 3 M & W 357). Mere joint ownership of property (as opposed to a joint venture) does not give rise to a partnership under the Partnership Act 1890, s 2(1) (*McKie v Luck* (1925) 9 TC 511) unless the joint property is used for a business (*Farrell v Sunderland SS Co Ltd* (1903) 4 TC 605).

In order to show the existence of a partnership it would normally be desirable to have a partnership agreement, despite those cases showing it not to be essential, and to have a partnership bank account on which all partners are signatories. It is often helpful to have formal partners' meetings, duly minuted. All partners should contribute to the capital of the firm, although not necessarily in profit-sharing proportions. The partnership should, where appropriate, be registered for value added tax. Partnership notepaper should be printed showing the names of the partners as required by the Business Names Act 1985, s 4(1)(*a*)(i) unless in the case of a partnership of more than 20 persons the notepaper states the principal place of business and a note to the effect that a list of partners is open to inspection at that place in accordance with s 4(3). It should also show the name of each partner and the business address on a notice displayed in accordance with the Business Names Act 1985, s 4(1)(*b*) on the business premises and in the case of a professional practice it should be registered with its appropriate professional body.

SALARIED PARTNERS

For tax purposes a distinction must be drawn between an equity partner who is a full partner with a proprietorial interest in the firm and a salaried partner who may be an employee and not a proprietor. A salaried partner would normally be assessed under Schedule E and be subject to the rules of Pay As You Earn, although occasionally such a partner might be assessed as a sole trader under Schedule D on his income from the partnership. A salaried partner may be held out as a partner to third parties and might thereby share in the firm's liability to third parties, but for *tax purposes* he does not share in the partnership assessment if he has no proprietary interest in the firm. The ability to apply to the Court to wind up the partnership under the Partnership Act 1890, s 39 is not conclusive (*Stekel v Ellice* [1973] 1 All ER 465). In that case a salaried partner with no further share of profits or losses was held not to be entitled to wind up the firm, even though a partnership existed under PA 1890, s 27, as he had no interest in the capital of the firm, its goodwill or in the clients, apart from those he introduced on joining and took with him on leaving.

It is possible to have a full equity partner with an interest in profits limited to a "salary" and therefore called a salaried partner. Such a person would share in the partnership tax assessment, if he were in reality in business on his own account, in partnership with others, rather than in a master and servant relationship; *Hall v Lorrimer* (1994) STC 23. The factors which will be particularly relevant in deciding whether the true relationship is that of a partnership or employment are as follows:

1. whether the form of the agreement is more akin to that of partnership than of master and servant;
2. whether the individual participates in profits (and losses) during the continuance of the partnership;
3. whether the individual participates in profits upon a dissolution;
4. whether the individual is in fact treated as a partner rather than as an employee, and is involved in discussions and decisions relating to the conduct of the partnership business;
5. whether the individual contributes to the partnership capital.

The impact of unlimited employer's National Insurance contributions and the change to a current year basis of assessment has caused a number of firms to vary their arrangements with salaried partners to change their status from Schedule E employees to Schedule D limited interest equity partners with self-employed status for National Insurance under Social Security Contributions and Benefits Act 1992, s 2.

LIMITED PARTNERS

A limited partner under the Limited Partnership Act 1907 is prohibited from taking part in the management of the firm under the terms of s 6 of that Act. This does not itself prevent the income being earned income for tax purposes provided that the limited partner is personally active in the business in another capacity. This is most commonly met with in the case of stockbrokers where a senior partner, on retirement, may become a limited partner but continue actively to deal with his clients and, therefore, qualify for his share of the profits to be treated as earned income. Where it cannot be shown that a partner is personally active in the partnership, his profit share will not be treated for tax purposes as relevant earnings for pension contribution purposes under TA 1988, s 623(2) or s 644.

EARNED INCOME

Normally a partnership would be carrying on a trade or profession and therefore assessed under Schedule D, Case I or II (and not under Case VI (*Fenston v Johnstone* (1940) 23 TC 29)) and the income of a partner would be earned income as defined by TA 1988, s 833(4)–(6) which refers to any income which is charged under Schedule A or Schedule D and is immediately derived by the individual from the carrying on or exercise by him of his trade, profession or vocation either as an individual or in the case of a partnership as a partner personally acting therein.

4 *The nature of partnerships*

It is not uncommon in professional partnerships to have income which, as a general rule, would be assessable under Schedule E, such as directors' fees in the case of a firm of accountants or solicitors or fees from a hospital appointment in a medical practice. Such income is excluded from the Schedule D computation and assessed under Schedule E on the holder of the office or employment. In certain cases, such as for directors' fees, it is possible to render a bill in the normal way, adding VAT as appropriate and bringing the income into the Schedule D computation, in which case there will be no Schedule E assessment and a "no tax" notice of coding would be obtained (see Extra Statutory Concession A37).

Chapter 2

The current year basis of assessment

GENERAL

The introduction of self-assessment in 1996/97 requires numerous changes to the taxation of income for income tax purposes and one of the most significant changes is the introduction of a current year basis of assessment for Schedule D Cases I and II which replaces the preceding year basis. The current year basis applies for new businesses commencing on or after 6 April 1994 and to existing businesses from 1997/98, with 1996/97 being a transitional year. In the case of partnerships, the changes are even more far-reaching in that the partnership itself ceases to be an assessable entity for tax purposes and there will no longer be an assessment in the partnership name but on each partner individually.

One of the problems of the current year basis of assessment is that the drafting seems to have been done in the most confusing manner possible by amendment of the existing legislation and inserting additional sections into TA 1988 and the Taxes Management Act (TMA) 1970 rather than to provide a new set of rules. This means that there are in effect two sections masquerading under the same section number, one of which applies to businesses on the preceding year basis and one of which applies to businesses on the current year basis. As it will not be until 1999/2000 that all businesses are dealt with on a current year basis this confusion could last for some time. In this book references to legislation in TA 1988 or TMA 1970 which apply both for the preceding year basis of assessment and in a modified form to the current year basis of assessment are followed by (new) after the reference, where the reference is to the legislation as amended by FA 1994 or FA 1995 and applicable to the current year basis of assessment.

The partnership will still produce partnership accounts and tax computations, adjusting the accounts to arrive at the taxable profit. Under the current year basis of assessment, capital allowances are treated as a deductible expense in arriving at the taxable profit. The partnership will prepare a partnership return of the partnership income, including the Schedule D Case I or II computation and any other income of the partnership. There will then be a partnership statement produced by the firm which will allocate the taxable income among the partners in accordance with their profit-sharing ratio in the accounting period. This ought, in most cases, to remove the requirement for an equitable adjustment among partners to take account of the fact that under the preceding year basis of assessment the profits were calculated by reference to the profits of the accounting year ending in the preceding fiscal year, but allocated among the partners in accordance with their profit-sharing arrangements in the fiscal year itself.

Having arrived at each partner's share of income from the partnership statement, each partner is then treated as an individual carrying on a sole trade and taxed accordingly. The effect of this is that a person joining a firm as an equity partner is treated as if he had commenced a new trade, profession or vocation at the date of joining and, on his death or retirement, as if that business had ceased. There is therefore no commencement or cessation of the partnership as a whole and thus no requirement for any elections for continuation, or there being a deemed cessation of the entire firm on a change of partners as under the preceding year basis of assessment.

Partners will be responsible for payment of their own tax liabilities and tax will cease to be a liability of the firm for which each partner is jointly and severally liable, and will become a liability of the individual partners personally. Many firms will continue to make payments to the Revenue centrally, in connection with the partners' tax liabilities in respect of the business, but this will be a payment on account of each partner's individual liabilities. It is probable that over time the practice of paying the partnership tax centrally will diminish as partnerships accept the fact that their co-partners are likely to meet what will be a personal liability at the due date of payment in the same way as they pay any other personal liability unconnected with the firm.

If there are non-resident partners, the partnership as a whole becomes automatically appointed as the agent of the non-resident partners and their U.K. representative for the payment of taxation, so that the joint and several liability of the partners for the tax liability of their co-partners continues to this limited degree.

Before looking at the specific problems of partnerships under the current year basis of assessment, it is necessary to look at the basic rules so far as they apply to sole traders. The theory behind the current year basis is that over the life of the business the profits as adjusted for tax purposes should equate to the profit actually assessed to income tax. This did not necessarily apply under the preceding year basis of assessment and over the life of the business assessable profits would normally have been less, but could have been more, than the total of the adjusted profit. This gave rise to tax planning seeking to exploit the rules and the current year basis seeks to do away with this problem. The original intention, when the change to the current year basis and self-assessment were known as simplified assessing, was that the new system would be clear, simple to understand, equitable and simple to administer. As will become apparent in this chapter, the goal of simplicity has been crowded out by the requirements of the Exchequer for an even flow of funds from taxpayers and by the requirements of the Revenue to prevent any abuse of the system or the avoidance of taxation, and to preserve equity among taxpayers. The Exchequer requirements mean that a minimum of twelve months' profits will be assessed in every fiscal year, except for the year in which the business commences or ceases.

YEAR OF COMMENCEMENT

Under the current year basis of assessment, the profits for the first fiscal year to be assessed or self-assessed are those of the period from commencement of the business to the following 5 April under TA 1988, s 61(1)(new). If the accounts are made up to 5 April following commencement the assessment will be on those profits as adjusted for tax purposes. If the first accounting period ends before 5 April the profits to be assessed will be the adjusted profits of that period and a proportion calculated on a daily basis of the profits for the next accounting period. If the first accounting date takes place after 5 April following commencement the assessment is based on the proportion of the profits again calculated on a daily basis. All such calculations for the current year basis of assessment are calculated on a daily basis, under TA 1988, s 72(2), unless, exceptionally, this would not give a just and reasonable result of the profits for the first accounting period (*Marshall Hus & Partners Ltd v Bolton* (1981) STC 18). There is therefore no major change in the current year basis compared with a preceding year basis for the first year of assessment, except that capital allowances are treated as an expense instead of a separate computation.

EXAMPLE 2.01

First accounts for less than 12 months ending in first fiscal year
Mr A started business in partnership on 1 August 1998 and the firm produced accounts to 31 December 1998, ie for a period of less than 12 months ending in the fiscal year of commencement, and annually thereafter.

His share of profits (as adjusted for tax purposes)

1.8.98 to 31.12.98		£10,000
y/e 31.12.1999		£33,000
y/e 31.12.2000		£45,000
y/e 31.12.2001		£57,000
Taxable		
1998/99	1.8.98 to 5.4.99	
	£10,000 + (95/365 × £33,000)	£18,589 (a)
1999/2000	y/e 31.12.1999	£33,000 (b)
2000/01	y/e 31.12.2000	£45,000 (c)
2001/02	y/e 31.12.2001	£57,000 (d)

Notes
(a) TA 1988, s 61(1)(new), commencement to 5 April.
(b) TA 1988, s 61(2) does not apply, although the second year of assessment, as the period from commencement 1.8.98 to the accounting date given by TA 1988, s 60(5)(new) of 31.12.99, is not less than 12 months. Therefore, this is the first year of assessment in which there is an accounting date and the basis period is fixed by TA 1988, s 60(3)(a)(new).
(c) TA 1988, s 60(3)(b)(new).
(d) TA 1988, s 60(3)(b)(new).

The period from 1.1.99 to 5.4.99 is taxed both for 1998/99 and 1999/2000 and is therefore an overlap period relievable under TA 1988, s 63A, resulting in overlap profits of £8,589 (95/365 × £33,000).

SECOND YEAR OF ASSESSMENT

In the second year of assessment there are a number of permutations possible for the assessable profit.

Fiscal year accounting

The simplest situation under the current year basis of assessment is where accounts are made up to 5 April in each year so that the adjusted profits for the accounting period form the basis of assessment for the fiscal year. There is, however, no requirement to make up accounts to 5 April and most businesses prefer a different date for commercial reasons or to maximise the period between earning profits and paying tax on those profits, and allowing the maximum time for the preparation of accounts and returns. Many businesses will therefore choose an accounting date ending early in the fiscal year such as 30 April.

EXAMPLE 2.02

Fiscal year accounting
Mr B joined a partnership on 1 August 1998 which produced accounts annually to 5 April.

His share of profits (as adjusted for tax purposes)

1.8.98 to 5.4.99		£16,000
y/e 5.4.2000		£36,000
y/e 5.4.2001		£48,000
y/e 5.4.2002		£60,000
Taxable		
1998/99	1.8.98 to 5.4.99	£16,000 (a)
1999/00	y/e 5.4.2000	£36,000 (b)
2000/01	y/e 5.4.2001	£48,000 (c)
2001/02	y/e 5.4.2002	£60,000 (d)

Notes
(a) TA 1988, s 61(1)(new), commencement to 5 April.
(b) TA 1988, s 61(2) is inapplicable, as period from commencement 1.8.98 to accounting date, 5.4.2000 is not less than 12 months. Therefore, TA 1988 s 60(3)(*a*)(new) applies as this is the first year of assessment in which the accounting date falls not less than 12 months after commencement.
(c) TA 1988, s 60(3)(*b*)(new).
(d) TA 1988, s 60(3)(*b*)(new).

Accounting date twelve months or more from commencement

If the accounting date ending in the second fiscal year is twelve months or more from the date of commencement of the business, the profits to be assessed in the second fiscal year are those for the twelve months ending on the accounting date, apportioning accounting periods as necessary under TA 1988, s 60(3)(*a*)(new). It will be appreciated that unless fiscal year accounting is adopted the twelve-month period ending in the second fiscal year must include some or all of the profit in the year of commencement when the profits for the period from commencement to the following 5 April were assessed. This gives rise to an overlap and the profits so doubly charged are the overlap profits of an overlap period, under TA 1988, s 63A(new).

EXAMPLE 2.03

First accounts for 12 months
Mr B joined a partnership on 1 August 1998 which produced accounts annually to 31 July.

His share of profits (as adjusted for tax purposes)
y/e 31.7.1999	£28,000
y/e 31.7.2000	£40,000
y/e 31.7.2001	£52,000

EXAMPLE 2.03 *(continued)*

Taxable
1998/99	1.8.98 to 5.4.99	
	(248/365 × £28,000)	£19,024 (a)
1999/00	y/e 31.7.1999	£28,000 (b)
2000/01	y/e 31.7.2000	£40,000 (c)
2001/02	y/e 31.7.2001	£52,000 (d)

Notes
(a) TA 1988, s 61(1)(new), commencement to 5 April.
(b) TA 1988, s 61(2) is inapplicable, as period from commencement 1.8.98 to the accounting date, 31.7.99 is not less than 12 months (TA 1988, s 61(2(a)(new)). Therefore, the basis period for the first year of assessment in which there is an accounting period under TA 1988, s 60(3)(a)(new) is the year ended 31.7.99.
(c) TA 1988, s 60(3)(b)(new).
(d) TA 1988, s 60(3)(b)(new).

The period from commencement on 1.8.98 to 5.4.99 is taxed both for 1998/99 and 1999/2000 and is therefore an overlap period relievable under TA 1988, s 63A, resulting in overlap profits of £19,024.

EXAMPLE 2.04

First accounts for more than 12 months ending in second fiscal year

Mr D started business in partnership on 1 August 1998 and the firm produced accounts to 31 December 1999, ie for a period of more than 12 months ending in the fiscal year following that of commencement, and annually thereafter.

His share of profits (as adjusted for tax purposes)
1.8.98 to 31.12.99		£43,000
y/e 31.12.2000		£45,000
y/e 31.12.2001		£57,000

Taxable
1998/99	1.1.98 to 5.4.99	
	(248/518 × £43,000)	£20,587 (a)
1999/00	1.1.99 to 31.12.99	
	(365/518 × £43,000)	£30,300 (b)
2000/01	y/e 31.12.2000	£45,000 (c)
2001/02	y/e 31.12.2001	£57,000 (d)

Notes
(a) TA 1988, s 61(1)(new), commencement to 5 April.
(b) TA 1988, s 61(3)(a)(new) applies, 12 months to first accounting date. TA 1988, s 61(2)(new) does not apply as the accounting period is not less than 12 months.
(c) TA 1988, s 60(3)(b)(new).
(d) TA 1988, s 60(3)(b)(new).

The period from 1.1.99 to 5.4.99 is taxed both in 1998/99 and 1999/2000 and is therefore an overlap period relievable under TA 1988, s 63A, resulting in overlap profits of £7,886 (95/518 × £43,000).

Accounting period of less than twelve months in second fiscal year

If the accounting date in the second fiscal year is less than twelve months from commencement, the profits to be assessed are those of the twelve-month period

10 The current year basis of assessment

from commencement, under TA 1988, s 61(2)(*a*)(new), again apportioning as necessary.

EXAMPLE 2.05

First accounts for less than 12 months ending in second fiscal year
Mr E started business in partnership on 1 August 1998 and the firm produced accounts to 30 June 1999, ie for a period of less than 12 months ending in the fiscal year following that of commencement, and annually thereafter.

His share of profits (as adjusted for tax purposes)
1.8.98 to 30.6.99		£25,000
y/e 30.6.2000		£39,000
y/e 30.6.2001		£51,000

Taxable
1998/99	1.1.98 to 5.4.99	
	(248/334 × £25,000)	£18,562 (a)
1999/00	1.8.98 to 31.7.99	
	£25,000 + (31/365 × £39,000)	£28,312 (b)
2000/01	y/e 30.6.2000	£39,000 (c)
2001/02	y/e 30.6.2001	£51,000 (d)

Notes
(a) TA 1988, s 61(1)(new), commencement to 5 April.
(b) TA 1988, s 61(3)(*a*)(new) does apply on the second year of assessment, because the period from commencement 1.8.98 to the accounting date is less than 12 months. The basis period given by TA 1988, s 61(2)(*a*)(new) is the 12 months from commencement, ie 1.8.98 to 31.7.99. This conforms to the requirement for at least 12 months' profits to be taxed in every year other than that of commencement of cessation.
(c) TA 1988, s 60(3)(*a*)(new) applies as 30.6.2000 is the first accounting date which falls not less than 12 months after commencement.
(d) TA 1988, s 60(3)(*b*)(new).

The period from commencement on 1.8.98 to 5.4.99 is taxed both in 1998/99 and 1999/2000 and is therefore an overlap period relieved under TA 1988, s 63A, with overlap profits of £18,562. The period from 1.7.99 to 31.7.99 is taxed both in 1999/2000 and 2000/01 and is therefore an overlap period relievable under TA 1988, s 63A, resulting in overlap profits of £3,312 (31/365 × £39,000), increasing the overlap profits to £21,874.

No accounting date in second fiscal year

If the business commences towards the end of the fiscal year, say on 1 January 1995, and accounts are to be made up to 30 April each year, it would not be unusual for the first set of accounts to be those of the sixteen-month period ending on 30 April 1996. In such a case the profits of the second fiscal year in which there is no accounting date will be those of the fiscal year, under TA 1988, s 60(1)(new), apportioned in the normal way.

EXAMPLE 2.06

First accounts for more than 12 months ending in third fiscal year
Mr F started business in partnership on 1 August 1998 and the firm produced accounts to 30 June 2000, ie for a period of more than 12 months ending in the second fiscal year following the years of commencement, and annually thereafter.

EXAMPLE 2.06 *(continued)*

His share of profits (as adjusted for tax purposes)
1.8.98 to 30.6.2000		£64,000
y/e 30.6.2001		£51,000

Taxable
1998/99	1.1.98 to 5.4.99	
	(248/700 × £64,000)	£22,674 (a)
1999/00	6.4.99 to 5.4.00	
	(365/700 × £64,000)	£33,371 (b)
2000/01	1.7.99 to 30.6.00	
	(365/700 × £64,000)	£33,371 (c)
2001/02	y/e 30.6.2001	£51,000 (d)

Notes
(a) TA 1988, s 61(1)(new), commencement to 5 April.
(b) TA 1988, s 60(1)(new) applies on the fiscal year basis as there is no accounting period ending in the second year of assessment, therefore TA 1988, s 60(3)(new) cannot apply, and therefore TA 1988, s 61(new) cannot apply either in view of TA 1988, s 61(2)(*a*)(new).
(c) TA 1988, s 60(3)(*b*)(new) applies, 12 months to first accounting date. TA 1988, s 61(2)(new) does not apply as it is the third year of assessment, nor does TA 1988, s 60(3)(*b*)(new) as TA 1988, s 60(3)(*a*)(new) applies.
(d) TA 1988, s 60(3)(*b*)(new).

The period from 1.7.99 to 5.4.2000 is taxed in both 1999/2000 and 2000/01 and is therefore an overlap period relievable under TA 1988, s 63A, resulting in overlap profits of £25,600 (280/700 × £64,000).

THIRD YEAR OF ASSESSMENT

If the first accounting period which ends more than twelve months after commencement ends in the third fiscal year, the assessment is on the profits for twelve months ending on that accounting date, under TA 1988, s 60(3)(*a*)(new).

Where the assessment for this twelve-month period includes profits that have already been assessed in the previous year there are further overlap profits of an overlap period.

In all other cases the assessment is on twelve months from the end of the accounting date in the preceding fiscal year, under TA 1988, s 60(3)(*b*)(new).

FOURTH AND SUBSEQUENT YEARS

The normal basis period for tax years is the twelve-month period from the end of the accounting period which ended in the preceding year. In the normal case of a business making up accounts for twelve months the assessment will therefore be on the profits of the accounting period ending in the current fiscal year, under TA 1988, s 60(3)(*b*)(new).

CHANGE OF ACCOUNTING DATE

The Revenue practice on a change of accounting date, set out in booklet IR 26, which applied for the preceding year basis of assessment, is replaced for the current year basis of assessment by more detailed statutory provisions in TA 1988, s 62(new). Where there is a change of accounting date, the resulting accounting period must either be less than twelve months, if the accounting date is moved forward to a period earlier in the fiscal year, or longer if it is moved back to a period ending later in the fiscal year. A change of accounting date is ignored for tax purposes unless certain specific requirements are met with, laid down by TA 1988, s 62A, or the change takes place in the second or third fiscal year. These requirements are that the accounting period to the new accounting date does not exceed a period of eighteen months, that notice of the change of accounting date is given to the Revenue by 31 January following the year of assessment in which the accounting change is deemed to take place and either there has been no accounting date change effective for tax purposes in any of the preceding five years of assessment (other than in the first three years), or the notice of the change sets out the reasons for the change, which the Revenue is satisfied are bona fide commercial reasons or where they do not signify their objection to the change within sixty days.

If these requirements cannot be met, or the taxpayer chooses not to make the election, the basis period for income tax purposes continues to be twelve months from the end of the previous basis period. It would be possible therefore to continue to have a different end of basis period for tax purposes than that used for accounts purposes. This would therefore require apportionment of the accounting figures to arrive at the results for the tax basis period and would make the administration of the current year basis of assessment needlessly complicated. It is likely, therefore, that in most cases taxpayers will make the appropriate election. If an election is not made in one fiscal year because, for example, the eighteen-month maximum period has been exceeded, a valid election can be made in the subsequent year because the conditions will now be capable of being met in that the actual accounting period in the year following the change is no more than a twelve-month period. In that case the change is deemed to have been made in the year in which it is accepted as a valid change.

Accounting period of less than twelve months

Where the change results in an accounting period of less than twelve months, the assessable profits are those of the twelve-month period ending with the new accounting date. This will result in further overlap profits of an additional overlap period.

EXAMPLE 2.07

Shortened accounting period
Mr G joined a partnership on 1 August 1998 which produced accounts to 5 April each year until 2001 when the accounting date was brought forward to 30 June and annually thereafter. The requirements of TA 1988, s 62A were met.

His share of profits (as adjusted for tax purposes)
1.8.98 to 5.4.99	£16,000
y/e 5.4.2000	£36,000
y/e 5.4.2001	£48,000
p/e 30.6.2001	£15,000
y/e 30.6.2002	£60,000

EXAMPLE 2.07 *(continued)*
Taxable

1998/99	1.8.98 to 5.4.99	£16,000 (a)
1999/00	y/e 5.4.2000	£36,000 (b)
2000/01	y/e 5.4.2001	£48,000 (c)
2001/02	y/e 30.6.2001	
	(9/12 × £64,000 + £15,000)	£51,000 (d)
2002/03	y/e 30.6.2002	£60,000 (e)

NOTES
(a) TA 1988, s 61(1).
(b) TA 1988, s 61(3)(*a*).
(c) TA 1988, s 60(3)(*b*).
(d) TA 1988, s 62(5) makes this the year in which the accounting date is deemed to change as accounts are made up to a new date in the fiscal year. The period is less than 12 months from the end of the previous accounting date (5.4.2001), therefore TA 1988, s 62(2)(*a*) determines the basis as 12 months ending with the new accounting date. The period 1.7.2000 to 5.4.20001 is taxed in both 2000/01 and 2001/02 and therefore there is an overlap period under TA 1988, s 63A, resulting in overlap profits of £36,000 (9/12 × £48,000).
(e) TA 1988, s 60(3)(*b*).

Accounting period of more than twelve months

If the period from the end of the previous basis period for tax purposes to the new accounting date is more than twelve months, the assessment will be based on the profits for the whole period. This means that more than twelve months' profits are assessed in the fiscal year subject to any relief for previous overlap. The cumulative overlap profits of the cumulative overlap period that have arisen in previous years and partially relieved in that the proportion by which the long period of account exceeds twelve months is calculated and applied to the cumulative overlap profits which are then treated as a deduction in the year of accounting change. This is arrived at by applying the statutory formula in TA 1988, s 63A(1); FA 1994, s 205 which is

$$A \times \frac{B - C}{D}$$

where A is the aggregate amount of the overlap profit which has not previously been allowed in an overlap adjustment, B is the number of days in the basis period, which must of course be more than 365 in a long period of account, C is the number of days in the year of assessment; ie 365 or 366 in a leap year, and D is the aggregate of the overlap periods arising on commencement or on an earlier change of accounting date or in transition to the current year basis, less any overlap periods which have already been relieved on a previous change of accounting date.

EXAMPLE 2.08

Extended accounting period ending in next fiscal year
Mr H joined a partnership on 1 August 1998 which produced accounts to 31 July each year until 2001/02 when the accounting date was extended to 31 January 2002 and annually thereafter. The requirements of TA 1988, s 62A were met.

His share of profits (as adjusted for tax purposes)

y/e 31.7.1999	£28,000
y/e 31.7.2000	£40,000
p/e 31.1.2002	£82,000
y/e 31.1.2003	£60,000

14   The current year basis of assessment

EXAMPLE 2.08 *(continued)*

Taxable
1998/99	1.8.98 to 5.4.99	£19,024 (a)
1999/2000	y/e 31.7.99	£28,000 (b)
2000/01	y/e 31.7.2000	£40,000 (c)
2001/02	1.8.00 to 31.1.02	
	(£82,000 – £14,114)	£67,886 (d)
2002/03	y/e 31.1.03	£60,000 (e)

Notes
(a) TA 1988, s 61(1), 248/365 × £28,000 = £19,024.
(b) TA 1988, s 60(3)(*a*), overlap 1.8.98 to 5.4.99 = £19,024 (248 days).
(c) TA 1988, s 60(3)(*b*).
(d) TA 1988, s 62(5) makes this the year in which the accounting date is deemed to change as accounts are made up to a new date in the fiscal year. The period is more than 12 months from the end of the previous basis period (31.7.2000), therefore TA 1988, s 62(2)(*b*) determines the basis as the period ending with the new accounting date (ie 31.1.02 falling in the fiscal year ended 5.4.02). This is an 18-month accounting period, subject to overlap relief under TA 1988, s 63A, of the appropriate proportion of the overlap brought forward, i e

$$A \times \frac{B-C}{D}$$

$$£19,024 \times \frac{549-365}{248} = £14,114 \text{ leaving } £19,024 - £14,114 = £4,910$$

to continue to be carried forward under TA 1988 s 63A.
(e) TA 1988, s 60(3)(*b*).

If the long period of account skips a complete fiscal year so that no accounting period ends in that year, in other words from say, 31 March in one year to 30 June in the following year, the change of accounting date is deemed to have taken place twelve months before the date of the actual change, ie the change of accounting date in the example above would be deemed to have taken place on 30 June in the previous year.

EXAMPLE 2.09

Extended accounting period skipping a fiscal year
Mr I joined a partnership on 1 August 1998 which produced accounts to 5 April each year until April 2001 when the accounting date was extended to 30 June 2002 and annually thereafter. The requirements of TA 1988, s 62A were met.

His share of profits (as adjusted for tax purposes)
1.8.98 to 5.4.99	£16,000
y/e 5.4.2000	£36,000
y/e 5.4.2001	£48,000
p/e 30.6.2002	£75,000

Taxable
1998/99	1.8.98 to 5.4.99	£16,000 (a)
1999/00	y/e 5.4.2000	£36,000 (b)
2000/01	y/e 5.4.2001	£48,000 (c)
2001/02	y/e 30.6.2001	
	(9/12 × £48,000 + 3/15 × £75,000)	£51,000 (d)

EXAMPLE 2.09 *(continued)*

2002/03	y/e 30.6.2002	
	(12/15 × £75,000)	£60,000 (e)

Notes
(a) TA 1988, s 61(1).
(b) TA 1988, s 61(3)(*a*).
(c) TA 1988, s 60(3)(*b*).
(d) TA 1988, s 62(5) makes this the year in which the accounting date is deemed to change as there is no accounting date in the fiscal year. The period is less than 12 months from the end of the previous accounting date (5.4.2001), therefore TA 1988, s 62(2)(*a*) determines the basis period as 12 months ending with the new accounting date. The period 1.7.2000 to 5.4.2001 is taxed in both 2000/01 and 20001/02 and therefore there is an overlap period relievable under TA 1988, s 63A, resulting in overlap profits of £36,000 (9/12 × £48,000).
(e) TA 1988, s 60(3)(*b*). Although this is the year in which the new accounting date actually falls, the change is deemed to take place in 2001/02 under TA 1988, s 62(5) (see above), therefore the basis period is 12 months from the end of the basis period for the previous year.

In order to prevent any year falling out of assessment where two accounting periods end in the same fiscal year, for example if the accounting period is changed from 30 April to 31 December in the same year, the results for the two periods are amalgamated and the calculations proceed as if there had been a valid change of accounting date to the second date in the fiscal year. It does not matter if this results in the amalgamated accounting period being in excess of eighteen months because the actual accounting period will clearly be for less than twelve months if there are two accounting periods ending in the same fiscal year. This assumes that the other requirements for a valid change are met.

EXAMPLE 2.10

Two accounting periods ending in the same fiscal year
Mr J started business in partnership on 1 August 1998 and the firm produced accounts to 31 July each year until 2001/02 when the accounting date was changed to 31 March 2002 and annually thereafter. The requirements of TA 1988, s 62A were met by preparing an account to 31 July 2001 and an eight-month account to 31 March 2002.

His share of profits (as adjusted for tax purposes)
y/e 31.7.1999		£56,000
y/e 31.7.2000		£80,000
y/e 31.7.2001		£100,000
1.8.2001 to 31.3.2002		£70,000
y/e 31.3.2003		£120,000
Taxable		
1998/99	1.8.98 to 5.4.99	£38,049 (a)
1999/00	y/e 31.7.99	£56,000 (b)
2000/01	y/e 31.7.00	£80,000 (c)
2001/02	1.8.00 to 31.3.02	
	£100,000 + £70,000 − £37,282 =	£132,718 (d)
2002/03	y/e 31.1.03	£120,000 (e)

Notes
(a) TA 1988, s 61(1), 248/365 × £56,000 = £38,049.
(b) TA 1988, s 60(3)(*a*), overlap 1.8.98 to 5.4.99 = £38,049.

16 The current year basis of assessment

EXAMPLE 2.10 *(continued)*

(c) TA 1988, s 60(3)(*b*).
(d) TA 1988, s 62(2)(*b*). The change of accounting date takes effect in 2001/02, the first year of assessment in which accounts are made up to the new date under TA 1988, s 62(5). TA 1988, s 60(5) amalgamates the two accounting periods and TA 1988, s 62(2)(*b*) applies to fix the basis period as the period from the end of the basis period in the previous fiscal year to the new accounting date. This is a 20-month basis period, subject to overlap relief under TA 1988, s 63A, of the appropriate proportion of the overlap relief brought forward, i e

$$A \times \frac{B-C}{D}$$

$$£38,049 \times \frac{608-365}{248} = £37,282 \text{ leaving } £767$$

to continue to be carried forward under TA 1988, s 63A.

(e) TA 1988, s 60(3)(*b*).

Accounting change in second or third year

If there is an accounting date change in the second year but still within twelve months of commencement, the profits assessable remain those for the first twelve months. If the change in the second year is more than twelve months from commencement the basis period in the second year is the twelve months to the new accounting date. If there is a change in the third year of assessment and no accounting period in the previous year, ie the second year, the normal change of accounting date rules deem the change to take place twelve months prior to the actual change, but if this results in the basis period being deemed to end in the second fiscal year less than twelve months after commencement the assessment is still on the twelve months from commencement.

EXAMPLE 2.11

Change of accounting date in second year
Mr K started business in partnership on 1 August 1998 and the firm produced accounts to 31 December 1998 and then to 30 April 1999 and annually thereafter.

His share of profits (as adjusted for tax purposes)
1.8.98 to 31.12.98		£20,000
1.1.99 to 30.4.99		£12,000
y/e 30.4.2000		£60,000
y/e 30.4.2001		£80,000
Taxable (subject to overlap relief under TA 1988, s 63A)		
1998/99	1.8.98 to 5.4.99	£29,500 (a)
1999/00	1.8.98 to 31.7.99	£47,122 (b)
2000/01	y/e 30.4.2000	£60,000 (c)
2001/02	y/e 30.4.2001	£80,000 (d)

Notes
(a) TA 1988, s 61(1), actual basis for year of commencement £20,000 + (95/120 × £12,000) = £29,500.
(b) TA 1988, s 61(2)(*b*), first 12 months £20,000 + £12,000 + (92/365 × £60,000) = £47,122.

EXAMPLE 2.11 *(continued)*

(c) TA 1988, s 60(3)(*a*), year ended on accounting date.
(d) TA 1988, s 60(3)(*b*).

The period from 1.8.98 to 5.4.99 is taxed in 1998/99 and 1999/2000. The period from 1.5.99 to 31.7.99 is taxed in 1999/2000 and 2000/01. The overlap period relievable under TA 1988, s 63A is therefore 248 days and 92 days, a total of 340 days, and the overlap profits of £29,500 and (92/365 × £60,000) £15,123 a total of £44,623.

EXAMPLE 2.12

Change of accounting date in second year more than 12 months from commencement
Mr L joined a partnership on 1 August 1998 which produced accounts to 31 December 1998 and then to 30 September 1999 and annually thereafter.

His share of profits (as adjusted for tax purposes)
1.8.98 to 31.12.98		£20,000
1.1.99 to 30.9.99		£54,000
y/e 30.9.2000		£70,000
y/e 30.9.2001		£80,000
Taxable (subject to overlap relief under TA 1988, s 63A)		
1998/99	1.8.98 to 5.4.99	£38,791 (a)
1999/2000	y/e 30.9.99	£66,026 (b)
2000/01	y/e 30.9.2000	£70,000 (c)
2001/02	y/e 30.9.2001	£80,000 (d)

Notes
(a) TA 1988, s 61(1), actual basis for year of commencement £20,000 + (95/273 × £54,000) = £38,791.
(b) TA 1988, s 61(3)(*a*), 12 months to new accounting date £54,000 + (92/153 × £20,000) = £66,026.
(c) TA 1988, s 60(3)(*b*).
(d) TA 1988, s 60(3)(*b*).

The period from 1.10.98 to 5.4.99 is taxed in 1998/99 and 1999/2000. The overlap period relievable under TA 1988, s 63A is therefore 187 days and the overlap profits are 92/153 × £20,000 and 95/273 × £54,000 – a total of £30,817.

EXAMPLE 2.13

Change of accounting date in third year
Mr M started business in partnership on 1 August 1998 and the firm produced accounts to 5 April 1999 and then to 30 June 2000, ie a period ending in the third year and not for 12 months from the first accounting date and within 2 years of commencement

His share of profits (as adjusted for tax purposes)
1.8.98 to 5.4.99		£22,000
p/e 30.6.2000		£42,000
y/e 30.6.2001		£51,000
Taxable		
1998/99	1.8.98 to 5.4.99	£22,000 (a)
1999/00	1.8.98 to 31.7.99	
	£22,000 + 117/452 × £42,000	£32,872 (b)
2000/01	1.7.99 to 30.6.2000	
	(366/452) × £42,000	£34,008 (c)
2001/02	y/e 30.6.2001	£51,000 (d)

EXAMPLE 2.13 *(continued)*

Notes
(a) TA 1988, s 61(1), commencement to 5 April.
(b) TA 1988, s 61(3)(*b*), first 12 months.
(c) TA 1988, s 62(3)(*b*) applies, 12 months to new accounting date.
(d) TA 1988, s 60(3)(*b*).

The period from 1.8.98 to 5.4.99 is taxed in both 1998/99 and 1999/2000 and is therefore an overlap period relievable under TA 1988, s 63A, resulting in overlap profits of £22,000. The period from 1.7.99 to 31.7.99 is taxed in both 1999/2000 and 2000/01 and is therefore a further overlap period resulting in additional overlap profits of £2,880 (31/452 × £42,000).

CESSATION

The basis period in the year of discontinuance ends with the date of discontinuance and starts on the day following the end of the basis period in the preceding fiscal year. This avoids any drop-out as on the preceding year basis of assessment under which the final period is from 6 April in the year of cessation to the date of cessation. However, on cessation any overlap profits of an overlap period that have not previously been relieved may be deducted from the profits for the period to cessation. An excess of overlap profits relievable on cessation over the chargeable profits, if any, of the cessation period results in a loss that may be relieved in the normal way.

EXAMPLE 2.14

Mr N had been a partner for many years in a firm which made up accounts to 30 April each year. He retired on 31 December 2002. He has available overlap relief of £18,000 brought forward.

His share of profits (as adjusted for tax purposes)
y/e 30.4.2001		£60,000
y/e 30.4.2002		£40,000
p/e 31.12.2002		£10,000
Taxable		
2001/02	y/e 30.4.2001	£60,000 (a)
2002/03	p/e 31.12.2002	£32,000 (b)

Notes
(a) TA 1988, s 60(3)(*b*).
(b) TA 1988, s 63(1)(*b*), beginning on 1.5.2001 immediately after the basis period for the preceding year of assessment (2001/02, 30.4.2001) and ending at the date of cessation, 31.12.2002 (£40,000 + £10,000 = £50,000). His available transitional overlap relief of £18,000 reduces the final assessment to £50,000 − £18,000 = £32,000.

In the case of a partnership the change of accounting date rules apply to the partnership as a whole and if the requirements are not met for a valid change, the end of the basis period for tax purposes continues to be twelve months from the end of the preceding period. If a new partner joins a partnership after an invalid change, the old accounting date is regarded as the applicable accounting date for the incoming partner, irrespective of the actual date to which accounts are made up, so that the incoming partner's date for self-assessment is coterminous with that of the existing partners (TA 1988, s 111(5); FA 1995, s 117).

LOSSES

The loss relief provisions for the current year basis of assessment are designed to mirror, so far as possible, the existing provisions under the preceding year basis and the existing loss relief provisions in TA 1988, ss 380 to 392 are modified to deal with losses on the current year basis of assessment. The revised loss provisions apply to businesses commencing, or deemed to commence, on or after 6 April 1994; but to continuing businesses which commenced prior to 6 April 1994, only from 1997/98. Care is needed to apply the right set of rules in any given set of circumstances.

Loss set-off

A loss under the current year basis of assessment is computed in the same manner as a profit ie, for the accounting period ending in the fiscal year. Under the preceding year basis of assessment, in strictness, the loss should be apportioned to the fiscal year in which it arises on a split accounts basis, although in practice it has been common to treat the loss for the accounting period ending in the fiscal year as the loss for the fiscal year. Under the current year basis there is no provision to calculate the loss for the fiscal year on a split accounts basis and the loss would only be for the fiscal year itself if the accounting period chosen was to 5 April. The loss for the accounting year ending in the fiscal year may be set against the total income for the year in which the loss arises, or the total income of the preceding fiscal year (TA 1988, s 380(1)(new)). This preserves the effective one-year carry back which applies for the preceding year basis of assessment. The same loss cannot be relieved more than once and it is not possible to claim part of the loss in order to preserve personal allowances, for example, except to the extent that the loss exceeds the available income against which it may be set. A loss claim must be made within one year of the filing date which is 31 January following the end of the year of assessment in which the loss arises. The tax payer has the option to use the loss against the current year's income in preference to the preceding year's income, or vice versa, with any balance of the loss being set against the total income of the other year.

Loss carried forward

To the extent the loss is not claimed for set-off against total income or exceeds total income, it may be carried forward against future income of the same trade under TA 1988, s 385(1)(new); FA 1994, s 209(4). Losses carried forward in this manner must be set against the first available income from the same trade, profession or vocation, and a single claim made within five years from the filing date is sufficient; it will no longer be necessary to claim for the unrelieved loss in each profitable year as under the preceding year basis (FA 1994, s 209(4),(5)). The time limit for a claim prior to 1996/97 is six years from the end of the fiscal year.

As losses under the current year basis are computed in the same way as profits, they are inclusive of capital allowances which are treated as trading expenses and therefore there is no need to add capital allowances to losses for loss relief purposes as was necessary under the preceding year basis of assessment.

EXAMPLE 2.15

Set-off and carry forward

Mr O became a partner on 1 August 1998 in a firm which produced accounts to 31 December 1998, ie for a period of less than 12 months ending in his fiscal year of commencement, and annually thereafter. He also had investment income of £4,000 a year.

EXAMPLE 2.15 (*continued*)

His share of profits and losses (as adjusted for tax purposes)

1.8.98 to 31.12.98		£10,000
y/e 31.12.1999		£33,000
y/e 31.12.2000 (loss)		£(45,000)
y/e 31.12.2001		£57,000

Taxable – subject to loss relief

1998/99	1.8.98 to 5.4.99		
	£10,000 + (3/12 × £33,000)	£18,250	(a)
1999/2000	y/e 31.12.99	£33,000	(b)
2000/01	y/e 31.12.2000	£NIL	(c)
2001/02	y/e 31.12.2001	£57,000	(d)

Notes
(a) TA 1988, s 61(1), commencement to 5 April.
(b) TA 1988, s 61(2) does not apply, although the second year of assessment, as the period from commencement 1.8.98 to the accounting date given by TA 1988, s 60(5), 31.12.99, is not less than 12 months. Therefore, this is the first year of assessment in which there is an accounting date which falls not less than 12 months after the commencement date and the basis period is fixed by TA 1988, s 60(3)(*a*).
(c) TA 1988, s 60(3)(*b*).
(d) TA 1988, s 60(3)(*b*).

The period from 1.1.99 to 5.4.99 is taxed both for 1998/99 and 1999/2000 and is therefore an overlap period relieved under TA 1988, s 63A, resulting in overlap profits of £8,250 (3/12 × £33,000).

Loss relief available

The loss for the year ended 31 December 2000 is £45,000. This may be relieved as follows (ignoring relief under TA 1988, s 381):

Against investment income in	
2000/01 [TA 1988, s 380(1)(*a*)]	4,000
Against trading profits and investment	
income in 1999/00	4,000
[TA 1988, s 380(1)(*b*)]	33,000
Against trading profits for the year ended	
31 December 2001 (balance) [TA 1988, s 385]	4,000
	£45,000

However, as the investment income in 2000/01 is covered by personal allowances, it is probably better not to claim relief against total income in that year (i e not to claim under TA 1988, s 380(1)(*a*)) which would increase the loss carried forward against the profits for the year ended 31 December 2001 to £8,000.

Loss in early years of trade

The provisions which enable a loss to be carried back and set against total income of the three preceding years under TA 1988, s 381(new) applies for the current year basis of assessment where the loss arises in the first four years of the trade.

EXAMPLE 2.16

Set-off, carry forward and early year losses

Mr P joined a partnerships on 1 August 1998 which produced accounts annually to 31 July 1999. He also had investment income of £6,000 a year and a salary of £12,000 a year up to 31.3.1998.

His share of profits and losses (as adjusted for tax purposes)
y/e 31.7.1999 (loss)		£(28,000)
y/e 31.7.2000		£40,000
y/e 31.7.2001		£52,000
Taxable – subject to loss relief		
1998/99	1.8.98 to 5.4.99	
	(8/12 × (£28,000))	£NIL (a)
1999/2000	y/e 31.7.99	£NIL (b)
2000/01	y/e 31.7.2000	£40,000 (c)
2001/02	y/e 31.7.2001	£52,000 (d)

Notes
(a) TA 1988, s 61(1), commencement to 5 April.
(b) TA 1988, s 61(2) is inapplicable as period from commencement 1.8.98 to accounting date 31.7.99 is not less than 12 months, TA 1988, s 61(2)(*a*). Therefore, the basis period for the first year of assessment in which there is an accounting period under TA 1988 s 60(3)(*a*).
(c) TA 1988, s 60(3)(*b*).
(d) TA 1988, s 60(3)(*b*).

The period from commencement on 1.8.98 to 5.4.99 is taxed both for 1998/99 and 1999/2000 and is therefore an overlap period relievable under TA 1988, s 63A, but no overlap profits arise.

Loss relief available

The loss of £28,000 for the year ended 31 July 1999 may be relieved as follows (ignoring relief under TA 1988, s 381):

Against total income in 1997/98 on the basis of the loss in 1998/99 of £18,667 (8/12 × £28,000 for 1.8.98 to 5.4.99) limited to total income [TA 1988, s 380(1)(*b*)]	18,000
Against total income in 1998/99 on loss as above unrelieved (£18,667 – £18,000) limited to total income of £6,000 [TA 1988, s 380(1)(*a*)]	667
Against the same income in respect of the loss for the year ended 31 July 1999 [TA 1988, s 380(1)] £9,333 limited to total income (£6,000 – £667)	5,333
Against future profits from the same trade under [TA 1988, s 385] £28,000 less relieved £24,000 leaving balance of £4,000 to be claimed against profits for the year ended 31 July 2000	4,000
	£28,000

22 The current year basis of assessment

EXAMPLE 2.16(a), *as above, but giving loss relief under TA 1988, s 381*

Loss for 1998/99		18,667
Loss for 1999/2000		9,333
Total losses available for relief		£28,000

Loss relief			
1995/96	Earned income		12,000
	Investment income		6,000
			18,000
	Loss arising 1998/99 £18,667		
	(limited to total income)		
	(Balance £667 c/f to 1996/97)		(18,000)
	Chargeable to tax		£NIL
1996/97	Earned income		12,000
	Investment income		6,000
			18,000
	Balance of loss arising 1998/99		
	(£18,667 – £18,000)		(667)
	Loss arising 1999/2000		(9,333)
	Chargeable to tax		£8,000

Terminal loss

A terminal loss relief claim enables the loss in the final twelve months of a business to be set against the total income of that year and of the three preceding fiscal years (TA 1988, s 388(new)). Where a loss would fall into a computation more than once, for example on a change of accounting date, relief is given in the first year for which it is available and it is treated as zero in the second year (TA 1988, s 382(4)(new)).

EXAMPLE 2.17

Mr Q was a partner in a firm which made up its accounts to 30 November each year until 31 August 2003 when he resigned. He had no other income until 1 January 2004 when he took a job which produced earnings of £20,000 in 2003/04.

His share of the results (as adjusted for tax purposes)
y/e 30.11.99	£170,000
y/e 30.11.2000	£130,000
y/e 30.11.2001	£100,000
y/e 30.11.2002 (loss)	£(40,000)
1.12.2002 to 31.8.2003 (loss)	£(220,000)

EXAMPLE 2.17 *(continued)*

Assessable/taxable before loss relief
1999/2000	Current year	£170,000
2000/01	Current year	£130,000
2001/02	Current year	£100,000
2002/03	Current year	£NIL
2003/04	Current year	£NIL

Loss relief available
2001/02	Current year	£100,000
	Less loss carried back under TA 1988, s 380(1)(*b*)	£40,000
	Amended assessment	£60,000

Terminal loss
2003/04	Loss in last 12 months of trading	
	1.12.02 to 31.8.03	220,000
	1.9.02 to 30.11.02	NIL
	(already relieved under TA 1988, s 380(1)(*b*))	
	Total terminal loss	220,000
	Set-off against income in 2003/04	20,000
	Loss carried back	200,000
	Set-off against income in 2002/03	NIL
	Loss carried back	200,000
	Set-off against income in 2001/02	60,000
	Loss carried back	140,000
	Set-off against income in 2000/01	130,000
	Loss unrelieved	£10,000

CAPITAL ALLOWANCES

The current year basis provisions which treat capital allowances as trading expenses apply to new businesses commencing or deemed to commence on or after 6 April 1994, but for existing businesses only from 1997/98. As with losses the old provisions apply for the transitional year 1996/97 to avoid complications of transitional year averaging (FA 1994, s 211(2)). Where, exceptionally, allowances are given by way of discharge or repayment of tax, the relief is given against the income of the specified class by reference to the period of account, not the fiscal year. Writing down and initial allowances are treated as a trading expense in the period of account and balancing charges as a trading receipt (CAA 1990, s 140(2)(new)). The claim for capital allowances is made in the tax return and not as a separate claim under TMA 1970, s 42 (CAA 1990, s 140(3)(new)). The actual rates and calculation of capital allowances remains basically the same under the current year basis as under the preceding year basis of assessment.

EXAMPLE 2.18

RS & Co. made up accounts to 30 June annually. In the year ended 30 June 1999 they incurred expenditure on plant and machinery of £80,000. Their capital allowances pool brought forward was £200,000 and they had disposals of £8,000. Their profits before capital allowances, but otherwise as adjusted for tax purposes were £104,000.

Capital allowances for y/e 30.6.99	200,000
Less disposals	8,000
	192,000
Additions	80,000
	272,000
Writing-down allowance at 25% pa	68,000
Written down value carried forward	204,000
Profits for accounting period	104,000
Less capital allowances	68,000
Taxable profit	£36,000

The adjusted profit of £36,000 for the year ended 30 June 1999 is assessed for 1999/2000 on the current year basis.

EXAMPLE 2.19

In the previous example, had RS & Co. started business on 1 July 1998 and incurred expenditure on plant of £280,000, less disposals of £8,000, the computation would have been:

Plant additions	280,000
Less disposals	8,000
	272,000
Writing-down allowance at 25% pa	68,000
Written down value carried forward	204,000
Profit for accounting period	104,000
Less capital allowances	68,000
Adjusted profit	£36,000

Assessable taxable		
1998/99	1.7.98 to 5.4.99 (9/12 × £36,000) Commencement to next 5 April TA 1988, s 61(1)	£27,000
1999/2000	y/e 30.6.99 12 months to accounting date, TA 1988, s 60(3)(a) Overlap relief £27,000 for overlap period 1.7.98 to 5.4.99	£36,000

The basis period rules for capital allowances are unnecessary under the current year basis of assessment as the chargeable period is the period for which accounts are made up. If, exceptionally, two periods of account overlap, for example if a partnership prepares accounts to the date of a partner's death and then for the normal accounting period including that period, the capital allowances for the common period fall in the first period only (CAA 1990, s 160(6)(new)). These rules only apply where the same period appears in two sets of accounts, not where there is an overlap of basis periods, for example where the same profits after capital allowances are charged to tax more than once under the transitional provisions or on a commencement or change of accounting date.

EXAMPLE 2.20

T and U were in partnership, making up accounts to 31 December annually until 1999 when T died on 30 June. Accounts were prepared to the date of death and for the year ended 31 December 1999.

The capital allowances pool at 1.1.1999 was £240,000 and there were acquisitions of plant and machinery of £18,000 and £24,000 in each half year, and disposals of £2,000 and £4,000 respectively.

The capital allowances are:
1.1.99 to 30.6.99

Written down value brought forward at 1.1.99	240,000
Additions 1.1.99 to 30.6.99	18,000
	258,000
Disposals 1.1.99 to 30.6.99	2,000
	256,000
Writing-down allowance £256,000 × 25% × 6/12	32,000
Written down value at 30.6.99	224,000
Additions 1.7.99 to 31.12.99	24,000
	248,000
Disposals 1.7.99 to 31.12.99	4,000
	244,000
Writing-down allowance £244,000 × 25% × 6/12	30,500
Written down value at 31.12.99	£213,500

The other possibility, which again would be fairly rare, would be where the trade continues but there is a gap between two sets of accounts. This could happen if a business went into suspended animation for a period, perhaps on a change of premises, or as a result of a fire or other disaster.

Writing down allowances are computed on the basis of an annualised rate where the accounting period is less than or more than twelve months (FA 1994, s 213(3)–(10)). However, if an accounting period exceeds eighteen months it is divided into periods of account of twelve months or less for the purposes of computing the capital allowances. It should be noted that capital allowances are computed by reference to the period of account, not the date within the accounting period that the asset is acquired or disposed of, and it is the profits or losses after capital allowances that come into the basis period calculations that have already been explained. Any overlap or overlap relief is therefore inclusive of capital allowances except under the transitional provisions dealt with below.

EXAMPLE 2.21

V & Co. made up accounts each year to 31 December until 1999 when they produced a short set of accounts to 30 June which was a valid change of accounting date for tax purposes and annually thereafter. In the six months to 30 June 1999 they incurred expenditure on plant and machinery of £50,000. Their capital allowances pool brought forward was £160,000 and disposals in the period realised £10,000.

Capital allowances for 6-month period ending 30.6.99:

Pool value brought forward	160,000
Less disposals	10,000
	150,000
Additions in period 1.1.99 to 30.6.99	50,000
	200,000
Writing-down allowance (£200,000 × 25% × 6/12)	25,000
Written down value carried forward at 30.6.99	175,000

Adjusted pre-capital allowances profits were:

y/e 31.12.98	120,000
1.1.99 to 30.6.99	55,000

Assessable/taxable

1998/99	y/e 31.12.98	
	(£120,000 less capital allowances £40,000)	80,000
1999/2000	Year to new accounting date	
	1.1.99 to 30.6.99	
	(£55,000 less capital allowances £25,000)	30,000
	1.7.98 to 31.12.98 (£80,000 × 6/12)	£40,000
	Assessment	£213,500

Where a trade is not being carried on but allowances are available, for example to a landed estate where the allowances are given by way of discharge or repayment, the period of account is the year of assessment (CAA 1990, s 160(5)(new)). The allowances given for patents and know-how are also adjusted pro-rata where the accounting period is more or less than twelve months (TA, 1988, s 520(4)(a)(ii)(new)).

TRANSITIONAL PROVISIONS

A business in existence at 5 April 1994 remains taxable under the preceding year basis of assessment for 1994/95 and 1995/96. If the business ceases before 6 April 1997 it also remains under the preceding year basis of assessment throughout (FA 1994, Sch. 20, para. 3(1)). A business which continues beyond 5 April 1997 is normally assessed under the current year basis of assessment rules from 1997/98 and under the transitional rules in 1996/97.

Transitional averaging

The 1996/97 assessment is based on an annualised average profit for the transitional period assuming there is an accounting date in 1996/97, the primary basis period is the year ending on the latest accounting date falling in that year (FA 1994, Sch. 20, para. 1(2)(*a*)). If there is no accounting period ending in 1996/97 the basis period is the year ended 5 April 1997 (FA 1994, Sch. 20, para. 1(2)(*b*)). To the profits of the primary basis period must be added the profits of the relevant period which begins immediately after the end of the basis period for 1995/96, computed under the preceding year basis of assessment rules, and ends immediately before the beginning of the primary basis period for 1996/97, computed under the current year basis of assessment rules (FA 1994, Sch. 20, para. 2(2)). The assessment is the appropriate percentage of the aggregate profits, which is 365 divided by the total number of days in the full basis period; that is the primary basis plus the relevant period. In the vast majority of cases where the business makes up accounts to the same date each year, the transitional provisions assess, in 1996/97, 50% of the aggregate profits for the two years ending on the normal accounting date in 1996/97.

EXAMPLE 2.22

Transitional averaging
W has been in partnership for many years and the firm produces accounts each year to 5 April.

His share of profits (as adjusted for tax purposes)
y/e 5.4.94	£40,000
y/e 5.4.95	£44,000
y/e 5.4.96	£52,000
y/e 5.4.97	£48,000
y/e 5.4.98	£60,000
y/e 5.4.99	£56,000

Assessable/taxable
1994/95	Preceding year basis	£40,000 (a)
1995/96	Preceding year basis	£44,000 (b)
1996/97	Transitional year	£49,932 (c)
1997/98	Current year basis	£60,000 (d)
1998/99	Current year basis	£56,000 (e)

Notes
(a) TA 1988, s 60(3) (original version).
(b) TA 1988, s 60(3) (original version).
(c) Primary basis period for 1996/97 under
TA 1988, s 60(3)(*b*)   48,000
Relevant period under FA 1994, Sch. 20, para. 2(2)(*b*),(5)
i.e. 6.4.95 to 5.4.96   52,000

Aggregate [FA 1994, Sch. 20, para. 2(2)]   £100,000

Appropriate percentage under FA 1994, Sch. 20, para. 2(5)

$$£100,000 \times \frac{365}{366 + 365} = £49,932$$

EXAMPLE 2.22 *(continued)*

There is no transitional overlap period under FA 1994, Sch. 20, para. 2(4) as the basis period for 1997/98 begins on 6 April 1997 under TA 1988, s 60(3)(*b*). 1996 is a leap year.
(d) Substituted TA 1988, s 60(3)(*b*).
(e) Substituted TA 1988, s 60(3)(*b*).

EXAMPLE 2.23

Transitional averaging

X is a partner in a firm which produces accounts to 31 December each year until 1996/97 when the accounting date is changed to 31 March as a result of a 15-month accounting period.

His share of profits (as adjusted for tax purposes)
y/e 31.12.94	£50,000
y/e 31.12.95	£60,000
1.1.96 to 31.3.97	£90,000
y/e 31.3.98	£80,000

Assessable/taxable
1995/96	Preceding year basis	£50,000 (a)
1996/97	Transitional year	£66,687 (b)
1997/98	Current year basis	£80,000 (c)

Notes
(a) TA 1988, s 60(3) (original version).
(b) Primary basis period for 1996/97 under FA 1994,
Sch. 20, para. 1(2)(*a*) (12 months to 31.3.97)
12/15 × £90,000 = ⟶ 72,000
Relevant period under FA 1994, Sch. 20, para. 2(2)(*b*)
ie 1.1.95 to 31.3.96
1.1.95 to 31.12.95 ⟶ 60,000
1.1.96 to 31.3.96 (3/15 × £390,000) ⟶ 18,000

Aggregate [FA 1994, Sch. 20, para. 2(2)] £150,000

Appropriate percentage under FA 1994, Sch. 20, para. 2(5)

$$£150,000 \times \frac{365}{365+456} = £66,687$$

Transitional overlap period under FA 1994, Sch. 20, para. 2(4) part of basis period for 1997/98, year ended 31 March 1998, which falls before 6 April 1997 and after 31 March 1997, ie 1.4.97 to 5.4.97, ie 5 days' overlap profits £80,000 × 5/365 = £1,095.
(c) TA 1988, s 60(3)(*b*); FA 1994, s 200.

Where, exceptionally, 1995/96 is assessed on an actual basis as a result of a deemed cessation and commencement on a partnership change, without a continuation election, after 5 April 1992, or on an election under TA 1988, s 62(4), after 5 April 1990, or on the taxpayer making the appropriate election to have a business commencing in the year ended 5 April 1994 assessed on an actual basis under TA 1988, s 62(2) or (4); the assessment for 1996/97 will also be on the profits for the fiscal year, apportioned as necessary.

Transitional provisions

The primary basis period for 1997/98 will be the twelve months from the end of the basis period for 1996/97 in the normal way, which will be the year ended with the accounting date ending in 1997/98, assuming there is no change in accounting date. If there is a change of accounting date in 1997/98 the assessment will be on the profits for the twelve months to the new accounting date with an appropriate overlap under TA 1988, s 63A, where the accounting date is brought forward, or from the end of the 1996/97 basis period to the new accounting date in 1997/98 if the accounting date is made later in the fiscal year.

EXAMPLE 2.24

Y is a partner in a firm which produces accounts to 31 December each year until 31 December 1996. The firm then produces accounts for the 6 months to 30 June 1997.

His share of profits (as adjusted for tax purposes)
y/e 31.12.95	£60,000
y/e 31.12.96	£80,000
p/e 30.6.97	£48,000
Assessable/taxable	
1996/97	£69,904 (a)
1997/98	£88,000 (b)

Notes
(a) Basis period for 1996/97 under TA 1988, s 60(3)(*b*)

Accounting year to 31.12.96 ending in current fiscal year	80,000
Relevant period under FA 1994, Sch. 20, para. 2(2)(*b*), (5), i e 1.1.95 to 31.12.95	60,000
Aggregate [FA 1994, Sch. 20, para. 2(2)]	£140,000

Appropriate percentage under FA 1994, Sch. 20, para. 2(5)

$$£140,000 \times \frac{365}{366+365} = £69,904$$

Transitional overlap period under FA 1994, Sch. 20, para. 2(4) part of basis period for 1997/98, year ended 30 June 1997, which falls before 6 April 1997 and after the end of the basis period for 1996/97, 31 December 1996, ie 1.1.97, ie 95 days, overlap profits £48,000 × 95/181 = £25,193

(c) TA 1988, s 62(5) makes 1997/98 the year in which the accounting date is deemed to change as accounts are made up to a new date in the fiscal year. The period is less than 12 months from the end of the previous basis period (31.12.96), therefore TA 1988, s 62(2)(*a*) determines the basis as 12 months ending with the new accounting date, ie £80,000 × 6/12 + £48,000 = £88,000, year ended 30 June 1997. The period 1.7.96 to 31.12.96 is taxed in both 1996/97 and 1997/98, and therefore there is a standard over-lap period under TA 1988, s 63A, resulting in overlap profits of £40,000 (6/12 × £80,000).

Transitional overlap

The purpose of the transitional relief is to recognise the fact that under the preceding year basis of assessment the opening period profits usually have been

30 *The current year basis of assessment*

assessed between two and three times. The transitional averaging effectively gives relief for one year's double charge on commencement (in terms of timing, not in terms of profits) and the balance of the double charge is taken into account by granting transitional overlap relief which consists of the apportioned profits for the period from the end of the basis period for 1996/97 to 5 April 1997, ie part of the profit assessable in 1997/98 (FA 1994, Sch. 20, para. 2(4)). Transitional overlap relief may be used on a change of accounting date resulting in a long period or on cessation, in the same way as ordinary overlap relief under TA 1988, s 63A(new).

EXAMPLE 2.25

Z has been a partner in a business for many years which produces accounts each year to 30 April.

His share of profits (as adjusted for tax purposes)
y/e 30.4.93		£40,000
y/e 30.4.94		£44,000
y/e 30.4.95		£52,000
y/e 30.4.96		£48,000
y/e 30.4.97		£60,000
y/e 30.4.98		£56,000
Assessable/taxable		
1994/95	Preceding year basis	£40,000 (a)
1995/96	Preceding year basis	£44,000 (b)
1996/97	Transitional year	£49,932 (c)
1997/98	Current year basis	£60,000 (d)
1998/99	Current year basis	£56,000 (e)

Notes
(a) TA 1988, s 60(3) (original version) accounting year ending in preceding fiscal year.
(b) TA 1988, s 60(3) (original version).
(c) Basis period for 1996/97 under TA 1988, s 60(3)(*b*)
    (accounting year to 30.4.96 ending in
    current fiscal year)   48,000
    Relevant period under FA 1994, Sch. 20, para. 2(2)(*b*),
    (5) ie 1.5.94 to 30.4.95   52,000

    Aggregate [FA 1994, Sch. 20, para. 2(2)]   £100,000

Appropriate percentage under FA 1994, Sch. 20, para. 2(5)
(1996 is a leap year)

$$£100,000 \times \frac{365}{366+365} = £49,932$$

Overlap period under FA 1994, Sch. 20, para. 2(4); part of basis period for 1997/98, year ending 30 April 1997, which falls before 6 April 1997 and after 30 April 1996, ie 1.5.96 to 5.4.97, ie 340 days, overlap profits £60,000 × 340/365 = £55,890.
(d) TA 1988, s 60(3)(*b*).
(e) TA 1988, s 60(3)(*b*).

In computing the transitional overlap the amount of overlap is calculated on the profits before capital allowances, notwithstanding that the 1997/98 assessment would be on the profits after deducting capital allowances as an expense. The reason for this is to prevent a loss of capital allowances because the basis periods under the preceding year basis of assessment do not give rise to any overlaps or gaps and therefore no adjustment is required under the transitional provisions. If, however, the business is a partnership with a corporate partner the capital allowances are calculated under TA 1988, s 114(3) and the correct figure is given by calculating the transitional overlap on the figure after capital allowances (FA 1994, Sch. 20, para. 2(4A) and (4B).

CESSATION PRIOR TO 6 APRIL 1998

Under the preceding year basis of assessment the Revenue have the option on cessation under TA 1988, s 63 to substitute the actual profits for a penultimate and ante-penultimate fiscal years for the profits previously assessable on the preceding year basis, as explained in Chapter 1. Where a cessation takes place in 1997/98 the current year basis rules are applied in the first instance for 1996/97 and 1997/98. However, the Revenue may direct that the old rules continue to apply which would revise 1995/96 and 1996/97 to the profits of the fiscal year in each case, apportioning the figures as necessary (FA 1994, Sch. 20, para. 3(2)). The year 1997/98 therefore becomes assessable on the profits from 6 April 1997 to the date of cessation. Clearly, the Revenue would only make a direction if it resulted in a higher tax charge.

EXAMPLE 2.26

Cessation in 1997/98
Mr AB had been a partner in a business for many years which produced accounts to 30 June each year until 31 January 1998 when he retired.

His share of profits (as adjusted for tax purposes)
y/e 30.6.93	£72,000
y/e 30.6.94	£60,000
y/e 30.6.95	£48,000
y/e 30.6.96	£36,000
y/e 30.6.97	£24,000
p/e 31.1.98	£10,000

Assessable/taxable
1994/95	Preceding year basis	£72,000 (a)
1995/96	Preceding year basis	£60,000 (b)
1996/97	Transitional year	£41,942 (c)
1997/98	Year of cessation	£17,644 (d)

Notes
(a) TA 1988, s 60(3) (original version) accounting year ending in preceding year of assessment.
(b) TA 1988, s 60(3) as above.
(c) Basis period for 1996/97 under TA 1988, s 60(3)(*b*)
accounting year ending 30 June 1996 in fiscal year	36,000
Relevant period under FA 1994, Sch. 20, para. 2(2)(*b*), (5) i.e. 1.7.94 to 30.6.95	48,000
Aggregate [FA 1994, Sch. 20, para. 2(2)]	£84,000

EXAMPLE 2.26 *(continued)*
Appropriate percentage under FA 1994, Sch. 20, para. 2(5)
(1996 is a leap year)

$$£84,000 \times \frac{365}{366+356} = £41,942$$

(d) TA 1988, s 63, period from end of basis period for 1996/97, 1 July to date of cessation 31 January 1998, ie £24,000 year ended 30 June 1997 plus £10,000 period ending 31 January 1998, ie £34,000 less overlap relief under TA 1988, s 63A(3), £16,356 (see below) = £17,644.
Transitional overlap period under FA 1994, Sch. 20, para. 2(4), part of basis period for 1997/98 which falls before 6 April 1997, 1.7.96 to 5.4.97, ie 279 days, overlap profits £34,000 × 279/580* = £16,356.

* period 1.7.96 to 31.1.98, 365 + 215 days

Revenue direction
The Revenue may direct that the new rules do not apply under TA 1994, Sch. 20 para. 3(2).
1994/95	Preceding year basis	£72,000 (a)
1995/96	Preceding year basis	£60,000 (b)
1996/97	Preceding year basis	£48,000 (c)
1997/98	6 April to date of cessation	£16,000 (d)

Notes
(a) TA 1988, s 60(3) (original version).
(b) TA 1988, s 60(3) (original version).
(c) TA 1988, s 60(3) (original version).
(d) TA 1988, s 63(1)(*a*) (original version), ie £6,000 (3/12 × £24,000) + £10,000. The total of 1996/97 and 1997/98 on this basis is £64,000 (£48,000 + £16,000) compared with £59,586 (£41,942 + £17,644) on the new basis so the Revenue are likely to make this direction.

The Revenue have a further option to compute 1995/96 and 1996/97 on an actual fiscal year basis under TA 1988, s 63(1)(*b*) (original version).

1995/96	Actual basis	
	3/12 × £48,000 =	12,000
	9/12 × £36,000 =	27,000
		39,000
1996/97	Actual basis	
	3/12 × £36,000 =	9,000
	9/12 × £24,000 =	18,000
		27,000
		£66,000

However, this is less than as originally computed under the old rules which amounted to £108,000 (£60,000 + £48,000) and this further option would not be exercised in this instance.

CESSATION IN 1998/99

If the cessation takes place in 1998/99 the Revenue may make a direction for 1996/97 to be assessed on the actual profits of the fiscal year instead of the normal average profits basis (FA 1994, Sch. 20, para. 3(3) and (4)). The Revenue would obviously make such a direction only if the result would be to increase the taxable profits in 1996/97. The years 1997/98 and 1998/99 are not affected by such a change but, clearly, if 1996/97 is adjusted to the profits for the fiscal year there would be no transitional overlap under FA 1994, Sch. 20, para. 2(4).

EXAMPLE 2.27

Cessation in 1998/99

Mr AC had carried on trading in partnership for many years, making up the firm's accounts to 30 June each year until he retired on 31 December 1998.

His share of profits (as adjusted for tax purposes)
y/e 30.6.94	£60,000
y/e 30.6.95	£56,000
y/e 30.6.96	£48,000
y/e 30.6.97	£44,000
y/e 30.6.98	£32,000
1.7.98 to 31.12.98	£6,000

Assessable/taxable
1995/96	Preceding year basis	£60,000 (a)
1996/97	Transitional year	£51,928 (b)
1997/98	Current year basis	£44,000 (c)
1998/99	Year of discontinuance	£4,368 (d)

Notes

(a) TA 1988, s 60(3) (original version).

(b) Basis period for 1996/97

y/e 30.6.96 [FA 1994, Sch. 20, para. (2)(*a*)]	48,000
Relevant period under FA 1994, Sch. 20, para. 2(2)(*b*)	
y/e 30.6.95	56,000
Aggregate [FA 1994, Sch. 20, para. 2(2)]	£104,000

Appropriate percentage under FA 1994, Sch. 20, para. 2(5)

$$£104,000 \times \frac{365}{366+365} = £51,928$$

(c) TA 1988, s 60(3)(*b*), y/e 30.6.97

(d) TA 1988, s 60(3)(*b*), y/e 30.6.98 = £32,000

+ p/e 31.12.98 £6,000 total	38,000
Less overlap relief, overlap period	
1.7.96 to 5.4.97, overlap profits 279/365 × £44,000 =	33,632
Final assessment £38,000 − £33,632 =	4,368
Possible Revenue direction under FA 1994, Sch. 20, para. 3(3), (4): 1996/97 on transitional rules (as above)	51,928

EXAMPLE 2.27 *(continued)*

```
1996/97 on actual basis
   3/12 × y/e 30.6.96 (£48,000)                    12,000
   9/12 × y/e 30.6.97 (£44,000)                    33,000
                                                  -------
                                                  £45,000
                                                  =======
```

PARTNERSHIPS – OTHER INCOME

The profits of the partnership are to be computed as if the partnership were an individual resident in the U.K. (TA 1988, s 111(2)(new)). The profits of the partnership as adjusted for tax purposes are allocated to the partners in their profit-sharing ratio for the accounting period under TA 1988, s 111(3)(new) and each partner is charged to tax on his share of those profits. The commencement provisions under the current year basis of assessment are applied as if a partner's individual deemed trade commenced on joining the partnership and ceased on leaving the partnership. A change of accounting date for the firm is treated as a change of accounting date of each of the individual partners (TA 1988, s 111(4)). This means that each partner has his overlap on commencement and overlap relief on cessation or a change of accounting date. It also means that a change of accounting date applicable for tax purposes must be made on behalf of the partnership by a nominated partner (TA 1988, s 111(6)). If the partnership is entitled to income from an overseas firm the income would be assessed under Schedule D, Case V. Under the current year basis of assessment profits of an overseas trade are computed applying Schedule D, Cases I and II rules, although they remain assessable under Schedule D, Case V. Income from property assessed under Schedule A, and investment income assessed under Schedule D, Cases III, IV or V, or sundry income assessed under Schedule D, Case VI would normally be assessed on a strict fiscal year basis for self-assessment purposes, as would income subject to deduction of tax at source. Where, however, such income is received by a partnership such non-trading income, other than that received under deduction of tax, is taxable by reference to the same basis periods as those which apply to the Schedule D, Cases I and II income, as if it were income of a second deemed trade (TA 1988, s 111(7) and (8)(new)). This treatment also brings in the overlap provisions on commencement or change of accounting date, and under the transitional provisions and overlap relief on a cessation or extension of accounting period. Each partner would again be assessable on his share of the partnership's other income, separately from any investment income receivable by him from non-partnership investment, taxed income is dealt with on a fiscal year basis.

EXAMPLE 2.28

Other income – transitional averaging

ADEF & Co. was a partnership consisting of AD and EF sharing profits equally, which has the following income, as adjusted for tax purposes, assumed to accrue evenly throughout the period.

	Total	Sch. D Case I	Sch. A	Sch. D Case III	Sch. D Case V
	£	£	£	£	£
y/e 30.4.94	226,000	160,000	40,000	10,000	16,000
y/e 30.4.95	260,000	180,000	48,000	12,000	20,000
y/e 30.4.96	282,000	200,000	50,000	8,000	24,000
y/e 30.4.97	258,000	170,000	44,000	4,000	40,000

EXAMPLE 2.28 *(continued)*

Assessable/taxable

	Total	AD	EF
1995/96 Schedule D, Case I – y/e 30.4.94	160,000	80,000	80,000

Schedule A – y/e 5.4.96
25/365 × £48,000 — 3,288
340/365 × £50,000 — 46,576

	49,864	24,932	24,932

Schedule D, Case III – y/e 5.4.95 (PYB)
25/365 × £10,000 — 685
340/365 × £12,000 — 11,178

	11,863	5,931	5,932

Schedule D, Case V – y/e 5.4.95 (PYB)
25/365 × £16,000 — 1,096
340 × £20,000 — 18,630

	19,726	9,863	9,863

1996/97 transitional year
Schedule D, Case I
Primary basis period
y/e 30.4.96 — 200,000
Relevant period y/e 30.4.95 — 180,000

Aggregate — £380,000

	Total	AD	EF

Appropriate percentage

$$£380,000 \times \frac{365}{365+365} =$$

	190,000	95,000	95,000

Schedule A – y/e 5.4.97
25/365 × £50,000 — 3,424
340/365 × £44,000 — 40,986

	44,410	22,205	22,205

Schedule D, Case III – y/e 5.4.96
25/365 × £12,000 — 822
340/365 × £8,000 — 7,452
y/e 5.4.97
25/365 × £8,000 — 548
340/365 × £4,000 — 3,726

Aggregate — £12,548

50% thereof	6,274	3,137	3,137

EXAMPLE 2.28 *(continued)*

		Total	AD	EF
Schedule D, Case V – y/e 5.4.96				
25/365 × £20,000	1,370			
340/365 × £24,000	22,356			
y/e 5.4.97				
25/365 × £24,000	1,644			
340/365 × £40,000	37,260			
Aggregate	£62,630			
50% thereof		31,315	15,658	15,657
1997/98				
Schedule D Case I – y/e 30.4.97		190,000	95,000	95,000
Transitional overlap relief [FA 1994, Sch. 20, para. 2(4)] £190,000 × 340/365		176,986	88,493	88,493
Schedule A – 30.4.97		44,000	22,000	22,000
Schedule D Case III – y/e 30.4.97		4,000	2,000	2,000
Schedule D Case V – y/e 30.4.97		40,000	20,000	20,000

Transitional overlap relief is given by TA 1988, s 111(8).

	£	£	£
Schedule A			
340/365 × £44,000	40,986	20,493	20,493
Schedule D, Case III			
340/365 × £4,000	3,726	1,863	1,863
Schedule D, Case V			
340/365 × £40,000	37,260	18,630	18,630

EXAMPLE 2.29

Other income – commencement

Mr GH joined the firm of IJK & Co. as a partner on 1 October 1998. The partnership made up accounts to 30 April each year and Mr GH's share of profits as adjusted for tax purposes was as follows:

Year ended 30 April 1999	
Schedule D, Case I	£70,000
Schedule D, Case III	£30,000
Schedule D, Case V	£20,000
Schedule A	£24,000
Year ended 30 April 2000	
Schedule D, Case I	£160,000
Schedule D, Case III	£20,000
Schedule D, Case V	£40,000
Schedule A	£48,000

Assessable/taxable
1998/99
  1 October 1998 to 5 April 1999 (a)
  Schedule D, Case I 187/212 × £70,000   61,746

Schedule D, Case III(b) 187/212 × £30,000		26,462
Schedule D, Case V(b) 187/212 × £20,000		17,642
Schedule A(b) 187/212 × £24,000		21,170
		£127,020

Notes
(a) TA 1988, s 61(1), commencement to 5 April.
(b) Other income included [TA 1988, s 111].

1999/2000 £ £
1 October 1998 to 30 September 1999 (a)

	£	£
Schedule D, Case I		
1.10.98 to 30.4.99	70,000	
1.5.99 to 30.9.99 153/365 × £160,000	67,068	
		137,068
Schedule D, Case III		
1.10.98 to 30.4.99	30,000	
1.5.99 to 30.9.99 153/365 × £20,000	8,384	
		38,384
Schedule D, Case V		
1.10.98 to 30.4.99	20,000	
1.5.99 to 30.9.99 153/265 × £40,000	16,768	
		36,768
Schedule A		
1.10.98 to 30.4.99	24,000	
1.5.99 to 30.9.99 153/365 × £48,000	20,120	
		44,120
		£256,340

Notes
(a) TA 1988, s 61(2)(a) applies because the period from commencement 1.10.98 to the accounting date is less than 12 months. The basis period is therefore 12 months from commencement.
(b) The period from commencement on 1.10.98 to 5.4.99 is taxed both in 1998/99 and 1999/2000 and is therefore an overlap period relieved under TA 1988, s 63A, extended to other income by TA 1988, s 111(8). Overlap profits are:

Schedule D, Case I	61,746
Schedule D, Case III	26,462
Schedule D, Case V	17,642
Schedule A	21,170
	£127,020

2000/01
Year ended 30 April 2000 (a)
Schedule D, Case I   160,000

EXAMPLE 2.29 *(continued)*

Schedule D, Case III	20,000
Schedule D, Case V	40,000
Schedule A	48,000
	£268,000

Notes
(a) TA 1988, s 60(3)(*a*) applies as 30.4.2000 is the first accounting date for Mr GH which falls not less than 12 months after his commencement on 1.10.98.
(b) The period from 1.5.99 to 30.9.99 is taxed in both 1999/2000 and 200/01 and is therefore an overlap profit relievable under TA 1988, s 63A, resulting in overlap profits of:

Schedule D, Case I	67,068
Schedule D, Case III	8,384
Schedule D, Case V	16,768
Schedule A	20,120
	£112,340

Total overlap profits are:

Schedule D, Case I £61,746 + £67,068	128,814
Schedule D, Case III £26,462 + £8,384	34,846
Schedule D, Case V £17,642 + £16,768	34,410
Schedule A £21,170 + £20,120	41,290
	£239,360

Overlap relief arising from this treatment of partnership investment income which cannot be relieved against such income may be set against total income (TA 1988, s 111(9)). Losses arising under the second deemed trade such as Schedule A losses are also calculated by reference to the partnership basis periods applicable to trading losses. A partner becomes or ceases to be a partner by reference to the actual trade or profession (TA 1988, s 111(13)(new)). This means that there would not be a cessation of the deemed second trade merely because some or all of the partnership investments were disposed of. The deemed cessation of a trade on a partner leaving the firm is treated as a cessation for the post-cessation receipt rules under FA 1995, s 117(3).

TRANSITIONAL ANTI-AVOIDANCE – TRANSITIONAL AVERAGING

Anti-avoidance measures are introduced by FA 1995, Sch. 22 to prevent the exploitation of the transitional rules. It will be appreciated that where transitional averaging applies the effect is that profits in the transitional period are taxed at a reduced rate which therefore gives the taxpayer an incentive to maximise the profits in the transitional period. This is countered by FA 1995, Sch. 22, para. 1 by providing that if there is a relevant change which is an accounting change or change of business practice, or where there is a relevant transaction, ie a self-cancelling or connected party transaction which increases the profit in the transitional period either by accelerating income or deferring income or expenses, the tax sought to be saved is recovered, together with a penalty element of 25% of that tax. The penalty element is avoided under FA 1995, Sch. 22, para. 13 if the taxpayer voluntarily discloses the transaction to the Revenue as falling, or possibly falling, within the transitional anti-avoidance provisions. The provisions only apply where there has been a deliberate attempt to exploit the transitional rules and the anti-avoidance measures do not apply if any of the escape routes are available. The escape routes consist of: (i) a motive test, FA 1995, Sch. 22, para. 14(1)(*a*), under which the anti-avoidance rules are not invoked if the relevant change or transaction was wholly and exclusively for bona fide commercial purposes; (ii) a benefit test, that is that the obtaining of a tax advantage was not the single or main benefit to be expected from the relevant change or transaction; or (iii) a de minimis test, where the tax saved as a result of the change or transaction falls below the de minimis limits. These limits in FA 1995, Sch. 22, para. 1(3) are not expected to be fixed until immediately prior to 5 April 1997, ie at the end of the transitional period, as it is the intention of the Revenue to deter taxpayers from attempting to exploit the transitional provisions rather than to seek to collect the penalty for them having done so.

In order to compute the anti-avoidance charge, it is necessary to calculate the appropriate percentage of the profits diverted, that is 365 divided by the number of days in the transitional period, from which the complementary percentage is calculated at 100 minus the appropriate percentage. The tax charge is 1.25 times the complementary percentage of the profits diverted into the transitional period which is taxed in addition to the appropriate percentage of the profits in the transitional period under the normal transitional averaging provisions.

EXAMPLE 2.30

Alpha & Co., a two-partner firm, has been in business for many years and produces accounts for each year to 30 April.

Profits (as adjusted for tax purposes)
y/e 30.4.94		£40,000
y/e 30.4.95		£80,000
y/e 30.4.96		£120,00
y/e 30.4.97		£110,000
Assessable/taxable		
1995/96	Preceding year basis	40,000 (a)
1996/97	Transitional year	112,500 (b)
1997/98	Current year basis	110,000 (c)
	Total	£262,500

Notes
(a) TA 1988, s 60(3), original version.
(b) Primary basis period for 1996/97 under TA 1988
    s 60 (3)(*b*) – y/e 30.4.96   120,000
    Relevant period under FA 1994,
    Sch. 20, para. 2(2)(*b*), (5), ie 1.5.94 to 30.4.95   80,000

    Aggregate FA 1994, Sch. 20, para. 2(2)   £200,000

However, it transpires that profits of £20,000 were artificially shifted from the year ended 30 April 1994 to the year ended 30 April 1995. Alpha & Co. is unable to demonstrate any bona fide commercial reasons for this shift. The Revenue therefore impose the anti-avoidance provisions.

40 The current year basis of assessment

Appropriate percentage [FA 1995, Sch. 22, para. 1(4)]	$\dfrac{365}{365+365} = 50\%$	
Complementary percentage	$100 - 50 = 50\%$	
[FA 1995, Sch. 22, para. 1(2)(a)]		
50% × £120,000		60,000
50% × £80,000		40,000
[FA 1995, Sch. 22 para. 1(2)(b)]		
1.25 × 50% × £20,000		12,500
		£112,500

Transitional overlap period under FA 1994, Sch. 20, para. 2(4): part of basis period for 1997/98, year ending 30 April 1997, which falls after 30 April 1996 and before 6 April 1997, i e 1.5.96 to 5.4.97, i e 340 days' overlap profits, £110,000 × 340/365 = £102,466

(c) TA 1988, s 60(3)(b).

Had no shift or profits taken place the profits (as adjusted for tax purposes) would have been:

y/e 30.4.94		£60,000
y/e 30.4.95		£60,000
y/e 30.4.96		£120,00
y/e 30.4.97		£110,000
Assessable/taxable		
1995/96	Preceding year basis	60,000 (d)
1996/97	Transitional year	90,000 (e)
1997/98	Current year basis	110,000 (f)
	Total	£260,000

NOTES
(d) TA 1988, s 60(3), original version.
(e) Primary basis for 1996/97 under TA 1988, s 60 (3)(b)

FA 1994, s 200–y/e 30.4.96	120,000
Relevant period under FA 1994, Sch. 20, para. 2(2)(b), (5) i.e. 1.5.94 to 30.4.95	60,000
Aggregate [FA 1994, Sch. 20, para. 2(2)]	£180,000

Appropriate percentage under FA 1994, Sch. 20, para. 2(5):

$$£180,000 \times \dfrac{365}{365+365} = £90,000$$

(f) TA 1988, s 60(3)(b):
The unjustified shift of profits into the transitional period results in additional profits being charge of £2,500 (£262,500 − £260,000), i e a penalty of tax on one-quarter of £10,000 which is the amount that would have escaped tax on averaging £20,000 (£20,000 × 365/730).

EXAMPLE 2.31

Beta & Co. a five-partner firm, has been in business for many years and produced accounts each year to 31 December until 1996 when it produced accounts for the 15 months to 31 March 1997.

Profits (as adjusted for tax purposes)
y/e 31.12.94	£200,000
y/e 31.12.95	£400,000
p/e 31.3.97	£600,000
y/e 31.3.98	£550,000

Assessable/taxable
1995/96	Preceding year basis	200,000 (a)
1996/97	Transitional year	514,480 (b)
1997/98	Current year basis	550,000 (c)
	Total	£1,264,480

Notes
(a) TA 1988, s 60(3), original version.
(b) Primary basis period for 1996/97 under TA 1988,
s 60 (3)(b) – y/e 31.3.97 (12/15 × £600,000)   480,000
Relevant period under FA 1994, Sch. 20,
para. 2(2)(b), (5), ie 1.1.95 to 31.3.96
y/e 31.12.95   400,000
1.1.96 to 31.3.96 (3/15 × £600,000)   120,000

Aggregate [FA 1994, Sch. 20, para. 2(2)]   £1,000,000

Appropriate percentage under FA 1994, Sch. 20, para. 2(5):

$$£1,000,000 \times \frac{365}{365+365+90} \qquad £445,122$$

However, it transpires that profits of £100,000 were artificially shifted from the year ended 31 December 1994 to the year ended 31 December 1995. Beta & Co. is unable to demonstrate any bona fide commercial reason for this shift. The Revenue therefore impose the anti avoidance provisions.

Appropriate percentage $\dfrac{365}{365+365+90} \times 100 = 44.512\%$

Complementary percentage 100 – 44.512% = 55.488%

Aggregate
FA 1995, Sch. 22, para. 1(2)(a)
44.512% × £480,000	213,658
44.512% × £400,000	178,048
44.512% × £120,000	53,414

FA 1995, Sch. 22, para. 1(2)(b)
1.25 × 55.488% × £100,000	69,360
	£514,480

42 The current year basis of assessment

EXAMPLE 2.31 (*continued*)

Transitional overlap period under FA 1994, Sch. 20, para. 2(4): part of basis period for 1997/98, year ending 31 March 1998, which falls after 31 March 1997 and before 6 April 1997, ie 1.4.97 to 5.4.97, ie 5 days' overlap profits £550,000 × 5/365 = £7,534

(c) TA 1988, s 60(3)(*b*).

Had no shift or profits taken place the profits (as adjusted for tax purposes) would have been:

y/e 31.12.94		£300,000
y/e 31.12.95		£300,000
y/e 31.3.97		£600,000
y/e 31.3.98		£550,000
Assessable/taxable		
1995/96	Preceding year basis	300,000 (d)
1996/97	Transitional year	400,610 (e)
1997/98	Current year basis	550,000 (f)
	Total	£1,250,610

Notes

(d) TA 1988, s 60(3), original version.
(e) Primary basis for 1996/97 under TA 1988, s 60 (3)(*b*);

p/e 30.4.96 (12/15 × £600,000)	480,000
Relevant period under FA 1994, Sch. 20, para. 2(2)(*b*), (5), ie 1.1.95 to 31.3.96	
y/e 31.12.95	300,000
1.1.96 to 31.3.96 (3/15 × £600,000)	120,000
Aggregate [FA 1994, Sch. 20, para. 2(2)]	£900,000

Appropriate percentage under FA 1994, Sch. 20, para. 2(5);

$$£900,000 \times \frac{365}{365+365+90} = £400,610$$

(f) TA 1988, s 60(3)(*b*):
The unjustified shift of profits into the transitional period results in additional profits being charge of £13,870 (£1,264,480 − £1,250,610), ie a penalty of tax on one-quarter of £55,488 which is the amount that would have escaped tax on averaging, £100,000—

$$(£100,000 \times \frac{365}{365+365+90})$$

RELEVANT CHANGES

An accounting change or change of business practice is defined by FA 1995, Sch. 22, para. 14 as any change in an established practice of a trade, profession or vocation as to timing of the supply of goods or services, the invoicing of customers or clients and the collection of outstanding debts, the obtaining of goods or services, the incurring of business expenses and the settlement of outstanding debts, or obtaining or making payments in advance or payments on account. An accounting change means any modification of an accounting policy or substitution of one policy for another but does not include a change of accounting date, which brings the end of the basis period for 1996/97 closer to 5 April 1997.

The Inland Revenue booklet published on 29 November 1994 entitled "Self Assessment – Transition to the Current Year Basis – Anti-avoidance Provisions" states in paras 3.14 to 3.24:

> **"Change in business practice**
> *Expenses as well as receipts*
> 3.14 The legislation refers to amounts included in the profits or gains of the periods in question. It is important to note that the profit shifting envisaged does not refer only to the movement of receipts from one period to another. As the definition of 'change of business practice' at paragraph 13(3) of the draft legislation makes clear, the rules target equally situations where expenses are shifted to increase profits.
>
> *Established business practices*
> 3.15 The rules refer to a change occurring in an **established** business practice.
> 3.16 Whether a practice is established or not is ultimately a question of fact, but expenditure of a largely discretionary nature (such as routine decoration arising **broadly** every say, 5–7 years) would not normally be included in this category. However,where there was, say, a regular annual routine maintenance task necessitated by the specific nature of the trade (Health and Safety Regulations applying to a food processing plant for example) bringing forward or deferring the related expenditure, exceptionally, to the (respectively) previous or following year would be likely to constitute a change in an established practice.
>
> *Timing is crucial*
> 3.17 The rules target specifically changes which impact on the timing of recognition of profits so changes in practices which are not, in themselves, directly timing oriented, will normally be outside the rules. An example would be a change from a policy of leasing to purchasing capital assets.
> 3.18 On the other hand, a farmer (for example) departing from his established practice and delaying the sale of his crops in order to gain a tax advantage by shifting the proceeds into the transitional basis period would be in a trigger situation.
>
> **Accounting change**
> 3.19 'Accounting change' includes both a change of accounting policy and a modification of an existing policy.
> 3.20 An example of a change of accounting policy would be a change in the time at which profits from long term contracts are recognised (for example from recognition on completion to recognition over the life of the contract).
> 3.21 An example of a modification of an existing policy would be a change in the basis of valuation of trading stock at the account end (involving perhaps a re-appraisal of what overhead costs are to be included in calculating the cost of the stock).
> 3.22 The accounting change trigger can include any change of accounting date other than (a statutorily prescribed exception) one which brings the end of the basis period for the year 1996/97 closer to 5 April 1997.
> 3.23 Also within the trigger situations would be a change, for a professional partnership, from a cash to, for example, an earnings basis of assessment.
> 3.24 Not all accounting changes, however, have an effect on the accounting **policy** of a business. An example would be a change, based on practical experience, in measuring the useful life of leased assets with the result that the expenditure passing through the profit and loss account is reduced. This would not be con-

sidered a change of accounting policy but merely a re-appraisal of the basic facts to which an accounting policy was applied."

An accounting change or change of business practice is a relevant change unless it is made solely for bona fide commercial reasons (the motive test), or the obtaining of a tax advantage is not the single main benefit, that could reasonably be expected to arise from the making of the change (the benefit test). "Tax advantage" is not defined and therefore has a wide meaning, and in the view of the Inland Revenue includes a timing advantage.

In the publication on 29 November 1994 "Self Assessment – Transition to the Current Year Basis–Anti-avoidance Provisions", the Revenue confirmed in relation to the motive test requiring the exclusion to be solely for bona fide commercial reasons that:

> "in interpreting and applying the test the Inland Revenue would regard the sole purpose test to be equivalent to the 'wholly and exclusively' test in TA 1988, s 74. The same well established principles relating to that test could therefore be applied in relation to this test in the anti-avoidance rules. In particular, the fact that consideration may have been given to the tax consequences of a trigger transaction would not of itself have to lead to the conclusion that the transaction was undertaken other than for solely commercial reasons."

RELEVANT TRANSACTIONS

A relevant transaction is defined by FA 1995, Sch. 22, paras 15–17 as any self-cancelling transaction or transaction with a connected person unless it is entered into solely for bona fide commercial reasons, or the obtaining of a tax advantage is not the main benefit that could reasonably be expected to arise from entering into the transaction.

A self-cancelling transaction is an agreement by which the person carrying on the trade, profession or vocation agrees to sell or transfer trading stock or workin progress, if under the agreement he agrees to buy back or re-acquire the trading stock or work in progress, or acquires or grants an option, which is subsequently exercised, for him to buy back or reacquire the trading stock or work in progress.

Trading stock is defined by reference to TA 1988, s 100, ie property of any description whether real or personal which is sold in the ordinary course of a trade, or would be so sold if it were mature or its manufacture, preparation or construction were complete, or materials used in the manufacture preparation or construction of any such property including work in progress. Work in progress in relation to a profession or vocation is defined as services performed in the ordinary course of the profession or vocation which is wholly or partly completed at the time of the sale or transfer and which would have been charged for on completion if the transfer had not been affected, and any articles produced or material used in the performance of such services. This definition is based on that in TA 1988, s 101.

Connected person is defined by reference to TA 1988, s 839, ie spouse, relative, spouse of a relative or relative of a spouse; relative being brother, sister, ancestor or lineal descendent. A trustee is connected with the settlor or anybody connected with him, or with a company connected with the settlement. Partners are connected with an individual if he controls the partnership and with a company if the company controls the partnership or the same person controls the company and the partnership, and partners of more than one partnership are connected if the same person controls both partnerships. Control of a company is defined in accordance with TA 1988, s 416, i e the close company definition of ability to control the votes or having the greater part of the share capital income or rights on winding up, and partnership control is defined by reference to TA 1988, s 840, i e the right to share in more than half the assets or more than half the income of the partnership. Control is determined by including persons connected with the controller.

TRANSITIONAL OVERLAP

The Revenue are also concerned about the diversion of profits into the transitional overlap period. The concern is that the profits of this period, that is from the end of the basis period for 1996/97, which is normally the accounting year ending in 1996/97 to 5 April 1997, i e part of the profits for the accounting year ending in 1997/98, will ultimately be tax-free as overlap relief on a cessation or change of accounting date. It is therefore provided by FA 1995, Sch. 22, paras 3–5 that if profits are diverted into this period as a result of a relevant change or transaction, the overlap relief is reduced by 1.25 times the amount diverted into the overlap period which results in a penalty of 25% of the tax sought to be saved. As with the anti-transitional averaging provisions the penalty element does not apply if the diversion is brought to the Revenue's attention and no adjustment is made where any of the escape routes apply, i e the motive test, the benefit test or the deminimis provisions. Again, the de minimis levels for the transitional overlap relief will not be announced until immediately before 5 April 1997.

EXAMPLE 2.32

Mr Gamma is a partner in Delta & Co. and his self-assessments for 1997/98 and 1998/99 are as follows:

1997/98 – y/e 30.4.97	£80,000
1998/99 – y/e 30.4.98	£40,000

His transitional overlap profits are £74,520 (340/365 × £80,000). However, it transpires that profits of £30,000 were shifted from the year ended 30 April 1998 into the year ended 30 April 1997, falling foul of the anti-avoidance provisions. The transitional overlap profits are therefore restricted as follows:

Transitional overlap profit [FA 1994, Sch. 1, para. 2(4)]	74,520
Less 1.25 times aggregate of amounts falling within [FA 1995, Sch. 22, para. 3(1)(*b*)], 340/365 × £30,000 × 1.25 =	34,932
Revised transitional overlap relief	£39,588

The unjustified shift of profits into the transitional overlap period results in an additional reduction in overlap relief of £6,986 (34,932 – (£30,000 × 340/365)), ie a penalty of tax on one-quarter of £27,945 (£30,000 × 340/365) which is the amount by which the transitional overlap relief was artificially inflated.

These anti-avoidance rules could eliminate a claim for transitional overlap relief but would not impose a charge to tax on a negative figure.

46 The current year basis of assessment

If a partner retires in 1996/97 he would never normally come within the current year basis of assessment, but to prevent the manipulation of profits in favour of such a partner in order to avoid the transitional overlap penalty, such a partner may be assessed on his share of the diverted overlap as if he had remained a partner, under FA 1995, Sch. 22, para. 4.

EXAMPLE 2.33

Messrs Epsilon, Zeta and Theta have for many years traded in partnership. Epsilon leaves the partnership on 31 December 1996. Accounts are made up annually to 30 June and profits are shared as follows:

Year ended	30.6.94	30.6.95	30.6.96	30.6.97		30.6.98
				Time apportioned		
				(1.7.96 to	*1.1.97 to*	
				31.12.96)	*30.6.97)*	
Profit sharing ratios	33:33:33	33:33:33	33:33:33	50:25:25	50:50	50:50
Profits adjusted for tax purposes	£200,000	£400,000	£600,000	£500,000	£500,000	£200,000
E	66,667	133,333	200,000	250,000	–	–
Z	66,666	133,334	200,000	125,000	250,000	100,000
T	66,667	133,333	200,000	125,000	250,000	100,000
	£200,000	£400,000	£600,000	£500,000	£500,000	£200,000

A continuation election (a) is made in respect of Epsilon's departure from the partnership and each partner is assessed to tax as follows:

	Total	E	Z	T
1995/96				
y/e 30.6.94 preceding year basis (b)				
Profit sharing ratio				
(6.4.95 to 30.6.95) 33:33:33 3/12	50,000	16,667	16,667	16,666
(1.7.96 to 5.4.96) 33: 33: 33 9/12	150,000	50,000	50,000	50,000
	£200,000	£66,667	£66,667	£66,666
1996/97				
Transitional year (c)				
Profit sharing ratio				
(6.4.96 to 30.6.96) 33:33:33 3/12	125,000	41,667	41,667	41,666
(1.7.96 to 31.12.96) 50:25:25 6/12	250,000	62,500	62,500	62,500
(1.1.97 to 5.4.97) 50:50 3/12	125,000	125,000	62,500	62,500
	£500,000	166,667	166,667	166,666
Anti-avoidance adjustment (f)		46,876		
		£213,543		

EXAMPLE 2.33 *(continued)*

	Total	Z	T
1997/98 y/e 30.6.97 current year basis (d) Profit sharing ratio			
(1.7.96 to 31.12.96) 50:25:25 6/12	250,000	125,000	125,000
1.1.97 to 30.6.97) 50:50 6/12	500,000	250,000	250,000
	£750,000	£375,000	£375,000
Transitional overlap relief (e) 9/12		281,250	281,250
Less anti-avoidance adjustment (f)		70,312	70,312
Revised overlap relief		£210,398	£210,938

Notes
(a) TA 1988, s 113(2).
(b) TA 1988, s 60(3), original version.
(c) Primary basis period for 1996/97 under TA 1988,
s 60(3)(*b*) – y/e 30.6.96   600,000
Relevant period under FA 1994, Sch. 20, para. 2(2)(*b*), (5),
ie 1.7.94 to 30.6.95   400,000

Aggregate [FA 1994, Sch. 20, para. 2(2)   £1,000,000

Appropriate percentage under FA 1994, Sch. 20, para. 2(5)

$$£1,000,000 \times \frac{365}{365+365} = £500,000$$

(d) Profit for year ended 30.6.97 = £1,000,000. Share of Zeta and Theta computed in accordance with current year basis under TA 1988, ss 60(3)(*b*), 111(3)(*a*). Epsilon retires on 31 December 1996 and therefore is not assessable in 1997/98.
(e) FA 1994, Sch. 20, para. 2(4).
(f) It transpires that profits of £200,000 were shifted from the year ended 30 June 1998 into the year ended 30 June 1997, falling foul of the anti-avoidance provisions. The transitional overlap profits are therefore restricted as follows:

Transitional overlap profit assuming Epsilon had not retired:

	Total	E	Z	T
Profit y/e 30.6.97	£1,000,000	£250,000	£375,000	£375,000
Transitional overlap profit 9/12 [FA 1994, Sch. 20, para. 2(4)]	750,000	187,500	281,250	281,250
Less 1.25 times aggregate of amounts falling within FA 1995, Sch. 22, para. 3(1)(*b*) 9/12 × £200,000 × 1.25 in deemed profit sharing proportion A's share is charged for 1996/97 under FA 1995, Sch. 22, para. 4	187,500	46,876	70,312	70,312

48   The current year basis of assessment

EXAMPLE 2.33 *(continued)*

The unjustified shift of profits into the transitional overlap period results in an additional reduction in overlap relief of £37,500 (£187,500 − (£200,000 × 9/12)), ie a penalty of tax on one quarter of £150,000 (£200,000 × 9/12) which is the amount by which the transitional overlap relief was artificially inflated.

EXAMPLE 2.34

This shows the calculation of partners' individual basis periods. A, B, C and D have been in partnership for many years making up accounts to 30 April. The results of the business for the 4 years to 30 April 2000 are shown below.

Year to 30 April	1997	1998	1999	2000
Adjusted profit	£155,000	£190,000	£230,000	£215,000
Sharing ratios	%	%	%	%
A	25	19	15	
B	25	22	25	40
C	25	22	25	30
D	25	22	20	30
E		15	15	
Joiners		E on 1.5.97		
Leavers			A and E on 30.4.99	

The assessments on the individual partners for the years 1997/98 to 2000/01 are shown below. For calculation purposes 5 April is assumed to be coterminous with 31 March.

1997/98

This is the first year of the current year basis of assessment. The basis period is the period of account ending in the year of assessment (30 April 1997). The profits are apportioned to the partners in the commercial PSR for the accounting period.

	Adjusted profits	A	B	C	D
PSR		25%	25%	25%	25%
Assessable 1997/98	£155,000	£38,750	£38,750	£38,750	£38,750

*As pre current year basis partners, A, B, C and D are entitled to "transitional relief".
*Transitional relief is that part of the basis period profit for 1997/98 falling before 6 April 1997.
*Transitional relief is carried forward as overlap relief.

The basis period used for 1997/98 is 1 May 1996 to 30 April 1997 and 340 days fall before 6 April 1997. Thus the transitional relief for each partner is:

1997/98 profit	£38,750	£38,750	£38,750	£38,750
Transitional relief is 340/365.	£36,095	£36,095	£36,095	£36,095

E becomes a partner on 1 May 1997 and thus will have a 1997/98 assessment. Under s 61(1) the actual basis will apply to him on his commencement. Thus his assessment will be the 11 months to 5 April 1998. This will not be capable of final calculation until after the 1998 accounts are prepared.

EXAMPLE 2.34 (continued)

1998/99

The basis period is the period of account ending in the year of assessment (30 April 1998). The profit must now be apportioned to the partners in the commercial PSR for the accounting period.

	Adjusted profits	A	B	C	D	E
PSR		19%	22%	22%	22%	15%
Assessable 1998/99	£190,000	£36,100	£41,800	£41,800	£41,800	£28,500

This is E's first accounts year and thus he is assessable on his profit for the 11 months to 5 April 1998.

His assessment is for 1997/98 and is 11/12 of £28,500.	£26,125
His assessment for 1998/99 (Year 2).	£28,500
Overlap relief is for the period 1 May 1997 to 5 April 1998.	£26,125

Overlap relief b/fwd & c/fwd	£36,095	£36,095	£36,095	£36,095	£26,125

This demonstrates the operation of the commencement provisions to E as he starts his deemed "own trade".

1999/2000

The basis period is the period of account ending in the year of assessment (30 April 1999). Note that both A and E retire on 30 April 1999, being during the tax year 1999/2000. A and E had their 1998/99 assessments based on the period ended 30 April 1998. Thus the 1999/2000 assessments will be based on the 12 months to 30 April 1999 (subject to overlap relief). The profit must now be apportioned to the partners in the commercial PSR for the accounting period.

	Adjusted profits	A	B	C	D	E
PSR		15%	25%	25%	20%	15%
Less: overlap relief	£230,000	£34,500	£57,500	£57,500	£46,000	£34,500
Assessable 1999/2000		£34,500				£26,125
		NIL	£57,500	£57,500	£46,000	£8,375

Note that A does not get the benefit of all his overlap relief as he has insufficient profits. However, the balance of £1,595 can be claimed under the "new" loss relief provisions.

Overlap relief					
Brought forward	£36,095	£36,095	£36,095	£36,095	£26,125
Used	£34,500				£26,125
Carried forward	NIL	£36,095	£36,095	£36,095	NIL
Available as loss relief	£1,595				

EXAMPLE 2.34 *(continued)*

2000/2001

A simple year at last!

	Adjusted profits	B 40%	C 30%	D 30%
PSR				
Assessable 2000/2001	£215,000	£86,000	£64,500	£64,500
Overlap relief b/fwd & c/fwd		£36,095	£36,095	£36,095

OVERSEAS INCOME

Income from a trade, profession or vocation carried on wholly abroad, assessable under Schedule D, Case V is dealt with along Schedule D, Case I lines under the current year basis of assessment and similar provisions apply to prevent the exploitation of transitional averaging or transitional overlap, and again a partner retiring in 1996/97 is deemed still to be a partner for the purpose of the transitional overlap anti-avoidance, FA 1995, Sch. 22, paras 6–8.

INTEREST PRIVATISATION

One of the ways in which it would have been possible to take advantage of the transitional provisions would have been to "privatise" partnership interest. Interest paid by a partnership would be allowed as a trading expense under TA 1988, s 74 on an ordinary accruals basis and interest falling into the transitional period would be subject to transitional averaging and effectively only part of the interest would be relieved. A way of increasing the profit in the transitional period is to reduce the expenses and if the partnership borrowings were repaid and replaced by borrowings by the individual partners on-lent interest-free to the partnership, the partners would be able to claim interest as a charge on income under TA 1988, ss 353, 362 and 363. Charges on income would not fall within the transitional averaging arrangements and full relief would therefore be obtained for the interest paid, even though only part of the profits were taxed under the transitional averaging. It is therefore provided by FA 1995, Sch. 22, para. 2 that unless the individual partners' loans to replace the partnership borrowing were taken out prior to 1 April 1994 (FA 1995, Sch. 22, para. 2(4)(*a*)), the charge on income deduction is restricted to the appropriate percentage of the interest paid by the partners in 1994/95 and 1995/96. There is no penalty element but the relief for interest is effectively reduced to that which would have applied had the interest been paid by the partnership and included in the transitional averaging computations. Indirect and multiple loans are naturally caught by the anti-avoidance provisions, but there are escape routes under FA 1995, Sch. 22, para. 2(2) where the borrowing by the individual partners is shown to be wholly or mainly for bona fide commercial reasons, or does not reduce the partnership borrowings. There will also be de minimis levels to be announced immediately prior to 5 April 1997 (FA 1995, Sch. 22, para. 2(4)(*b*)).

The privatisation of partnership borrowings in this way would also have an effect on the partnership overlap as the charge on income would not reduce the taxable profits falling in the transitional overlap period, and therefore eligible for overlap relief. In order to counter the perceived avoidance the overlap is reduced under FA 1995, Sch. 22, para. 5 by the interest not paid by the firm as a result of the loans by partners replacing the partnership borrowings. There is no penalty element but the overlap relief is reduced to what it would have been had the loans not been privatised.

EXAMPLE 2.35

Mr Nu is a partner in Omega & Co. which draws up accounts to 30 April each year. On 1 May 1994 he borrows £200,000 and introduces it to the partnership to reduce the partnership overdraft. In each of the years 1994/95 to 1996/97 he claims relief under TA 1988, s 353 for interest paid of £20,000, the interest being payable quarterly in advance.

Mr Nu is unable to provide evidence that the refinancing was undertaken for bona fide commercial reasons. His relief under TA 1988, s 353 is therefore reduced as follows:

"Appropriate percentage" FA 1995, Sch. 22, para. 1(4)	365 ÷ No. of days in transitional period (730)
"Relevant period" FA 1995, Sch. 22, para. 2(a)	Any period falling within the transitional period
Transitional period	Basis period for 1996/97 (year ended 30 April 1996) and the relevant period (defined by FA 1994, Sch. 20, para. 2(5) (year ended 30 April 1995))

Therefore relief for interest paid in 1994/95 and 1995/97 (i e the years in which the interest for the transitional period is actually paid) is restricted to:

£20,000 × 365/730 = £10,000 for each year.

EXAMPLE 2.36

Messrs Sigma, Tau and Kappa have for many years traded in partnership together. Sigma makes a loan to the partnership on 1 May 1996 of £200,000 to reduce partnership borrowings. He pays interest on that loan of £20,000 each year (the interest that the partnership would otherwise have paid) and claims the appropriate relief under TA 1988, s 353 for 1997/98 and 1998/99. Sigma's share of the partnership profits amount to £110,000. However, this arrangement falls foul of the anti-avoidance provisions and Sigma's transitional overlap relief is adjusted as follows:

Transitional overlap profits (FA 1994, Sch. 20, para. 2(4))	110,000
Amounts not included in the overlap profit as a result of Sigma's loan to the partnership (FA 1995, Sch. 22, para. 5(2) 11/12 × £20,000) =	18,333
Revised overlap relief c/fwd	£91,667

OTHER INCOME – SCHEDULE A

Although the other income of a partnership, including rental income, is assessed by reference to the partnership basis period as a deemed second trade, this is purely for computational purposes and the income remains investment income assessable under Schedule A in the case of rents or Schedule D, Cases III, IV, V or VI for other investment or non-trading income.

FA 1995, s 33–34 and Sch. 6 change totally the income tax provisions relating to rental income assessed under Schedule A and bring furnished letting income wholly within Schedule A and out of Schedule D, Case VI. The changes apply from 1995/96 and the changes are made largely by amending the Schedule A provisions of TA 1988. As the changes do not apply for corporation tax, the farcical situation results in the same section of TA 1988 having totally different meanings for 1994/95 and earlier years, for 1995/96 and later years for income tax purposes, and for the continuing purposes of corporation tax.

The main change for Schedule A is to compute the profits from renting property in the U.K. as if it were a Schedule A business under Schedule D, Case I rules under new TA 1988, s 21(3) inserted by FA 1995, s 39(4)(2), which means that the accruals basis is applied. Under the old Schedule A rules which applied up to 5 April 1995, the income has been assessed on the basis of the rents receivable in the year, irrespective of whether the period covered by the rent was in advance or in arrears. Expenses were normally allowed on a payments basis under TA 1988, s 25, although in some cases accrued expenses would have been allowed except for interest. Interest would have been charged on the basis of the interest paid in the fiscal year, irrespective of whether the period covered by the interest was in advance or in arrears, under TA 1988, s 353.

Schedule A is also dealt with on a strict fiscal year basis from 1995/96 except in the case of partnership income which is dealt with by reference to the Schedule D, Case I or II accounting period under TA 1988, s 111(7) and (8). Personal rental income of partners will therefore be on a fiscal year basis, but not their share of the partnership rents.

TRANSITIONAL SCHEDULE A RULES

Up to 1994/95, a considerable number of variations on the strict statutory position were accepted by the Revenue. In particular, it was not unusual to assess income arising under Schedule A on the basis of accounts prepared for a year ending in the fiscal year or even the accounting year ending in the preceding fiscal year. Furnished lettings assessable under Schedule D, Case VI up until 1994/95 were also often dealt with on a non-statutory basis and are brought into the Schedule A net for 1995/96 onwards. The 10% wear and tear allowance for furnished lettings based on the rents less water rates or council tax and other obligations of the tenant, continues to apply under extra statutory concession A19.

Because of the numerous non-statutory bases applied for Schedule A there are no statutory transitional provisions. This means that 1994/95 should be assessed on the old strict statutory basis and 1995/96 on the new statutory basis. The Revenue are however prepared to accept 1994/95 as a non-statutory transitional year. This means that 1993/94 will be assessed on the old basis agreed with the Revenue, applied consistently, and 1995/96 on the strict statutory basis of fully accrued income and expenses. The year 1994/95 would begin immediately after the end of the basis period for 1993/94 and continue to 5 April 1995. Any income that would also be taxable in 1995/96 on an accruals basis is excluded, as would be any expenses for which relief would be claimed for 1995/96. Any interest covering the period up to 5 April 1995 that remains unrelieved on this basis is treated as payable in 1995/96 and relieved in that year.

Where the period from the end of the 1993/94 basis period to 5 April 1995 is a period in excess of a year, the annualised equivalent of the net income is taken so that one year's income is assessed in each fiscal year. This takes account of the fact that in order to have got on to a non-statutory preceding year or non-5 April year end basis, earlier profits would have been doubly counted. Similarly, the capital allowances basis period for 1994/95, for example for plant and machinery used in estate management, includes all additions and disposals in the period from the end of the 1993/94 basis period to 5 April 1995, with a twelve-month writing down allowance, irrespective of the length of the basis period. The non-statutory transitional treatment for 1994/95 is explained in the Inland Revenue Press Release of 10 February 1995. The old Schedule A allowance for expenditure on maintenance, repairs, insurance and management is widened to include all expenses allowable under Schedule D, Case I or II, but the provisions of TA 1988, s 82 which restrict relief or interest on borrowings outside the U.K. are disapplied for Schedule A purposes, by FA 1995, Sch. 6, para. 13.

The Schedule D rules applied for Schedule A include the post-cessation receipt provisions and the treatment of capital allowances as an expense. The Schedule D, Case VI charge on premiums treated as rent, the assignment of a lease granted at an undervalue, or a sale of land with the right to reconveyance are brought into Schedule A. The land managed as one estate provisions are retained and the Schedule A assessment will be on the aggregate of the rents less expenses of all properties. The mortgage interest relief at source rules do not apply and a new regime is introduced for Schedule A losses under TA 1988, s 379A inserted by FA 1995, Sch. 6, para. 19, allowing relief for losses on one property against profits on another and carrying forward any unused losses against future Schedule A income. The Schedule A losses remain ring-fenced and only allowable against Schedule A profits. except for certain agricultural estates where a deficit may be set against total income. Pre-1995/96 deficits are treated as a Schedule A loss or unrelieved interest as appropriate, and the pre-trading loss provisions appropriate to Schedule D are introduced into Schedule A. The furnished letting rules remain and an industrial building that is temporarily unused still qualifies for industrial buildings allowances as if the Schedule A business were actually being carried on.

Income from overseas properties is taxable under TA 1988, ss 65 and 65A as amended and inserted by FA 1995, s 41, under Schedule D, Case V, although Schedule A, and therefore Schedule D, Case I, lines, on a full accruals basis. Although the Schedule A rules are applied the assessment is actually still under Schedule D, Case V which means that a non-U.K. domiciled U.K. resident is still eligible for the remittance basis. The Schedule D provisions giving relief for foreign travel are disapplied for overseas properties. The foreign properties are treated as separate sources of Schedule D, Case V income for 1995/96 and 1996/97, and are then aggregated as income from a single source in 1997/98. This is because transitional provisions might apply on the Schedule D, Case V basis for some properties but not others. Because the assessment is under Schedule D, Case V, it is still on the preceding year basis for 1995/96 and follows the normal Schedule D, Case V transitional provisions for 1996/97, that is on the average of the income for the two years ending on 5 April 1997. The Schedule A loss provisions will not apply to Schedule D, Case V losses until 1998/99, any loss relief available prior to that date being restricted to that available under extra statutory concession B25.

As the Schedule A transitional measures for 1994/95 are non-statutory it is necessary to agree them with the Inland Revenue. As explained in the Press Release of 10 February 1995, any appeal must be internally within the Revenue with the final appeal to the Inland Revenue Adjudicator, as any referral to the

Commissioners would of necessity result in the strict application of the law with no relief for any double charges. As the transitional relief can only be given by agreement with the Revenue, there is clearly no need for any statutory anti-avoidance provisions to prevent taxpayers exploiting the transitional rules.

OTHER INVESTMENT INCOME

Untaxed interest and income from foreign securities and possessions taxed respectively under Schedule D, Cases III, IV and V are dealt with following the Schedule D, Case I rules for basis periods, transitional averaging, overlap and commencement and cessation, and not by reference to the income in the fiscal year. The commencement and cessation provisions only apply where a partner joins or leaves the partnership, not where the investment income first arises or ceases. Investment income of the partners outside the partnership is taxed on the strict fiscal year basis on the income of the fiscal year. Where the income first arises on or after 5 April 1994 the income is assessed on the income arising in the current fiscal year throughout, except in the case of a non-domiciled individual whose Schedule D, Case IV or V income is on remittances in the fiscal year. Additional deposits to existing accounts can be, and if substantial will be, treated by the Revenue as new sources of income assessed on the current fiscal year basis, following *Hart v Sangster* (1957) 37 TC 231. Pre-6 April 1994 sources of income which continue into 1997/98 are assessed on the preceding year basis of assessment up to and including 1995/96, that is the income arising in the preceding fiscal year.

For 1997/98 the assessment is on the income of the current fiscal year. This means that the assessment for 1996/97 is a transitional year assessed on 50% of the aggregate income arising in 1995/96 and 1996/97. These rules obviously give the taxpayer the incentive of trying to divert income into the 1996/97 basis period. Where relevant arrangements as defined by FA 1995, Sch. 22, paras 18–20 have been entered into to divert income into the transitional period, tax is charged not only on 50% of the income arising in 1995/96 and 1996/97, but also on 62.5% of income diverted into the transitional period as a result of the relevant arrangements under FA 1995, Sch. 22, paras 9 and 10. This results in an effective penalty of 25% of the tax on the income of which the taxpayer was attempting to save tax. There is a let-out if the taxpayer can meet the benefit test in that the main benefit to be arrived from the relevant arrangements was not the avoidance of tax, FA 1995, Sch. 22, paras 18(1) and 19(2)(*b*), or if the amount diverted is within the de minimis limits, which will be announced prior to 5 April 1997, under FA 1995, Sch. 22, paras 9(3) and 10(3). For non-interest income there is also a motive test, under FA 1995, Sch. 22, para. 19(2)(*a*).

The penalty element may be avoided by bringing the relevant arrangements to the notice of the Inland Revenue and accepting a tax charge to eliminate the advantage without penalty if the requirements of the escape routes cannot be met, under FA 1995, Sch. 22, para. 13(2).

In the case of interest, relevant arrangements exist under FA 1995, Sch. 22, para. 18 where the interest arises at irregular intervals during 1994/95 to 1997/98, or there are artificial variations in the rate of interest applicable during those years. Variations in the interest rate are artificial unless based on variations in regularly published variable interest rates. The Revenue in their publication of 29 November 1994 "Self assessment transition to the current year basis, anti-avoidance provisions" at para 3.26 confirm that "savings, profits (offered by for example building societies) providing increasing amounts of interest in successive years would not be caught by the rules provided the savings arrangements had not been entered into with a view of exploiting the transitional arrangements".

In the case of income other than interest assessable under Schedule D, Cases III, IV or V, relevant arrangements exist under FA 1995, Sch. 22, paras 19 and 20 if the income arises at irregular intervals during the years 1994/95 to 1997/98, and any transaction with a connected person as defined by TA 1988, s 839 is a relevant transaction unless the escape provisions apply.

EXAMPLE 2.37

Mr Pi received, personally, untaxed interest assessable under Schedule D, Case III as follows:

Year ended 5 April 1995	£20,000
Year ended 5 April 1996	£16,000
Year ended 5 April 1997	£8,000

His assessments for 1995/96 and 1996/97 would therefore be as follows:

1995/96 preceding year
TA 1988, s 64 (original version)
Year ended 5 April 1995 £20,000

1996/97 transitional year
FA 1994, Sch. 20, para. 4(2)

Year ended 5 April 1996	16,000	
Year ended 5 April 1997	8,000	
	£24,000 × 50% =	£12,000

However, it transpires that the receipt of interest due in the year ended 5 April 1995 totalling £12,000 was delayed until the year ended 5 April 1996, thus falling within the anti-avoidance provisions. Pi's 1996/97 assessment is therefore adjusted as follows:

FA 1995, Sch. 22, para. 9(2)
50% of the amounts in FA 1994, Sch. 20, para 4(2)

Year ended 5 April 1996	16,000	
Year ended 5 April 1997	8,000	
	£24,000 × 50% =	12,000

Plus amounts falling within		
FA 1995, Sch. 22, para. 9(1)(*b*)	£12,000 × 62.5% =	7,500
		£19,500

Had there been no delay in the payment of interest, Pi's assessments for 1995/96 and 1996/97 would have been as follows:

1995/96 TA 1988, s 64 (original version)
Year ended 5 April 1995   32,000
1996/97 FA 1994, Sch. 20, para 4(2)

Year ended 5 April 1996   4,000
Year ended 5 April 1997   8,000

£12,000 × 50% =   6,000

£38,000

However, as a result of the anti-avoidance provisions an extra £1,500 is assessed:
1995/96   20,000
1996/97   19,500

£39,500

The shift of interest into the transitional period results in an additional amount being charged of £1,500 (£39,500 − £38,000), i e a penalty of tax on one-quarter of the amount that would have escaped tax on averaging (£12,000 × 50%).

PARTNERSHIP RETURNS

The Revenue will normally issue a partnership return to the firm under TMA 1970, s 12AA(2) or to a particular partner, under TMA 1970, s 12AA(3), who has been nominated by the firm or identified by the Revenue; requiring the delivery of the return, together with a partnership statement, accounts and computations.

The income would include all income of the partnership including chargeable gains and the individual partners' names, addresses and tax reference numbers. The filing date as for an individual is not later than 31 January following the end of the year of assessment or three months from the date of issue of the return where it is issued late (TMA 1970, s 12AA(4)). Where there is a corporate partner the filing date is not later than one year after the period in respect of which the return is issued or three months from the issue of the return if later (TMA 1970, s 12AA(5)).

The partnership statement is a statement of the income or loss from each source which has accrued or been sustained by the partnership for each period of account ending in the period covered by the tax return, and any changes on income for the period, identifying each partner's share of such income, loss or charge, to enable him to self-assess as an individual (TMA 1970, s 12AB(1)).

The rules relating to the filing by individual partners of their own tax returns and the payment of tax thereon is outside the scope of this book.

Chapter 3

Taxable income and allowable expenditure

GENERAL

Partners assessed to tax under Schedule D, Cases I or II are taxed on their share of its total world-wide income (*Davies v Braithwaite* (1993) 18 TC 198), less the expenses wholly and exclusively laid out or expended for the purposes of the trade or profession under TA 1988, s 74(*a*).

TAXABLE INCOME

Most trading receipts are easily recognised as such but it is not always clear whether the sale of a capital asset gives rise to a capital profit or to a trading receipt.

The sale of land in particular can give rise to a problem. Land bought and re-sold has been treated as giving rise to a trading receipt in several cases (such as *Californian Copper Syndicate Ltd v Harris* (1904) 5 TC 159; *Turner v Last* (1965) 42 TC 517; *Bowie v Reg Dunn (Builders) Ltd* (1974) STC 234), except where as in *Taylor v Good* (1974) 49 TC 277; *Marson v Morton* (1986) STC 436 and *Kirkham v Williams* (1991) STC 342) it can be shown that there was no trading intention at acquisition or subsequently.

The sale of investments on the other hand will normally give rise to a capital profit (following such cases as *Glasgow Heritable Trust Ltd v IRC* (1954) 35 TC 196; *Royal Mutual Benefit Building Society v Walker* (1968) 45 TC 171; *Salt v Chamberlain* [1979] STC 750; *Simmons v IRC* (1980) STC 350) although, exceptionally, a sale of investments can give rise to a trading profit, (*IRC v Toll Property Co Ltd* (1952) 34 TC 13), the critical point being whether the asset was acquired as a trading asset. Trading implies a continuing business but isolated transactions can give rise to trading profits where the transaction is "an adventure in the nature of trade" (*Edwards v Bairstow and Harrison* (1955) 36 TC 207, purchase and sale of cotton spinning plant; *Wisdom v Chamberlain* (1968) 45 TC 92, purchase and sale of silver bullion).

Compensation received in respect of damage to the business, loss of agencies or breach of contract will nearly always be taxable as a trading receipt (see *Anglo French Exploration Co Ltd v Clayson* (1956) 36 TC 545; *IRC v David MacDonald & Co* (1955) 36 TC 388). Compensation for a fundamental revenue loss which affected the entire basis of the business has been held to be capital (*Van den Berghs Ltd v Clark* (1935) 19 TC 390; *Sabine v Lookers Ltd* (1958) 38 TC 120; *British Borneo Petroleum Syndicate Ltd v Cropper* (1968) 45 TC 201; *Barr*

Crombie & Co Ltd v IRC (1945) 26 TC 406). Compensation for the loss of a capital asset is capital (*Glenboig Union Fireclay Co Ltd v IRC* (1922) 12 TC 427).

Ex gratia receipts may be tax fee if unsolicited and if all work done has been properly remunerated. This is illustrated in the case of *Murray v Goodhews* [1978] STC 207 where *ex gratia* payments made on giving up tenancies of tied houses were not taxable, contrasted with *McGowan v Brown and Cousins* (*trading as Stuart Edwards*) [1977] STC 342 in which an estate agency was voluntarily compensated after complaining about the failure to obtain a letting agency which they would normally have expected to obtain, having negotiated the original purchase for development. An *ex gratia* payment as compensation to the managers of a shipping company was held to be not taxable in *Chibbett v Joseph Robinson & Sons* (1924) 9 TC 48 but not where there was a valid claim to compensation (*Blackburn v Close Bros Ltd* (1960) 39 TC 164) or where there is an *ex gratia* payment made to compensate for loss of revenue. An interesting case is that of *Ellis v Lucas* (1966) 43 TC 276 where it was held that compensation for a loss of an auditorship was assessable under Schedule E and taxable in accordance with the golden handshake provisions of TA 1988, s 148, except that it was covered by the exemption under TA 1988, s 188(4) and (5) as being below the taxable limits. This case was followed in *Walker v Carnaby Harrower Barham and Pykett* (1969) 46 TC 561 and extended to the loss of a secretaryship in *IRC v Brander and Cruikshank* (1970) 46 TC 574. These cases imply that strictly speaking income from holding an office such as company auditor or secretary should be assessable under Schedule E and not under Schedule D, Case II. In practice, such income is assessed under Schedule D if invoiced by the firm except in respect of compensation payments which are claimed under Schedule E and would only be taxable if the amount apportioned to any one partner was in excess of £30,000, which is the exemption limit under TA 1988, s 188(4) and (5).

Directors' fees are assessed under Schedule D if extra-statutory concession A 37 applies, which provides:

"1. Where fees are received in respect of directorships held by members of a professional partnership they are in strictness assessable on the individual partners under Schedule E. It is however the practice of the Inland Revenue to accede to a request from the partnership for the inclusion of the fees in the Schedule D assessment provided that:

—the directorship is a normal incident of the profession and of that particular practice concerned;

—the fees are only a small part of the profits; and

—under the partnership agreement the fees are pooled for division among the partners.

Partnerships seeking such treatment are expected to provide the Revenue with a written undertaking that directors' fees received in full will be included in the gross income or receipts of the basis period, whether or not the directorship is still held in the year of assessment and whether or not the partner concerned is still a partner."

Income forgone by a gift or sale at less than market value is taxable within a trade on the basis of the difference between the normal sale value and the amount received (*Sharkey v Wernher* (1955) 36 TC 275; *Petrotim Securities Ltd v Ayres* (1963) 41 TC 389) although this does not apply to a profession (*Mason v Innes* (1967) 44 TC 326).

Partnership income from non-trading sources will be assessed separately as explained in Chapter 2 and Appendix I, such as rents under Schedule A and interest received under Schedule D, Case III. Rental income under Schedule A would be apportioned to the partners and taxed on a current year basis. Normally, up to 1994/95, the assessment would be based on the rents receivable in the accounting period ending in the year of assessment in accordance with Revenue booklet IR 27, para. 101. Such treatment becomes statutory under TA 1988, s 111(7), where the current year basis of assessment applies, as explained in Chapter 2. By concession, if part of the practice premises are sub-let the rent may sometimes be treated as trading income under Schedule D, Case I, which can be helpful in the increasingly rare cases where it is allowed by the Revenue: it would follow from this treatment that where the surplus property is let at a loss this is treated as a trading expense. Note that under TA 1988, s 15(4), was possible prior to 1995/96, to apportion the rent received from furnished lettings and claim the proportion relating to the property as assessable under Schedule A. As this reduces the concessionary 10% depreciation allowance given by SP/A19 as a deduction in lieu of capital allowances, it is not usually worthwhile unless there is a deficit on other unfurnished properties which can be offset against the furnished lettings income to greater advantage than the 10% reduction provides. From 1995/96 this treatment will no longer be necessary as furnished lettings are moved from Schedule D, Case VI to Schedule A as explained in Chapter 2.

Schedule D, Case III deposit interest is calculated by taking the actual deposit interest received in the preceding fiscal year, or accounting period where the current year basis of assessment applies, and apportioning it among the partners in accordance with their profit-sharing ratios in the year of receipt. An assessment is made on each partner individually on his share of the deposit interest on an actual or preceding year basis as appropriate for each partner, rather than there being a single assessment in the partnership name divided amongst the partners as applies for Schedule D, Case I or II under the preceding year basis. Deposit interest received is not earned income (*Northend v White and Leonard and Corbin Greener*) (1975) 50 TC 121) and is not, therefore, relevant earnings for pension purposes under TA 1988, ss 623(2) or 644(2). It should be noted however that Schedule D, Case III deposit interest on designated clients' deposits belong to the clients and is taxable on them and not on the partners (*Brown v IRC* (1964) 42 TC 42). Interest paid out to clients of solicitors in lieu of interest on undesignated deposit accounts is a deduction from such interest received and taxed as the clients income (see Law Society's Gazette, 19 April 1978).

Deposit interest received by a partnership from a U.K. bank will suffer tax at source at the basic rate, in the same way as building society interest received. Such interest is assessed to higher rates on the interest actually received in the fiscal year or accounting period grossed up at the basic rate. Deposits with banks offshore, for example, in the Isle of Man, Jersey or Guernsey, would be assessed under Schedule D, Case V.

Although partnership deposit interest is taxed as investment income of the partners, as explained in Chapter 2 and Appendix I, there can be cases where it is advantageous for a wealthy client to lend money to a professional partnership which will, provided that professional rules so allow, place the money on deposit and will effectively give credit for the deposit interest received when fixing the fee which would otherwise be charged to the client. In this way the client has effectively foregone investment income which would have been taxed at say 40% and has received a reduction in the fees which he would have been charged and which he would have had to meet out of taxed income. In view of the case of *Mason v Innes* (1967) 44 TC 326 there is no requirement for the partnership to bring into credit for income tax purposes a market value fee which they would otherwise have charged, and the transaction is not caught by the anti-avoidance provisions of TA 1988, s 786.

So far as Solicitors and the Solicitors Account Rules are concerned it is not necessary to place clients' money in a designated deposit account if the client specifically requests otherwise. It might be necessary to assume a notional fee for VAT purposes (*Customs and Excise Comrs v Exeter Golf and Country Club Ltd* [1980] STC 162).

A partnership might be in receipt of Schedule D, Case VI income from say, furnished lettings up to 1994/95 (*Shop Investments Ltd v Sweet* (1940) 23 TC 38) or other income not connected with the trade, for example, commodity dealing (*Cooper v Stubbs* (1925) 10 TC 29), or insurance commission (*Hugh v Rogers* (1958) 38 TC 270). Whether such income will be part of the trading income or be assessable under Schedule D, Case VI will depend on the facts of each case. A Case VI assessment should properly be based on the partnership accounts for the year ending in the current fiscal year, but if the income is received regularly the Revenue may agree a non-statutory preceding year basis of assessment under Schedule D, Case VI.

Tax deferral

A feature of the taxation system in the United Kingdom is the ability to obtain an immediate tax write-off for certain limited forms of capital or revenue expenditure; the most obvious case being the 100% scientific research allowance and 100% allowance for expenditure on commercial and industrial buildings in enterprise zones. This enables expenditure to qualify for tax relief when incurred and, if that expenditure produces profits in due course, these will be taxed as they arise. To the extent that the excess of the expenditure over income can be set off against other income as a trading loss, it is said to shelter that income and the tax liability is deferred until a future period.

If it is necessary to pay out all the expenditure to obtain the loss there is a net cash outflow in that the investment is greater than the tax saved. This may still make commercial sense if the assets are acquired out of gross income, in view of the allowances, and produce a worthwhile commercial return.

Even under the current rate of writing down allowances, if long life plant can be acquired on hire-purchase or deferred terms, the tax shelter may also produce a cash flow advantage, particularly if the asset earns sufficient to cover the interest payable. Such an arrangement is said to have a gearing effect.

It is necessary with a tax shelter to appreciate that it is a mere deferral of tax and it could make the overall tax payable greater if the expenditure produced taxable income in future, which would be added to the primary source of income and suffer the highest rates of tax.

The immediate tax saving may, however, be sufficient to outweigh future problems, particularly if the loss can be carried back to an earlier year, for example under TA 1988, s 381 (as explained on p. 20) when high rates of tax are repaid together with a tax free repayment supplement.

It is also worth bearing in mind that high levels of inflation, if they were to recur, make it particularly attractive to defer tax as, when it is eventually payable, the real cost is significantly less than it would have been if paid on the normal due date.

One of the problems of using a highly geared tax shelter is that although there is an allowance in the first period, in subsequent periods income will be received which will be taxable as additional income, thus exacerbating the tax problem. Although a tax shelter can be a useful means of spreading exceptional profits the future taxable income must be taken into account.

TA 1988, s 381 may enable profits to be sheltered retrospectively by using capital allowances in a trade to produce a loss which can be set against the income of the three fiscal years before the trade commenced beginning with the earliest, although the phasing out of the first year allowance makes it difficult to achieve a worthwhile tax saving in a reasonable commercial operation (see Example 2.16 at p. 21).

Allowable expenditure

TA 1988, s 74 allows as a deduction all expenses wholly and exclusively laid out or expended for the purposes of the trade or profession, excluding those relating to private premises or otherwise not relating to the business, such as partners' removal expenses (*MacKinlay v Arthur Young McClelland Moores & Co* (1989) STC 898), repairs to a flat occupied as a residence (*Mason v Tyson* (1980) STC 284 and medical expenses (*Norman v Golder*) (1944) 26 TC 293). Capital expenditure and depreciation thereon is disallowed (although capital allowances may be available by reference to that expenditure, which under the current year basis of assessment are treated as a business expense). Annual payments such as annuities or royalties are allowed as a charge on total income and not as a trading expense.

Dual purpose expenses partly for business purposes and partly for private purposes are not deductible (*Bowden v Russell and Russell* (1965) 42 TC 310; *Caillebotte v Quinn* [1975] STC 265; *Prior v Saunders* (1993) STC 562; *Murgatroyd v Evans-Jackson* (1966) 43 TC 581; *Prince v Mapp* (1969) 46 TC 169; *Mallalieu v Drummond* [1983] STC 665; *Watkis v Ashford, Sparkes & Harward* (a firm) [1985] STC 451 except where the private benefit is purely incidental (*Bentleys Stokes and Lowless v Beeson* (1952) 33 TC 491). Apportionment between business and private use is allowed where part of the total expense is wholly for the trade such as the business use of a car or house where the whole of the running costs relating to the business use are allowed and the whole of such costs relating to private use disallowed *Nolder v Walters* (1930) 15 TC 380 (a Schedule E case).

Ordinary principles of commercial accountancy are usually followed by the courts in deciding whether or not an expense is allowable, unless there is some provision of statute or case law which precludes a deduction, for example under TA 1988, s 74 (as in *Odeon Associated Theatres v Jones* (1971) 48 TC 257; *Chancery Lane Safe Deposit and Offices Co Ltd v IRC* (1965) 43 TC 83; *Gallagher v Jones* (1993) STC 537; *Johnston v Britannia Airways* (1994) STC 763; *Owen v Southern Railway of Peru Ltd* (1954) 36 TC 602), but they may depart from the accounting treatment if they think it appropriate to do so in order to show a correct statement of profits for tax purposes (*Willingale v International Commercial Bank Ltd* [1978] STC 75; *Patrick v Broadstone Mills Ltd* (1953) 35 TC 44; *Minister of National Revenue v Anaconda American Brass Co Ltd* (1955) 34 ATC 330, which rejected the accounting treatment actually used for discounts receivable on bills, base stock valuation and last-in first-out stock valuations, respectively).

In *Johnston v Britannia Airways* (1994) STC 763 at 778, Knox J quoted with approval Sir John Pennycuick V-C's judgment in *Odeon Associated Theatres Ltd v Jones (Inspector of Taxes)* (1971) 1 WLR 442 at 454, 48 TC 275 at 273 where the meaning and effect of the time honoured expression "ordinary principles of commercial accountancy" was explained in the following terms:

"The concern of the court in this connection is to ascertain the true profit of the taxpayer. That and nothing else, apart from express statutory adjustments, is the subject of taxation in respect of trade. In so ascertaining the true profit of a trade the court applies the correct principles of the prevailing system of commercial accountancy. I use the word 'correct' deliberately. In order to ascertain what are the correct principles it has recourse to the evidence of accountants. That evidence is conclusive on the practice of accountants in the sense of the principles on which accountants act in practice. That is a question of pure fact, but the court itself has to make a final decision as to whether that practice corresponds to the correct principles of commercial accountancy. No doubt in the vast proportion of cases the court will agree with the accountants but it will not necessarily do so. Again there may be a divergency of view between the accountants, or there may be alternative principles, none of which can be said to be incorrect, or, of course, there may be no accountancy evidence at all. The cases illustrate these various points. At the end of the day the court must determine what is the correct principle of commercial accountancy to be applied. Having done so, it will ascertain the true profit of the trade according to that principle, and the profit so ascertained is the subject of taxation. The expression 'ordinary principles of commercial accountancy' is, as I understand it, employed to denote what is involved in this composite process."

That passage, already much quoted even at the time of the Special Commissioners' decision, has since received the express approval of the Court of Appeal in *Gallagher v Jones (Inspector of Taxes)* [1993] STC 537, [1994] 2 WLR 160.

Bad debts

Specific provision may be made for trading debts which are or may prove bad and they are thereby relieved (*Anderton and Halsted Ltd v Birrell* (1931) 16 TC 200), however, bad debt recoveries are taxed when recovered (*Bristow v William Dickinson & Co Ltd* (1946) 27 TC 157). Non-trading bad debts are non-allowable capital losses (*English Crown Spelter Co Ltd v Baker* (1908) 5 TC 327) although capital gains tax relief may be available under TCGA 1992, s 253 in respect of loans to traders and in respect of losses on guarantees of such loans.

Compensation for loss of office

Compensation payments may be allowed (*Mitchel v BW Noble Ltd* (1927) 11 TC 372), unless in connection with the sale of a business or on cessation of trade (*James Snook & Co Ltd v Blasdale* (1952) 33 TC 244) or in relation to a capital asset (*Devon Mutual Steamship Insurance Association v Ogg* (1927) 13 TC 184).

Wages and salaries

Employee remuneration is an allowable deduction provided it is reasonable for the work done (*Copeman v William Flood & Sons Ltd* (1940) 24 TC 53; *L G Berry Investments Ltd v Attwooll* (1964) 41 TC 547; *Earlspring Properties Ltd v Guest* (1993) STC 473). Even an *ex gratia* payment to an employee can be allowable if for the purposes of the trade (*Smith v Incorporated Council of Law Reporting for England and Wales* (1914) 6 TC 477). Redundancy payments, however, may be considered to be paid otherwise than for the purposes of the trade (TA 1988, s 90).

Professional practices may well find it desirable to employ wives of partners and pay them reasonable remuneration for the work done. However care should be taken not to fix the level of remuneration at a figure which produces a National Insurance liability in excess of the tax saving.

In view of the opening year's provisions, under the preceding year basis of assessment, it was often advantageous to employ future partners in the first year of trading so that a deduction was obtained to the remuneration as a trading expense. If the first year's profits formed the basis of nearly three years of assessment it will be appreciated that the remuneration was effectively allowed against three years profits as explained in Chapter 1. After the first year's assessment the employee could be brought into the partnership as a profit sharing partner and if a continuation election was made, he would have apportioned to him in the second and third years the profits which were reduced by his salary. In deciding whether to keep a future partner as an employee for the first year, the cost of the employer's National Insurance Contributions had to be taken into account. Under the current year basis of assessment it is still beneficial to keep the first year's profit as low as possible to minimise the overlap profits carried forward, but this cannot be achieved by making future partner employees, because on becoming partners they are deemed to have commenced a deemed trade and would have their own overlap. Renting rather than buying the business premises could be a sensible method of minimising the opening profits.

Staff pension scheme contributions will be an allowable expense, although the initial costs of setting up a scheme were held to be capital in *Atherton v British Insulated and Helsby Cables Ltd* (1925) 10 TC 155. The Revenue will usually allow a normal contribution in the year of payment and spread forward the tax relief on any special contribution in excess of £25,000 over a maximum period of four years under the provisions of the Occupational Pension Scheme Practice Notes IR12, para. 5 (*J H Clark & Co Ltd v Musker* (1956) 37 TC 1).

The period of spread is determined by the size of the special contribution, with between £25,000 and £50,000 being spread over two years, £50,001 and £100,000 over three years and over £100,000 over four years. A special contribution made solely to finance cost of living pension increases for existing pensioners will not normally be spread. Expenses of establishing and running a scheme are allowed as expenses of the chargeable period in which they are paid, but are not scheme contributions.

The expenses of providing accommodation and equipment for running the scheme are allowable. Contributions to, or expenses in connection with, an approved scheme which is not exempt approved are allowable if wholly and exclusively for the purpose of the trade.

Under TA 1988, s 84 payments for technical education are specifically deductible whether or not any direct advantage is obtained by the trader. In *Wickwar v Berry* (1963) 41 TC 33 a payment by a farmer for his son's training at an agricultural college was an allowable deduction for tax purposes.

Interest

Short interest, that is on loans of less than one year, would normally be an allowable deduction following *Scottish Northern American Trust Ltd v Farmer* (1911) 5 TC 693. Annual interest will also be deductible as a trading expense except where it is payable to a non-resident and it is, therefore, disallowed under TA 1988, s 82 unless paid under deduction of tax, or otherwise allowable under that section.

Annual interest, other than on an overdraft, paid by partners personally, may be treated as a charge on income under TA 1988, ss 349, 350 and 353 and deducted from each partner's total income.

Relief for such interest may be given not only in respect of interest paid by the partnership itself but also in respect of interest on a loan taken out by a partner for the purchase of plant used in a trade under TA 1988, Sch. 19 paras. 3–6 albeit for a limited period of three fiscal years following that in which the advance was made, and for a loan taken out to purchase a share in a partnership or to contribute capital in a partnership or lend money to a partnership provided the partner has not recovered any capital under TA 1988, ss 362 and 363.

Interest paid by the firm can only be claimed as an expense, not as a charge on income, *Wilcock v Frigate Investments Ltd* (1982) STC 198.

Legal expenses

Legal expenses in relation to capital assets are disallowed (*Texas Land and Mortgage Co v Holtham* (1894) 3 TC 255) although costs of protecting business assets are allowable (*Southern v Borax Consolidated Ltd* (1940) 23 TC 597). Hence the legal expenses on new lease are disallowed but on renewal of an existing short lease are allowed.

Provisions

Provisions against specific liabilities are allowable (*James Spencer & Co v IRC* (1950) 32 TC 111), but general provisions are only permitted where they can be arrived at with sufficient accuracy to give a true and fair view of the profits of the business (*Johnston v Britannia Airways Ltd* (1994) STC 763; *Owen v Southern Railway of Peru Ltd* (1956) 36 TC 602).

Rent

Rent payable would normally be allowable following *IRC v Falkirk Iron Co Ltd* (1933) 17 TC 625 unless an asset is thereby acquired (*IRC v Land Securities Investment Trust Ltd* (1969) 45 TC 495) or the property is not used for the purposes of the trade (*Allied Newspapers Ltd v Hindsley* (1937) 21 TC 422). Payments on cancellation of a lease are, however, capital (*Cowcher v Richard Mills & Co Ltd* (1927) 13 TC 216) and commutation of a revenue liability is generally capital (*IRC v William Sharp & Son* (1959) 38 TC 341). It is, therefore, normally not desirable to pay a premium on a lease, although part of the premium payable on grant, but not assignment, of a lease may be allowable under TA 1988, s 87.

Repairs

Repair expenditure is generally allowable (*Samuel Jones & Co (Devonvale) Ltd v IRC* (1951) 32 TC 513) unless a new asset arises as a result of the expenditure (*O'Grady v Bullcroft Main Collieries Ltd* (1932) 17 TC 93). Expenditure relating to dilapidations prior to ownership is capital if the asset cannot be used in the condition in which it is acquired (*Law Shipping Co Ltd v IRC* (1923) 12 TC 621), but not if it is capable of being used (*Odeon Associated Theatres Ltd v Jones* (1971) 48 TC 257). Where premises were leased in a bad state of repair it was held, in *Jackson v Laskers Home Furnishers Ltd* (1956) 37 TC 69, that expenditure on accumulated repairs was capital.

Specific deductions

Deductions specifically allowable include patent expenses under TA 1988, s 83, the annual equivalent of the premium on land under TA 1988, s 87, where the premium itself would be taxable on the recipient under the provisions of TA 1988, s 34, pre-trading expenses under TA 1988, s 401 and counselling services for employees under TA 1988, ss 589A and 589B.

Entertaining

Expenses specifically disallowed include business entertaining expenses under TA 1988, s 577. Such expenditure, including capital allowances on assets used for providing business entertainment, is not an allowable deduction for tax purposes. Entertaining expenditure is usually disallowed in the Schedule D computation, although if an employee is given a round sum allowance to cover, inter alia, entertaining it would normally be an allowable expense of the payer and would be charged as income of the employee subject to his claim for expenses other than entertaining under TA 1988, s 198. There is an exception for business entertaining of staff which is allowable, as is expenditure on staff parties of no more than £50 per head, under extra-statutory concession A70(B). There is a disallowance of gifts except those which do not exceed £10 per donee on cost and incorporate a conspicuous advertisement for the firm so long as the gift consists neither of tokens, vouchers, food, drink nor tobacco.

Travelling expenses

Travelling expenses for trading purposes are allowed (*Edwards v Warmsley Henshall & Co* (1967) 44 TC 431) but not between home and place of work (*Newsom v Robertson* (1952) 33 TC 452; *Sargent v Barnes* [1978] STC 322) unless the home is also the base of operations (*Horton v Young* (1971) 47 TC 60).

Appropriations

Salaries to equity partners and interest on partners' capital are appropriations of profit and not allowable expenses. Interest on loans from partners and rent paid to a partner for business premises would be allowable trading expenses. They would, however, be assessed on the recipient partner as unearned income and it is often possible to give such a partner a larger share of profits which would be taxable on him as earned income and have the interest free use of money and rent free use of property. There would be no income tax assessment on income foregone and no inheritance tax problem in view of IHTA 1984, s 56(4). The payment of rent could have adverse consequences for both capital gains tax, retirement relief (see p. 111), and business property relief and inheritance tax (see p. 92).

Capital expenditure

Expenditure disallowed as being capital may nonetheless qualify for capital allowances if it is expenditure on an industrial building or hotel, a mine or oil well, on dredging, agricultural buildings or works, crematoria, or plant and machinery. All except the last are extremely unlikely in a professional partnership. A detailed consideration of capital allowances provisions is outside the scope of this book but one or two practical points may be mentioned.

A 40% first year allowance was available in connection with plant and machinery under the provisions of CAA 1990, s 22 as amended by FA 1993, s 115 and Sch. 13, in respect of expenditure incurred (CAA 1990, ss 24 and 25) between 1 November 1992 and 31 October 1993, but not thereafter. An individual or partnership cannot disclaim first year allowances but may omit to claim them in which case annual allowances are available on the basis of 25% of the written-down value (CAA 1990, s 24). Under CAA 1990, s 75, which also applies where there is no entitlement to a first year allowance, first year allowances are not available on transfers from connected persons or where it appears that the sole or main benefit of the transaction might be the first year allowance that would otherwise be available, and in certain other circumstances. These restrictions however do not apply if the plant and machinery is new in view of the provisions of CAA 1990, s 76(5). A first year allowance is also not available for certain leased plant under CAA 1990, ss 39–41, which are unlikely to apply to professional partnerships. Under the provisions of CAA 1990, s 34, a first year allowance is not available in respect of an ordinary motor car even though it is used for business purposes. The writing down allowance is restricted to a maximum of £3,000 per annum for expenditure incurred after 10 March 1992 (previously £2,000 per annum) for a car costing more than £12,000 (previously £8,000), although on sale a balancing allowance would be given if necessary to write off any unrelieved balance. If the car or other plant is leased and the lessee has an option to purchase; under the provisions of CAA 1990, ss 35(3) and 60 the lessee is entitled to the allowances as if he were the owner. If there is no such option to purchase there might be a restriction on the rent deductible in view of CAA 1990, s 35(2). Where the car cost more than £12,000 it is necessary to disallow a proportion of the rent represented by half the excess of the retail price of the car when new over £12,000.

If there is any private usage of the car there is no benefit in kind assessable on the partner as there would be on a Schedule E employee, but there will be a proportionate disallowance in the running costs of the car and on the capital allowances or lease rental paid so that an allowance can only be claimed for the business proportion. It is not possible to obtain a tax benefit by transferring a car at a nominal value to an individual partner at the end of the lease because CAA 1990, s 26(1)(b) would substitute the market value, a view confirmed by the Inland Revenue Press Release of 26 July 1978.

Plant has been held to include such items as law books (*Munby v Furlong* [1977] STC 232), movable office partitioning (*Jarrold v John Good & Sons Ltd* (1962) 40 TC 681) and flooring (*Hunt v Henry Quick Ltd* (1992) STC 633), loose tools, knives and lasts (*Hinton v Maden and Ireland Ltd* (1959) 38 TC 391), grain silos (*Schofield v R and H Hall Ltd* [1975] STC 353), a dry dock (*IRC v Barclay Curle & Co Ltd* (1969) 45 TC 221), a swimming pool (*Cook v Beech Station Caravans Ltd* [1974] STC 402) and a horse (*Yarmouth v France* (1887) 19 QBD 647). The definition cannot be extended to include a building within which the trading takes place even if a prefabricated building (*St John's School v Ward* [1974] STC 69) or a ship used as a floating restaurant (*Benson v Yard Arm Club Ltd* [1979] STC 266) or a garage canopy (*Dixon v Fitch's Garage Ltd* [1975] STC 480, but see the Irish case of *O'Culachain v McMullon Brothers* (1991) 1 IR 363, or suspended ceilings (*Hampton v Forte Autogrill Ltd* [1980] STC 80), or fixed kennels (*Carr v Sayer & Sayer* (1992) STC 396), or a glasshouse used as a garden centre (*Gray v Seymours Garden Centre (Horticulture)* (1993) STC 354.

It is, however, perfectly permissible to allocate expenditure on a building between the building itself and plant incorporated in the building such as decorative lighting (*IRC v Scottish & Newcastle Breweries Ltd* (1982) STC 296; *Leeds Permanent Building Society v Proctor* (1982) STC 821. Such plant will qualify for capital allowances under CAA 1990, s 51, but does not include lighting (*J. Lyons & Co Ltd v Attorney General* (1944) 1 All ER 477; *Hunt v Henry Quick Ltd* (1992) STC 633; *Cole Bros Ltd v Phillips* (1982) STC 307; *Wimpey International Ltd v Warland, Associated Restaurants Ltd v Warland* (1989) STC 273). The Revenue view on such expenditure as published in the CCAB Press Release in August 1977 is as follows:

> "Expenditure on the provision of main services to a building such as electrical wiring, cold water piping and gas piping is regarded as part of the cost of the building and therefore does not qualify for capital allowances. We do, however, regard as eligible for capital allowances expenditure on apparatus to provide electric light or power, hot water, central heating, ventilation or air-conditioning and expenditure on alarm and sprinkler systems. Relief is also given on the cost of all hot water pipes and on the cost of baths, wash basins etc., although the St John's School case suggests that the Courts might regard such expenditure as part of the cost of the building. We do not, however, propose any change in practice in this respect."

These rules were codified in CAA 1990, Sch. AA1 which provides that expenditure on plant does not include expenditure incurred on a building after 29 November 1993, unless incurred before 6 April 1996 in pursuance of a contract made by 29 November 1993. "Building" includes any asset incorporated into it, or which (being moveable) is of a kind normally incorporated in buildings. "Building" includes particular items in Table 1, column 1, namely (*a*) walls, floors, ceilings, doors, gates, shutters, windows and stairs (*b*) main services, and systems of water, electricity and gas (*c*) waste disposal systems (*d*) sewerage and drainage systems (*e*) shafts and other structures in which lifts, hoists, escalators and moving walkways are installed and (*f*) fire safety systems.

Table 1, column 2 lists sixteen categories of assets which are included in the expression "building" but not affected by these rules so they may still qualify as plant under existing case law, but not if their principal purpose is to insulate or enclose the interior of a building, or provide a permanent wall, floor or ceiling.

Similarly, a cold store, an aero engine test bed, a caravan provided mainly for holiday lets, and any moveable building intended to be moved in the course of a trade (such as a contractor's Portakabin) may qualify as plant.

Under CAA 1990, Sch. AA1, para. 4 expenditure still qualifies as plant where it relates to thermal insulation (CAA 1990, s 67), computer software (CAA 1990, s 67A), fire safety (CAA 1990, s 69), safety at sports grounds (CAA 1990, s 70) or security (CAA 1990, s 71). Films, tapes and discs (CAA 1990, s 68) still qualify as revenue expenditure

Chapter 4
The sole proprietor

GENERAL

Partnerships quite frequently begin by an individual setting up a business of his own and subsequently bringing in to the business assistants who in time become fully-fledged partners.

The business may start as a part-time activity, very often from home, and it is necessary to consider whether a claim can be made for the use of the home partly for business purposes. Under the apportionment ruling in *Nolder v Walters* (1930) 15 TC 380, an apportionment of the running costs of the home should be claimable. If say one room is set aside for business purposes and there are eight usable rooms in the house, excluding bathrooms and lavatories, the expenses allowable would usually be calculated as one-eighth of the expenditure on heating, lighting, cleaning, exterior repairs and decoration, rent and rates, together with capital allowances on equipment bought particularly for business purposes and the cost of decorating the study for business purposes.

It is worth bearing in mind that if the room is used exclusively for the purposes of the trade or profession part of the capital gain on the disposal of the property would become chargeable in view of TCGA 1992, s 224. It is frequently possible to ensure, however, that the room is not used exclusively for the purposes of the business so that for example non-business books as well as business books may be kept in the study. In this way it should be possible to obtain both a deduction for the running expenses as a trading expense under TA 1988, s 74 and avoid a capital gains tax charge on disposal of the property. If, however, part of the property is set aside exclusively for business purposes as for example, a doctor's surgery, a capital gains tax charge on that proportion of the profit on sale would be inevitable. However, the problem may be postponed, in some cases indefinitely, by taking advantage of roll-over relief under TCGA 1992, s 152 and retirement relief under TCGA ss 163, 164 and Sch. 6, or reinvestment relief under TCGA 1994, ss 164A–N.

Wife's salary

The sole practitioner will very often be assisted by his wife to whom he can pay a salary. This salary must be reasonable for the work actually involved and the National Insurance costs must not be overlooked (*Stott & Ingham v Trehearne* (1924) 9 TC 69; *Johnson Bros & Co v IRC* (1919) 12 TC 147; *Copeman v William Flood & Sons Ltd* (1940) 24 TC 53; *Earlspring Properties Ltd v Guest* (1993) STC 473; *Dollar & Dollar v Lyon* (1981) STC 333).

In a non-professional practice or where the wife is professionally qualified it might be desirable to bring her into partnership, because if she is actively involved as a partner her share of the partnership assessment will be based on the profit sharing arrangement between the husband and wife and not restricted to reasonable remuneration for the work actually involved. So long as the wife is actively involved in the partnership the income will be treated as her income.

Losses

If the business incurs losses on commencement in a year of assessment which is either the year of assessment in which the trade, profession or vocation commenced, or any of the following three years of assessment a claim may be made under TA 1988, s 381 within one year of the self-assessment filing date for the year of assessment containing the end of the relevant accounts (or within two years of the end of the year of assessment under the preceding year basis) to set the loss against the taxpayer's total income for the three years of assessment preceding that in which the loss is sustained. Relief is given for the earliest available year first. Relief cannot be claimed under this section and also under any other section of the Taxes Acts. It is necessary to show that the trade was being carried on on a commercial basis with a view to profits. It is not, however, possible to switch a trade from husband to wife or *vice versa* and claim loss relief on commencement under this section. Relief is available where the trade is carried on in partnership and continues for those actively engaged in the partnership notwithstanding a change in the partners, so that a deemed cessation on a change in partners under the preceding year basis would not give rise to commencement loss relief. Capital allowances have to be used in the first instance to cover balancing charges but any excess may be used to augment a loss for which relief is claimed (TA 1988, s 383). The relief is also available under the current year basis, with capital allowances treated as an expense for business commencing on or after 6 April 1994 (FA 1994, s 211(2)).

EXAMPLE 4.01

Algernon commenced practice as a sole practitioner on 6 April 1995 and made losses after capital allowances as follows:

1995–96	£5,000
1996–97	£2,000

Prior to commencing on his own he had been employed and his total taxable income for the previous three years has been:

1992–93	£4,000
1993–94	£5,000
1994–95	£6,000

He claims relief under TA 1988, s 381 and the assessments are adjusted as follows:

1992–93	£4,000 – £5,000	NIL
1993–94	£5,000 – £1,000 – £2,000 = £2,000	
1994–95		£6,000
1995–96		NIL
1996–97		NIL

Cash basis

Under the Inland Revenue statement of practice A27 the Revenue will not allow a cash basis as opposed to a full earnings basis for the first three years, or four years where the first three years are assessed on an actual basis from the date of commencement or following any change treated as a cessation. Profits are therefore computed on the earnings basis in determining all tax liabilities affected by the profits of those years. However, in practice, a sole trader commencing business in a small way is very often assessed on a cash basis. Further consideration of the cash and earnings basis is contained in Chapter 5.

Shared expenses

When a sole trader begins to go into full-time practice it is not uncommon to enter into an arrangement with another trader in a similar circumstance or with a larger firm to share certain of the running expenses, such as office accommodation, telephone, receptionist and secretarial facilities. The sharing of expenses would not normally give rise to a partnership arrangement and the individual would remain taxable on his profits and claims as a trading expense his proportion of the jointly incurred expenses.

Blocks of fees

The sole trader wishing to expand may consider purchasing an interest in a business that is already in existence and, for example, buy a block of fees in a professional practice. Such a purchase must be looked at carefully because if it is a purchase of goodwill as opposed to a purchase of work-in-progress it will be a capital item and not allowable as a trading expense. The cost would be allowable in any capital gains tax computation on any subsequent disposal of the business but this is not normally of any immediate advantage. An annuity paid to a former proprietor on the acquisition of a business or to his widow would be an allowable charge on income for both basic and higher rate tax purposes under the provisions of TA 1988, s 683.

So far as the recipient is concerned a sale of goodwill would be a capital receipt subject to capital gains tax and the annuity would be taxed as investment income following *Pegler v Abell* (1972) 48 TC 564 unless it was part of a partnership arrangement under the provisions of TA 1988, s 628 (see Chapter 9).

The sole practitioner or small partnership is frequently in need of specialist assistance. He might buy this assistance as principal in which case the cost would be treated as a trading expense. He might alternatively introduce his client to the specialist in return for some introductory commission. The introductory fee would be a profit of the trade and the specialist costs would be met direct by the clients. Occasionally such arrangements might be made on a fee sharing basis but these are relatively uncommon as it could lead to the specialist being regarded as being in partnership with the sole practitioner.

It should be remembered that in some businesses it is necessary to have a practicing certificate before commencing to trade or to be professionally qualified or registered.

Chapter 5
Cash basis

GENERAL

Partnership accounts are usually prepared on the full "earnings basis" in the same way as accounts for a limited company. In other words, debtors, stock and work-in-progress are evaluated at each year end and brought into the accounts and creditors for expenses incurred but not yet paid are similarly evaluated and included in the accounts. Accounts prepared on the earnings basis will be accepted by the Revenue as the starting point for adjustment of the profit for taxation purposes.

In certain circumstances the Revenue will also accept accounts prepared on what they term "the conventional basis" which is usually referred to colloquially as the "cash basis". On a strict cash basis income is brought into the accounts only when actually received and expenses are debited only when paid. The Revenue will also accept various forms of semi-cash accounting provided that the accounting principles are consistently applied. It is quite common to include income on a cash received basis but to provide for expenses on a normal accruals method as for an earnings basis. It is also quite common practice, particularly in many professions, to include debtors but to exclude stock and work-in-progress. This basis seems especially favoured by solicitors and is sometimes known as the bills delivered basis.

The courts have approved accounts prepared on the cash basis in *Wetton Page & Co v Attwooll* (1962) 40 TC 619; *McCash and Hunter v IRC* (1955) 36 TC 170 and *D and G R Rankine v IRC* (1952) 32 TC 520.

FIRST THREE YEARS AND CHANGE IN BASIS

One particular problem with the cash basis is that the Revenue will not accept accounts prepared on a cash basis in respect of the assessments based on the accounts for the first three years of a business. Such accounts must therefore be prepared on a full earnings basis. The Revenue policy was published in a Press Release issued by the Allied Accountancy Bodies dated 11 November 1969 and published in *The Accountant* on 20 November 1969 (now SP/A.27). The Press Release reads as follows with section references updated to the current legislation:

> "*Accounts on a cash basis*
> At the request of the allied accountancy bodies, the Board of Inland Revenue have authorised publication of a statement of the circumstances in which the accounts of an individual or a partnership carrying on a profession or vocation, prepared otherwise than on a full earnings basis, may be acceptable. Readers are reminded that the statement

reproduced in the following paragraphs should be read in conjunction with the provisions of (TA 1988, s 104).

A company, whether limited or unlimited, is normally required to prepare accounts for tax purposes on an earnings basis, as defined in (TA 1988, s 110). An individual or a partnership carrying on a trade is similarly required to prepare accounts on an earnings basis, but in the circumstances set out below accounts prepared on a cash basis, or on a conventional basis such as bills issued or work completed which is neither full 'earnings' nor pure 'cash', may be accepted from an individual or partnership carrying on a profession or vocation.

Where a profession or vocation is newly set up, or is treated as new for tax purposes (e.g. under TA 1988, s 113), the profits of the first three years from the date of setting up or the change to which TA 1988, s 113 applies are required to be computed on the earnings basis in determining all tax liabilities affected by the profits of those years. For this purpose, 'earnings basis' is given the meaning set out in TA 1988, s 110.

The computation of subsequent profits will continue on the earnings basis until the taxpayer asks to change to a cash or other conventional basis. Such a change will be accepted if the new basis seems likely to provide a reasonable measure of the taxpayer's profit and on the understanding, that the change is a complete one. For example, receipts after the change for work done before the change must be brought into the computation of profits on the cash basis notwithstanding that they have already been brought into account in the computations on the earnings basis; similarly, expenses accrued due but unpaid which were debited in the accounts on the earnings basis may again be debited in the subsequent accounts on the case basis when they are paid.

A further condition is that the taxpayer wishing to make such a change is required to give a written undertaking that he will issue bills for services rendered or work done (that is, in the normal way, completed work but also including work in progress where interim payments or payment on account are contemplated by the terms of the contract or the custom of the particular profession) at regular and frequent intervals. The intervals may be chosen by the taxpayer, but they should normally be quarterly or more often, and they should be specified in the undertaking. Attention is drawn to the possibility of liability under TA 1988, s 104, wherever accounts are prepared on a basis other than earnings: in computing such liability there is no provision for any relief in respect of any profits which may have been brought into the computation twice when the change from the compulsory initial earnings basis was made.

Where accounts are prepared on a cash or other conventional basis and it is desired to change to an earnings basis, no objection will be raised, but attention is again drawn to the liability that will arise under TA 1988, s 104. A subsequent claim to revert to a conventional basis would be resisted.

The statement is not applicable to barristers: a separate statement regarding that profession was issued in January 1969 (SP/A.3)."

DOUBLE CHARGE

The problem with changing from an earnings basis to a cash basis is that the debtors and work-in-progress that have already been taxed under the earnings basis will again be taxed when encashed under the cash basis. This means that the same profits are effectively taxed twice with no relief for the double taxation (*IRC v Morrison* (1932) 17 TC 325).

FACTORING DEBTORS

It is sometimes suggested that the factoring of debtors immediately prior to changing to a cash basis is a useful way of reducing the value of debtors to an absolute minimum. Because the majority of the cash will already have been received from the factoring company there will be less cash to receive after the changeover which will reduce the profits in the first year of accounts on the cash basis and thereby minimise the double taxation. However, unless the debts are consistently factored the accounts on a cash basis would not give a reasonable approximation to the true results and would not be accepted by the Revenue for tax purposes.

Although on a change from the earnings basis to a cash basis there is double taxation in that the profit from the same work may be assessed twice there is no double taxation in the sense that for each year of assessment there is only one assessable profit so that for example the accounts to 30 April 1997 prepared on a full earnings basis would form the basis of assessment for 1997–98, whereas the accounts for 30 April 1998 prepared on a cash basis would form the basis of assessment for 1998–99.

POST-CESSATION RECEIPTS

If, however, the cash basis comes to an end for any reason, for example, on the cessation of business or under the preceding year basis on a deemed cessation on a change of partners without there being a continuation election, the debtors and work-in-progress at cessation will be taxed as post cessation receipts.

There can be a post-cessation receipts charge in respect of accounts prepared on the full earnings basis under TA 1988, s 103. This section will levy tax under Schedule D, Case VI on amounts received after cessation not included in an earnings basis, such as royalties received after cessation which would otherwise be exempt from tax following *Purchase v Stainer's Executors* (1951) 32 TC 367; *Carson v Cheyney's Executors* (1958) 38 TC 240 and *Hume v Asquith* (1968) 45 TC 251. The section includes all sums received after cessation so far as their value was not brought into account in computing the profits before cessation.

The section also applies to profits computed on a cash basis which would have escaped taxation had the accounts been prepared on an earnings basis, in other words income not ascertained at the date of cessation such as a share of profits from a joint venture which has not yet been completed. If the amount due is ascertained at the date of cessation but the cash has not yet been received the amount would have been included in accounts prepared on an earnings basis and the post cessation receipt is not caught under TA 1988, s 103, but under TA 1988, s 104 which applies only where the accounts are prepared on the cash basis. TA 1988, s 103 does not apply to income from outside the United Kingdom received by a non-resident or his agent or from the sale of copyright by the personal representatives of an artist or author, or to sums realised from the sale of work-in-progress. Transfers of work-in-progress at cessation are deemed to take place at the open market value under TA 1988, s 100(1)(*b*) and TA 1988, s 101(1)(*b*), except where the work-in-progress is transferred for valuable consideration (but not necessarily for full value) to a transferee who carries on the trade or profession and will deduct the cost in computing his trading profits, in which case the work-in-progress is valued at the amount paid for the work-in-progress irrespective of its true market value under TA 1988, s 101(1)(*a*). A similar rule for stock in TA 1988, s 100 ceased to apply for transfers between connected parties on any discontinuance occurring after 29 November 1994 as a result of TA 1988, s 100(1A), subject to a joint election to take the higher of the price paid on the acquisition value (cost) of the transfer as the disposal value if less than the arm's length price which would otherwise apply under TA 1988, s 100(1C)–(1F) inserted by FA 1995, s 140.

Election

Under TA 1988, s 101(2), the partners in a professional practice can elect by notice in writing sent to the Inspector at any time within twelve months after a discontinuance that the excess of the sale price of work-in-progress over cost should be excluded from the profits of the final accounting period and included as a post-cessation receipt under TA 1988, s 103.

Assessment

Under TA 1988, s 104 where there has been a cessation under Schedule D, Cases I and II and the accounts have been computed on a cash basis or semi-cash basis, post-cessation receipts ascertained but not received at the date of cessation are charged to tax under Schedule D, Case VI. Although the charge is under Schedule D, Case VI it is nonetheless earned income under TA 1988, s 107. TA 1988, s 110(2) confirms that a notional discontinuance on a change in partners under the preceding year basis where there has been no election for continuation under TA 1988, s 113(2) is a discontinuance for post-cessation receipts purposes. In computing post-cessation receipts any expenses or capital allowances which could have been deducted had the business continued will be allowed under TA 1988, s 105. For example, bad debts would be allowed and the administrative costs of collecting debtors would be treated as an allowable expense. It is possible to have a post-cessation loss and loss relief can be claimed against post-cessation profits but, other than under TA 1988, s 109A, not against total income under TA 1988, s 380. Nor used it to be possible for such losses be carried back to a period before the loss was was incurred unless the accounts are re-opened or an error or mistake claim made under TMA 1970, s 33. However, TA 1988, s 109A introduced by FA 1995, s 90 provides limited relief for the cost of remedying defective work, damages and legal and other costs associated therewith, post-cessation and professional indemnity insurance cover incurred with seven years of cessation. Similar relief is available for debts regarded as recoverable at cessation which subsequently turn out to be bad. The relief is not carried back but set against total income of the year in which the expenditure is incurred, on a claim made within twelve months of 31 January following the fiscal year end (or two years for 1994–95 and 1995–96). Any excess expenditure may not be carried back and can only be carried forward against later post-cessation receipts under TA 1988, s 105. However, the tax payer may specify in his claim that any excess may be set against capital gains of the same year (but not carried forward), in which case it would be relieved before any capital losses brought forward, the annual exemption and any trading losses set against gains under FA 1991, s 72. Insurance recoveries are post-cessation receipts under TA 1988, s 103 (TA 1988, s 109A(3)), but related to the year in which the associated expenditure is incurred. Any claim under TA 1988, s 109A is reduced by any provision for expenses at the date of cessation which remains unpaid at the end of the year in which the expenditure is incurred, but if paid subsequently it in turn would qualify for relief (TA 1988, s 109A(5). It is not possible to claim double relief.

Sale of business

On a cessation on sale the right to the post-cessation receipts is often transferred to the purchaser and TA 1988, s 106 provides that in such circumstances the post-cessation receipts are not taxable on the business ceasing, but the sale proceeds are charged as if they were post-cessation receipts. Similarly on a notional discontinuance on a change in partnership under the preceding year basis there is no post-cessation receipt if the post-cessation income is credited to the continuing partners and any charge on post-cessation receipts is limited to any amount credited to the outgoing partner under TA 1988, s 106(2). This does not, however, get round the problem that such a cessation would mean that for the next three accounting years the accounts would have to be prepared on the earnings basis.

Carry-back election

Under TA 1988, s 108 the taxpayer can elect within two years from the date of a post-cessation receipt assessment to carry back the amount chargeable and have it assessed as if it was received on the last day of trading instead of being assessed under schedule D, Case VI on a current year basis in the year of receipt. It would normally be desirable to elect for carry-back where for example there are losses or unused capital allowances at the date of cessation which cannot be carried forward and set against post-cessation receipts, but may be used against such receipts on an election to carry back under TA 1988, s 108.

Transitional provisions

Prior to the introduction of the taxation of post-cessation receipts many partners were relying on the tax-free post-cessation receipts to provide for their retirement. There is therefore a transitional arrangement under TA 1988, s 109 for taxpayers born before 6 April 1917 who were being assessed on a basis other than earnings on 18 March 1968. If the taxpayer was sixty-five or more on 5 April 1967 only 5/20ths of the post-cessation receipt is chargeable. If he was on that date aged less than fifty-two, 19/20ths of the post-cessation receipt would be taxable and for intermediate ages 18/24ths is taxable if aged fifty-two, 17/24ths if aged fifty-three and so on up to age sixty-four on that date. This relief is unlikely to apply in many cases now.

The relief is available for sole traders as well as partners. The old extra-statutory top-slicing relief on mergers of firms on a cash basis in ESC A18 was withdrawn on 15 March 1988.

Chapter 6

Capital taxes

INHERITANCE TAX

General

In order to understand the impact of inheritance tax on partnerships it is necessary to reconsider the definition of a partnership which is, by the Partnership Act 1890, s 1 "the relation which subsists between persons carrying on a business in common with a view to profit." Section 4 of the Act goes on to state that persons who have entered into partnership with one another are called collectively a firm, but only in Scotland does a firm constitute a legal person distinct from the individual partners of whom it is composed; an English partnership is not a distinct entity separate from the individuals which comprise it (see, for example, *Meyer & Co v Faber (No 2)* [1923] 2 Ch 421; *Sadler v Whiteman* [1910] AC 514; *R v Holden* [1912] 1 KB 483). The particular problems and planning possibilities associated with Scottish partnerships are not considered in this book.

A partner has no direct interest in the assets of the firm – called partnership property by the Partnership Act 1890, s 20 – because no such interest is given by s 24 of that Act. This is also confirmed in the somewhat ancient case of *Lingen v Simpson* (1824) 1 Sim & St 600.

But, although he has no direct interest in the partnership assets as such, he does have a *chose in action*. This right, or series of rights, consists of a share of the income during the life of the partnership under Partnership Act 1890, s 24(1), a right to the repayment of capital on dissolution (Partnership Act 1890, s 44(3)(*b*)), and the right to a share in any surplus arising on dissolution (Partnership Act 1890, s 44(4)(*b*); *Rodriguez v Speyer Bros* [1919] AC 68).

For inheritance tax purposes partners are connected persons except in relation to transfers of partnership assets pursuant to bona fide commercial arrangements, which would in any event be outside the scope of inheritance tax. They are also connected with their spouse or relative, including brothers, sisters, ancestors and lineal descendants, uncles, aunts, nephews and nieces (IHTA 1984, s 270, TCGA 1992, s 286).

In all partnership transactions it is worth bearing in mind that IHTA 1984, s 10(1) provides that a disposition is not a transfer value if it is shown that it was not intended, and was not made in a transaction intended, to confer any gratuitous benefit on any person and either:
 (*a*) that it was made in a transaction at arm's length between persons not connected with each other; or
 (*b*) that it was such as might be expected to be made in a transaction at arm's length between persons not connected with each other.

Formation

On commencement of a partnership a partner may provide capital to the partnership in which case he has converted one asset *viz.* cash into another asset *viz.* an interest in partnership and as there would be no gratuitous intent involved there would be no inheritance tax liability.

Introduction of new partners

If a new partner is introduced into a partnership he will normally be required to provide capital but may be allowed to do this over a period of time. He will, however, be required to work in the partnership and although the existing partners' interest in the partnership is diluted there would normally be no inheritance tax liability provided that the introduction of the new partner was on normal commercial terms.

Automatic accruer

It is often provided that within a partnership, goodwill belongs to the partners for the time being and on the death or retirement of any partner his share of goodwill passes to the continuing partners automatically without payment. Similar arrangements are sometimes made in connection with a partner's share of capital. In a normal commercial arrangement there should be no gratuitous transfer of value, because although each partner stands to lose his share of goodwill and/or capital on retirement, he also stands to gain from his own partners' death or retirement on reciprocal arrangements. If, however, there is a marked disparity of ages of partners it could be that there is an intended transfer of value from the older to the younger partners. In such cases it may be possible to show following the case of *A-G v Boden* [1912] 1 KB 539 that the younger partners are taking over some of the responsibility from the older partners and this is a commercial justification for transferring to them part of the older partners' share in the partnership. It is quite common for a partnership agreement to specify that senior partners have to devote such time and attention to the business as they deem necessary while the junior partners have to devote the whole of their time and attention to the business. These clauses are known as "time and attention" or "Boden" clauses. The fact that the senior partner may not devote the whole of his time to the business could cause a problem if he becomes entitled to a partnership annuity. In order for the annuity to be classified as earned income it is necessary for a partner to have devoted substantially the whole of his time to the business TA 1988, s 628(2).

The question of time spent on the business of the partnership is relevant also for other tax considerations. First, TA 1988, s 833(4)–(6) requires a partner to be personally acting in the partnership before his partnership income is treated as earned income. Secondly under TA 1988, s 628 the last seven years of assessment in which the partner *was required to devote substantially the whole of his time to acting as a partner* ... figure prominently in determining the amount of a partnership annuity which is treated as earned income of the partners in retirement (see Chapter 12).

If a family member is brought into the partnership followed by a transfer of a partnership interest (for example, the senior partner's son, is taken into partnership and part of the senior partner's interest is transferred to the son) there is a *prime facie* transfer of value, because there would be a presumption of gratuitous intent between father and son. This presumption would be capable of being rebutted either relying on the Boden principle or by showing that the arrangements were similar to the arrangements involved when a non-family partner is introduced. However, between connected parties the onus is on the taxpayer to prove that there was no gift element. If in any event there is a transfer of value on the introduction of a partner the transferor partner has to value the reduction in his estate as a result of the introduction of the new partner. This means that his partnership interest has to be valued before and after the introduction, except where the entire interest qualifies for business property relief of 100% under IHTA 1984, ss 104(1)(*a*) and 105(1)(*a*).

Annuities

Partnership arrangements very often provide that after retirement an annuity is paid to the retiring partner for a period of time or occasionally for life, and this annuity may or may not continue for the retired partner's widow. The mere grant of an annuity would not of itself be a disposition, being only the assumption of a liability, but any payment made under the annuity would be a chargeable transfer. Normally the annuity would not be granted in isolation but would be part of the overall arrangement among the partners and as such would only be a chargeable transfer if it could not be shown that there was no gratuitous intent. There would be no such transfer if it were part of the normal commercial arrangements, as would normally be the case. In such cases there would be no inheritance tax charge on the payment of the annuity as this would be under a liability incurred for full consideration.

Retirement and dissolution

On retirement or dissolution the outgoing partner again exchanges as part of the commercial arrangements among the partners his share in the partnership for whatever he is entitled to under the agreement. This would not give rise to an inheritance tax charge as there is no gratuitous intent on anybody's part, and this would apply whether or not he was entitled to a share in any profit on any of the partnership property or to payment for goodwill, or even to repayment of his capital account. Whereas he previously had a share in the partnership he now has cash or assets transferred to him from the partnership. If, however, the outgoing partner does not receive his full entitlement there would normally be a chargeable transfer on the difference between the amount to which he would have been entitled under the partnership arrangements and the amount he actually receives. It would normally be difficult to prove lack of gratuitous intent where an outgoing partner did not receive his full entitlement, provided that the entitlement was realistic and it could be met by the continuing partners. A failure to take his full entitlement must be distinguished from a variation in that entitlement, for example, by agreeing to waive repayment of his capital account in return for an increased annuity. Sums due to a retired partner from the firm, after his retirement, would not constitute business property under IHTA 1984, s 105 for the purpose of business property relief.

Death

On death a partner has an asset, being his interest in the partnership, which is part of his estate and would normally constitute business property under IHTA 1984, s 105. That asset would be his entitlement under the partnership arrangements to repayment on death and would only, for example, reflect the increase in value of underlying assets in the partnership if he would be entitled to share in such increase. It must be emphasised that the asset to be valued is the share in the partnership, not a proportion of the partnership assets less liabilities, unless his death precipitates a dissolution of the partnership in which case his partnership share would represent his pro rata share in the assets less liabilities of the partnership. If payable over a set period of time the present value at the date of death would be chargeable.

Gifts made by the firm

A partnership has no legal identity distinct from the partners and, therefore, a gift by the firm would be treated as a disposal by each of the individual partners. The quantum of the gift however would be the reduction in each partner's share in the partnership as a result of the gift and this may not be the same as a proportionate share of the asset given away. If a partner was only entitled to a share in surplus assets on a dissolution, a disposal of an asset by the firm may have only a marginal depreciatory effect on the value of any one partner's interest in the firm. It is worth emphasising that the only interest of any partner in a partnership is his share in the firm and partnership assets do not themselves form part of his estate (*Lingen v Simpson* (1824) 1 Sim & St 600; *Dreyfus v IRC* (1929) 14 TC 560)).

Partner's own property used by the firm

Loans at less than the normal commercial rate of interest or the use of property at less than the commercial rent is not now a chargeable transfer for inheritance tax purposes (IHTA 1984, s 56(4)).

Exemptions and reliefs

A partner's interest in a partnership is relevant business property and currently qualifies for a 100% deduction for inheritance tax purposes under IHTA 1984, ss 104(1)(*a*) and 105(1)(*a*). There are exceptions for businesses carried on otherwise than for gain or which are share dealing, property dealing or investment partnerships.

Property used by a partnership for the purpose of its business which is provided by a partner will qualify for business relief of 50% under IHTA 1984, ss 104(1)(*b*) and 105(1)(*d*). Note that a loan of assets by a spouse of a partner would not qualify for business relief.

For business relief purposes the value of an interest in a business is the net value as determined under IHTA 1984, s 110(*b*) and (*c*) which provides:

> "For the purpose of this section—(b) the net value of a business is the value of the assets used in the business (including goodwill) reduced by the aggregate amount of any liabilities incurred for the purposes of the business; (c) in ascertaining the net value of an interest in a business, no regard shall be had to assets or liabilities other than those by reference to which the net value of the business would have fallen to be ascertained if the tax had been attributed to the entire business."

In spite of this wording it is maintained that the partner's interest in the business is the value of his partnership share in accordance with the partnership agreement and Partnership Act 1890. This is not necessarily a proportion of the partnership assets less liabilities as he might, for example, not be entitled to a share in good-

Inheritance tax

will or to any share in the excess of market value over book value of properties. Any contrary interpretation would mean that on any gratuitous transfer of the partnership interest, or on death, the business relief could be calculated on a different figure from the reduction in the estate as a result of the transfer of the value of the partnership inherited on death, which would presumably not be the intention of the legislation. There are, however, provisions in IHTA 1984, s 112(2) which exclude business relief for assets owned by the firm but which are not used for the purposes of the partnership, for example, excess accommodation sub-let to third parties, or where the partnership property has been held for less than two years and does not replace earlier property so that the total period of ownership is at least two out of five years prior to the transfer. Surplus cash balances could be excluded under these provisions but not normal working capital used in the partnership business.

It is understood that the Revenue will accept that a partial assignment from one partner's capital account to another will qualify for business relief.

See p. 222 on the problems of buy/sell arrangements.

EXAMPLE 6.01

Lotus Blossom & Co. owned its freehold office block worth £50,000. On 11 August 1995 the four partners gave the property jointly to their sons. It is considered that the office block of itself is not an interest in a business, but the asset is used wholly for the purpose of the partnership business.

	Transfer £	Business relief 50% £	Transfer of value £	Less annual exemption* £	Chargeable £
Partner A	12,500	6,250	6,250	2,870	3,380
B	12,500	6,250	6,250	4,100	2,150
C	12,500	6,250	6,250	1,470	4,780
D	12,500	6,250	6,250	2,100	4,150
	£50,000	£25,000	£25,000	£10,540	£14,460

* The "annual" exemption is the £6,000 maximum that could possibly apply (i e, £3,000 previous year's exemption not utilised, plus £3,000 current year's exemption), less, an assumed utilisation of, for A, £3,130, for B, £1,900, for C £4,530 and for D £3,900.

Transaction	Date	Cumulative net value transferred £	Band £	IHT on transfer £
A				
Brought forward	6.4.95 (say)	150,000		
Transfer of value £3,380	11.8.95	153,380		Nil
B				
Brought forward	6.4.95 (say)	160,000		
Transfer of value £2,150	11.8.95	162,150	40%	£860

EXAMPLE 6.01 *(continued)*

C					
Brought forward	6.4.95 (say)	180,000			
Transfer of value £4,780	11.8.95	184,780		40%	£1,912
D					
Brought forward	12.7.95 (say)	152,000			
Transfer of value £4,150	11.8.95	156,150		0–154,000	Nil
				154,000–156,150	
				2,150 @ 40%	£860

Payment by instalments

Inheritance tax payable on an interest in a partnership passing on death or where the tax is payable by the transferee, may be paid by ten equal yearly instalments under IHTA 1984, s 227. It is necessary to make an election in writing and the first instalment is due six months after the end of the month in which the death occurred, or when it would be payable on a lifetime transfer if not paid by instalments. Interest on unpaid tax accrues only from the date each instalment becomes due under IHTA 1984, s 234.

For this purpose only the value of the interest in the partnership is determined (IHTA 1984, s 227(7)) on the basis of the *proportionate* interest in the net value of the partnership (ie the partnership assets less liabilities) *as a whole* ignoring rights or liabilities as between the partners themselves.

Valuation

The valuation of an interest in a partnership follows the normal valuation principles as the price which the property might reasonably be expected to fetch if sold in the open market at the appropriate time under IHTA 1984, s 160. The interest is, therefore, valued in accordance with the rights attaching to the partnership share (but see above for rules applying for purposes of payment by instalments). This means that if a retiring partner is entitled to a share of the goodwill, for example, it will be calculated in accordance with the partnership agreement irrespective of its actual value in the absence of such agreement. Therefore, in a professional partnership goodwill might still be valued on the basis of, say, one and a half years' purchase of the gross recurring fees. If the goodwill has to be valued on a straightforward commercial basis this is usually calculated on a total capitalisation basis or on a super profits basis. Total capitalisation involves estimating the annual recurring profit after deducting reasonable remuneration for the partners and taking a number of years' purchase of these profits. From this is deducted the net tangible assets to give the value of goodwill. Alternatively, the calculation may be made on a super profits basis which involves taking the anticipated recurring profits of the partnership less the partner's remuneration and less a reasonable return on the capital employed in the partnership. This is then multiplied by a number of years purchase. In the case of *Findlay's Trustees v IRC* (1938) 22 ATC 437 the total capitalisation method was preferred to the super profits method.

EXAMPLE 6.02

ABC Co.
Balance Sheet at 30 June 1995

	£	£
CURRENT ASSETS		
Stock		120,000
Debtors		100,000
Balance at Bank		50,000
		270,000
Less: CURRENT LIABILITIES		
Sundry creditors		90,000
		£180,000
Financed by:		
CAPITAL ACCOUNTS: AS		25,000
ES		25,000
		50,000
CURRENT ACCOUNT: AS		70,000
ES		60,000
		£180,000

Profit record before tax:
Year ended 30.6.93		50,000
30.6.94		40,000
30.6.95		10,000
		£100,000

Super profits basis:

		£
Average profits: 50,000 × 3		150,000
40,000 × 2		80,000
10,000 × 1		10,000
6		£240,000
$\dfrac{24,000}{6} =$		40,000
Less: Economic rent of property (say)		3,750
		36,250
Less: Notional remuneration		
AS	12,000	
ES	6,000	18,000
		18,250
Less: Capital employed		
Stock + debtors – creditors		
£130,000, say, @ 11%		14,300
		£ 3,950

EXAMPLE 6.02 *(continued)*

Goodwill 4 years purchase of super profits	£15,800

Total capitalisation basis

	£
Average maintainable profits as adjusted as before	£18,250

Required yield 12½%	
Years purchase $\dfrac{100}{12\frac{1}{2}} = 8$	146,000
Less: stock + debtors − creditors	130,000
Goodwill	£ 16,000

CAPITAL GAINS TAX

The capital gains tax legislation dealing with partnership is, to say the least, somewhat deficient. The legislation in TCGA 1992, s 59 merely provides that:

> "Where two or more persons carry on a trade or business in partnership
> (a) tax in respect of chargeable gains accruing to them on the disposal of any partnership assets shall in Scotland as well as elsewhere in the United Kingdom be assessed and charged on them separately; and
> (b) any partnership dealings shall be treated as dealings by the partners and not by the firm as such; and
> (c) Section 112(1) and (2) of the Taxes Act 1988 (residence of partnerships) shall apply in relation to tax chargeable in pursuance of this part of this Act as it applies in relation to income tax."

It is also provided by TCGA 1992, s 286(4) that:

> "Except in relation to acquisitions or disposals of partnership assets pursuant to bona fide commercial arrangements a person is connected with any person with whom he is in partnership and with the husband and wife or a relative of any individual with whom he is in partnership."

A relative for this purpose includes brother, sister, ancestor, or lineal descendant, but unlike for inheritance tax purposes, does not include uncles and aunts, nephews and nieces.

As has been shown, when considering inheritance tax, the only asset that a partner actually possesses in connection with a partnership is a *chose in action* but the capital gains tax legislation reconstitutes the assets in the hands of the partners by providing that gains attributable to partners are allocated to them in the proportion in which they share surplus assets. This is usually known as the asset sharing ratio and in many cases, although not invariably will be the same as the profit sharing ratio for dividing income profits among the partners.

It will be noted that the legislation does not provide that the partners will cease to have their interest in the partnership as a separate *chose in action*, which is important when considering aspects of partnership goodwill.

As a result of the inadequate legislation to deal with capital gains tax on partnerships the Inland Revenue published a statement of practice on 17 January 1975 (SP/D12) and although this has no statutory force it nonetheless deals with most partnership capital gains tax situations. The statement of practice followed discussions with the Law Society and the Allied Accountancy Bodies and provides as follows (as updated for TCGA 1992 references and with examples supplied by the authors):

"REVENUE STATEMENT OF PRACTICE

1. *Nature of the asset liable to tax*

TCGA 1992, s 59 treats any partnership dealings in chargeable assets for capital gains tax purposes as dealings by the individual partners rather than by the firm as such. Each partner has, therefore, to be regarded as owning a fractional share of each of the partnership assets and not for this purpose an interest in the partnership.

Where it is necessary to ascertain the market value of a partner's share in the partnership asset for capital gains tax purposes, it will be taken as a fraction of the value of the total partnership interest in the asset without any discount for the size of his share. If, for example, a partnership owned all the issued shares in a company, the value of the interest in that holding of a partner with a one-tenth share would be one-tenth of the value of the partnership's 100% holding."

The capital gains tax examples in this chapter ignore indexation relief unless otherwise stated.

EXAMPLE 6.03

			£
1984 Hereclese bought the goodwill of a business for			8,000
1992 Hereclese took Theseus into equal partnership when the goodwill was worth			14,000
1998 Sale of entire goodwill of business			12,000
Hereclese	£	£	
1992 Sale 50% of £14,000		7,000	
Less: 50% of £8,000	4,000		
plus indexation (say) 60%	2,400		
	———	6,400	
Gain		———	600
1998 Sale 50% of £12,000		6,000	
Less: 50% of £8,000	4,000		
plus indexation (say) 75%	3,000		
	———	7,000	
No gain or loss		———	Nil
Theseus			
1998 Sale 50% of £12,000		6,000	
Cost (50% of £14,000)	7,000		
plus indexation (say) 15%	1,050		
	———	8,050	
Loss restricted to non-indexation element		———	(1,000)

EXAMPLE 6.03 (continued)

If the goodwill had not ben revalued in 1992 there would have been no chargeable gain at that stage, unless the parties were related, in which case there would normally be a disposal at market value.

1992 Sale 50% × book value £8,000		4,000	
Less: 50% × £8,000	4,000		
plus indexation at 60%	2,400		
		6,400	
Gain			Nil
Loss restricted to non-indexed loss			Nil

Note: Indexation can reduce a gain but not create or add to a loss; FA 1994, s 93, amending TCGA 1992, and Sch. 12.

"2. *Disposals of assets by a partnership*

Where an asset is disposed of by a partnership to an outside party each of the partners will be treated as disposing of his fractional share of the asset. Similarly if a partnership makes a part disposal of an asset each partner will be treated as making a part disposal of his fractional share. In computing gains or losses the proceeds of disposal will be allocated between the partners in the ratio of their shares in asset surpluses at the time of disposal. Where this is not specifically laid down the allocation will follow the actual destination of the surplus as shown in the partnership accounts; regard will of course have to be paid to any agreement outside the accounts. If the surplus is not allocated among the partners but, for example, put to a common reserve, regard will be had to the ordinary profit-sharing ratios in the absence of a specified asset-surplus-sharing ratio. Expenditure on the acquisition of assets by a partnership will be allocated between the partners in the same way at the time of the acquisition. This allocation may require adjustment, however, if there is a subsequent change in the partnership sharing ratio (see para. 4)."

EXAMPLE 6.04

Orpheus acquired his interest in the partnership freehold property in 1990 from a former partner Lute for £7,000. Value in books not adjusted.

	Firm 100% £ (1977)	Jason 50% £ (1980)	Perseus 30% £ (1984)	Orpheus 20% £
Cost of freehold property (1985)	20,000	10,000	6,000	
Acquisition from former partner				7,000
1995 Part disposal:				
Proceeds	16,000	8,000	4,800	3,200
Value retained	18,000	9,000	5,400	3,600

EXAMPLE 6.04 *(continued)*

Computation

Cost plus indexation (say)	10,000	6,000	7,000
Attributable portion: $\left(\dfrac{A}{A+B}\right)$	7,500	3,600	1,400
Proceeds ÷ (proceeds + value retained)	$\times\,^{8}/_{17}$	$\times\,^{48}/_{102}$	$\times\,^{32}/_{68}$
Attributable cost, indexed	8,235	4,517	3,952
Proceeds	8,000	4,800	3,200
Chargeable gain	Nil	283	Nil
Loss limited by indexation	Nil		Nil

"3. *Partnership assets divided in kind among the partners*

Where a partnership distributes an asset in kind to one or more of the partners, for example, on dissolution, a partner who receives the asset will not be regarded as disposing of his fractional share in it. A computation will first be necessary of the gains which would be chargeable on the individual partners if the asset had been disposed of at its current market value. Where this results in a gain being attributed to a partner not receiving the asset the gain will be charged at the time of the distribution of the asset. Where, however, the gain is allocated to a partner receiving the asset concerned there will be no charge on distribution. Instead, his capital gains tax cost to be carried forward will be the market value of the asset at the date of distribution as reduced by the amount of his gain. The same principles will be applied where the computation results in a loss."

EXAMPLE 6.05

Homer, Ovid and Virgil shared assets and surplus profits 40:35:25. On 1 July 1995 Homer retired and took with him the freehold property.

	Book value (and cost) £	*Market value* £
Freehold property	8,000	30,000
Goodwill	25,000	5,000
Non-chargeable assets	40,000	40,000
	£73,000	£75,000

Chargeable gains	*Ovid* (35%) £	*Virgil* (25%) £
Proceeds (% of Freehold value)	10,500	7,500
Cost (%)	2,800	2,000
Indexation (say)	1,400	1,000
Gain	£6,300	£4,500

EXAMPLE 6.05 (*continued*)

	£
Allowable loss – Homer	
disposal of 40% goodwill	2,000
Cost (40% of £25,000)	10,000
Indexation (say)	5,000
Allowable loss* excluding indexation	£(8,000)
Acquisition Cost of Freehold – Homer	
Market value	30,000
Less: notional gain	
40% × (30,000 −(8,000 + 4,000 indexation))	7,200
	£22,800

*Losses with connected persons are restricted and can only be set against gains with the same persons (TCGA 1992, s 286(3)). Partners are connected persons except in relation to disposals of partnership assets pursuant to bona fide commercial restrictions. (TCGA 1992, s 286(4)). It is considered that Homer's disposal is such as to escape restrictions under these provisions.

"4. *Changes in partnership sharing ratios*

An occasion of charge also arises when there is a change in partnership sharing ratios including changes arising from a partner joining or leaving the partnership. In these circumstances a partner who reduces or gives up his share in asset surpluses will be treated as disposing of part or the whole of his share in each of the partnership assets and a partner who increases his share will be treated as making a similar acquisition. Subject to the qualifications mentioned at 6 and 7 below the disposal consideration will be a fraction (equal to the fractional share changing hands) of the current balance sheet value of each chargeable asset provided that there is no direct payment or consideration outside the partnership. Where no adjustment is made through the partnership accounts (for example, by revaluation of the assets coupled with a corresponding increase or decrease in the partner's current or capital account at some date between the partner's acquisition and the reduction in his share) the disposal is treated as made for a consideration equal to his capital gains tax cost and thus there will be neither a chargeable gain nor an allowable loss at that point. A partner whose share reduces will carry forward a smaller proportion of cost to set against a subsequent disposal of the asset and a partner whose share increases will carry forward a larger proportion of cost.

The general rules in TCGA 1992, s 42, for apportioning the total acquisition cost on a part disposal of an asset will not be applied in the case of a partner reducing his asset-surplus share. Instead, the cost of the part disposed of will be calculated on a fractional basis."

EXAMPLE 6.06

BALANCE SHEET

	Capital A/C £	Current A/C £	Surplus asset share Old %	Surplus asset share New %
Achilles	25,000	20,000	50	40
Bacchus	15,000	20,000	30	30
Cheiron	10,000	15,000	20	30
	£50,000	£55,000	100%	100%

EXAMPLE 6.06 (*continued*)

	Assets £
Freehold property at cost	65,000
Goodwill at cost	Nil
Non-chargeable assets	40,000
	£105,000

Disposal by Achilles

	£
Proceeds	9,500
Cost (50% − 40% × £65,000)	6,500
Indexation (say)	3,000
Gain/loss	Nil

Acquisition by Cheiron

Cost	£9,500

Note:
The proceeds (and cost to Cheiron) are calculated as the same as the indexed cost to give a no gain/no loss position as this paragraph is extended by SP1/89 as follows:

> *Rebasing*
> The Board of Inland Revenue have agreed that a disposal of a share of partnership assets to which paragraph 4 of the Statement of Practice of 17 January 1975 [Statement D12] applies so that neither a chargeable gain nor an allowable loss accrues (before indexation for disposals before 6 April 1988) may be treated for the purposes of [TCGA 1992, s 35, Sch. 3] as if it were a no gain/no loss disposal within [TCGA 1992, Sch. 3, para. 1].
>
> *Deferred charges*
> A disposal of a share of partnership assets to which paragraph 4 of the Statement of Practice of 17 January 1975 [Statement D12] applies so that neither a chargeable gain nor an allowable loss accrues (before indexation for disposals before 6 April 1988) may be treated for the purposes of [TCGA 1992, s 36, Sch. 4], as if it were a no gain/no loss disposal within [TCGA 1992, Sch. 3, para. 1].
>
> *Indexation*
> When, on or after 6 April 1988, a partner disposes of all or part of his share of partnership assets in circumstances to which paragraph 4 of the Statement of Practice of 17 January 1975 [Statement D12] applies so that neither a chargeable gain nor an allowable loss accrues, the amount of the consideration will be calculated on the assumption that an unindexed gain will accrue to the transferor equal to the indexation allowance, so that after taking account of the indexation allowance, neither a gain nor a loss accrues.
>
> Where a partner disposes on or after 6 April 1988 of all or part of his share of partnership assets, and he is treated by virtue of this Statement as having owned the share on 31 March 1982, the indexation allowance on the disposal may be computed as if he had acquired the share on 31 March 1982. A disposal of a share in a partnership asset on or after 31 March 1982 to which paragraph 4 of the Statement of Practice of 17 January 1975 [Statement D12] applies so that neither a chargeable gain nor an allowable loss accrues may be treated for the purposes of [TCGA 1992, s 55(5)] as if it were

a no gain/no loss disposal within [TCGA 1992, s 35(3)(d)]. A special rule will however apply where the share changed hands on or after 6 April 1985 (1 April in the case of an acquisition from a company) and before 6 April 1988: in these circumstances the indexation allowance will be computed by reference to the 31 March 1982 value *but* from the date of the last disposal of the share before 6 April 1988."

"5. *Adjustments through the accounts*

Where a partnership asset is revalued a partner will be credited in his current or capital account with a sum equal to his fractional share of the increase in value. An upward revaluation of chargeable assets is not itself an occasion of charge. If, however, there were to be a subsequent reduction in the partner's asset-surplus share, the effect would be to reduce his potential liability to capital gains tax on the eventual disposal of the assets without an equivalent reduction of the credit he has received in the accounts. Consequently at the time of the reduction in sharing ratio he will be regarded as disposing of the fractional share of the partnership asset represented by the difference between his old and his new share for a consideration equal to that fraction of the increased value at the revaluation. The partner whose share correspondingly increases will have his acquisition cost to be carried forward for the asset increased by the same amount. The same principles will be applied in the case of a downward revaluation.

(*Note*: A revaluation can be avoided by providing by agreement that the profit on an asset such as a freehold property should be divided in the old profit sharing ratio up to the value at the date of change and thereafter any future increase in value would be divided in the new profit sharing ratio.)"

EXAMPLE 6.07

Castor and Pollux share assets and profits 60:40

	£
Freehold property: cost 1985	40,000
revalued	120,000

Profit and asset sharing ratios changed to 50:50 on 1.10.95 when the property was worth £140,000 but was not revalued.

Castor	£
1992 – no disposal	
1995 – Proceeds (60% – 50% × £120,000)	12,000
Cost (60% – 50% × £40,000)	4,000
Indexation (say 50%)	2,000
Gain	£6,000
Cost carried forward 50% × 40,000, subject to indexation	£20,000

Pollux	£
1985 – Cost 40% × 40,000	16,000
1995 – Cost 10 % × 120,000	12,000
Cost carried forward, subject to indexation	£28,000

"*Payment outside the accounts*

Where on a change of partnership sharing ratios payments are made directly between two or more partners outside the framework of the partnership accounts, the payments represent consideration for the disposal of the whole or part of a partner's share in partnership assets in addition to any consideration calculated on the bases described in 4 and 5 above. Often such payments will be for goodwill not included in the balance sheet. In such cases the partner receiving the payment will have no capital gains tax cost to set against it unless he made a similar payment for his share in the asset (for example, on entering the partnership) or elects to have the market value at 31 March 1982 treated as his acquisition cost. The partner making the payment will only be allowed to deduct the amount in computing gains or losses on a subsequent disposal of his share in the asset. He will be able to claim a loss when he finally leaves the partnership or when his share is reduced provided that he then receives either no consideration or a lesser consideration for his share of the asset. Where the payment clearly constitutes payment for a share in assets included in the partnership accounts, the partner receiving it will be able to deduct the amount of the partnership acquisition cost represented by the fraction he is disposing of. Special treatment, as outlined in 7 below, may be necessary for transfers between persons not at arm's length."

EXAMPLE 6.08

Electra and Ganymede were in partnership sharing profits 50:50. On 1 January 1994 Hebe was admitted into partnership with a 20% share for which she paid £12,000 to Electra.

The profit shares become:

	Old%	New%
Electra	50	30
Ganymede	50	50
Hebe	–	20
	100	100

	£
Electra	
Sale proceeds – goodwill	12,000
Cost NIL 31 March 1982 value – say –	4,000
Indexation (say 75%)	3,000
Gain	£5,000
Hebe	
Cost of goodwill	£12,000

Note:
The revaluation at 6 April 1965 would normally be superseded by a revaluation at 31 March 1982 under the rebasing provisions of TCGA 1995, s 35. Partners may make rebasing elections individually and separately in respect of partnership assets as opposed to wholly owned assets, IR Tax Bulletin Issue 1, page 5.

"7. *Transfers between persons not at arm's length*

Where no payment is made either through or outside the accounts in connection with a change in partnership sharing ratio, a capital gains tax charge will only arise if the transaction is otherwise than by way of a bargain made at arm's-length and falls therefore within TCGA 1992, s 18, as a transaction between connected persons. Under TCGA 1992, s 286(4) transfers of partnership assets between partners are not regarded as transactions between connected persons if they are pursuant to bona fide commercial arrangements. This treatment will also be given to transactions between an incoming partner and the existing partners.

Where the partners (including incoming partners) are connected other than by partnership (for example, father and son) or are otherwise not at arm's-length (for example, uncle and nephew) the transfer of a share in the partnership assets may fall to be treated as having been made at market value. Market value will not be substituted, however, if nothing would have been paid had the parties been at arm's-length. Similarly if consideration of less than market value passes between partners connected other than by partnership or otherwise not at arm's-length, the transfer will only be regarded as having been made for full market value if the consideration actually paid was less than that which would have been paid by parties at arm's-length. Where a transfer has to be treated as if it had taken place for market value, the deemed disposal proceeds will fall to be treated in the same way as payments outside the accounts."

EXAMPLE 6.09

Gordius, a sole trader, introduced his son Midas into partnership, without charge, as a 25% partner and transferred £10,000 from his capital account. The transfer could not be justified on commercial grounds. Partners would only be eligible for repayment of their capital and current accounts on retirement or death, without revaluing the assets.

	Book value (and cost) £	Market value £	
Freehold property	20,000	60,000	
Goodwill	25,000	40,000	
Non-chargeable assets	30,000	30,000	
Capital a/c	£75,000	£130,000	

	£	£
Gordius		
Freehold property: proceeds (25% × £60,000)	15,000	
cost (25% × £20,000 + indexation)	8,000	
		7,000
Goodwill: proceeds (25% × £40,000)	10,000	
cost (25% × £25,000 + indexation)	8,000	
		2,000
Chargeable gain		£9,000

Estate before transfer 100% × £130,000 =	130,000
Less: estate after transfer (limited to repayment of capital and current accounts)	
£75,000 − £10,000 =	65,000
	65,000
Less 100% business relief	65,000
Value transferred for IHT purposes	Nil

"8. *Annuities provided by partnerships*

A lump sum which is paid to a partner on leaving the partnership or on a reduction of his share in the partnership represents consideration for the disposal by the partner concerned of the whole or part of his share in the partnership assets and will be subject to the rules in 6 above. The same treatment will apply when a partnership buys a purchased life annuity for a partner, the measure of the consideration being the actual cost of the annuity.

Where a partnership makes annual payments to a retired partner (whether under covenant or not) the capitalised value of the annuity will only be treated as consideration for the disposal of his share in the partnership assets under TCGA 1992, s 37(3) if it is more than can be regarded as a reasonable recognition of the past contribution of work and effort by the partner to the partnership. Provided that the former partner had been in the partnership for at least ten years an annuity will be regarded as reasonable for this purpose if it is no more than two-thirds of his average share of the profits in the best three of the last seven years in which he was required to devote substantially the whole of his time to acting as a partner. In arriving at a partner's share of the profits regard will be had to the partnership profits assessed before deduction of any capital allowances or charges. The ten year period will include any period during which the partner was a member of another firm whose business has been merged with that of the present firm. For lesser periods the following fractions will be used instead of the two thirds:

Complete years in partnership	Fraction
1–5	1/60 for each year
6	8/60
7	16/60
8	24/60
9	32/60

Where the capitalised value of an annuity is treated as consideration received by the retired partner, it will also be regarded as allowable expenditure by the remaining partners on the acquisition of their fractional shares in partnership assets from him."

(see reference to writing off goodwill on p. 116 and automatic accruer, p. 145)

"This provision was extended by SP1/79 published on 12 January 1979. 'Paragraph 8 of the Statement of Practice issued by the Board of Inland Revenue on 17 January 1975 explains the circumstances in which the capitalised value of an annuity paid by a partnership to a retired partner will not be treated as consideration for the disposal of his share in the partnership assets. The Board have now agreed that this practice will be extended to certain cases in which a lump sum is paid in addition to an annuity. Where the aggregate of the annuity and one-ninth of the lump sum does not exceed the appropriate fraction (as indicated in the Statement) of the retired partner's average share of the profits, the capitalised value of the annuity will not be treated as consideration in the hands of the retired partner. The lump sum, however, will continue to be so treated.

This extension of the practice will be applied to all cases in which the liability has not been finally determined at the date of this Notice.'"

"9. *Mergers*

When the members of two or more existing partnerships come together to form a new one, the capital gains tax treatment will follow the same lines as that for changes in partnership sharing ratios. If gains arise for reasons similar to those covered in 5 and 6 above, it may be possible for roll-over relief under TCGA 1992, ss 152–158, to be claimed by any partner continuing in the partnership insofar as he disposes of part of his share in the assets of the old firm and acquires a share in other assets put into the 'merged' firm. Where, however, in such cases the consideration given for the shares in chargeable assets acquired is less than the consideration for those disposed of, relief will be restricted under TCGA 1992, s 153(1)."

EXAMPLE 6.10

Pluto and Pallas (50:50 partners) merged with Notus and Nemesis (60:40 partners). Profits are shared equally after the merger.

	P & P £	N & N £
Goodwill		
Cost	Nil	£10,000
Market value	£25,000	£30,000
Cost in balance sheet of merged practice	£55,000	

Computation	Pluto £	Pallas £	Notus £	Nemesis £
Disposal				
25% × £25,000 (each)	6,250	6,250		
35% × £30,000			10,500	
15% × £30,000				4,500
Cost				
25% × Nil (each)	–	–		
35% × £10,000 + indexation		5,250		
15% × £10,000 + indexation				2,250
Gain	£6,250	£6,250	£5,250	£2,250
Acquisition				
25% × £30,000 (each)	7,500	7,500		
25% × £25,000 (each)			6,250	6,250
TCGA 1992, ss 152–158				
Roll-over relief	6,250	6,250	2,750*	2,250
	1,250	1,250	3,500	4,000
Original goodwill retained				
25% × Nil (each)	–	–		
25% × £10,000 (each)			2,500	2,500
Revised cost for goodwill, subject to indexation	£1,250	£1,250	£6,000	£6,500
Chargeable gain	Nil	Nil	£4,250	Nil

*Under TCGA 1992, s 153, where the reinvestment (£6,250) is less than the consideration for the earlier disposal (£10,500), and is also less than the gain (£5,250), that deficit (£4,250) is treated as the gain, and the difference (£2,750) between that and the actual gain is deducted from the consideration for the reinvestment.

"10. *Shares acquired in stages*

Where a share in a partnership is acquired in stages wholly after 5 April 1965, the acquisition costs of the various chargeable assets will be calculated by pooling the expenditure relating to each asset. Where a share built up in stages was acquired wholly or partly before 6 April 1965 the rules in TCGA 1992, Sch. 2, para. 18 will normally be followed to identify the acquisition cost of the share in each asset which is disposed of on the occasion of a reduction in the partnership's share; i.e. the disposal will normally be identified with shares acquired on a 'first in, first out' basis. Special considerations will be given, however, to any case in which this rule appears to produce an unreasonable result when applied to temporary changes in the shares in a partnership, for example, those occurring when a partner's departure and new partner's arrival are out of step by a few months."

Note: This paragraph will normally be superseded by rebasing revaluation at 31 March 1992 under TCGA 1992, s 35, which will supplant any pre 6 April 1965 acquisitions.

"11. *Elections under TCGA 1992, Sch. 2, para. 4*

Where the assets disposed of are quoted securities eligible for a pooling election under TCGA 1992, Sch. 2, para. 4, partners will be allowed to make separate elections in respect of shares or fixed interest securities held by the partnership as distinct from shares or securities which they hold on a personal basis. Each partner will have a separate right of election for his proportion of the partnership securities and the time limit for the purposes of Sch. 2 will run from the earlier of:
(*a*) the first relevant disposal of shares or securities by the partnership; and
(*b*) the first reduction of the particular partner's share in the partnership assets after 19 March 1968."

"12. *Transitional arrangements*

The practices set out in this statement will be applied to all capital gains tax assessments after 17 January 1975. Where tax liabilities have already been settled on other reasonable bases the assessment will not be upset. Often gains and losses on previous disposals will have been computed on a different basis and the acquisition costs allocated as a result to partners to set against future disposals will be different from those which would have arisen had the new practices been followed. Such costs will only be recalculated in exceptional circumstances."

Roll-over relief (TCGA 1992, ss 152–158)

If a chargeable gain arises to a partnership from the disposal of a qualifying asset used only for the purposes of the trade throughout the period of ownership and a new qualifying asset is acquired, the gain may be rolled over into the new assets. The old asset is treated as being sold for a price giving rise to neither a chargeable gain nor an allowable loss and the acquisition value of the new asset is reduced by the amount of the chargeable gain. The asset must have been used for the trade (*Temperley v Visibell Ltd* [1974] STC 64), land must have been occupied for the purposes of the trade, *Anderton v Lamb* (1981) STC 43, and the new asset must be used for the purposes of the trade immediately on acquisition, *Campbell Connelly & Co Ltd v Barnett* (1994) STC 50, or as soon thereafter as possible IR Tax Bulletin Issue 1, page 5.

If the asset is only partly replaced the gain immediately chargeable is limited to the amount of the consideration for the disposal of the old asset not reinvested in the new asset, i e there is no relief unless at least the base cost is reinvested. The new asset must be contracted for during a period beginning one year before and ending three years after the disposal of the old asset, although extension of this time limit may be given by the Revenue at their discretion. The qualifying assets include land and buildings occupied for the purposes of the trade except for a trade of dealing in or developing land, or providing services for the occupier of land. The other qualifying assets are fixed plant and machinery, ships, aircraft, goodwill, hovercraft, milk and potato quotas, and ewe and suckler cow premium quotas. Fixed plant and machinery means fixed plant and fixed machinery as confirmed in *Williams v Evans* (1982) STC 498. There are provisions for apportionment when the old asset has been used only partly for the purposes of the trade or has been so used for only part of the period of ownership. The relief applies to professions in the same way as to trades.

Roll-over relief is allowed between two trades and is also allowable in respect of an asset owned by an individual which is used by his family company (*Gordon v IRC* (1991) STC 174). Apportionment is necessary for assets used only partly for the trade, *Tod v Mudd* (1987) STC 141, or only used for part of the period, *Richart v J Lyons & Co* (1989) STC 665. An asset let to a partnership by a partner qualifies for roll-over relief if used in the partnership trade, SP/D11. By concession, roll-over relief is extended to partitions of land on dissolution of a partnership, ESC D23, improvements of existing assets, ESC D22, assets not brought immediately into use if work is being done on the asset, ESC D24, acquisition of a further interest in an asset already used for the trade, such as the acquisition of the freehold reversion of leasehold property, ESC D25, after indexation based on the total from the date of acquisition of the lease, ESC D42, and a repurchase of an old asset, ESC D16.

If the new asset is a wasting asset the gain is merely held-over under the provisions of TCGA 1992, s 154.

Roll-over into wasting assets

TCGA 1992, s 154 provides that where roll-over relief would otherwise be available except that the new asset (called Asset No. 2) is a depreciating asset the chargeable gain on Asset No. 1 is not rolled-over completely but is held over for a maximum period of ten years.

The hold-over period comes to an end at the earliest of the disposal of Asset No. 2, Asset No. 2 ceasing to be used for the purposes of the trade otherwise than on death, ESC D45, or 10 years from the acquisition of Asset No. 2.

If during the hold-over period and before the held over gain becomes assessable a non-depreciating Asset No. 3 is acquired a claim may be made to drop the hold-over relief and roll over the gain on Asset No. 1 into Asset No. 3.

There are provisions for a gain being partly held-over and partly rolled-over. A depreciating asset is one which is or will within ten years of acquisition become a wasting asset, ie one with a predictable life not exceeding fifty years as defined by TCGA 1992, s 44. Plant and machinery is regarded as always having a life of less than fifty years.

EXAMPLE 6.11

	£
XYZ Ltd	
Sale of trade premises 31 December 1995	100,000
Indexed cost 31 March 1982	60,000
Gain	40,000
Purchase of computer 30 September 1995 for £90,000	
Chargeable gain limited to proceeds not reinvested	10,000
Gain held over	£30,000

EXAMPLE 6.11 *(continued)*

Purchase of goodwill of additional business 1 May 1997	125,000
Less: Gain held over	30,000
Deemed acquisition cost of goodwill for capital gains purposes	£95,000

Although the purchase of the computer in 1995 qualifies for capital allowances this does not prevent the chargeable gain on the disposal of the premises being held over against the proceeds reinvested in the computer.

Transfer of business to a company

TCGA 1992, s 162 gives deferment to capital gains tax arising on a disposal by partners of a business as a going concern, *Gordon v IRC* (1991) STC 174, to a company wholly or partly in exchange for shares (the new assets) in the transferee company which must be issued to the transferors. It is essential that all the assets in the business (the old assets) are transferred to the transferee company, except cash which may be excluded if desired.

It is first of all necessary to calculate the aggregate chargeable gains which would accrue on the disposal of the business being transferred. The part of the total consideration for the disposal which is attributable to shares is deferred by way of deduction from the allowable cost of those shares to the transferors. It is, therefore, necessary to apportion the chargeable gains between the share consideration and any other consideration for example, cash, but excluding any liability taken over, ESC D32. This apportionment is made on the basis of the following calculation:

$$\text{Chargeable gains} \times \frac{\text{cost of shares in transferee company (ie market value of the shares issued on transfer of the business)}}{\text{total consideration received by transferor for business}}$$

The amount so calculated is deducted from the cost of the shares and cannot exceed that sum. When the shares so received are disposed of the gain is computed in accordance with the reduced cost. If the consideration for the transfer of the business is wholly shares capital gains tax will be entirely deferred until the shares themselves are disposed of, as explained in Chapter 10.

EXAMPLE 6.12

Mr EE ran a business as a retail grocer; he transferred his business to GH Ltd in consideration for the issue of 10,000 shares of £1 each fully paid in that company and £2,000 in cash. The value of the 10,000 shares was £11,600.

The assets and liabilities of the business were as follows:

	Cost £	Market value £
Assets		
Freehold property	5,000	8,000
Furniture and fittings	1,000	800
Trading stock	1,400	1,700
Goodwill	500	3,000
Debtors	–	600
	7,900	14,100
Liabilities		
Trade and expense creditors	–	500
	£7,900	£13,600

All of those assets and liabilities were taken over by GH Ltd.
The chargeable gains arising on the disposal of the business to GH Ltd are as follows:

	Sale price £	Cost £	Indexation £	Chargeable gain £
Freehold property	8,000	5,000	1,900	1,100
Goodwill	3,000	500	190	2,310
Gain on the old assets				3,410
Deduct: $\frac{11,600}{13,600} \times £3,410$				2,909
Gain chargeable				£501

The allowable cost of the shares will be £11,600 – £2,909 = £8,691.

RETIREMENT RELIEF

Retirement relief is available to an individual who has attained the age of fifty-five, or who has retired on grounds of ill health below the age of fifty-five, where there is both a material disposal of business assets and the qualifying period relating to the disposal ends after 30 November 1993. TCGA 1992, ss 163, 164 and Sch. 6 set out the detailed rules relating to the relief.

A material disposal of business assets is a disposal of the whole or part of a business which has been carried on for at least one year (*McGregor v Adcock* (1977) STC 206; *Atkinson v Dancer, Manion v Johnston* (1988) STC 758; *Pepper v Daffurn* (1993) STC 466); or it is a disposal of shares in a personal trading company or a member of a trading group in which the holding company is the individual's personal company and the individual is a full-time working director of the company or group, see *IRC v D. Devine & Sons Ltd* (1963) 41 TC 21D. The Revenue usually regard twenty-eight hours a week or more as full time. A personal trading company is one in which at least 5% of the voting shares are held (TCGA 1992, Sch. 6, para. 1(2)). A material disposal of business assets also includes a disposal of assets which were in use for the purpose of a business that had ceased, if it has been carried on for at least one year and it ceased on the retirement, at age fifty-five or later, or on grounds of ill health provided that the disposal takes place no more than twelve months after the cessation. The twelve-month required period can be traced through on a transfer of a business to a family company. Retirement relief is also available where the company ceased to qualify as a trading company or member of a trading group, for example, on becoming an investment company, and at that time the shareholder was aged over fifty-five or had retired on grounds of ill health, in which case the relief is still available if it would have been available had the disposal taken place at the date the company ceased to qualify, provided that the disposal takes place within twelve months following the cessation.

If the individual making the disposal ceases to be a full-time working director he can still qualify for retirement relief provided that the company qualified as his personal trading company, or holding company of a trading group, and provided that he devoted at least ten hours per week to the company in a technical or managerial capacity during the period from ceasing to be a full-time working director to the date of disposal.

Retirement relief is extended to partners in respect of a disposal of their interest in the partnership, or partnership assets.

Retirement relief is also extended to include assets owned by the individual and used by a partnership in which he was a partner or a personal trading company or group of which he was a full-time working director. The disposal must be associated with the individual's withdrawal from the business.

Retirement relief on the grounds of ill health is available where the individual is incapable of doing the kind of work done previously and this incapacity is likely to be permanent. The taxpayer must produce the necessary evidence of ill health to the satisfaction of the Board whose decision is final.

The relief does not have to be claimed in respect of somebody reaching the appropriate age but in cases of ill health, or on a trustee's disposal, a claim must be made within two years of the disposal.

Gains qualifying for relief

In the case of a disposal of an interest in a business or of assets the aggregate of the gains less losses on the disposal qualifies for retirement relief.

In the case of an associated disposal of an asset used by a company or partnership if it has been used for any part of the period or ownership or where the individual has not been a partner or full-time working director during part of the period of ownership, or where rent has been charged for the use of the asset the amount eligible for retirement relief is proportionately reduced. Where a rent has been charged the proportion is based on the rent paid compared with an open market rent. Whether a prior share of profit to a landlord partner in lieu of rent would be caught is not clear but it could be deemed to be "any form of consideration" (Sch. 6, para. 10(3)).

Gains and losses on the individual assets are computed in the normal way. Chargeable business assets include goodwill but exclude shares held as investments. Otherwise they are only assets used for the purpose of a trade or profession, carried on by the partner in a partnership of which he was a member. An asset on which a gain would not be a chargeable gain is not a chargeable business asset.

112 *Capital taxes*

The maximum retirement relief is £250,000 plus half the excess over £250,000 and below £1 million which is available where the qualifying period is at least ten years. The relief is reduced proportionately where the qualifying period is less than ten years subject to a minimum of one year at which date the maximum relief is £250,000 plus half of £75,000.

If the qualifying period is less than ten years but is preceded by an earlier business period which falls wholly or partly within the ten-year period it is possible to aggregate the two periods provided that any gap between them is no more than two years and that the maximum period is ten years. The gap, if any, between the two periods is transferred to the beginning of the earlier business period. There may be more than one earlier business period.

If retirement relief has already been given on an earlier disposal the relief on the later disposal is limited to the relief that would have been available on the later disposal if its qualifying period had begun at the beginning of the qualifying period for the earlier period and the relief actually given on the earlier disposal. Similar adjustments are made if there are several earlier disposals.

Where the assets disposed of have been acquired from a spouse by way of gift or on death the qualifying period for the individual's disposal may be extended to cover the period of ownership by the spouse. The whole of the spouse's interest must have been acquired and they must have been living together at the time of the gift or death. An election must be made within two years of the disposal. On a lifetime transfer the relief by reference to the extended qualifying period is restricted to the maximum for one individual, less any retirement relief given to the spouse up to and including the gift, and any trustees disposals in respect of which the spouse was the beneficiary. The second limit is the amount of relief that would have been available if the disposal had been made by the spouse and the individual's acts in relation to the business or as a full-time working director or partner were those of the spouse.

EXAMPLE 6.13

Messrs Lee, Vee and Earl are in business as surveyors trading as Lee Vearly & Co sharing profits equally. They own the freeholds of their branch offices and their head office is owned personally by Lee. No rent is charged by Lee but in consideration for the use of the property he receives a prior share of profits, which is equivalent to two-thirds of the rental value. The partnership commenced on 1 January 1978 and Lee retired on 31 December 1995 at the age of 58. Goodwill and freehold premises were revalued on that date. The office was purchased by Lee on 1 January 1983 for £80,000, but not used by the partnership until 1 January 1986, and on retirement Lee sold it to a third party for £180,000. The balance sheet, after revaluation, at 31 December 1995 was as below. On retirement Lee sold his partnership interest to Sharp for full value.

	£		£
Freeholds	300,000	Partners Capital a/cs	400,000
(cost 1978 £210,000)			
Goodwill			
(cost 1978 NIL)	90,000		
Other assets less			
liabilities	10,000		
	400,000		400,000

Lee's capital gains tax position is as follows:

Sale of offices £
Proceeds 180,000
Cost 80,000
Indexation (say) 50,000

130,000

Gross gain £50,000

Period of ownership 13 years
Period of business use 10 years

Business use period $\dfrac{10 \text{ years}}{13 \text{ years}} \times £50,000$ £38,461

Consideration received for use
$^2/_3 \times$ market rent
Thus retirement relief limited to
$^1/_3 \times £38,461 =$ £12,280

Retirement Relief not available on £37,180
(£50,000 less £12,820)

In view of the qualifying period all of the gain on the disposal of the Freehold and the Goodwill rank for retirement relief subject to maximum limits.

Freehold £
Proceeds $^1/_3 \times 1,300,000$ 433,333
Cost $^1/_3 \times 210,000$ 70,000
Indexation (say) 49,000

119,000

Gain £314,333

Goodwill
Proceeds $^1/_3 \times 90,000$ 30,000
MV at 31.3.1982 5,000
Indexation 3,500

8,500

Gain £21,500

	Total	Office	Freehold	Goodwill
Total gains	385,833	50,000	314,333	21,500
Retirement relief not available on	37,180	37,180	–	–
Gains available for retirement relief	348,653	£12,820	£314,333	£21,500

EXAMPLE 6.13 *(continued)*

Retirement relief[1]	299,327
After retirement relief	49,326
Add non qualifying gain	37,180
Net gains	£86,506

Note:
[1] £250,000 + ½ (£348,653 – £250,000)

Reinvestment relief

It is possible to roll-over the gain on any asset to the extent that the gain is reinvested in qualifying unquoted shares, under TCGA 1992, ss 164A to N. The provisions are complex and hedged about with many anti-avoidance provisions. Only the gain (and not the whole proceeds) need to be reinvested.

The relief applies where the reinvestor makes a disposal and acquires a qualifying investment within the qualifying period, ie a period beginning twelve months before the disposal and ending three years thereafter, subject to Revenue discretion to extend this period.

The qualifying reinvestment must be in ordinary shares, not within the business expansion scheme, in a qualifying unquoted company which carries on one or more qualifying trades or is a holding company of qualifying subsidiaries carrying on qualifying trades. Where the asset disposed of consisted of shares or securities in a company, the qualifying company cannot be the same company or in the same group as that company. There is no requirement that the reinvestor is an officer or employee of the new company nor, from 1 December 1993, that the reinvestor hold a minimum number of shares.

The activities of the company follow the extensive restrictions of the former business expansion scheme. The company does not have to be incorporated in the U.K. however.

Reinvestment relief is calculated without regard to any retirement relief. Where only a proportion of a taxpayer's gains are eligible for retirement relief, reinvestment rollover relief is set first against the part of the gain which is not eligible for retirement relief.

The roll-over relief is clawed back if a triggering event occurs within the relevant three-year period after the acquisition of the eligible shares in the qualifying reinvestment company unless the shares have already been disposed of, or the disposal is to the reinvestor's spouse who takes over the reinvestor's position. A triggering event is the shares in the reinvestment company ceasing to be eligible or the company ceasing to be a qualifying company, or the reinvestor becoming non-resident other than on taking up a full-time employment lasting for less than three years, or if the shares are exchanged for qualifying corporate bonds under TCGA 1992, s 116. The reinvestment relief therefore cannot be used to roll-over a gain with a view to eliminating it by subsequently going non-resident within three years.

Any chargeable gain arising under the clawback provisions can be rolled over, provided that the gain is reinvested in an unquoted trading company within the period of twelve months before and three years after the time the gain accrues, extendable by the Revenue.

A qualifying company is an unquoted company carrying on one or more qualifying trades or a holding company of a qualifying company which may itself carry on a qualifying trade, or may be a pure holding company. Incidental matters have no significant effect on the extent of the company's activities may be ignored. The company is not a qualifying company if it controls a non-qualifying subsidiary or is under the control of another company, or if it is being wound up.

A company is not a qualifying company where the value of its interests in land exceeds half the value of either the company's chargeable assets or its assets as a whole, whichever is greater. Interests in land are gross interests in land at market value less debts secured on those interests, unsecured debts not repayable within twelve months and preferential shares. Interests in land do not include interests as mortgagee and exclude the value of any machinery or plant installed in the building which is legally part of the building. Certain mineral rights are ignored and a corporate partner is deemed to have a direct interest in its share of partnership land. A group of companies is treated as a single company and intra-group debts are ignored.

The comparison with either chargeable assets or total assets applies from 30 November 1993 and removes the difficulty that where a company had no goodwill, plant or other chargeable assets, *any* interest in land without deductible debts or preference shares precluded relief. Total assets are as used for the enterprise investment scheme, TA 1988, s 294.

The former business expansion scheme rules are largely incorporated into the reinvestment provisions, and research and development activities leading to trading are included.

Forbidden activities include dealing in land or securities, dealing in goods otherwise than wholesaling or retailing, banking, insurance and financing, leasing licensing, providing legal or accountancy services or providing services to such activities, property development and farming. Retail and wholesale trades are defined. The licence restriction does not apply to film-making companies or research and development companies, and certain shipping activities are permissible.

The trade must be conducted on a commercial basis and with a view to profits.

Indexation

For capital gains tax purposes an indexation allowance is available under TCGA 1992, s 53 on the relevant allowable expenditure to reduce or extinguish a gain. It may not, after 30 November 1993, create or increase an allowable loss but transitional relief on or up to £10,000 is available (except for companies) in 1993–94 and 1994–95: FA 1994, Sch. 12.

The allowance is calculated by multiplying each of the separate items of base cost and improvement expenditure (under TCGA 1992, s 38(1)(*a*) and (*b*)) by a decimal factor (to the nearest third decimal place) determined by the formula:

$$\left[\frac{RD - RI}{RI} \right]$$

(*a*) Where RD is the retail prices index for the month in which the disposal occurs; and

(b) RI is the retail prices index for the later of March 1982 or the month in which the item of expenditure was incurred.

In respect of disposals on or after 6 April 1988 indexation of assets held on 31 March 1982 is to be calculated as if the asset were sold and immediately reacquired at market value on 31 March 1982. There are the usual tracing provisions to deal with assets that have been merged or divided.

When a transferee disposes of an asset acquired on a no gain/no loss basis from a transferor who owned the asset on 31 March 1982, indexation is available, from that date, by reference to the value on that date.

Rebasing

Assets held on 31 March 1982 and disposed of after 5 April 1988 are deemed to have been sold and reacquired at the market value at 31 March 1982 but not if this produces a gain where there would otherwise be a smaller gain or a loss, or if it produces a loss where there would otherwise be a smaller loss or a gain, or if there would otherwise be no gain and no loss under the previous positions. Nor does it apply to no gain/no loss disposals. Where the use of the market value at 31 March 1982 substitutes a gain for a loss or a loss for a gain it is treated as a no gain/no loss disposal.

A taxpayer can elect for capital gains and losses on all assets held at 31 March 1982 to be calculated by reference to 31 March 1982 values only. This avoids the need to maintain earlier records and simplifies the tax computations. Separate elections are made in different capacities (partner, trustees, etc.), see IR Tax Bulletin Issue 1, page 5.

An election once made is irrevocable. It applies to all disposals after 5 April 1988 of assets held at 31 March 1982. It can be made up to two years after the end of the accounting period or tax year in which the first relevant disposal after 5 April 1988 of an asset held at 31 March 1982 takes place. Disposals of certain non-chargeable assets do not trigger the two-year time limit, and the meaning of first relevant disposal is amplified in SP4/92.

Goodwill written off

It is common practice these days for professional partnerships to agree that the share of an outgoing partner in the goodwill, if any, of the partnership shall automatically accrue to the continuing partners without payment. When goodwill is written off in this manner after a partner has previously purchased the goodwill or acquired it by gift at a time when it had a commercial value, it has to be considered whether there may be a claim for a capital gains tax loss under the provisions of TCGA 1992, s 24(2) on the grounds that the value of the asset has become negligible. In such a case the asset is treated as having been disposed of and reacquired for capital gains tax purposes at the then value, which in the case of goodwill written off would arguably be nil. If the asset has a base value for capital gains tax purposes this would clearly give rise to a capital loss which could be set against other capital gains in the year in which the goodwill was written off or in any subsequent year.

TCGA 1992, s 24(2) reads as follows:

"If on a claim by the owner of an asset the Inspector is satisfied that the value of an asset has become negligible, he may allow a claim and thereupon this part of this Act shall have effect as if the claimant had sold and immediately reacquired the asset for a consideration of an amount equal to the value specified in the claim."

The claim must be made within two years after the end of the financial year in which the asset became of negligible value. (Inland Revenue press release 4 August 1975.) In December 1973 an appeal was heard before the Commissioners of Taxes for the London City Division made under TMA 1970 s 42(3), against the Inspector of Taxes decision concerning the value of partnership goodwill for the purposes of TCGA 1992, s 24(2). As a case before the General Commissioners the decision has not been reported.

The facts of the case were straightforward and common to many professional practices in that over a number of years partners had bought goodwill on joining the partnership which had been purchased by successors on death or retirement. It was, however, recognised that it was becoming increasingly difficult to introduce suitable young partners who were both able and willing to find not only their share of the capital required to run the partnership, but also to pay a capital sum for the purchase of goodwill, which in the absence of inherited wealth would require to be borrowed and repaid out of taxed income. On 1 November 1967 a partnership minute was passed recording the simple decision that it was agreed to value goodwill at nil. The appellant's argument was that his share of partnership goodwill ceased to become of any commercial value after 1 November 1967 and, therefore, should be regarded as having become of negligible value. The partners concerned were unrelated and their only connection for capital gains tax purposes was as partners in a professional practice.

The appellant quoted the definition of goodwill from the *Practice Administration Booklet No. 11* published by the Institute of Chartered Accountants in England and Wales and written by E. Kenneth Wright, M.A., F.C.A. Mr. Wright defined goodwill as follows:

> "To being with, goodwill has its orthodox meaning of the benefit of an established connection, the expectation that customers will return to the old firm, and in this sense its value must be linked with some concept of super-profit. Closely allied with this is the idea of an entrance fee: key money to gain admission to a desirable means of earning a living. Thirdly it is in many cases an accepted tradition, a survival buoyed up by the vested interests of existing partners who, having themselves paid capital for their shares, not unnaturally wish to be paid out in the same coin. An finally there is the widespread notion that goodwill is in some way tied up with the provision for retirement – hence the growing practice of providing pensions or annuities for retired partners or their dependants instead of paying outright capital sums for the purchase of their goodwill."

The appellant proceeded to establish first of all that there were no super-profits over and above a reasonable remuneration for the professional activities of the partners and a reasonable return on capital employed in running the business. Secondly, the idea of an entrance fee was demolished on the grounds that it was necessary to replace retiring partners and to introduce further partners as the business expanded, and if the incoming partners were unwilling to pay for goodwill, as was the case, there was clearly no possibility of charging an entrance fee for goodwill. So far as the question of an accepted tradition was concerned it was shown that partners retiring prior to the date goodwill as written off were in fact paid for goodwill on a formula basis of one and a half years purchase of their then share of profits, whereas partners retiring after 1 November, 1967 were not paid anything for a share of goodwill. Finally it was pointed out that goodwill as a means of providing for retirement had become obsolescent with the introduction of self-employed deferred annuities in 1956 and it was now the practice for partners to provide for their own retirement.

Certain partners in the case before the Commissioners may in future receive annuities which would be much less than the amount allowable under paragraph 8 of the Inland Revenue Statement of Practice of 17 January, 1975 relating to partnership annuities under which the Revenue will accept that an annuity of up to two-thirds of the average share of profits due to a partner for the best three out of the last seven years prior to his retirement after ten years service as a partner will not be treated as a payment for goodwill on the capitalised value of the annuity under the provisions of the TCGA 1992, s 37(3).

The Revenue arguments against allowing goodwill written off to be treated as having become of negligible value were, first of all, that if in the future circumstances changed the partners could meet and agree between themselves that goodwill should be restored. The Revenue view was that the partners in a professional practice cannot merely by making a statement destroy the goodwill of the firm, and it was difficult to accept that if an offer was made for the practice as a going concern, however unlikely that might be, they would agree there was no goodwill. The counter argument was that the appellant's share of goodwill on 1 November, 1967 had become valueless in the circumstances appertaining from that date; it was unnecessary and wrong to consider possible future circumstances.

The second Revenue argument was that as partners were connected, transactions between them were on the basis of market value and market value is normally the price an asset might reasonably be expected to fetch on a sale in the open market. In the Revenue view the market value is the purchase price which might have been expected on a full commercial basis from a successor to the appellant's share in the partnership, and that the admission of two junior partners without payment for goodwill was not conclusive evidence that the market value of the practice was nil. This argument was demolished on the basis that the only potential purchasers of the appellant's share of goodwill were incoming partners and if they were unwilling to pay for goodwill it must by definition be worthless. The Revenue made some interesting comments on the question of goodwill:

> "You appear to equate goodwill with the profit over and above a commercial wage which a partner or a prospective partner could expect as his share of the profits. I would suggest that this view of goodwill is a very narrow one and goodwill is more usually regarded as embracing the benefits arising from the existence, reputation and connections of the professional practice. It reflects the use of the firm's name, its knowledge and experience and in the event of a change of proprietorship the likelihood that the established customers will be retained. It may be that by an internal arrangement the partners agree that in future no value is placed on partnership goodwill and consequently partners admitted following the decision are not charged for the goodwill, but in my view this is quite different from saying that if a change of proprietorship occurred on the sale of the practice on a going concern its reputation, connections, knowledge, experience and established clientele would necessarily be valued at nil."

The appellant accepted the definition of the Revenue, but pointed out that the commercial valuation of such an asset as goodwill was based on considerations such as super-profits if any, and the terms that could be negotiated on a commercial basis consequent upon negotiations conducted at arm's length.

The Revenue also placed considerable reliance on a number of advertisements appearing in magazines such as The Accountant where sole practitioners or small firms were advertising for sale professional practices on the basis of a multiple of the gross fees, or some similar basis. It was pointed out that one partner out of many cannot unilaterally offer for sale his share of partnership goodwill, as any incoming partner would have to be acceptable to the remaining partners, and therefore it was impossible to compare a sole practitioner with a case such as the appellant's where he was one partner out of nine at that time.

The commissioners having heard the case gave a written judgment in favour of the appellant in terms which recognised that the goodwill of such an accountancy practice in the City of London might have had value if offered for sale as a whole. The appeal was, however, concerned with the value at 1 November 1967 of one partner's share or interest in that goodwill. From the evidence before them the Commissioners found that the value of such a share or interest had become negligible at that date by reason of it being unsaleable, and it was in consequence of that fact that the arrangements between the partners for carrying on the partnership business and for the retirement or death of partners and the introduction of new partners were made without regard to goodwill.

This case was not taken beyond the Commissioners' stage, but the practice of the Revenue in such cases did not change and it is understood that the Revenue were in fact successful before other bodies of Commissioners although no details are known to the authors of the facts behind these cases. However a further case was taken, this time to the Special Commissioners on the identical argument. Again the Special Commissioner decided in favour of the taxpayer and he found on the basis of the facts that the partner's interest in goodwill had become of negligible value on the date of the resolution under which the partners agreed to write it off and as a result a loss had crystallised under what is now TCGA 1992, s 24(2). The Revenue have intimated that they do not intend to take this case to the High Court.

The case before the Special Commissioners was heard by Mr. T. H. K. Everett and concerned a partner in a London firm of chartered accountants, Mr. G. W. D. James.

The original partnership deed provided that a deceased partner should be paid a percentage of the goodwill of the business equal to his percentage share of the profits of the business at the date of death and that goodwill was to be calculated on the basis of two and a quarter times the average net profits of the firm for the three complete years of the partnership immediately preceding the date on which the goodwill had to be calculated. In both the case of Mr. James and the 1973 case before the General Commissioners which concerned a Mr. J. C. Smethers, who coincidentally was also a partner in another firm of city chartered accountants, there were proposals which were subsequently put into effect whereby the partners who had originally paid for goodwill, which was now declared to be worthless, would qualify for an annuity from the firm on their eventual retirement.

In both cases the agreement to write off goodwill was contained in either a partnership minute or informal decision signed by all partners and was only incorporated in a full partnership deed at a later stage.

The contentions for Mr. James may be summarised as follows:
(a) The partnership memorandum and agreement eliminated goodwill from the firm and this memorandum and agreement was subsequently confirmed by the Supplemental Deed of Partnership.

(b) Mr. James's share of goodwill ceased to have any commercial value after the date of the agreement and should therefore be regarded as having become of negligible value in accordance with the provisions of TCGA 1992, s 24(2).

(c) Goodwill has been defined by Mr. E. Kenneth Wright MA FCA in practice Administration Booklet number 11 (published by the Institute of Chartered Accountants in England and Wales) as follows:

> "To begin with, goodwill has its orthodox meaning of the benefit of an established connection, the expectation that customers will return to the old firm, and in this sense its value must be linked with some concept of super-profit. Closely allied with this is the idea of an entrance fee: key money to gain admission to a desirable means of earning a living. Thirdly it is in many cases an accepted tradition, a survival buoyed up by the vested interests of existing partners who, having themselves paid capital for their shares, not unnaturally wish to be paid out in the same coin. And finally there is the widespread notion that goodwill is in some way tied up with the provision for retirement – hence the growing practice of providing pensions or annuities for retired partners or their dependents instead of paying outright capital sums for the purchase of their goodwill."

The partnership did not earn super-profits but provided only a reasonable remuneration for the professional activities of the partners and a reasonable return on capital employed in running the business. It was no longer able to charge an entrance fee as incoming partners of the required ability were unwilling or unable to pay an entrance fee. Similarly the tradition relating to the payment for goodwill had become untenable in the absence of willing purchasers. Finally the existence of goodwill as a means of providing for retirement has become obsolescent in recent years as it is increasingly the practice for the self-employed to make their own retirement provision by means of purchased retirement annuity contracts.

(d) The Inland Revenue Practice Statement dated 17 January 1975 relating to partnership annuities make it clear that it is the practice of the Inland Revenue not to treat the capitalised value of an annuity of a reasonable amount (as therein defined) as payment for goodwill.

(e) Until the date of the agreement for writing off goodwill Mr. James had only a right to be paid a certain sum of money in certain events pursuant to the terms of clause 18(3) of the Main Deed. He had no direct interest in the goodwill of the partnership itself. He was entitled only to choose inaction. Despite the provisions of [section 59(a) and (b) of the Capital Gains Tax Act 1979] the position remains unchanged. The rights of the partners pursuant to clause 18 of the Main deed did not affect in any way the value of the goodwill of the partnership.

(f) Although TCGA 1992, s 24(2) refers to "value" not "market value" such value must be assessed in money terms in the context of a taxing statute.

(g) The asset which Mr. James had purchased (ie "goodwill") was an entitlement to receive certain sums in certain eventualities in accordance with the provisions of clause 18 and Schedule 3 of the Main Deed. With effect from the date of the agreement such asset became of negligible value and accordingly Mr. James was entitled to the relief for losses which he has claimed.

The submissions of H.M. Inspector of Taxes may be summarised as follows:

(a) When surrendering his right to repayment for past expenditure on goodwill Mr. James acquired a valuable asset in the shape of a right to a pension. This can be illustrated most effectively by reference to the case of *Lawrence v Ridsdale's Executrix* ((1976) 51 TC 376) where Walton J. says (at 401):

"For what, then, are they being paid? The economic answer is quite obvious: they are being paid for their shares of the goodwill of the partnership, shares which they leave behind them when they go and for which they are not otherwise compensated under the terms of the partnership agreement. In economic substance, the annuities are the purchase price of the goodwill – nothing more and nothing less."

(b) Section TCGA 1992, s 24(2) speaks of "value" not "market value". In this context it is useful to refer to the speech of Lord Russell of Killowen in the case of *O'Brien v Benson's Hosiery (Holdings) Ltd* where he says ((1977) 53 TC 241 at 270):

"In my opinion it is erroneous to deduce from section 22(4) [of the Finance Act 1965], the language of which has no direct application to the present case, a principle of general application for the purposes of capital gains tax that an asset must have a market value."

Accordingly although there has been a change in the asset held by Mr. James the present asset represents the original cost of the goodwill it replaced and has clearly not become negligible in value.

(c) Further or in the alternative it must be recognised that the partnership itself has an asset in the shape of valuable goodwill whether or not such asset is saleable. Accordingly, by virtue of the provisions of [TCGA 1992, s 59] Mr. James is deemed to be the owner of a share of such goodwill.

(d) Accordingly as Mr. James' entitlement to goodwill has not become of negligible value, his appeal should be dismissed.

The relevant parts of the decision were as follows:

"I must first consider the nature of the asset which Mr. James acquired. In doing so I can have reference only to the Main Deed as no evidence was adduced concerning the contents of earlier partnership deeds.

Clause 18(3) of the Main Deed provides for certain payments to be made in certain events and also provides that the amount of such payments is to be calculated in accordance with the terms of the Third Schedule to the deed. This schedule provides an arithmetical formula agreed by the partners and pursuant to which all transactions affecting goodwill were to be made.

The formula is related to the average net profits of the partnership and to that extent may be said to reflect the value of the partnership from time to time. Nevertheless the formula pays no regard to the actual market value of the practice.

The value of the partnership business as a whole is the price for which the business can be sold at any given moment to a willing purchaser. That this value bears little if any direct relationship to the value as assessed in accordance with the Third Schedule to the Main Deed becomes apparent when it is seen that the Third Schedule formula is based on average net profits covering a period of three years. Such a process of averaging would have a cushioning effect serving to iron out any fluctuations in the amounts of annual net profits. It also ignores the consequences of factors which could have a very considerable effect upon the value of the goodwill of the partnership as a whole to a willing purchaser, such as for example the death of a well-known very active partner, the loss of a major client or adverse publicity attaching to a substantial claim for negligence.

The formula contained in the Third Schedule of the Main Deed formed a convenient basis for ascertaining sums to be paid by incoming partners on admission to the practice and to outgoing partners on death or retirement. In addition transactions on the same basis could take place between continuing partners when it was necessary or desirable to alter profit sharing ratios in any way. It is my belief that such a formula has little direct or consequential connection with the value of the goodwill of the business as a whole and I hold accordingly. Until its amendment, Mr. James possessed under the provisions of the Main Deed an asset which he had acquired by purchase and which consisted of his right to receive a certain sum of money upon the happening of certain events.

In consequence of such findings on the facts of this case I reject the Crown's submission pursuant to [TGCA 1992, s 59]. The Crown concedes that Mr. James surrendered his right to any repayment of his past expenditure on goodwill by the Supplemental Deed. It maintains however that Mr. James retained a valuable asset in the shape of an interest in the value of the practice as such, whether or not it was saleable or marketable, placing reliance upon the dictum of Lord Russell of Killowen in *Benson's Hosiery*. Fortunately it is not necessary for me to distinguish *Benson* in the light of my finding that Mr. James' asset which is the subject of this appeal was separate and distinct from the goodwill of the practice as a whole. During the whole time that Mr. James was a member of the partnership he was entitled to receive, on a dissolution of the partnership or a sale of the practice, his share of the net value of the assets of the partnership. Such a right was unaffected by the terms of either the Supplemental Deed or the document (writing off goodwill).

What then was the effect of the memorandum and agreement circulated to and signed by the partners.

The Crown accepts the definition of goodwill as advanced on behalf of Mr. James and going further the Crown does not dispute the proposition that economic circumstances have compelled the foregoing of an entry payment by incoming partners to professional practices. The Crown also concedes that Mr. James incurred expense in acquiring an asset labelled 'goodwill' and that he surrendered his right to any repayment of his past expenditure on such asset by the terms of the Supplemental Deed. It is contended on behalf of the Crown however that Mr. James surrendered his asset in return for the granting of valuable pension rights. This is perhaps a somewhat surprising submission when considered in the light of the Inland Revenue Practice Statement dated 17 January 1975, but that is of course an extra-statutory concession.

Examining the terms of the document which the partners signed on 18 March 1977 and relating it to the terms of the Main Deed it is curious that the deed contains no omnibus provision permitting amendment of its terms by means of a memorandum signed by all the partners. Clause 15(1) permits amendment of the provisions of the Second Schedule by such means and Clause 18(3) permits amendment of the Third Schedule by such means. It is of course possible that amendment may not include deletion but fortunately the position is saved by the provisions of Section 19 Partnership Act 1890 which provides expressly that the mutual rights and duties of the partners may be varied by the consent of all the partners. It is clear therefore that the contents of the first paragraph of the memorandum and agreement signed by the partners on 18 March 1977, effectively destroyed the provisions of Clause 18(3) and the Third Schedule of the Main Deed. From that moment those provisions ceased to have effect and I hold accordingly. I find that in the events which happened there was no direct relationship between Mr. James surrendering his entitlement to receive payments for goodwill and his becoming entitled to payment of an annuity of his eventual retirement.

Thus on the facts found Mr. James' asset became of negligible value on (the date of signing the document writing off goodwill) within the meaning of TCGA 1992, s 24(2). Accordingly I allow the appeal and grant Mr. James the relief for losses which he claims."

Even today it still remains to be seen whether the Revenue will accept that a partner's interest in goodwill in a professional practice is an asset distinct from the goodwill of the firm as such and can become of negligible value by an appropriate agreement among the partners, or whether they will continue to argue that the cases they have lost before the Commissioners on this point are in each case dependent upon an appropriate finding of fact by the Commissioners and therefore each case will require to be argued before the Commissioners.

Chapter 7

Overseas activities

UNITED KINGDOM PARTNERSHIPS WITH A FOREIGN ELEMENT

Although a United Kingdom partnership is not a separate legal entity (unless it is a Scottish Partnership under Partnership Act 1890, s 4(2)), it is nonetheless deemed to carry on a single trade for United Kingdom tax purposes if the partnership is managed and controlled from the United Kingdom (TA 1988, s 111). Each partner is deemed to carry on a separate trade under self-assessment. However, it is possible for a U.K. resident to carry on a trade abroad and not participate in the control and management of the business, and therefore avoid a liability under Schedule D, Case I or II (*Colquhoun v Brooks* (1889) 2 TC 490 and *Ferguson's Trustees v Donovan* [1929] IR 489, Sup Ct). On the other hand the cases of *Ogilvie v Kitton* (1908) 5 TC 338 and *Spiers v MacKinnon* (1929) 14 TC 386 show that where the *head and brain* of the business is resident in the United Kingdom the profits would be assessed under Schedule D, Case I or II.

The whole of the worldwide profits of a profession carried on by a U.K. resident is assessable to U.K. tax under Schedule D, Case II (*Davies v Braithwaite* (1933) 18 TC 198). Similarly a Schedule D, Case I trade carried on partly in the U.K. and partly abroad by a U.K. resident is wholly liable to U.K. tax under Schedule D, Case I (*London Bank of Mexico v Apthorpe* (1891) 2 TC 143).

The effect of all these cases is that a partnership carrying on a business partly in the United Kingdom and partly overseas will be liable to U.K. tax on the whole of the overseas income. If the overseas income arises from a permanent establishment in the foreign country it is probable that there will be a foreign tax liability on the overseas profits which will be credited against the U.K. tax liability either under the terms of the double taxation treaty with the overseas country, or unilaterally in the U.K. under TA 1988, s 790. When considering the foreign activities of a U.K. resident it is important to bear in mind that the double taxation treaties, which, following TA 1988, s 788(1) and *Ostime v Australian Mutual Provident Society* (1959) 38 TC 492, would over-rule the U.K. legislation, may provide that a dual resident is deemed to be not resident in the United Kingdom. For example, a Spanish national with a home in both the United Kingdom and Spain and business interests in both countries would be deemed under Article 4(2)(*c*) of the Anglo Spanish Double Taxation Agreement, S.I. 1976, No. 1919 to be resident in Spain and not in the United Kingdom. Similar provisions are to be found in other agreements, for example that with the Irish Republic, S.I. 1976, No. 2151, and the U.S.A., S.I. 1980, No. 568.

A non-resident or deemed non-resident trading in the United Kingdom would only be taxed under Schedule D, Case I on profits arising in the United Kingdom (see *Erichsen v Last* (1881) 1 TC 351; on appeal 4 TC 422, CA; *Firestone Tyre & Rubber Ltd v Llewellin* (1957) 37 TC 111; *Pommery and Greno v Apthorpe* (1886) 2 TC 182; *Werle & Co v Colquhoun* (1888) 2 TC 402). The profits are arrived at as if the non-resident were trading with an independent business resident in the U.K., at arm's length, in accordance with Article 7(2) and (3) of the OECD model tax treaty.

TA 1988, s 18(1)(*a*)(ii) provides that tax under Schedule D shall be charged in respect of any person residing in the United Kingdom from any trade, profession or vocation whether carried on in the United Kingdom or elsewhere. TA 1988, s 18(1)(*a*)(iii) provides that tax shall be charged under Schedule D on any person, whether a British subject or not, although not resident in the United Kingdom from any property whatever in the United Kingdom or from any trade, profession or vocation exercised within the United Kingdom.

A non-domiciled individual is taxed in the same way as a U.K. domiciled individual under Schedule D, Case I and II.

If the trade is being carried on by U.K. residents and the world-wide profits are taxable they will be computed on normal Schedule D, Case I or II lines in exactly the same way as if the whole of the income arose in the United Kingdom.

CHANGE OF RESIDENCE

If a U.K. resident partner becomes non-resident or a non-resident partner becomes U.K. resident, there is deemed to be a cessation for the purposes of Schedule D, Cases I, II or V for that partner for all tax purposes other than the carry forward of losses which may be carried through the change, TA 1988, ss 110A and 112(1B)(new).

This is necessitated by the fact that a U.K. resident partner is taxable on his worldwide income, whereas a non-resident partner is taxable only on income arising in the U.K. (*Pommery & Greno v Apthorpe* (1886) 2 TC 182 at 189). A change of residence crystallises a cessation if the change takes place in 1997/98 or subsequently, or if in 1995/96 or 1996/97 where the partner is assessable under the current year basis, in other words for a business commencing on or after 6 April 1994. The strict authority position is that an individual cannot be resident for part only of a fiscal year (*Neubergh v IRC* (1958) STC 181; *Gubay v Kington* (1984) STC 99) which means that he would be treated as non-resident from 6 April following the date of departure with the cessation deeming to take place on 5 April. Conversely, for a partner becoming resident in the U.K., he would be treated as resident from 6 April in the year in which he arrives. However, under extra statutory concession A11 an individual is normally treated for tax purposes as resident from the day of arrival to take up residence in the U.K. or is treated as non-resident from the day following the day of departure. The Revenue will normally apply the concession where a partner changes residence.

Where the individual is not domiciled in the U.K. the remittance basis applies, under TA 1988, s 112 (1A)(new) which means that a partner becoming a resident in the U.K. can safely remit income from the partnership any time after the end of the fiscal year in which he arrives as the source of that income would have ceased at the time of remittance (*Kneen v Martin* (1935) 19 TC 33). This rule does not apply to Schedule E income of a salaried partner which would be caught under TA 1988, s 19(4A). If it were not for the deemed cessation, remittances from a continuing source would be assessed to the U.K. even though arising from a period prior to becoming resident following *Back v Whitlock* (1932) 16 TC 73 and *Carter v Sharon* (1936) 20 TC 29.

Because of the deemed cessation and commencement, a partner changing residence would, where appropriate, be able to claim loss relief against total income for the previous three years for the first four years of the income following the change of residence under TA 1988, s 381.

FOREIGN PARTNERSHIPS

Where a partnership is managed and controlled abroad, the profits of a U.K. resident partner are taxable under Schedule D, Case V on his share of the worldwide income of the partnership. If he is not domiciled in the U.K. he would be taxable only on his share of the income arising in the U.K. and on any remittances from the remaining worldwide profits. A non-resident partner is taxed on his share of the U.K. income as if the partnership were an individual not resident in the U.K. (TA 1988, s 112(1)).

Corporate partners resident in the U.K. are likewise taxable on their share of the worldwide profits, whereas non-resident corporate partners are taxable only on their share of U.K. profits, TA 1988, ss 112(5) and 115(5).

The U.K. Revenue do not like the rule in TA 1988, s 111(3), which provides that the profits of the U.K. branch of a worldwide partnership are allocated among the partners generally, as each partner's share of profits is relatively small and is often covered by personal allowances given under many double tax treaties. The U.K. resident partners running the U.K. branch would, however, often be non-U.K. domiciled and therefore taxable only on their very small share of the U.K. profits and remittances from the worldwide profits of the firm. It is clearly beneficial to arrange profit-sharing in this manner rather than to give the U.K. resident partners the lion's share of the U.K. profits, all of which would be fully taxed.

The U.K. resident partners of a non-resident partner are made that partner's U.K. representative, responsible for the payment of tax on his share of the partnership income and gains, under FA 1995, s 126(7) and are therefore jointly and severally liable for the non-resident partner's U.K. tax. It is essential, therefore, to take this into account in calculating the drawings that may be made by a non-resident partner which should be limited to his share of profits net of U.K. tax.

REMITTANCES

Assessments under Schedule D Case V on a remittance basis include not only direct remittances to the United Kingdom but constructive remittances such as the satisfaction of a debt incurred in the United Kingdom under TA 1988, s 65(4)–(9). A cheque drawn on a U.S.A. bank account in favour of a U.K. bank was held to be a constructive remittance when the dollars were sold by the U.K. bank to the Bank of England the customer being credited with the sterling proceeds (*Thomson v Moyse* (1960) 39 TC 291) as was a loan enjoyed in the United Kingdom (*Harmel v Wright* (1973) 49 TC 149). Remittances of the proceeds of foreign securities could be remittances of capital if the securities were acquired before the taxpayer became resident in the United Kingdom (*Kneen v Martin* (1934) 19 TC 33) unless purchased out of foreign income while the taxpayer was resident in the United Kingdom (*Walsh v Randall* (1940) 23 TC 55).

A non-domiciled individual taxable on the remittance basis could make gifts to his wife and family overseas free of inheritance tax and if, for example, the wife bought a fur coat or otherwise spent the money, and provided that her husband derived no benefit, or if the children paid for their own school fees, it is considered that these would not be constructive remittances although the matter is not entirely free from doubt. There could be inheritance tax problems, however, if the non-domiciled individual was deemed to be domiciled under the provisions of IHTA 1984, s 267.

If a non-U.K. domiciled individual is assessable on a remittance basis it is important to ensure that so far as possible remittances to the United Kingdom are out of capital which means that he may require several overseas bank accounts. The account containing his capital prior to becoming resident in the United Kingdom may be freely remitted. An account containing the proceeds of disposals of overseas investments could be remitted, but any chargeable gain element would be taxable on the remittance basis under TCGA 1992, s 12. However, as a result of indexation of capital gains a remittance from such an account may be preferable to a remittance of income assessable under Schedule D, Case V and gains should therefore be kept in yet another bank account. Alternatively the total proceeds of investments sold at a profit or loss may be segregated and remittances made from the latter only. It may also be helpful to segregate overseas income which has suffered tax at source and is available for U.K. double taxation relief if remitted. Interestingly the Revenue have confirmed that the concentration of remittances into the basis period for 1996–97, where transitional averaging applies, does not call for any anti-avoidance measures even though, in many cases, the result would be to tax the remittances at an effective rate of half the higher rate or less.

In order to ensure that the control and management of a foreign partnership is outside the United Kingdom it is desirable to have a majority of non-U.K. resident partners and provision in the partnership agreement that partnership meetings must be held outside the United Kingdom. It is not essential to have a majority in number of non-resident partners provided that the voting control is such that they control the partnership. See in this respect the case of *Newstead v Frost* [1980] STC 123 in which the U.K. resident partner had 95% of the profits of the partnership but was still assessed under Schedule D, Case V as the control and management of the partnership was outside the United Kingdom.

Under TA 1988, s 65(4) a U.K. resident partner's share of the profits arising from a non-resident partnership will be subject to tax on a remittance basis, not only if he is not domiciled in the United Kingdom, but also if he is a British subject or a citizen of the Republic of Ireland not ordinarily resident in the United Kingdom. A Schedule D, Case V assessment on income from a foreign partnership is computed along the normal Schedule D, Case II lines.

If goods or services are transferred between a foreign partnership and an associated United Kingdom firm under common control, TA 1988, s 770 will enable the Revenue to substitute market value for the price charged for such goods or services. Similarly transfer pricing provisions are contained in most double taxation agreements in art. 9 of the O.E.C.D. model double tax treaty.

TRANSFER OF ASSETS ABROAD

Since the introduction of income tax, U.K. residents have been trying to arrange for income producing assets be held outside the United Kingdom while the owner remains resident. If the income is assessed on an arising basis, as would normally be the case, there is obviously little merit in such a manoeuvre. If more complex arrangements are entered into to ensure that the income arises to some overseas entity to be paid to the U.K. individual in a capital form at some later date, the scheme might appear to become rather more attractive. Unfortunately, such a desirable state of affairs is rather difficult to achieve, particularly in view of the anti-avoidance provisions of TA 1988, s 739. This particular section applies to individuals ordinarily resident in the United Kingdom where as a result of a transfer of assets anywhere in the world and in consequence thereof directly or indirectly income becomes payable to a non-resident or non-domiciled person, which includes a company or a trust. The U.K. individual will be subject to U.K. tax if he retains power to enjoy that income now or at some future date. The section is exceedingly widely drawn and covers for example the receipt of a capital sum including a loan or gift. There is, however, an exemption if it can be shown that there was no intention to avoid U.K. tax or that the operations were *bona fide* commercial transactions not designed to avoid United Kingdom taxation. One of the merits of a foreign partnership is that it might, therefore, be possible to show that overseas income accrues to the foreign partnership as part of a *bona fide* commercial arrangement not designed to avoid U.K. tax, while nonetheless mitigating the tax that would otherwise be payable.

Prior to the case of *Vestey v IRC (Nos 1 and 2)* [1980] STC 10 the Revenue used to argue that an assessment under TA 1988, s 739 could be made on an individual who had absolutely nothing to do with the original transfer of assets, but this argument was not upheld by the House of Lords. In the *Vestey* case beneficiaries under a trust avoided assessments under TA 1988, s 739 as they had not been concerned with the settlement or transfer of assets overseas. As a result the provisions of TA 1988, s 740 were enacted to tax non-transferors in receipt of benefits as distribution on the value received by them.

If TA 1988, s 739 applies, the income of the non-resident can be apportioned to the U.K taxpayer and he would be charged to tax as if the income were his. It should be noted that in certain cases the transfer of assets need not be by the U.K. taxpayer (see *Philippi v IRC* (1971) 47 TC 75 but note *Vestey v IRC (Nos 1 and 2)* [1980] STC 10). The income to be apportioned is the gross income before expenses (*Lord Chetwode v IRC* [1977] STC 64) and the Inland Revenue have very wide powers to serve a notice under TA 1988, s 745 to obtain particulars of such transactions from any person, including professional advisers. Attempts to refute such a notice failed in the case of *Royal Bank of Canada v IRC* (1971) 47 TC 565 and *Clinch v IRC* (1973) 49 TC 52. There has been a considerable number of cases on TA 1988, s 739 which range from the simple transfer of assets to an investment company such as *Cottingham's Executors v IRC* (1938) 22 TC 334 to the very much more complex situations extending over a period of years, such as in the case of *Lord Howard de Walden v IRC* (1941) 25 TC 121.

Most professions will allow overseas activities to be carried on through the medium of a corporate body, either a limited or unlimited company or the foreign equivalent.

A transfer of overseas activities to such a foreign company would normally ensure that the profits of the overseas activity would be subject to foreign tax in the overseas country of operation, but would not be liable to U.K. tax except on dividends remitted to the United Kingdom shareholders. Although TA 1988, s 739 may in theory apply to such a case the commercial motive and the need to retain profits overseas for development of the business would normally avoid any change in view of the exemption for *bona fide* commercial activities not designed to avoid tax. TA 1988, s 765, which restricts the ability of a U.K. resident company to transfer its residence or the whole part of its trade overseas does not apply to a partnership transferring part of its activities to a foreign country. It is also necessary to consider whether there could be any charge to tax under TA 1988, s 739 on a transfer of assets abroad, or on the foreign company profits under the controlled foreign company rules in TA 1988, ss 747–756 and Schs. 24–26. A foreign company directly owned by the partners or partnership would not be within the controlled foreign company provisions as the profits would not be apportioned to a U.K. company within TA 1988, s 747(4).

Although it might be possible to avoid some of the rigours of TA 1988, ss 739 and 740 by holding shares in a foreign company through a complex overseas trust structure, it is perhaps unlikely that many foreign businesses will generate sufficient income to justify such an arrangement, although each case would need to be considered on its merits. The advantage of an overseas trust or company to avoid capital gains tax are severely limited by TCGA 1992, ss 80, exit charge on trustees ceasing to be resident, 83, exit charge on trustees ceasing to be liable to U.K. tax, 85, disposal of interests in non-resident settlement, 86, attribution of gains to settlors, 87, attribution of gains to beneficiaries, 91, notional interest on accumulating gains, and 13 attributions of gains to member of non-residential companies.

A possible advantage of having an overseas company is that the United Kingdom partners might receive income from the overseas company by way of income from an overseas employment.

OVERSEAS EMPLOYMENTS

The tax legislation relating to overseas employments is now mainly contained in TA 1988, s 19 as modified by TA 1988, s 192, which defines foreign emoluments as those of an employment where the duties are carried on outside the U.K. (and not in the Republic of Ireland) and the employer is not resident.

Sch. E is divided into three cases:
(a) Case I applies where the employee is resident and ordinarily resident in the United Kingdom and charges any emoluments world-wide subject to deductions for a year of absence under TA 1988, s 193 or where the emoluments are foreign emoluments.
(b) Case II assesses a person who is not resident or if resident is not ordinarily resident to the U.K. tax on any emoluments in respect of duties performed in the United Kingdom, unless they are incidental duties arising from foreign emoluments, TA 1988, Sch. 12, para 6.
(c) Case III assesses a U.K. resident (whether originally resident or not) on remittances to the United Kingdom of foreign emoluments where all the duties are performed abroad.

Long absences

Duties performed wholly or partly outside the United Kingdom during a qualifying period that consists of at least 365 days and which are taxable under Schedule E, Case I are subject to a deduction of 100% of the amount arising under TA 1988, s 193(1). The qualifying period is one which consists entirely of days of absence from the United Kingdom, except for no more than sixty-two intervening days spent in the United Kingdom and provided that the total number of days in the United Kingdom does not exceed one-sixth of the total number of days in the qualifying period. Terminal leave pay may be added to the emoluments for the qualifying period, and terminal leave spent outside the United Kingdom could be a period of absence.

Supplementary

A person is regarded as absent from the United Kingdom on any day if he is absent at the end of it; *Hoye v Forsdyke* [1981] STC 711.

Any duties merely incidental to the performance of duties in the United Kingdom will be regarded as being performed in the United Kingdom.

TA 1988, s 132(2) provides that duties performed in the United Kingdom purely incidental to duties performed abroad are deemed to be performed outside the United Kingdom. This does not however deem the employee to be absent from the United Kingdom for the purposes of TA 1988, s 193; see *Robson v Dixon* (1972) 48 TC 527 on the meaning of incidental, which is a qualitative test.

EXPENSES IN CONNECTION WITH WORK DONE ABROAD

The U.K. resident and ordinary resident employee not in receipt of foreign emoluments, ie emoluments received by a non-domiciled employee from a non-resident employer, is entitled to a deduction for any travelling expenses where the duties are wholly performed outside the United Kingdom under TA 1988, ss 193 and 194. If the travel is only partly for business purposes, an apportionment may be made. Board and lodging paid for by the employer direct or by reimbursement is also an allowable expense.

Where the employee is absent from the United Kingdom for a continuous period of sixty days or more, the travelling expenses of a spouse and children for up to two return journeys in any year of assessment, provided that the cost is paid or reimbursed by the employer, is allowable as an expense to the employee.

Chapter 8
Miscellaneous taxes

VAT

Under VATA 1994, s 45 a partnership is treated as a single taxable person for value added tax purposes irrespective of any change in the individuals making up the partnership. It is the joint and several liability of all partners to give any VAT notice that is required by law, but if the notice is given by any one partner this will be sufficient compliance with the requirement. VAT (General) Regulations 1985, S.I. 1985, No. 886, reg. 9.

In spite of VATA 1994, s 45, however, Customs & Excise require, under notice 700, para. 94, changes in regulation particulars to be notified to them within thirty days. Such changes include a change in the name or trading name of the business where the proprietor of the business takes one or more other persons into partnership, where a partnership ceases to exist but one of the former partners becomes a sole proprietor of the business, where there is a change in the registered address of a partnership or where a company is incorporated to take over a business previously carried on by a proprietor, partnership or an incorporated body.

Where the same persons in partnership carry on more than one business there is only one registration for VAT purposes in spite of the fact that the businesses may be totally dissimilar (*Customs and Excise Cmrs v Glassborow* [1974] STC 142). It would seem that a Scottish Partnership as a distinct legal entity has to be registered separately for VAT purposes and two Scottish Partnerships carried on by the same persons would be separately registered.

In other respects a partnership for VAT purposes is treated in the same way as any other business. The partnership will charge VAT on chargeable supplies to third parties.

Under VATA 1994, Sch. 8, Group 7, para. 2(c) international services are zero-rated if they consist of the supply of services outside a member state of the European Community. Those services which are supplied where received are defined by VATA 1994, Sch. 5:

1. Transfers and assignments of copyright, patents, licences, trade marks and similar rights.
2. Advertising services.
3. Services of consultants, engineers, consultancy bureaux, lawyers, accountants and other similar services, data processing and provision of information (but excluding from this head any services relating to land).
4. Acceptance of any obligation to refrain from pursuing or exercising in whole or part any business activity or any such rights as are referred to in paragraph 1 above.

5   Banking, financial and insurance services (including reinsurance, but not including the provision of safe deposit facilities).
6   The supply of staff.
7   The letting or hire of goods other than means of transport.
8   The services rendered by one person to another in procuring for the other any of the services mentioned in paragraphs 1–7 above.
9   Any services not of a description specified in paragraphs 1 to 8 above when supplied to a recipient who is registered for VAT.

The services of a solicitor or accountant engaged in tax planning advice for a non-resident would therefore be free of value added tax as zero-rated supplies unless the client were resident in the EEC, in which case the services would only be zero-rated to the extent that they related to the business activities of the client.

On a change in rate of VAT continuous services may be apportioned and the proportion up to the date of change charged at the old rate. There would be a reverse charge on the import of services from abroad under VATA 1994, s 8.

STAMP DUTY

The partnership agreement for an unlimited partnership is not subject to stamp duty unless under seal in which case a fixed duty of 50p is chargeable under Stamp Act 1891, s 1 and Sch. 1.

If an incoming partner purchases an interest in a partnership and there is a document evidencing the sale there will be a 1% ad valorem in the same way as for any other conveyance or transfer on sale. If the incoming partner merely introduces capital to the firm no stamp duty would be payable unless a similar amount of capital was immediately withdrawn by the other partners, which would imply a sale, and any documentation would require stamping as such. If a partner joins a firm without introducing capital there is no sale to him and therefore no dutiable transfer.

A partner withdrawing his capital on retirement would not be subject to stamp duty but if he sold his interest there could again be 1% ad valorem duty on a conveyance or transfer on sale. A dissolution of the partnership could be a conveyance or transfer on sale subject to ad valorem stamp duty unless it is so worded as to qualify as a partition or division of the partnership assets in which case it would be exempt from stamp duty under FA 1985, s 85(1).

A lifetime gift is exempt from stamp duty under FA 1985, s 82.

Chapter 9

The partnership agreement

In this chapter a model partnership agreement, drafted with the assistance of Ralph P. Ray, B.Sc.(Econ) F.T.I.I., Solicitor, is analysed.

BLOGGS & CO. – PARTNERSHIP AGREEMENT

1. The parties

This partnership agreement is made the 1 day of May 1993 between Abel Bloggs of 15 Ship Street, Walden, Essex (hereinafter called AB) of the first part Charles Dunn of 23 The Avenue, North Minnis, Hertfordshire (hereinafter called CD) of the second part Edward Farley of The Orchards, Grove Road, Mowdun, Essex (hereinafter called EF) of the third part Graham Heather of Mount Pleasant Road, Chigwell, Essex (hereinafter called GH) of the fourth part and Ian Jacobs of The Fox, Bambers Green, Essex (hereinafter called IJ) of the fifth part.

2. The business

NOW THIS AGREEMENT WITNESSETH that it is hereby mutually agreed that the parties hereto (hereinafter collectively called "The Partners") have for many years been engaged in the practice as Chartered Accountants and are desirous of entering into a fresh partnership agreement to regulate the conduct of the business upon the following terms.

3. Duration

The partnership shall continue for the minimum term of two years from the date hereof and thereafter may be determined by any partner giving to the others not less than six months' notice in writing expiring at or any time after the said period of two years and so that in the event of any partner ceasing to be a partner by reason of such determination, his death or retirement, or expulsion in accordance with the provisions of this agreement, the partnership shall not determine as regards the surviving or continuing partners.

4. Name

The name of the firm is Bloggs & Co. A list of the names of the partners and address of the firm shall be written or printed on all letters of the firm and displayed as required by section 4 of the Business Names Act 1985.

5. Place of business

The business of the firm shall be carried on at 97 New Broad Street, London EC2 or at such other place or places as the partners shall from time to time determine.

6. Tenancy agreements/leases

The said leasehold premises at which the partnership business is now carried on are held for the residue of the term of nine years from the 1st day of January 1993 granted by a lease dated the 20th day of December 1992 and made between London Landlords Ltd. of the one part and AB, CD & EF of the other part at an initial rent of £40,000 per annum and shall be held by them in trust for the partners of the firm for the time being as part of the partnership property and they shall be indemnified by such other partners of the firm against such rent and the covenants and conditions contained in the said lease.

7. Capital

The capital of the partnership shall be in the sum of £100,000 and shall be provided by and belong to the partners in the following shares.

AB	£25,000
CD	£20,000
EF	£20,000
GH	£20,000
IJ	£15,000

If at any time hereafter any further capital shall be required for the purposes of the partnership the same shall, unless otherwise agreed, be contributed by the partners in the same shares.

8. Interest

Each partner shall be entitled to interest at the rate of 3% above the Barcloyds Bank base rate ruling on 1 May in each year on the amount of capital for the time being standing to his credit in the books of the firm and such interest shall be paid or credited before any division of profits is made.

9. No goodwill

The share of an outgoing partner in the goodwill (if any) of the partnership shall automatically accrue and belong to the continuing partners and no outgoing partner or his estate shall have any claim in respect thereof.

10. Profits

All profits and losses of the said business (including loss of capital) shall be divided and borne by the partners in the following shares.

AB	25%
CD	20%
EF	20%
GH	20%
IJ	15%

11. Drawings

A budget shall be produced prior to the commencement of each year for which partnership accounts are produced and shall serve as the basis of drawings for that ensuing year, unless revised by the partners during the course of the partnership year in which case references to the partnership budget shall refer to the revised budget. Each partner will calculate his entitlement on the assumption that 85% of the budgeted profit is achieved. The tax liability of each partner shall be calculated on his share of 85% of the budgeted profit. 85% of the budgeted profit less the tax provisions so calculated will be known as the budgeted drawable profit. Each partner shall leave in the firm 7½% of his share of 85% of the budgeted profit, which sum shall be used for the purchase of a retirement annuity or personal pension policy in the name of each partner and shall be known as the retirement annuity retention as referred to in clause 22. Each partner may draw each month his share of the budgeted drawable profit less the retirement annuity retention. When the partnership account is taken at the end of each year if it shall appear that any partner has drawn on account of his share of profits any sum in excess of his actual share therefore he shall forthwith repay the excess to the firm. Any profits remaining undrawn when the said partnership account is taken shall be credited to each partner's current account and unless required for the provision of further partnership capital shall be available to be withdrawn in two equal instalments within one month of the partnership account becoming available and within six months thereafter. No interest will be paid on undrawn current account balances.

12(*a*) Preliminary salaries

For the divisions of net profits in accordance with the provision of clause 10 hereof there shall be paid in each year the following sums by way of gross annual salaries which shall be deemed to accrue from day to day and shall be paid monthly or as the partners may from time to time agree.

AB	£16,000
CD	£14,000
EF	£12,000
GH	£10,000
IJ	£15,000

12(*b*) Other remuneration

All directors' remuneration, fees or emoluments and benefits of whatsoever nature which shall be received or derived by any partner while a member of the firm or services rendered or otherwise in respect of any office of profit or appointment held by him shall be treated and accounted for in the books of the firm as profits of the partnership.

12(*c*) Legacies

Legacies of up to £1,000 received by partners from clients of the firm will belong to the recipient. Legacies in excess of this amount will be apportioned with half belonging to the recipient and half divided among the remaining partners in profit sharing ratio at the date of death of the donor.

13. Accounts

All necessary and proper books of account shall be kept by the firm and on the 30th day of April 1994 and on the 30th day of April in each succeeding year a partnership account shall be produced consisting of a balance sheet and profit and loss account. Such account when signed shall be conclusive and final among the partners as to all matters therein unless some manifest error shall be discovered within three months after the signing thereof, in which case such error shall be rectified. So soon as the annual accounts shall have been signed by the partners the net profits (if any) of the business shall be divisible among them in accordance with the provisions of this agreement.

14. Clients' accounts

All monies and securities for money received by the partners or any of them on behalf of or as the property of a client or third person except such of the same as shall be required for the matter in hand on behalf of such client or third person shall forthwith be paid or delivered to such client or third person or paid into or deposited with the bank to an account separate and distinct from any account relating to the property of the firm.

15. Accountants of the partnership

Messrs. Ping, Pong & Co., chartered accountants of 14 The Square, Isleworth, Middlesex shall be appointed as the accountants of the partnership.

16. Bankers

The bankers of the firm shall be Barcloyds Bank plc and all cheques shall be signed by at least two of the partners.

17. The duties of the partners

Each partner shall at all times devote the whole of his time and attention to the partnership business except during holidays. Each partner shall be entitled to a total of five weeks holiday in each year, no more than three of which shall be taken consecutively.

Each partner shall punctually pay and discharge his separate debts and engagements and indemnify the other partners and the partnership assets against the same, and all proceedings, costs, claims or demands in respect thereof.

Each partner shall be just and faithful to the other partners in all transactions resulting to the partnership business and at all times shall give to the others a true account of all such dealings.

18. Negative covenants

No partner shall, except with the consent of the others:
- (*a*) Engage or be concerned or interested either directly or indirectly in any other business or occupation.
- (*b*) Compound, release or discharge any debt which shall be due or owing to the partnership without receiving the full amount thereof if in excess of £1,000.

(c) Engage, make contract with or dismiss any employee.
(d) Enter into any engagement whereby the partners may risk the loss or be made liable for one sum or any number of sums in respect of the same transaction amounting to £2,000.
(e) Except in the ordinary course of trade dispose by loan, pledge, sale or otherwise any part of the partnership property.
(f) Become a guarantor or surety for any person or to do or knowingly suffer anything whereby the partnership property may be endangered.
(g) Assign or mortgage a share or interest in the firm.
(h) Draw or accept or endorse any bill of exchange or promissory note on account of the partnership or employ any of the monies or effects thereof or in any manner pledge the credit thereof except in the usual and regular course of business.
(i) Lend any money belonging to or give any credit on behalf of the firm in any case in which the other partners shall have forbidden him to do so, or undertake any professional business of any kind on behalf of any person or company after having been required by the other parties not to do so.

19. Motor cars

Each partner shall be provided with a partnership car as partnership property. The car will be registered in the name of the individual partner and insured in the name of the partnership. Only the registered partner and his spouse will be insured to drive each partnership car. Each partner shall choose a partnership car at a cost to the firm not exceeding £20,000 increasing monthly at 0.2% from the date hereof. Such car may be either new or second-hand, subject to the majority of the partners declaring the proposed car unsuitable in which case the partner concerned will be required to purchase a car considered suitable for its use in the partnership.

Should any partner wish to buy a more expensive car than the limit permits he can provide the excess out of his own resources. Where a partner has paid such excess and the car in question is later traded in or sold by the firm, the firm shall only have a pro rata entitlement to the amount of the trade-in or sale price on the following formula:

$$\frac{\text{ceiling price on purchase}}{\text{actual purchase price}} \times \text{trade-in or sale price.}$$

in which case the car will appear in the Balance Sheet at the amount paid by the firm and depreciation provided on this figure.

Partnership cars will be replaced at three-yearly or shorter intervals. At the date of this agreement partners are due to replace partnership cars as follows:

AB	June 1993
CD	December 1993
EF	June 1994
GH	December 1994
IJ	June 1995

20. Car running expenses

Partners will be reimbursed for the full running expenses of partnership cars, including excise tax, insurance premiums, petrol, maintenance and repairs.

21. Outgoing partners

(a) If during the continuance of the partnership any partner shall die or become bankrupt or become a patient under the Mental Health Act 1959 or shall retire or otherwise cease to be a partner (hereinafter referred to as the outgoing partner) the outgoing partner or his legal personal representatives or assigns shall be entitled to repayment of the amounts (if any) standing to the credit of his capital, current or loan accounts with the firm as shown on the balance sheet produced under clause 13 hereof for the accounting partner period ending prior to the date when he became an outgoing partner less any withdrawals, repayments or drawings, together with a proportionate share calculated on a time basis of the profit or loss for the accounting period ending next after his becoming an outgoing partner.

(b) The amount so payable shall be made in 12 equal instalments at three monthly intervals, the first instalment to be paid within one month of the partner becoming an outgoing partner.

(c) The whole of the amount due to an outgoing partner or the balance thereof for the time being remaining unpaid shall be paid on the due dates with interest at the rate of 3% per annum above Barcloyds Bank base rate ruling at the date of retirement and at annual anniversaries thereafter on the amount for the time being outstanding.

(d) The continuing partners shall personally enter into a proper covenant to indemnify the outgoing partner and his estate, his personal representatives, trustees in bankruptcy or receiver of a patient as aforesaid against all proceedings, costs, claims and expenses in respect of the partnership arising after the date when the outgoing partner became an outgoing partner (other than acts or omissions for which the outgoing partner was responsible).

22. Pensions etc

Each partner shall effect for his own benefit a retirement annuity policy or personal pension under Chapters III or IV of Part XIV of the Income and Corporation Taxes Act 1988, as amended for not less than $7\frac{1}{2}\%$ of the budgeted drawable profit as provided for in clause 11 and it is hereby agreed that no liability will fall upon the remaining partners in respect of supplementing a retired partner's pension.

23. Life assurance

Partners shall effect such insurance arrangements as may appear expedient from time to time.

24. Accident or sickness insurance

There shall be effected for each partner a policy of insurance providing that in the event of his being totally incapacitated by illness or injury from attending to his partnership duties for a period of more than twelve months, there shall be paid to him in respect of each subsequent month thereafter until he attains the age of 65 or dies a sum equal to not less than half his current monthly drawings.

25. Tax election

An outgoing partner or his personal representatives shall if so requested by the continuing partners join with them in giving to Her Majesty's Inspector of Taxes a notice under (*a*) sub-section (2) of section 113 of the Income and Corporation Taxes Act 1988 (income tax) or section 77 of the Capital Allowances Act 1990 (capital allowances) or any statutory replacements or modifications thereof respectively for the time being in force and the outgoing partner or his personal representatives shall be indemnified by the continuing partner; against any basic or higher rates of income tax which may be payable by him as the result of giving any such notice in excess of the income tax which should have been payable if no such notice had been given.

26. Covenant in restraint of trade

An outgoing partner shall not for a period of eighteen months from the date he ceases to be a partner either on his own account or for any other person firm or company or as servant, agent or officer of any person or company carry on or be in any way engaged or interest in the business of chartered accountants within a radius of one mile from 97 New Broad Street, London, EC2, and as a separate covenant such outgoing partner will not on his own behalf or on behalf of any other person, firm or company canvass, solicit or endeavour to entice away from the partnership, any person, firm or company who, at any time during the last two years whilst he was a partner hereunder, has been a client of or in the habit of dealing with the partnership.

27. Dissolution

Subject and without prejudice to the express provisions contained in this Agreement on the dissolution of the partnership hereby constituted the same shall be wound up and the assets thereof sold as provided by the Partnership Act 1890 or any statutory modification or re-enactment thereof for the time being in force but so that each partner shall be at liberty to bid at any sale of any partnership assets.

28. Notice

Any notice required to be given hereunder shall be duly given if the same shall be delivered personally to the person to whom the same is intended to be given or left for him at or sent by registered letter to his usual or last known place of address in the United Kingdom or in the case of a notice to a partner left for him at the office of the partnership.

AS WITNESS whereof this agreement has been entered into the day and year first above written.

Signed by the said AB ....

in the presence of ....

Signed by the said CD ....

in the presence of ....

Signed by the said EF ....

in the presence of ....

Signed by the said GH ....

in the presence of ....

Signed by the said IJ ....

in the presence of ....

COMMENTARY ON PARTNERSHIP AGREEMENT

1. The parties

A partner's spouse can often usefully be included as a partner which would be neutral for capital transfer tax under IHTA 1984, s 18 and for capital gains tax under TCGA 1992, s 58. Her share of profit could be covered by her personal allowance in whole or part. In order for a spouse to be treated as an active partner however it is necessary for her to be engaged in the business in a real as opposed to purely nominal sense. In a professional practice it is usually only possible to include as partners those professionally qualified, although in such circumstances it can sometimes be advantageous to set up a service partnership in which the partners' spouses would be partners, as opposed to the more usual service company.

Children and grand-children are sometimes included as partners, but unless they are adult and actively engaged in the partnership the Revenue are likely to view their participation with some scepticism as for example in the case of *Alexander Bulloch & Co v IRC* [1976] STC 514. Other relatives included as partners such as nephews and nieces may be connected for inheritance tax purposes under IHTA 1984, s 270 in which case the onus is on the taxpayer to show there is no transfer of value with gratuitous intent. Trustees of, for example, an accumulation and maintenance settlement could be partners, possibly even limited partners under the Limited Partnership Act 1907, although not usually in a professional partnership. Whether or not to include employees as partners has been considered at some length in Chapter 1.

The introduction of a corporate partner is dealt with in Chapter 10.

2. The business

It is important that the partnership carries on a business as the mere holding of joint property is not necessarily a partnership, *Bucks v Bowers* (1969) 46 TC 267. It is also important to define the activities of the partnership where it might not otherwise be clear, for example, whether properties are held as part of the stock in trade of a property dealing partnership or as investments of an investment managing partnership.

If the partnership is to be a foreign partnership managed and controlled from overseas this fact should be made clear in the partnership agreement.

3. Duration

If the partnership is not already in being the duration clause could be as follows:

> "The partnership shall be deemed to have commenced on the 1st day of May 1993 and shall continue for the term of two years from that date and thereafter until determined

as hereinafter provided. After the expiration of the said term of two years the partnership may be determined by six months notice in writing expiring at or at any time after the said period of two years and so that a retirement or expulsion in accordance with the provisions of this agreement the partnership shall not determine as regards the surviving or continuing partners."

The important point to make on duration is that in the absence of a clause showing a contrary intention and continuing the partnership so far as the other parties are concerned any one partner can dissolve the partnership under the Partnership Act 1890, s 26 on the retirement of a partner, under s 32 by expiration of time or notice, under s 33 by bankruptcy, debt or mortgage of the partnership share, under s 34 by illegality of the partnership business or under s 35 by the court. Under the terms of the Partnership Act 1890, s 44 the partnership assets are used first to pay the debts and liabilities of the firm, then to pay each partner's loans and advances to the firm, then to repay each partner's capital account and finally to divide any surplus among the partners in profit sharing ratio. This would normally involve the end of the business as a commercial entity, hence the provision of the partnership agreement.

4. Name

The partnership name should obviously be relevant to the business being carried on and it is possible to have different partnerships with the same persons involved. Note however that for VAT purposes under the case of *Customs and Excise Comrs v Glassborow* [1974] STC 142 a number of partnerships of the same individuals can only have one VAT registration, so that it is necessary to have at least one different individual if separate VAT registration is required unless the partnership is constituted as a Scottish partnership, in which case as a Scottish partnership is a separate legal entity under the Partnership Act 1890, s 4(2), separate VAT registration would be available for each partnership, notwithstanding the fact that the same individuals were partners in each firm.

The requirements regarding business names are contained in the Business Names Act 1985.

5. and 6.   Place of business and leases

If the partnership premises are owned by one or more of the partners it is normally desirable to avoid paying rent as this is unearned income of the recipient. Instead the partnership would be given a licence to occupy the premises and the owner partner would be paid a salary in lieu of rent or given a higher share in the profits. If a rent is to be paid the repairing obligations should usually be placed on the lessee partnership which will reduce the rent payable and therefore reduce the Schedule A charge on the recipient. The situation is to be avoided where the landlord partner receives a rent of less than the repair costs and therefore has a Schedule A deficiency which cannot be set against his other income. The other disadvantage of paying rent to a landlord partner is the reduction or elimination of retirement relief under TCGA 1992, ss 163, 164 and Sch. 6.

There should be no inheritance tax problems of allowing the partnership to use the property rent-free. Where the partnership owns the premises, or indeed where one or more of the partners individually owns the premises, it might be desirable to consider a sale and lease back of the premises. A suitable lease could be entered into with the partnership and the let property sold for a capital sum. It is necessary in view of TA 1988, s 779 to limit the rent paid to a reasonable commercial rent and the sale and lease back of short leases where the lease back is for less than fifteen years is to be avoided in view of the swingeing anti-avoidance provisions in TA 1988, s 780.

Another point to note in the case of partnership property is the Partnership Act 1890 s 22 which, under the doctrine of conversion, provides that freehold property owned by a partnership is treated as personalty. This might affect the burden of inheritance tax under IHTA 1984, s 211 in view of IHTA 1984, s 237(3) which excludes personal property from the Inland Revenue charge. Provided that the point is appreciated the Partnership Act 1890, s 22 can easily be overcome by a suitable clause in the partnership agreement excluding its application, which would leave the partnership freehold as realty.

7. Capital

The amount of capital required and the manner in which it is to be divided will obviously depend on the business being carried on by the partnership. Fixing the required amount of capital is considered in more detail in Chapter 13.

Consideration might be given to partners providing that the capital of the firm once subscribed becomes partnership property and is not repayable to partners on dissolution (see Chapter 11). If so, the clause could read as follows:

> "The capital of the partnership shall be the sum of £100,000 and shall be provided by the partners in the following shares
>
> | | |
> |---|---|
> | AB | £20,000 |
> | CD | £20,000 |
> | EF | £20,000 |
> | GH | £20,000 |
> | IJ | £20,000 |
>
> If at any time hereafter any further capital shall be required for the purposes of the partnership the same shall, unless otherwise agreed, be contributed by the partners in the same shares. The share of an out-going partner in the capital of the partnership shall automatically accrue and belong to the partnership as a firm as such and no individual partner shall have any claim in respect thereof."

8. Interest

Although it might be desirable to separate partnership capital from partnership loans any interest payable on a partnership loan could be assessed under Schedule D, Case III as unearned income, whereas interest on partnership capital would be an appropriation of profits assessable under Schedule D, Cases I or II as earned income. The only advantage so far as the lender is concerned is that on a dissolution partnership loans would be repaid in priority to partnership capital.

In a family partnership adjustments among the partners' capital accounts can often overcome the liquidity problem of taking advantage of annual exemptions for inheritance tax purposes. Interest paid on a loan to provide partnership capital is allowable under TA 1988, s 362.

9. Goodwill

So far as partnership goodwill is concerned, it is becoming increasingly difficult to persuade incoming partners to raise the necessary capital to purchase an interest in the goodwill of a partnership, and it is, therefore, commonly provided that goodwill will pass to the surviving partners under what is known as an automatic accruer. If goodwill is retained the case of *A–G v Boden* [1912] 1 KB 539 should be noted in which it was held that a junior partner's acceptance of additional responsibility was good consideration for the transfer to him of a share in the goodwill of the partnership. As the automatic accruer of goodwill is a commercial arrangement there should not be any inheritance tax or capital gains tax problems arising, although there might be a capital gains tax loss on the grounds that the goodwill has become of negligible value under TCGA 1992, s 24(2) for a partner who has previously paid for goodwill. This aspect is considered in more detail in Chapter 6. If the partners are connected as relatives it will be necessary to show to the Revenue that the write-off of goodwill was a proper commercial transaction under the connected person provisions for inheritance tax purposes under TCGA 1992, s 286 as applied by IHTA 1984, ss 10 and 270. For capital gains tax purposes the provisions of the Inland Revenue SP/D12, paragraph 7 would have to be considered (see Chapter 6).

Providing for the automatic accrual of goodwill or capital might be accompanied by the provision of an annuity to the retired partner. This would have been ineffective for estate duty purposes in view of FA 1950, s 46, but does not give rise to an inheritance tax problem. For capital gains tax however, under TCGA 1992, s 37(3) the capitalised value of the annuity could be regarded as consideration for the disposal of goodwill. According to the Inland Revenue SP/D12, paragraph 8 however, annuities within the allowable limits set out in that paragraph will not be regarded as capitalised consideration on the disposal (see Chapter 6).

10. Profit sharing arrangements

Partnership agreements should make it clear the manner in which profits and losses are to be shared among the partners as this might be rather more complex than suggested in the draft agreement. For example, partners with considerable income outside the partnership might be prepared to accept a larger proportion of losses which they could immediately relieve against other income. In order to spread the burden of taxation it is sometimes desirable to agree a more equal distribution of profits than would normally be the case but ensure that younger partners draw out less than their full entitlement and build up further capital, whereas older partners draw out their full profit entitlement and begin to withdraw capital. The cash effect may therefore equate to the desired profit distribution while preserving the benefits of an equal distribution for tax purposes. In the model agreement revenue and capital profits and losses are shared in the same proportions. If desired these can be shared in different proportions for revenue profits, revenue losses, capital profits and capital losses. Deposit interest might be divided in a different ratio to profits if some partners are highly taxed.

These matters are considered in more detail in Chapter 12.

11. Drawings

The suggested method of calculating drawings would be suitable for most partnerships and emphasises the importance of budgetary control to each individual partner. A more rough and ready method of calculating drawings is to fix a monthly sum which may be drawn by each partner and then to deal with any surplus or deficit at the end of the accounting year. This monthly sum is often arrived at on the basis of the preceding year's accounts, but in times of inflation can lead to material underdrawing of monetary profits and consequent cash flow problems for the partners.

In this agreement partners' drawings are calculated after a deduction for taxation which will be assessed and payable by the firm until 1996–97. From 1997–98 each partner will be solely liable for his own taxation and it might therefore be decided that partners should draw the gross equivalent of the amount drawn previously. Many partnerships will, however, prefer to retain the tax reserve within the firm to ensure that the funds will be available to pay each partner's tax liability when due.

The requirement that a partner shall provide a minimum amount under the retirement annuity or personal pension provisions is enforced by a compulsory restriction on drawings enabling the firm to pay the premiums.

12. Salaries

There can be advantages in a senior partner becoming a salaried partner assessable under Schedule E (see Chapter 1) for a period prior to retirement in order to take advantage of the occupational pension scheme arrangements as described in Chapter 11.

Payment of a salary to a partner as a prior share of profits can be part of an insurance arrangement as described in Chapter 13 in lieu of rent or interest on a loan, or merely to ensure that a junior partner with a small share of the profit has sufficient income to live on.

13. Books of account

The partnership agreement provides for an accounting date of 30 April which is normally one of the best for tax purposes, but can of course be adapted for any other suitable accounting date. Whether the partnership accounts should be assessed on a cash or earnings basis will be a matter of some importance and has been considered in some detail in Chapter 5. It should be noted that if accounts are prepared on a cash basis the partnership will have hidden assets such as debtors and work in progress outside the books of account and the partnership agreement should make clear whether and to what extent an outgoing partner will share in such hidden assets.

14. Clients' accounts

The maintenance of clients' accounts is recommended as a matter of commercial prudence even where not required by the professional governing body or statute.

15. Accountants of the partnership

It is generally recommended that the agreement should state who is to act as the accountants of the partnership.

16. Bankers

The bankers to the partnership can be changed at will by the partners and it is sometimes advantageous to discuss the partnership finance requirements with alternative bankers from time to time. It is normally desirable to borrow as much as is commercially prudent from the bank rather than to provide for increased working capital through restriction of partners' drawings, because interest paid on a bank overdraft incurred by the partnership would be for the business and allowable for tax purposes, whereas partners' personal borrowings, which might be necessary if drawings were unduly restricted, would suffer interest not only at a higher rate in view of the individual's weaker borrowing powers, but also in a non-tax deductible form unless for qualifying purposes such as house purchase.

17. Duties of partners

The suggestion that all partners should be compelled to devote their whole time and attention to the partnership practice might be modified in the case of a senior partner if it were desired to couple this with a transfer of an interest in the partnership relying on the *A–G v Boden* [1912] 1 KB 539 decision, as discussed at p. 90.

19. and 20. Motor Cars

The suggested treatment of motor cars in the partnership agreement is fairly common but alternatives might be preferable in certain cases. Some firms will no doubt desire to lease motor cars rather than purchase them outright and whether it is advantageous to do so will depend on the terms of the lease. Artificial leases designed to give particular benefit to individual partners should be avoided in view of the Inland Revenue Press Release of 26 July 1978. A lessor will expect to make a profit which increases the cost compared with outright purchase. There may, on the other hand, be commercial advantages of leasing in that alternative cars may be made available if the leased car is out of action or contract maintenance may be provided. There may also be cash flow advantages from leasing in reducing the capital requirements of the firm.

An alternative book-keeping arrangement is where any excess amount paid by a partner above the ceiling price would be credited to the partner's current account, which would be debited with the excess depreciation and his share of any loss on sale. The full cost of the car would be shown on the firm's balance sheet. The excess on the current account would not be drawable by the contributing partner.

In some firms each partner owns his own car and pays his own car running expenses. He will then claim a share of the capital allowances appropriate to the business usage and claim the car running expenses as a deduction from the share of profits. Alternatively the partner may charge the business usage of the car he owns to the firm on a mileage basis, perhaps using AA mileage rates appropriate to the car.

A combination of these arrangements might be where the individual partner owns the car but the firm pays the running expenses. In some cases where the partnership owns the majority of the partners' cars as suggested in the model partnership agreement, certain partners may wish to stay outside the scheme, for example, because they wish to run a car not considered suitable by the majority of the partners. One of the main advantages of the partnership providing the car is that interest on money borrowed for the purchase of the car will be tax deductible in the partnership, but would not be tax deductible if incurred by each individual partner, except to a limited extent under TA 1988, ss 362 and 363.

21. Provisions for outgoing partner

Under the suggested partnership agreement the retirement of a partner does not dissolve the partnership and the retiring partner is not entitled to a share in the partnership goodwill or to share in any assets not reflected in the partnership accounts. In a continuing partnership this is perfectly fair in that the theoretical advantage to the remaining partners on a dissolution would not become a practical advantage so long as the business continues, and each partner in turn as he retires will be giving up his share in the assets outside the partnership to the benefit of incoming partners who in turn will do likewise when their retirement date comes. However, in some cases it is not acceptable to the senior partners to provide for their retirement without entitling them to a share in the increase in the value of the assets of the partnership. If this is the case the partnership agreement should make it clear as to the manner in which they are to participate. If, for example, the partnership accounts are on a cash basis it might be that the outgoing partners are entitled to share in the surplus on revaluation of capital assets, but are not entitled to a share in the debtors and work in progress as the firm will continue to make up accounts on a cash basis in future. If the outgoing partner is to share in a proportion of the work in progress and debtors he would normally only do so as and when these were encashed in spite of the fact that they would then be taxable on the continuing partners and tax free in the hands of the retiring partner, apart from capital gains tax if regarded as a disposal of goodwill paid by instalments.

22, 23, and 24. Pension/Annuity/Insurance provisions

Provisions for partnership retirement is dealt with in some detail in Chapter 11 and partnership insurance arrangements in Chapter 13. Pensions from the firm are usually to be avoided so far as possible, except possibly for older partners who have been unable to provide for adequate pensions under the retirement annuity arrangements. If they are to be included they should be on the personal covenant of the continuing partners and not secured on the partnership property, as this might give rise to a settlement for capital transfer tax purposes. A simple clause providing for annuities would be as follows:

> "The continuing partners jointly and severally covenant with the outgoing partner up to a period of ten years following his retirement they will pay to him an annuity of £5,000 per annum. If he should die during that ten year period they will pay to his widow a separate and distinct pension of £3,000 per annum for the remainder of that period."

Such an annuity should be a deduction from the earned income, of the paying partners under TA 1988, s 628, to the extent that it is taxable as earned income of the recipient.

25. Election for continuation

The importance of a continuation election for tax purposes under the preceding year basis of assessment is considered in Appendix II and it is normal to make the signing of such an election compulsory, as otherwise it would not be possible to persuade a partner adversely affected by such an election to sign even though there was an overall benefit to the majority of the partners. The draft agreement includes an indemnity clause which might be extended to provide for an equitable adjustment. This might read as follows:

> "The taxation saved as a result of a continuation election compared with a cessation and re-commencement will be calculated and apportioned among the partners in the fiscal years which would have been affected by a cessation and re-commencement in accordance with each partner's average profit sharing ratio during the years in question.

Any under- or over-payment of taxation resulting from the equitable adjustments will be adjusted through the partners current accounts."

Under self-assessment a partner leaving the firm will not cause a cessation other than in respect of own profit share as a deemed sole trade, and therefore continuation elections will cease to apply and can be left out of partnership agreements once the preceding year basis has ceased to apply, ie from 6 April 1997, or for new firms commencing after 6 April 1994.

26. Covenant in restraint of trade

Such covenants should normally be avoided as they could increase the commercial value of goodwill as applicable to the partnership, and are in any event difficult to enforce. A compromise might be some form of gentlemen's agreement only.

PROFIT SHARING

The sharing of profits is decided by reference to the Partnership Deed; if none, by mutual agreement, and in the absence of such agreement profits are shared equally (Partnership Act 1890, s 24(1)). Payments made to partners by way of salary, prior charge or interest on capital are appropriations of profit and must be added back to arrive at the Schedule D, Case I or Case II profit; although reference is then made to such appropriations when allocating the agreed taxable profit.

An example of the difference between the accounts sharing and the tax sharing of profits is shown in the following example:

EXAMPLE 9.01

A, B and C have been in partnership for many years and after receiving interest on capital of 10% and salaries of £5,000, £3,000 and £2,000 respectively they share the profits for the year ended 5 April 1993 in the ratio of 3:3:2. For the year ended 5 April 1994 it is decided to increase salaries by £1,000 each, increase interest to 15% and change the sharing ratio to 2:2:1. Capital accounts have remained at £30,000 for many years.

Accounts
Profit after interest and salaries   £80,000

Shares as to   A: 3/8ths   £30,000
                B: 3/8ths   £30,000
                C: 2/8ths   £20,000

                             £80,000

EXTRACT FROM PARTNERS' ACCOUNTS

Current Account	A £	B £	C £	Total
Balance 6 April 1992	1,000	300	(250)	
Salary 1992–93	5,000	3,000	2,000	10,000
Interest 1992–93	3,000	3,000	3,000	9,000
Shares 1992–93	30,000	30,000	20,000	80,000
	39,000	36,300	24,750	£99,000

EXAMPLE 9.01 *(continued)*

Current Account	A £	B £	C £	Total
Taxation provision	(12,000)	(11,000)	(6,000)	
Drawings 1992–93	(18,000)	(16,100)	(10,000)	
Balance 5 April 1993	9,000	9,200	8,750	
Capital account	30,000	30,000	30,000	
Total balance 5 April 1993	£39,000	£39,200	£38,750	

	A £	B £	C £	Total
Taxation Apportionment (for 1993–94)				
Profit before salaries and interest, p.y. basis				99,000
Interest at 15% (1993–94)	4,500	4,500	4,500	(13,500)
Salaries 1993–94	6,000	4,000	3,000	(13,000)
Balance 2:2:1	29,000	29,000	14,500	72,500
Assessment 1993–94	£39,500	£37,500	£22,000	£99,000

Traditionally an incoming partner would purchase a share of the goodwill and his share of profits would flow accordingly. His share would only alter as more senior partners retire and he purchased a further interest in the business. The more senior partners received a higher share of profits because of their larger share of goodwill, their seniority and their greater knowledge of the business. However, the trend towards larger professional practices with younger partners, the abolition of goodwill in many cases and the need for specialisation in single disciplines within a practice has led in many instances to an evening-out of profit shares. More senior partners tend to have larger capital accounts than their junior colleagues and this is taken care of by granting interest on capital. Capital accounts may fluctuate because of the withdrawal of surplus capital or indeed by accretions caused by profit retentions in the case of under-capitalised partner. Accordingly a date for the calculation of the interest should be fixed and it is not uncommon to choose the beginning of the period of account. The rate of interest to be applied should be commercial and could be quoted as so many points over the clearing bank's base rate. In times of rapidly changing base rates it may be advisable to credit interest quarterly using as a base the rate applicable to the quarter days chosen.

Undoubtedly partnerships still exist where there is a great disparity between the shares of the senior and junior partners. Senior partners may be unwilling to give up a part of their profits immediately as it would have a material effect upon their income. One way round this problem is to adopt the "increasing points" system.

EXAMPLE 9.02

In this example the higher share is 206.25% of the lowest share and it is wished to achieve a closer parity in sharing ratios. The partners wish to achieve this end over a number of years rather than immediately. Under an "increasing points" system the percentage share of profits is translated into points and each year a certain number of points are added to each partner's share. The number of points added would be the same for each partner.

The net effect of such a system is that the sharing ratios would come closer although they would never equate. Effectively the highest share and the lowest share would converge. The rate at which they would converge would depend upon the number of points added each year. There follows an illustrative schedule showing what the position would be on the assumption of 1, 2 and 3 points being added each year. The position is shown after five and after ten years. It can be seen that under the illustration the quickest convergence is achieved by using three points and after ten years the ratio of highest share to lowest becomes 122.36%. Obviously the rate at which the partners wish to reduce the disparity is a matter for them to decide but this decision having been taken a system could be devised to achieve the desired result. The illustration ignores the admission of future partners, but a system could be designed to take account of such admissions.

PROFIT SHARING – THE POINTS SYSTEM

(1) 1 Point per annum

Partners	Now	After 5 years Shares	%	After 10 years Shares	%
A	16	21	15.00	26	14.44
B	16.5	21.5	15.36	26.5	14.73
C	15	20	14.29	25	13.89
D	14.5	19.5	13.93	24.5	13.61
E	10	15	10.71	20	11.11
F	10	15	10.71	20	11.11
G	10	15	10.71	20	11.11
H	8	13	9.29	18	10.00
	100	140	100	180	100

Highest / Lowest   206.25%   163.34%   147.3%

(2) 2 Points per annum

A	16	26	14.44	36	13.85
B	16.5	26.5	14.73	36.5	14.04
C	15	25	13.89	35	13.46
D	14.5	24.5	13.61	34.5	13.27
E	10	20	11.11	30	11.54
F	10	20	11.11	30	11.54
G	10	20	11.11	30	11.54
H	8	18	10.00	28	10.76
	100	180	100	260	100

Highest / Lowest   206.25%   147.3%   130.48%

152   *The partnership agreement*

EXAMPLE 9.02 *(continued)*

(3) 3 Points per annum

Partners	Now	After 5 years		After 10 years	
		Shares	%	Shares	%
A	16	31	14.10	46	13.53
B	16.5	31.5	14.32	46.5	13.68
C	15	30	13.64	45	13.24
D	14.5	29.5	13.41	44.5	13.09
E	10	25	11.36	40	11.76
F	10	25	11.36	40	11.76
G	10	25	11.36	40	11.76
H	8	23	10.45	38	11.18
	100	220	100	340	100
Highest Lowest	206.25%		137.03%		122.36%

PARTNERSHIP ADMISSION

There are many and varied methods of remunerating the newly admitted partner. He may take an immediate share in equity at a lower level and move onto a higher scale after a suitable period. Alternatively he may take a guaranteed minimum with a very small equity stake on top. In practice the difficulty arises not so much on fixing the new partner's share but rather in deciding how the existing partners are to contribute to that share. There follows an example of an attempt to design a revised sharing system whilst presenting alternatives to the partnership concerned. The example is by no means exhaustive as the possible alternatives are endless.

EXAMPLE 9.03

1. It is understood that A, B, C and D would contribute one percentage point each to I and that a balance of £4,000 would be contributed by the partnership as a whole and that I was to receive the same share as H. Table 1 is calculated on this basis assuming a profit level of £150,000. It will be seen that under this method H and I are not equal and indeed by using this formula it would be impossible to guarantee equality. Rising profits would have the effect of reducing I's share relative to the other partners. The final column of Table 1 shows the equivalent percentage of total profits.
2. In an attempt to remove this anomaly a sharing system is required which grants full equity to I, equates his interest to that of H and maintains his share relative to his other partners in times of rising profits. Table 2 outlines the system devised, and it can be seen that it has been assumed that H and I are to have 8%, being H's present entitlement. The major feature of this method is that H does not contribute to I's share.
3. Table 3 is a refined version of Table 2 insofar as it seeks to design a sharing system whereby I has a full equity stake but in this case H contributes towards I's share. It does require a certain amount of algebraic manipulation to arrive at the figures. Using the sharing ratios in Table 3 and assuming again a profit of £150,000 the profit shares become as follows:

EXAMPLE 9.03 (*continued*)

	£
A	21,635
B	22,356
C	20,191
D	19,476
E	14,424
F	14,424
G	14,424
H	11,535
I	11,535
	£150,000

It should be noted that at a profit level of £150,000 the greatest loss to any one partner in adopting method 3 over method 1 is £274.

At the end of the day the method of sharing profits must be a decision reached by the firm. The calculations are an illustration of how matters might proceed under a full equity system.

TABLE 1

Assuming profits of £150,000

	%	Prior Charge £	Share £	Total £	Equivalent % of total profits
A	15		21,900	21,900	14.61
B	15.5		22,630	22,630	15.09
C	14		20,440	20,440	13.63
D	13.5		19,710	19,710	13.14
E	10		14,600	14,600	9.73
F	10		14,600	14,600	9.73
G	10		14,600	14,600	9.73
H	8		11,680	11,680	7.78
I	4	4,000	5,840	9,840	6.56
				£150,000	100.00

TABLE 2

Step 1
A, B, C and D give up one point to I. I to have same share as H, i e 8%.
Step 2
Exclude H and I shares, totalling 16%, leaving a balance available of 84%.
Step 3
After Step 1, the shares (excluding I and H) are:

		Share of 84%
A	15	14.32
B	15.5	14.79
C	14	13.36
D	13.5	12.88
E	10	9.55
F	10	9.55
G	10	9.55
	88	84

EXAMPLE 9.03 (continued)
Therefore final sharing becomes:

		% lost (gained)
A	14.32	1.68
B	14.79	1.71
C	13.36	1.64
D	12.88	1.62
E	9.55	0.45
F	9.55	0.45
G	9.55	0.45
H	8.00	
I	8.00	(8.00)
	100	

TABLE 3

Step 1
A, B, C and D to give up one point to I. I to have same shares as H, who is to contribute along with other partners in increasing I's share.

Step 2
After Step 1, the percentages are:

A	15
B	15.5
C	14
D	13.5
E	10
F	10
G	10
H	8
I	4
	100

Step 3
The total further contribution to I must be such that H's contribution will reduce his share to what I's will become. Thus if total further contribution is x, I's final share is 4 + x.

H's share of x is $\frac{8}{96}$ ths and his new profit share is thus $8 - \frac{8}{96}x$.

Thus x = 3.96 (to two decimal places).
Thus I's and H's final shares become 7.69%.

*Step 4**
Final sharing becomes:

		% lost (gained)
A	14.423	1.577
B	14.904	1.96
C	13.461	1.539
D	12.984	1.516
E	9.616	0.384
F	9.616	0.384
G	9.616	0.384
H	7.690	0.310
I	7.690	(7.690)
	100.00	—

PARTNERSHIP RETIREMENT

If a new partner is not to be admitted upon the occasion of a retirement and if the remaining partners are on the desired ratios relative to each other, then the retiring partner's share may be split amongst them in proportion to their existing shares. If a new partner is being admitted or if the partners wish to take the opportunity to revise sharing ratios, then some other system will be required. Again the possible alternatives are endless, and the only criterion is that the new system be acceptable to all.

Chapter 10

Service and associated trading companies

PROFESSIONAL RULES

The first point to consider with a service company for a professional partnership is the regulations which the appropriate professional body may have made concerning service companies. In some professions such as solicitors there are restrictions on the manner in which shares in a service company may be held and most professions will regulate the work that can be done by a service company. The main professional rules are summarised below.

Accountants

Accountants are, subject to various conditions, now allowed to carry out auditing work through the medium of a company, whether limited or unlimited, as well as other services such as management accounting advice, taxation and book-keeping services. There are, however, requirements that at least 75% of the shares are held by qualified accountants. Accountants may also set up service companies whether limited or unlimited, and there is no requirement that the shares have to be held by members of the partnership for whom the company provides services.

Actuaries

Actuaries may form a company, either limited or unlimited, and may do any professional work through such a company.

Architects

The Royal Institute of British Architects allows architects to trade through a limited company subject to various conditions.

Barristers

Barristers may not exercise their profession through a company, whether limited or unlimited, but may, if they so desire, form a service company to run a set of chambers, although to do so would apparently be unusual. There is no restriction on the manner in which the shares in such a service company would have to be held.

Dentists

Dentists do not carry on the business of dentistry through a body corporate unless they were already doing so on the 21 July 1955, as it is illegal so to carry on business under the Dentists Act 1957, ss 38 and 39.

As with doctors, there seems to be no reason why a dental practice should not utilise a service company, and again there is no specific restriction on the holding of the shares, although for professional purposes it would probably be desirable for the shares to be held by the partners in the practice.

Doctors

Doctors are not specifically precluded from carrying out their professions through a company, whether limited or unlimited, but they must pay particular regard to the provision of adequate precautions so as to ensure that:
  (a) The relationship between the medical practitioners and their patients is safeguarded and that treatment is given only by a registered medical practitioner or by persons working under his direction.
  (b) The company would be prevented from passing under non-professional control so that the company could exert no influence over the registered medical practitioners in clinical matters.
  (c) Advertising of the registered medical practitioners by the company would be prevented.

It would, however, be unusual for doctors to carry on their profession through a company, although a service company, for the benefit of a group practice, would appear to be unexceptionable.

There are no specific directions as to the manner in which shares in the service company must be held, although in practice it would probably be necessary to ensure that the active medical practitioners in the practice were the shareholders of the service company.

Engineers

Engineers are normally allowed to carry on their business through a company in whole or in part, and in most cases there is no requirement that the shares have to be held by qualified engineers. It is also permissible to set up a service company, whether limited or unlimited, and again there is normally no restriction as to the shareholdings.

Estate Agents

Estate agents and valuers may normally carry on business through a limited or unlimited company subject to various restrictions, including that the majority of the voting rights in the company must remain with professionally qualified directors and all directors must be professionally qualified. A limited company also has to have certain professional indemnity insurance cover.

A firm of estate agents may also set up a service company, whether limited or unlimited, and if the services are provided purely for the firm there appear to be no restrictions as to the manner in which the shares are held.

Insurance brokers

Insurance brokers are allowed to carry on their business through a company whether limited or unlimited or through a partnership, and many form a service company without restriction. There is no restriction as to the manner in which the shares may be held, but the directors, or some of them, should be registered.

Patent agents

Patent agents may only set up an unlimited company or may have a service company. There is no restriction on the manner in which the shares may be held.

Shipbrokers

Shipbrokers may, and usually do, trade as limited companies.

Solicitors

Solicitors cannot carry on any part of their professional activities through the medium of a company, but may form a service company, whether limited or unlimited, to carry out necessary services in connection with the running of the solicitors' practice such as the provision of staff and premises, furniture, equipment and general maintenance. So far as professional conduct is concerned, there is no objection to this provided membership of the company is restricted to members or partners of the firm, admitted solicitors holding practicing certificates, retired partners of the firm and dependants of retired or deceased partners.

Chartered surveyors

Chartered surveyors may, and, subject to certain restrictions, practice as limited companies both within and outside the United Kingdom, and without permission as unlimited companies inside the United Kingdom. They may also form service companies, whether limited or unlimited but shareholders should be limited to partners of the firm.

Quantity surveyors

Quantity surveyors like architects may carry on business through a limited company. They may also form service companies, either limited or unlimited, and no restrictions are made as to who may or may not be shareholders or directors.

This list is by no means exhaustive, but it does give a general indication of the room for manoeuvre within the various professions. Many of the professional bodies have detailed rules as to the use of companies either for part of the trading activities or for service companies and the rules are modified from time to time. It is therefore essential to check in any particular case that the proposed action is in accordance with the current rules of the appropriate professional body.

SERVICE COMPANY FUNCTIONS

As well as employing staff the service company will normally provide the premises and other services such as provision of stationery, telephones, library facilities etc.

The service company will normally agree a charge with the partnership which would recover its costs and leave it with a modest profit margin. This means a charge of anything up to about 15% on turnover, although the Revenue might begin to challenge the allowability of a service charge at this level in the partnership accounts. The more normal level of service charge profit loading would be between 5% and 10% on turnover.

In the case of *Stephenson v Payne Stone & Co* (1967) 44 TC 507 it was held that the partnership deduction for the payment to the service company should be limited to the cost to the service company plus a nominal profit for that company. In this particular case the taxpayer had been trying to obtain an advantage under the opening year provisions by having a large payment to the service company in the first year of the partnership following a cessation for tax purposes in order to obtain tax relief for the large payment to the service company more than once under the opening year provisions which then applied. The point to be noted however is that payment to the service company must be reasonable for the services provided and if it is excessive there is the danger of the Revenue assessing the service company on the whole of the service charge, but disallowing the excessive amount in the partnership accounts. This would obviously lead to double taxation.

CESSATION

On a cessation under the preceding year basis of assessment there is a disadvantage in that the company profit is taxed but there is no relief for the payment to it as the partnership results drop out of assessment under the cessation provisions.

If the cessation can be anticipated it might be possible to reduce the service company charge to the partnership to give rise to neither profit nor loss in the service company for the period where the partnership accounts will fall out of assessment on a cessation, which should eliminate the disadvantage that would otherwise arise of there being a profit in the service company taxed on a current year basis without a corresponding deduction in the partnership because the accounts for that period do not form the basis of any assessment. Although the Revenue could disallow an excessive service charge there is no provision to enable them to insist on a profit being made in the service company, unless they could show that the service company's charges to the partnership were materially less than at market value, in which case market value could possibly be substituted under the decisions in such cases as *Sharkey v Wernher* (1955) 36 TC 275 and *Petrotim Securities Ltd v Ayres* (1963) 41 TC 389.

This problem on cessation will not occur under the current year basis of assessment because there is no drop out of profits merely overlap relief, if any.

SMALL COMPANY RATES

The main advantage of using a service company is that partners individually suffer tax rates up to 40% whereas a service company would be subject to corporation tax at 33% for the year ended 31 March 1995. Provided that there are no associated companies the profits of the service company of up to £300,000 (for the year ended 31 March 1995) will suffer corporation tax at only 25%.

There is a marginal relief if the company's profits liable to corporation tax exceed the lower maximum amount of £300,000 for the year ended 31 March 1995, but do not exceed the higher maximum amount of £1,500,000 for that year. If the company has any associated companies the maximum amounts are divided by one plus the number of associated companies. Non-trading companies are ignored, as are companies controlled by relatives other than the spouse and minor children but otherwise non-associated and with no material trading interdependence, ESC C9. The maximum amounts are also proportionately reduced where the accounting period is less than twelve months. An associated company for part of the year is however included. A company is associated with another if both are under common control or one is controlled by the other, control being defined in TA 1988, s 416.

The formula to be applied for the year ended 31 March 1995 is $\frac{1}{50}(M-P)\times\frac{I}{P}$ where M is the higher maximum amount, P is the profits i e the income plus the assessable portion of chargeable gains, and for this section only including non group franked investment income, but not including group income. I is the income as defined in TA 1988, s 239(6), ie the profits assessable to corporation tax less any assessable capital gains.

EXAMPLE 10.01

Profits for the year ended 31 March 1995 including chargeable proportion of chargeable gains and FII	£400,000	
FII	40,000	
Corporation tax chargeable on (£400,000 less £40,000) = £360,000 at 33% =		£118,800
Less: $^1\!/_{50}$ (£1,500,000 – £400,000) × $\frac{£360,000}{400.000}$ =		£19,800
Total tax payable		£99,000

If an accounting period straddles 31 March when there has been a change in small company relief, it is necessary to split the accounting period into two, apportion the profits on a time basis and apply the appropriate fraction to each portion reducing the maximum amounts proportionately.

In calculating profits for this section FII in respect of distributions within a group may be ignored if they would have qualified as group income had the company so elected.

HOLDING THE SHARES

In professions where there is no restriction on the manner in which the shares in a service company are held it might be desirable to have the shares owned by the partners' wives rather than by the partners, because partners' wives are not associated with each other under the provisions of TA 1988, s 417(3), which, in turn, means that if there are at least eleven non-associated shareholders involved the company need not be a close company within the meaning of TA 1988, s 414. In practice, commercial considerations seem in any event, to make such a theoretical solution unacceptable in most cases.

The other considerations with regard to the shares in the service company are whether to hold them by the partnership itself as partnership property or by the partners individually.

If the shares are held as partnership property by the partnership there would be an inheritance tax advantage in that the value reflected in the partners' interest at death or retirement would qualify for business property relief of 100% as part of the interest in a business under IHTA 1984, ss 104(1)(a) and 105(1)(a), para. 2(1)(a) and 3(1)(a).

As partnership property, any change in the asset sharing ratio would not give rise to a capital gains tax charge provided that these shares were not revalued in view of paragraph 4 of the Inland Revenue SP/D12, unless possibly if the partners were related other than as partners, in which case a compulsory revaluation might take place under paragraph 7 of the same statement. If the shares in the service company are not to be revalued on partnership changes therefore, it will normally be desirable to hold the shares as partnership property. Even if the shares are revalued any chargeable gains may be within the small gains limits of TCGA 1992, s 3.

However, it sometimes happens that the service company shares are of considerable value, particularly where, for example, the service company owns a freehold property or a valuable lease, or has substantial work-in-progress. In such cases the existing partners are quite likely to require the shares to be revalued so that their share of the increase in value may be received by them. In such circumstances it is often desirable for the shares in the service company to be owned by the partners individually. For inheritance tax purposes business relief would only be available at 50% (100% after 5 April 1996) under IHTA 1984, ss 104(1)(*b*) and 105(1)(*c*) and any disposal of shares would give rise to a capital gains tax charge on the excess of the proceeds over the base cost, or 31 March 1982 value if appropriate.

If the partners hold the shares individually there will normally be an agreement for valuing the shares on any disposal. These arrangements would normally provide that the shares should be transferred on a basis reflecting a proportionate share of the total net assets of the company, including if thought desirable the revaluation of properties, work-in-progress or goodwill in the company. This would mean that a partner with 10% of the shares would be paid an amount based on 10% of the total value of the service company. It will be appreciated that under the normal method of valuing shares in a private company, a minority interest of 10% of the shares would be valued at substantially less than 10% of the value of the whole, hence the necessity for such an agreement. The Revenue have confirmed that the existence of such an agreement would not give rise to a Schedule E charge on any excess of the amount received over the normal market value under the provisions of TA 1988, s 162.

Where the partner individually owns the shares in the service company, he may retain such shares after ceasing to be a partner in the firm and conversely an incoming partner need not acquire shares in the service company as well as providing for his capital in the partnership immediately he joins. It is often quite convenient to arrange for the shares to be disposed of, say, within five years of ceasing to be a partner and to require the existing partners to buy and the retiring one to sell the shares at the agreed market value within this period.

Any capital gains tax charge would be limited to the partner disposing of his shares, but he would have the cash available to meet the liability. When considering the advantages and disadvantages of a service company where it is intended to give the outgoing partner the benefit of the increased value of the shares this capital gains tax charge on what is effectively the accumulated undistributed profits of the service company should not be forgotten. If a partner's share of the undistributed profits amounts to say £20,000, which have suffered corporation tax at 25%, the value of his shares should have increased by £15,000, which would give a capital gains tax liability at 40% of £6,000 making a total tax charge on that share of the profits of £11,000, or 55%. It is not, however, correct to infer from this that profits taxable on the individuals should be distributed as profits subject to income tax rather than retained in the service company as the capital gains tax on retained profits only becomes payable on a disposal which may be many years after the immediate tax saving, and a true comparison should be made with the current rate of corporation tax and the discounted present value of any subsequent capital gains tax compared with the income tax charge. The discounted present value of capital gains tax at 40% discounted at 15% per annum for twenty years is 2.44% and, therefore, the potential future capital gains tax liability, although it should not be overlooked, may be relatively insignificant when considering the immediate advantages of a lower rate of corporation tax compared with income tax on current profits.

PAYMENT OF TAX

One disadvantage of setting up a new service company is that the payment of tax on the profits will be accelerated, in that corporation tax will be due nine months after the end of the accounting period under TA 1988, s 10(1). It will be appreciated that if the partnership has an accounting period ending on the 30 April it currently has an average period of credit between the end of the accounting period and the due date of payment of tax of twenty-three months compared with the company's period of nine months. This will shorten under self-assessment but with a judicious choice of accounting date will still be a much longer period than nine months.

REMUNERATION

The desirability of employing partner's spouses has already been dealt with and if the service company employs the staff generally it should also employ the partners' spouse where they actually work for the business. Whether in such circumstances they should become members of an occupational pension scheme is considered in Chapter 11.

Partners and their spouses may, as directors or employees of a service company, draw remuneration taxable under Schedule E, which in turn might make membership of an occupational pension scheme attractive. The Revenue, however, argue in most cases that the only allowable remuneration as director is a modest responsibility fee of, say £5,000 per annum per director as his other profit-earning activities are in his capacity of partner in the firm. In some cases it can be shown as a matter of fact that the main duties of, say, a staff partner relate properly to the service company and should be remunerated therefrom. An associated trading company – see below – may overcome this problem.

EXPENSES

Although the majority of the expenses of running the firm could be paid through the service company certain items such as professional indemnity insurance would continue to be paid by the partnership. Partners' cars should normally be provided by the partnership rather than by the service company. The benefit in kind chargeable under Schedule E is now 35% of its list price, in most cases under TA 1988, s 157 and Sch 6 as amended. Car fuel is taxed under TA 1988, s 158 as an additional benefit which may also influence the ownership of business cars. The whole of the cost of the car should be allowable where it is provided by a company as the private usage is covered by the benefit in kind under the benefit provisions. The company would claim capital allowances on the car in full with no disallowance subject to the limitation of £12,000 per annum under F (No.2)A 1992, s 71164

It has been suggested that business use by the partner is not on account of the business of the service company, but the counter argument is that the business of the service company is to supply all forms of assistance to the partnership including the provision of cars for the partners and it is not thought that there should be any difficulty in practice in limiting the benefit to the scale charge.

PARTNERSHIP PREMISES

The treatment of the partnership premises when they are owned by one or more of the partners has already been considered. Where the premises are owned by all the partners, or where a lease is held in trust for all the partners for the time being, the premises are normally held by the firm as partnership property. One problem of owning the premises in this way is where a retiring partner requires to receive a share of any increase in the value of the property on retirement or death. This would require the premises to be revalued which would give rise to a chargeable gain on those partners whose shares reduce even though the revaluation of the property produces no cash to meet the liability. It can sometimes be simpler to own the property through the service company where the partners own the shares individually as any increase in value in the premises can be reflected in the price at which the shares are sold to incoming partners. In this way only the partner who actually sells his shares for cash has a chargeable transfer for capital gains tax purposes and he would have the cash available to meet the liability. At first glance it may seem silly to place the partnership premises in the service company in view of the potential double capital gains tax charge arising from corporate ownership. If the property were to be sold, the chargeable gain, less corporation tax payable thereon, would be reflected in the increased value of the shares, and if the service company were then to be liquidated the net chargeable gain would again be subject to capital gains tax as an increase in the value of shares. However, in practice, there is normally no intention to liquidate the service company and if the partnership premises were to be sold they would almost certainly be replaced and any chargeable gain arising would be rolled over under the provisions of TCGA 1992, ss 154 to 158.

If the service company does provide the premises it would normally not charge a rent to the partnership which would give rise to Schedule A income in the service company. It would charge an overall service fee to include the provision of premises. The service charge by a service company to the partnership would be subject to value added tax. This might give rise to a disallowance of input tax if the partnership is itself partially exempt, for example, providing insurance services as an insurance broker. In such cases, therefore, the service company has manufactured a partially disallowed VAT charge on such items as staff salaries and rent which would not have been subject to VAT if paid direct by the partnership.

If the partnership has a substantial premium on the acquisition of a lease for the partnership premises it might be worth considering owning that lease through a separate company, so that if it becomes worthless at the end of the lease the loss would be reflected in the fall in value of the shares which could then be disposed of and reacquired to crystallise a capital loss. It might be possible to deem the shares to be sold and immediately reacquired on the grounds that they have become of negligible value under the provisions of TCGA 1992, s 24(2). The lease itself would not give rise to a capital loss as the cost would have depreciated under the curved line depreciation provisions of TCGA 1992, Sch. 8.

MODE OF OPERATION

When a service company is set up various practical points have to be considered.

1. Fixed assets

(a) Property and leases

If a property is already owned by the partnership there could be a capital gains tax charge if it were transferred to a company although it would equally be sold at cost and the gain rolled over under TCGA 1992, s 165. Any leases could be transferred into the name of the company but if this involves considerable expense in legal or other fees it is felt that the leases could remain as they are and the company simply reimburse the partnership for the rent, rates and insurance as necessary at the appropriate time.

(b) Fixtures and fittings etc.

Fixtures, fittings and equipment would be transferred to the company at their written-down values at the appropriate date. As the company would be entitled to capital allowances there is no need to substitute market value, CAA 1990, s 26(1)(b) and the company would not be eligible for first year allowances on the assets transferred, CAA 1990, s 75.

(c) Motor cars

All cars may be owned by the firm and this could continue as far as partners' cars are concerned. Staff cars will normally be transferred to the company at their written-down value for tax purposes.

2. Current assets

(a) Any insurance policies on partners' lives will remain in the partnership.
(b) Work-in-progress may be transferred to the company at its market value.
(c) Stocks of stationery will be held by the company.
(d) Debtors will remain in the partnership as bills will continue to be rendered by and fees received by the partnership.
(e) Bank balances and cash in hand will flow from the detailed operation of both the company and the partnership and will find their appropriate places in the respective Balance Sheets.

3. Current liabilities

In the main it is envisaged that creditors will be transferred to the company although where certain items of expenditure are left in the partnership there may be creditors which will have to appear in the partnership Balance Sheet as opposed to the company.

4. Bank overdraft

As mentioned above bank and cash balances will find their appropriate places in the Balance Sheets as a result of the detailed operation of the two concerns.

5. Taxation

This will in the main remain a partnership liability except insofar as profits are transferred to the company in a particular year where the appropriate tax liability will be shown as a company liability.

6. Profit and Loss Account items

(a) Income

(1) *Fees.* It is envisaged that bills for work done will continue to be rendered by the partnership so that this item will remain substantially unchanged and sundry debtors referred to above will remain in the partnership Balance Sheet as before. If it is considered desirable for the company to generate its own fee income apart from the bills rendered to the partnership in respect of services rendered this could be done if the professional body so allows (see under associated trading companies below).

(2) *Commission, etc.* The receipt of this income from whatever sources should be left within the partnership.

(3) *Directors' fees, trustees fees, lecture fees, etc.* These will fall to be treated in the same way as ordinary fees.

(b) Expenditure

(1) *Staff.* It is suggested that all staff would be employed by the company and all costs relating to staff paid through the company. This would seem to cause no particular problem, there would normally be no difficulty as far as the pension scheme is concerned, in the transfer to the company with the approval of the Inland Revenue Pension Schemes Office. In addition, the Department of Employment have confirmed that there is no redundancy problem on the transfer of staff from the partnership to the company. The costs relating to staff would of course include the actual salaries, employer's national insurance contributions, agency fees, luncheon vouchers and the company's share of pension scheme contributions.

(2) *Property expenses.* This has already been referred to briefly under the heading "property" in the Balance Sheet section but there would appear to be no difficulty in the rent, rates, lighting, heating, cleaning and other expenses being charged through the company.

(3) *General expenses.* A broad analysis of the heading may include postage and telephone, library, vending machine, repairs to premises, equipment repairs and hire, printing and stationery, computer services, subscriptions and donations, travelling expenses, entertaining, motor expenses and miscellaneous other expenses. Most of these expenses can be transferred to the company without any problem, the exceptions are as follows:

(i) *Subscriptions and donations*
Subscriptions paid on behalf of staff would be transferred to the company but those relating to partners would remain in the firm. Donations could be made either by the company or the partnership.

(ii) *Travelling expenses*
This relates to expenditure by partners and staff not chargeable to clients. In addition there is also the question of travelling expenses charged to clients and these must be paid by the company and charged as disbursements onto work in progress. General travelling expenditure not charged to clients will be paid by the partnership insofar as this relates to partners' expenses and by the company insofar as this relates to staff.

(iii) *Entertaining*
Exactly the same situation would apply to entertaining, which would be disallowed under TA 1988, s 577, unless directly recharged to clients.

(iv) *Motor expenses*
Here again exactly the same situation applies and an analysis of motor expenses would follow the ownership of cars as indicated previously.

(v) *Miscellaneous other expenses*
In the main this relates to the numerous small items of expenditure which may be incurred in any form and it is suggested that these could be transferred to the company.

(vi) *Petty cash*
It is envisaged that only one petty cash account and book would be kept by each office, but that this would have analysed expenditure columns in it relating to partnership expenses and company expenses and that the totals of these columns would be reimbursed on an imprest system at appropriate intervals.

(4) *Depreciation.* This would follow the ownership of fixed assets.

(5) *Consultants' fees.* These would remain in the partnership.

(6) *Insurance.* This would be divided as appropriate. Professional indemnity insurance would remain in the partnership, insurance of buildings and fixed assets would follow the ownership of the assets basically being in the company and the insurance of cars would be split between partners and staff cars and charged accordingly.

(7) *Payments to widows of former partners.* These would remain in the partnership.

(8) *Bank interest.* This would be charged as appropriate according to where the overdraft was.

COMPUTER SYSTEMS

The sales ledger system would remain exactly as if there were no service company, all bills being rendered and all cash paid to the partnership. If the situation arose whereby the limited company was raising bills in its own name, these would be the subject of a separate sales ledger system.

The work-in-progress lists would be in the name of the company but apart from that would be identical in form and detail to a partnership without a service company. As all staff time and disbursements would be paid through the company this should not create any particular problem.

The company would render interim bills to the partnership during the course of the year based on a pre-determined percentage of partnership billing in any particular month and if this method is adopted it would ensure that the work-in-progress remains in the service company.

STRUCTURE OF THE COMPANY

It is suggested that the service company should be an unlimited company, to avoid having to file accounts with the Registrar of Companies.

ASSOCIATED TRADING COMPANIES

In many professions the activities of the service company are not confined merely to providing services to the partnership but extend to providing certain services to clients. An accountancy practice, for example, might provide management accounting advice or taxation services through a company. In such cases the profits of the company may be considerably increased and the remuneration paid to partners in their capacity as directors and employees of the service company could also be increased. This might enable an occupational pension fund to be set up for the partners as explained in Chapter 11, which can be very beneficial.

In cases where the partnership business could be carried on by a company, whether a limited or unlimited company, it might be worthwhile considering trading in corporate form and transferring the business of the partnership to a limited company. If all the assets of the partnership, or at least all the assets excluding cash, are transferred to the company wholly or partly in exchange for shares, capital gains tax roll-over relief can be claimed under the provisions of TCGA 1992, s 162.

TRANSFER OF A BUSINESS INTO A COMPANY

The transfer of the whole of a business carried on by a partnership to a company in exchange for an issue of shares in that company ("the transferee company") is a useful method of turning the business into a limited company or amalgamating the business which is being transferred with the business which is already being carried on by the transferee company. The capital gains tax on the disposal of the business assets at the date of the transfer is postponed (possibly indefinitely). Deferment is given in respect of chargeable gains arising on the disposal of the business as a going concern to the company wholly or partly in the exchange for shares issued to the transferor under TCGA 1992, s 162. The shares issued are described as the new assets and the business assets transferred are known as the old assets.

For the relief to operate it is necessary for all the old assets to be transferred to the company other than cash which may be excluded if desired. Normally it would be recommended that the cash should not be transferred to the company. Stamp duty saving schemes, whereby the debts are left with the transferor for collection, should be avoided as this would prevent the relief being available.

Initially it is necessary to calculate the aggregate chargeable gains, less losses which would accrue on the disposal of the business at open market value. That part of the total consideration for the disposal received from the company which is attributable to the shares issued is deferred by way of a deduction from the allowable base cost of those shares. Therefore, it is necessary to apportion the chargeable gains between the shares and any other consideration such as cash or a loan. The apportionment formula to be applied is:

$$\text{Chargeable gains} \times \frac{\text{Market value of the shares issued}}{\text{Total consideration received}}$$

It should be noted that this formula is applied to the chargeable gains *less* losses on the whole of the business assets being transferred. The amount of the deferral so calculated is deducted from the cost of the shares in the company issued for the business. When the shares are eventually sold the gain is computed by reference to the reduced cost.

If the consideration for the transfer of the business is wholly shares, capital gains tax will be deferred completely until the shares are eventually sold, or until the transferor dies, in which case the deferment becomes an exemption.

The following precedent has been prepared by Ralph P. Ray in accordance with the capital gains tax provision of TCGA 1992, s 162 and assumes that the business which is being transferred is owned by a small partnership, although it can easily be adapted where there are more proprietors of the business or for a sole proprietor.

THIS agreement[1] is made the 1st day of April 1996 BETWEEN John James of 14 New Street, Carlow, Sussex and James Johns of 41 Old Street, Lowcar, Sussex (hereinafter called "the Transferors") of the one part and James Johns Limited having its registered office at 14 New Street, Carlow, Sussex (hereinafter called "the Company") of the other part.

WHEREAS
(A) The transferors have for some years past carried on in partnership the business of estate agents at 14 New Street, Carlow, Sussex and elsewhere under the style of James John & Co. (hereinafter called "the business").
(B) The Company was duly incorporated under the Companies Act 1985 on the 14th day of February 1996 as a private company and as at the date hereof has a nominal share capital of £10,000 divided into 10,000 ordinary shares of £1 each of which two ordinary shares have been issued and are fully paid.[2]

NOW IT IS HEREBY AGREED as follows:
1. The Transferors shall transfer to the Company the business of the Transferors as a going concern as from the 1st of April 1996 together with all the assets thereof including:[3]
    (i) the goodwill
    (ii) the freehold and leasehold property specified in Schedule 1 hereto (and subject to the charges stated therein)
    (iii) the full benefit of all subsisting the pending contracts engagements and orders to which the Transferors were entitled
    (iv) the stock in trade all plant machinery tools vehicles implements utensils equipment books of account books of reference to customers and other books documents and effects
    (v) any trade marks designs patents and licences and policies of insurance of any kind (subject where necessary to the consent of the relevant office)
    (vi) all debts cheques bills notes and securities due to the Transferors in connection with the business

(vii) all other property and assets of the Transferors relating to the business.

2. The Company shall acquire the business subject to all debts owing by the Transferors in respect thereof and all liabilities subsisting at the said 1 April 1996.[4]

3. The Transferors hereby warrant that they have a good and marketable title to the assets of the business referred to in clause 1 hereof and each of them has a good right to transfer the same to the Company free from any incumbrance or interest in favour of any person.[5]

4. The Company shall accept without investigation requisition or objection the title of the Transferors to the assets hereby agreed to be transferred.

5. The consideration for the foregoing is represented by an aggregate value of £40,000 which shall be satisfied (as to the sum of £40,000) by the issue[6] to the Transferors of 4998 new shares of £1 each in the capital of the Company credited as fully paid up and in exchange for the said business agreed to be transferred to the Company upon the terms and conditions hereof.[7]

6. (*a*) It is hereby declared that for the purpose of this Agreement the values of the assets hereby agreed to be transferred shall be those set out in the accounts of the business as at the said 1 April 1996 and prepared by Cross Keys & Co., chartered accountants, a copy of which is attached to this Agreement and subscribed by or on behalf of the parties hereto for identification purposes.

(*b*) In particular the values of the respective assets referred to in Clause 1 hereof shall be those set out in Schedule II hereto.

(*c*) For purposes of stamp duty the property and effects hereby agreed to be transferred capable of passing by manual delivery shall so pass and shall be taken to be the value of £10,000.[8]

7. This Agreement shall be completed on or before the 1 April 1996 when possession of the several assets shall as far as practicable be given to the Company and the Company shall thereupon issue the said ordinary shares as aforesaid and the Transferors and all other necessary parties shall execute and do all such deeds and things as may be necessary for effectually vesting the said business in the Company.

8. The Transferors hereby irrevocably appoint the Company and its substitutes to be their Attorney for executing all documents and for perfecting any registration and for giving and signing all notices on behalf of the Transferors for carrying into effect in all respects the aforesaid transfer to the Company and also for demanding and recovering and giving receipts for all debts due to the Transferors in respect of the business and for bringing all necessary proceedings for the recovery of the same and in respect of all other assets of the business.[9]

9. The Company shall pay all the costs of and incidental to the preparation and execution of this Agreement and any further instruments necessary and proper for carrying this Agreement into effect and shall pursuant to section 88 of the Companies Act 1985 cause all necessary documents to be duly filed with the Registrar of Companies.[10]

10. It is hereby certified that the transaction hereby effected does not form part of a larger transaction or of a series of transactions in respect of which the amount or value or the aggregate amount or value of the consideration exceeds £60,000 exclusive of assets passing by delivery pursuant to Finance Act 1958 Sections 34(4).

IN WITNESS etc.

SCHEDULE I
(Particulars of freehold and leasehold property and any charges)

SCHEDULE II
(Particulars of assets being transferred with values as per attached accounts)
(Signature and seal of Transferors and seal of Company)[11]

NOTES:

(1) *Ad valorem* stamp duty on all assets transferred (Stamp Act 1891, ss 54–61 Sch. 1, see *Kelly's Draftsman* (13th ed.) p. 131 footnote (b)), except chattels transferable by manual delivery (see note to clause 5(c) below). No stamp duty relief under FA 1927, s 55, since a transferor in a transfer under TCGA 1992, s 162 must *not* be a company. Duty to be adjudicated.

(2) Ensure that the company has sufficient unissued capital or that its nominal capital is increased accordingly. Shares of different classes may be issued in TCGA 1992, s 162 transfer – see note to Clause 5 below on apportionment of consideration.

(3) TCGA 1992, s 162(1) cash may be excluded from the transfer. It is necessary to transfer all other assets in the business.

(4) An indemnity may be treated as consideration other than shares, creating a *pro tanto* capital gains tax liability; therefore avoid if possible.

(5) For more extensive warranties see Butterworths *Encyclopaedia of Forms and Precedents* (4th ed.), vol. 9, pp. 668–669.

(6) Register the consideration shares on transfer.

(7) TCGA 1992, s 162(3) where shares are of a different class or classes apportionment of capital gains tax relief must be made in accordance with the market values of such shares at date of transfer.

(8) FA 1958, s 34(4) any goods wares or merchandise may be disregarded for stamp duty, provided that these items are expressly excluded from the Agreement. Form Stamps No. 22 (apportionment of consideration under Agreement for Sale) should be completed and certified.

(9) A clause could be inserted here whereby the Company is to retain employees of the business (see Butterworths *Encyclopaedia of Forms and Precedents* (4th ed.), vol. 9, p. 603).

(10) Company within one month of first allotment of shares file with the Registrar of Companies contract in writing constituting title of allottee, and any contract of sale and return stating relevant particulars of shares allotted.

(11) Agreement under seal if power of attorney in Clause 8 is to include execution of deeds.

EXAMPLE 10.02

Aphrodite Ltd. was formed to take over the business of Aphrodite & Co. on 1 January 1995. Aphrodite & Co's balance sheet of 31 December 1994 was as follows:

	£			£
Capital accounts	34,000	Freehold property (at cost 1.1.86)		10,000
Current liabilities:		Current assets:		
Creditors	15,000	Stock	12,000	
		Debtors	18,000	
		Cash	9,000	39,000
	£49,000			£49,000

The freehold property was worth £25,000 and goodwill £20,000.
The partners received 10,000 shares of £1 each, retained the £9,000 cash and left £20,000 on loan account with the company.

The balance sheet of the company at 1 January 1995 was as follows:

	£			£
Share capital	10,000	Freehold property		25,000
Share premium	30,000	Goodwill		20,000
Current liabilities:		Current assets:		
Creditors	15,000	Stock	12,000	
Loan	20,000	Debtors	18,000	30,000
	£75,000			£75,000

EXAMPLE 10.02 *(continued)*

The chargeable gains on the transfer were:

	£	£
Freehold property	25,000	
Less: cost	10,000	
indexation, say	5,000	
	15,000	10,000
Goodwill	20,000	
Less: market value 31.3.1982	10,000	
indexation, say	8,000	
	18,000	2,000
Total chargeable gains		£12,000

$$\text{Chargeable gain} \times \frac{\text{Market value of shares in transferee company (share capital + premium)}}{\text{Total consideration received (share capital + premium + loan)}}$$

$$£12,000 \times \frac{£10,000 + £30,000}{£10,000 + £30,000 + £20,000}$$

$$£12,000 \times \frac{40,000}{60,000} = £8,000$$

Chargeable gain on disposal	12,000
Less: deferred	8,000
Assessable capital gain	£4,000
Cost of shares for capital gains tax purposes:	
Market value	40,000
Less: deferred gain	8,000
Net cost	£32,000

Although TCGA 1992, s 162 is the section designed to avoid capital gains tax on the transfer of a business to a company it does mean that all assets have to be transferred (except for cash) which can be inconvenient and expensive in terms of stamp duty.

It might, for example, be desirable to retain freehold property outside the company. This means that the property would have to be extracted from the business some time before the transfer, or sold back to the proprietors at market value immediately following the transfer.

Alternatively it might be preferable to take advantage of the gift of business asset relief available in TCGA 1992, s 165. Under these provisions, on a transfer of a business to a company, the shares would be issued to the proprietors for cash and the business assets which it was desired to transfer would be given to the company. There would then be an election jointly by the partners and the company under which the company would take over the base value of the partners for any future capital gains computation.

EXAMPLE 10.03

On the same facts as in example 10.02 the partner's desire to retain the freehold property and transfer the goodwill for no consideration, which is written up to market value in the company's books. To save stamp duty the debtors will be collected and the creditors paid by Aphrodite & Co.

The balance sheet of Aphrodite Ltd. at 1 January 1995 becomes.

	£			£
Share capital	2,000	Goodwill		20,000
Capital reserve	20,000	(cost Nil)		
Loan	10,000	Current assets:		
		Stock	12,000	
		Debtors	Nil	12,000
	£32,000			£32,000

Chargeable gain on partners in Aphrodite & Co.: Nil.

Cost of shares for capital gains tax purposes: £12,000

On 20 February 1995 the Institute of Chartered Accountants in England and Wales published a guidance note (TAX 7/95) on the tax implications of certain aspects of the incorporation of professional partnerships, as follows:

"Incorporation of professional partnerships: tax implications of certain aspects– guidance note (TAX 7/95)

INTRODUCTION

The incorporation of a professional partnership by means of the transfer of its business as a going concern to a company owned by the former partners gives rise to a number of potential tax problems. Some are recognised by the tax legislation, some dealt with by concession and others not dealt with at all.

The Tax Faculty has been in correspondence with the Inland Revenue about certain aspects of this matter the text of which is set out in the following pages. It included reference to the problems arising from the two points referred to in the last paragraph below and the statements mentioned were issued by the Revenue during the course of this correspondence.

For convenience this has been divided in sections as follows—
- A transfer of work in progress and debtors
- B interest relief
- C partnership annuities
- D corporate partnerships and TCGA 1992, s 162.

Particular attention is drawn to the issue on 20 June 1994 of the revised text of Concession A43 referred to at section B and to the article on page 151 of *Tax Bulletin* No 12 (August 1994) in respect of paragraph 5(*a*) of section C.

INCORPORATION OF PROFESSIONAL PARTNERSHIPS – TAX IMPLICATIONS
A   Transfer of work in progress and debtors
Partnership on earnings basis

1. The first potential problem is that there will practically always be an uplift in the basis of valuation because, for a variety of reasons, the partnership basis of valuation will fall short of a full earnings basis of a company. An example is when work in

progress (WIP) excludes partners' time in the partnership, but will include their salaries as employees of the company. The rate of tax and its timing will depend upon which of three treatments applies—

(*a*) transfer at partnership valuation, following which the uplift is taken in the company on revaluation of its opening WIP. (This would not normally be good accounting practice, but might nonetheless be adopted.);
(*b*) transfer at partnership valuation but, since the asset is purchased, the company does not revalue its opening WIP; and
(*c*) transfer at company valuation, so the uplift is taken in the closing WIP of the partnership.

2. If there is a revaluation of opening WIP in the company under (*a*), confirmation is sought that the uplift would fall within Case I, not Case VI. In that event, the only difference from the company not revaluing its WIP as under (*b*) would be that the profits would be deferred to the extent that the work is unbilled at the end of the company's first accounting period.

3. Please confirm that you would normally accept any of these three treatments as valid for taxation purposes provided that in cases (*a*) and (*b*) partnership valuation should be on the basis consistently used in the partnership accounts.

Revenue response
TA 1988 s 102(2) determines that if s 101(1)(*a*) applies the same figure is to be used for both parties to the agreement. If the terms of the transfer agreement are accepted and they provide that the WIP is transferred to the company at the partnership's closing valuation, scenario (*a*), then we will accept that s 101(1)(*a*) will apply. If the company revalues the WIP on acquisition the legislation overrides the company's accounts treatment so the uplift and the eventual profit arising out of that WIP will be assessed Case I on the company. Therefore the uplift could not be assessed Case VI at the Revenue's instigation. But under s 101(2) the partnership could elect that the difference between the original cost of the WIP and the s 101(1) valuation, in (*a*) the partners' closing valuation, should be assessed Case VI. With (*b*) the position is similar.

As the above is likely to apply in most cases we can generally provide the confirmation sought. Inspectors, however, will look closely at the application of s 101(1)(*a*), the transfer valuation basis adopted and the terms of the transfer agreement where the transfer valuation basis is not consistent with the basis previously used by the partnership, which itself must be acceptable. Subject to that we would accept that all three treatments are valid bases for transfer under s 101(1)(*a*).

4. Please also confirm that the transfer of the WIP in exchange for shares where TCGA 1992 s 162 rollover applies does not necessarily determine the transfer price of the WIP at market value for Case I/II purposes, and that inspectors will normally accept the price allocated to it in the sale agreement where it follows the basis of valuation consistently used in the partnership accounts.

Revenue response
Where an agreement for the sale of a professional business to a company in consideration for the issue of shares provides for an apportionment of the overall value of the business as between the various assets transferred, inspectors will normally accept such an apportionment unless it is clearly illusory, colourable or fraudulent. The value apportioned to professional WIP would therefore be accepted for TA 1988 s 101(1)(*a*) purposes if it represented the cost of the work on the basis consistently used to value the work for accounting purposes.

Partnership on conventional (eg bills delivered or cash) basis
5. Where the partnership does not account for WIP, the consideration (if any) paid for it by the company is assessable under Case VI (TA 1988 s 104(6)). Please confirm,

in consistency with [para] 4 above, that no consideration is assessable where the partnership assets are transferred for shares and a nil consideration is allocated to the WIP in the sale agreement.

6. Similarly, where the partnership does not account for debtors, please confirm that no consideration is assessable if the debtors are transferred in consideration for shares and a nil consideration is allocated in the sale agreement.

7. Please confirm that the same principles apply to any other conventional basis, i e one which is not an earnings basis.

Revenue response
If, as seems to be the case in cash or conventional bases cases, the consistent basis adopted has been not to value WIP and if the terms of the bargain are that the WIP is transferred for nil consideration then we would not seek to challenge the agreement. Then s 101(1) would not apply because 'in computing for any tax purpose the profits or gains of a profession' (this would not include the capital gains of the partners or the individual proprietor) there would not be 'a valuation . . . taken of the work . . . in progress at the discontinuance' (s 101(1)). TA 1988 ss 104(2), 106(2) (see our next two paras) have similar effect.

TA 1988 s 104 applies to tax the partners under Case VI on any sums received on or after discontinuance unless the sums were "otherwise chargeable to tax" (s 104(2)). If all the profit on the partnership's closing WIP is assessable on the company we would accept it would be excluded from Case VI charged by s 104(2). Thus if for the Company's tax purposes the opening WIP of the company is nil then there will be no Case VI charge on the WIP. TA 1988 s 106(2) (see our next para) has a similar effect.

If the terms of the bargain are that all the rights to the debts of the partnership are transferred to the company then under s 106(2), sums received which would otherwise be chargeable on the predecessor under Schedule D Case VI by virtue of s 104(1) are to be treated as business receipts of the successor. Therefore if the terms of the bargain are that nil consideration is given then for the company's tax purposes all receipts from those debtors would be the taxable business receipts.

INCORPORATION OF PROFESSIONAL PARTNERSHIPS – TAX IMPLICTIONS
B   Interest relief
1. Unless the company is close, the lack of interest relief on the working shareholders' borrowings for subscription or purchase of shares or for lending money to the company is a major bar to incorporation. The size of many professional companies will be such that they will not, in the normal way, be close.

2. Most professions restrict the amount of equity that may be held by non-members. For instance, an accountancy business carrying out a regulated audit has to have 75% of its equity owned by regulated individuals. Outside finance is generally limited by the lack of tangible asset cover. Accordingly, a professional company will tend to be under-capitalised if it cannot look to its shareholders for funds on a tax-effective basis. An owner-managed company of this sort cannot be compared with a quoted company that has institutional and portfolio investors and can offer good security. Under-capitalisation also reduces the ability of clients and the investing public to have effective redress when professional indemnity claims are made, particularly as insurance capacity in this market is severely limited. As the company would be owner-managed there is no good reason in principle why interest relief should not be given to working shareholders. Otherwise, it will make it very difficult for the equivalent of new partners to share in the ownership by becoming shareholders unless they have substantial private wealth – a retrogressive step.

3. In previous correspondence we asked if you would accept the case for an extension of Concession A43 so that partners who became the working shareholders of an owner-managed professional company would continue to obtain interest relief even if

the company was not close. You rejected this request (which itself would not help new working shareholders) on the grounds that it would introduce a radical extension to interest relief.

4. As an alternative, we asked if you would grant concessionary relief where the company is employee-controlled and the loan would satisfy TA 1988, s 361. You responded that s 361 was designed to cover an employee *buy-out*, involving a change of control, so extending Concession A43 would be too far removed from the aims of the legislation. This would, incidentally, introduce an anomaly – new working shareholders of the incorporated firm would gain relief for the first 12 months after incorporation under s 361, whereas their colleagues who were partners before, and working shareholders after, the incorporation, or who become shareholders more than 12 months after incorporation, would not.

5. We appreciate that the political climate is presently unsympathetic to any extension of interest relief, however deserving the cause. We therefore invite you to consider another approach to the problem. This is that given that it is not difficult to make a company close, you should be prepared to agree that certain methods of doing this would not be challenged.

6. Broadly speaking, a company is close if it is controlled by five or fewer individuals or by its directors, with shareholdings of associates of the relevant individuals being counted in. There are three basic ways in which this test might be met –

(*a*) have all the working shareholders (or sufficient of them to give voting control) as *directors*. Because the definition of a director contained in TA 1988 s 417 is not exclusive, someone formally appointed director would be a director for the purpose of s 414(1), even if there was an inner core of directors who had real responsibility for the company's policy;
(*b*) have all the working shareholders associates of one another by making them *partners* in a parallel partnership carrying on a segment of the business (although in this event care would have to be taken not to jeopardise s 162 relief in its entirety);
(*c*) have all the working shareholders associates of one another by making them trustees of a settlement of which they are themselves settlors, which holds shares in the company (see s 417(3)(*b*)). An example is an employee share trust.

The above solutions are artificial and conflict with commercial objectives. Nevertheless there will be a strong incentive for the larger firms to use one of them. Please would you confirm, therefore, that in the absence of any relieving provision you would not find them intrinsically objectionable.

Revenue response
Whether a company is close, for the purpose of s 414, depends on the particular facts. It is not necessarily the case that everyone who is styled a director is actually a director for these purposes. It is possible, however, for a company to have directors who, within the powers bestowed by the Articles of Association, exercise different degrees of power and responsibility within the company. Similarly, whether someone is actually a member of a partnership is a question of fact. As far as trustees are concerned, a participator in a company can be attributed with the rights and powers of the trustees of a settlement of which he or she is the settlor. The attribution is, however, only of those rights and powers which the trustees hold as trustees of that settlement and does not extend to those they hold in a personal capacity or as trustees of another settlement.

Note:
As stated above, in earlier correspondence the Institute requested that Concession A43 (issued in 1985) should be extended to meet the difficulties outlined above. This was not accepted by the Revenue and subsequent correspondence sought to explore other means of overcoming these difficulties.

On 20 June 1994, after the above exchange of correspondence, the Revenue issued a revised version of Concession A43 which extends the concession to cover cases where a partnership is incorporated into an employee controlled company.

This matter has, therefore, now been satisfactorily resolved in nearly all cases.

INCORPORATION OF PROFESSIONAL PARTNERSHIPS – TAX IMPLICATIONS
C Partnership annuities
Partners already retired
1. Please confirm your view that –

(*a*) where TCGA 1992 s 162 rollover applies on incorporation (assets exchanged for shares), the undertaking by the company to pay annuities, although strictly non-share consideration which would restrict the relief, by concession is treated as a payment for liabilities and therefore excluded from the consideration given for the chargeable assets; and

(*b*) where TCGA 1992 s 165 holdover is claimed (gift of business assets), the value of the undertaking to pay annuities (valued by reference to the cost of purchasing them from an insurance company) would produce a gain to the extent that it exceeded the base cost of the goodwill. In this connection we are unclear why it cannot be treated as payment for liabilities, as where s 162 applies.

Partners still working
2. You have told us that –

(*a*) under s 162, the undertaking by the company to pay annuities that commence in the future is not payment for an existing liability but part of the consideration given for the business transferred, thus restricting relief; and

(*b*) under s 165, there is also consideration so that relief is restricted.

3. This is regrettable. We have pointed out that in a typical situation the value of an annuity might be such that rollover relief is restricted by two-thirds – by contrast, if incorporation did not take place, Statement of Practice D12 para 8 would normally prevent capital gains tax being chargeable on retirement.

4. Very many professional practices still undertake to pay annuities to partners when they retire. If such a practice were to incorporate today, it would have substantial goodwill for which, typically, two forms of consideration would be regarded as having been given – the issue of shares and the undertaking to pay annuities in the figure. If deferment of the gain on the second element is denied, this will be a serious impediment to incorporation. The fact that you have not seen cases in which these give rise to a difficulty suggests either that partnerships have been prevented from incorporating, or – much more seriously – that the point has not been noticed by either the firm or the Revenue. It seems to us inevitable that the point does exist and is potentially damaging.

Revenue response
Where a business is transferred in exchange for shares, any gains are deferred by reducing the acquisition cost of those shares, but relief is restricted where any other consideration is given. An undertaking to pay an annuity involves taking on a liability, and in strictness s 162(4) will apply, since taking over a liability represents other consideration. This is, of course, amended by Concession D32. Concession D32, however, only applies where relief is due under s 162, and is not relevant for s 165 purposes.

It is worth noting although s 162 is automatically applied against any chargeable gain where the conditions are met, if a taxpayer makes a claim to, or is entitled to, relief under ss 152, 163 and 164, such relief will be given in priority to s 162.

A claim may also be made under s 165 although, in practice, this would not apply where full consideration was given for the assets or the transfer was by way of a bargain at arm's length. In those circumstances, and subject to any relief being given under s 152 etc, the only relief would be under s 162.

In the circumstances you describe, an agreement to pay an annuity would probably restrict relief under s 165 in practice.

Where the annuity relates to future payments to existing partners, there is no existing liability, and Concession D32 does not apply, but represents consideration within either ss 162 or 165. Statement of Practice D12, to which you refer, relates to the payment of annuities to retiring partners and has no relevance to gains made on incorporation by the continuing partners.

Post-incorporation annuity payments
5. Please confirm you view that –
   (a) the payment of annuities is allowable as an annual charge of the company under s 338;
   (b) the payment of an annuity to a former member of a partnership is excluded from TA 1988 s 125 – (annual payments for non-taxable consideration) – similarly, annuities payable by the company as a result of having taken over the obligation to pay them are in practice so excluded.

Revenue response
Item (a)
An annuity is not treated as a charge for the purpose of s 338 if it is not made under a liability incurred for a valuable and sufficient consideration. Where a company undertakes to pay an annuity as part of the deal whereby it acquires the business of a partnership, there is no reason in principle why such an annuity should not be treated as a charge on these grounds.

Item (b)
We can confirm that annuities paid by a partnership to a former member for the acquisition of a business or a share in a partnership are excluded from the scope of s 125.

Where a company takes over an obligation to pay the annuities, provided the payments are made in respect of bona fide commercial transactions, we can confirm that it is our practice to regard the payments as outside the scope of s 125.

INCORPORATION OF PROFESSIONAL PARTNERSHIPS – TAX IMPLICATIONS
D   Corporate partnerships and TCGA 1992 s 162
1. Capital gains tax rollover under s 162 depends upon the whole of the business being transferred by an individual. Having one or more corporate partners is not uncommon in professions such as those of surveyors and consulting engineers. Strictly, s 162 cannot apply to the individuals who are partners in such a partnership because part of the business is carried on by a company. Please confirm that the Revenue continue to apply the concession . . . [reproduced below] that s 162 relief is available to partners who are individuals where the partnership includes a company.

Revenue response
We can confirm that this applies to individuals. (Corporate partners are excluded under s 162(1).)

EXTRACT REFERRED TO UNDER SECTION D
Rollover relief – incorporation of business with individual and corporate partners
Where a sole trader or partnership incorporates a business. CGTA 1979 s 123 provides relief where the whole of the business is transferred by a person who is not a company for shares and cash. Where one of the partners is a company, s 123 could strictly not apply because those partners who are individuals are not transferring the whole business, but only their collective shares.

Somerset House have confirmed however, that provided the whole of the business has been transferred to a company, the Revenue will view each partner separately, thus enabling the individuals to have relief, but not the company. In addition, relief will be granted where one partner takes cash and another shares. This means a degree of flexibility could exist over the proportion of shares and cash which is taken in exchange for the business, so long as the whole of the business is exchanged wholly or partly for shares."

Extra statutory concession A43 referred to above provides:

"*A43. Interest relief: investment in partnerships and close companies*
1   Under TA 1988, ss 360–363 income tax relief is available for interest paid by individuals on a loan taken out to invest in, or on-lend to, a partnership or close company. The relief is subject to various conditions and ceases to be available when the conditions are no longer met. Relief is also reduced or withdrawn if the borrower recovers any capital from the partnership or close company without using it to repay the loan – for example, if he sells or exchanges his interest or shares.
2   Strictly relief ceases to be due where (*a*) the partnership is incorporated into a close company, or (*b*) as a result of a company reorganisation shares in one close company are exchanged for shares in another. In practice, however, relief for interest on the loan is not discontinued in such circumstances, provided that the general conditions for relief would be met if the loan had been a new loan taken out to invest in the new company. The rules restricting or withdrawing relief where the borrower recovers any capital continue to apply in the normal way."

CORPORATE PARTNERS

As an alternative to having a service company, on transferring the whole of the partnership business to a company, it can, if allowed by the appropriate professional body, be worth considering having a corporate partner in the partnership. The partners could, therefore, own shares in a company which was itself a partner in the partnership. Surplus profits could be channelled into the corporate partner where they would be subject to corporation tax. TA 1988, s 114 provides that where one of the partners in the partnership is a company its share of profits is subject to corporation tax in the accounting period as if it were a separate Schedule D, Case I source of income. If the accounting period of the company differs from that of the partnership the company's share of the partnership profits is apportioned on a time basis to the company's accounting period. Partners who are individuals in a company partnership are assessed on their share of the profits in the normal manner, although corporation tax rules apply in calculating the adjusted profits and in computing capital allowances. Because companies are assessed to tax on a current year basis and individuals on a preceding year basis there can be scope for mitigating tax by changing the profit sharing allocation between a company and individuals in partnership, although the blatant exploitation of these rules is now limited by TA 1988, s 116 which is an anti-avoidance section aimed at preventing the exploitation of group relief and capital allowances in a trading partnership where a limited company is one of the partners.

TA 1988, s 116 applies where a company partner's share in the profits or losses of the accounting period are enjoyed by other members of the partnership, or where the company partner receives any payment or benefit other than a payment for group relief in respect of its share of the loss of the partnership. In such circumstances the company will only be able to take its share of any trading loss or charges on income against its share of partnership profits. A company cannot set non-partnership trading losses against its share of partnership profits TA 1988, s 116(2)(*a*). That section carries further restrictions, the partnership profits will not be available to cover non-partnership charges on income. The company cannot set advance corporation tax against the corporation tax liability on its share of partnership profits. Casual partnership profits assessed under Schedule D, Case VI are treated in the same way as those that formed the profit or losses of a trade under Schedule D, Case I. The company's share of profits is determined in accordance with TA 1988, s 114 except that capital allowances and charges are also taken into account.

There is no automatic cessation under TA 1988, s 113(1) where there is a change in a corporate partner (TA 1988, 114(3)(*b*)), although the normal rules apply where changes in individual partners occur. Although in most cases the shares in a service company or in the corporate member of a company partnership will be held by the partners or by their spouses, there could be advantages in holding the shares through family trusts such as a maintenance and accumulation settlement in favour of the partner's children, which might be particularly valuable if the company owns the partnership premises or in other cases where the value is likely to be substantial.

Chapter 11

Provision for retirement

GENERAL

It is common for a partnership deed to be specific in directing that each partner make retirement provision for himself.

A minimum level of contribution may even be prescribed. The most tax efficient way of making such a contribution will, therefore, quite naturally be at the forefront of each partner's mind. As a self-employed person, a partner will not be entitled to the State earnings related pension (SERPS) and can, therefore, only look forward to the basic retirement pension from the State. The various methods by which retirement provision can be made are now considered in turn.

PERSONAL PENSION PLANS

Personal pension plans (PPPs) are issued in accordance with Inland Revenue requirements set out in TA 1988, ss 630 to 653 and the guidance notes IR76. A wide range of institutions are authorised to issue these plans including life companies, unit trust managers, building societies, banking organisations and friendly societies.

The contributions paid into such a plan are invested and the funds accumulated at retirement age to provide the partner with a lifetime pension. This pension can include provision for either full or limited inflation increases and can continue on death in part or whole to the surviving spouse. Up to 25% of the fund at retirement can be paid out as a tax-free cash sum with the pension being reduced accordingly.

The fund into which personal pension contributions are paid is a tax-free one, considerably improving the compound growth and making such an investment highly attractive. Furthermore, the plan holder is allowed to claim his contributions as a deduction from his total income for tax purposes. The Revenue require form PPCC in support of such a claim and there are limits on the level of premiums that will qualify for the relief. For the tax year 1995–96, the limitation is based on the following percentages of net relevant earnings:

Age at 6 April 1995	Percentage of net relevant earnings
Up to 35	17.5
36 to 45	20
46 to 50	25
51 to 55	30
56 to 60	35
Over 60	40

Net relevant earnings consist of earnings from the self-employed occupation or partnership or from a non-pensionable employment. Non-pensionable, in this context, merely means that there is no occupational scheme as defined by TA 1988, s 623(3) available for the employment concerned. A partner's net relevant earnings will be his share of the profits for the year of assessment as computed for income tax purposes after deducting capital allowances. Net relevant earnings are limited to a maximum of £82,200 for the tax year 1996–97.

The contribution is deducted primarily from the earnings to which it relates and relief is given against the assessable profits for the year in which it is paid.

If the qualifying contribution paid, or deemed to have been paid, in a tax year is less than the permissible percentage of net relevant earnings there is a balance of unused relief which may be carried forward. If in one of the following six years a contribution is paid in excess of the appropriate percentage of net relevant earnings for that year, part of the unused relief brought forward from an earlier year may be used up. The relief is given in the year in which the contribution is paid, or is deemed to be paid, and is not backdated to the year in which the unused relief arose. Unused relief is absorbed on a first in first out basis.

Backdating is otherwise severely restricted and the only option is to elect for a payment to be treated as having been paid in the previous tax year to that in which it was actually paid. If there were no net relevant earnings in that year, the election can go back one further year, i e to the tax year two years before that in which the contribution was actually paid. This election must be made by 6 July following the year of actual payment.

By carefully planning to use this combination of backdating and the carry forward of unused relief, tax relief on pension contributions can be maximised by shifting into those years in which the highest rate of tax is payable. Care should also be taken where feasible to ensure that earlier years' relief is utilised before it goes out of time.

The tax relief on the contributions, together with growth within a tax-free fund, combine to make a personal pension plan one of the most attractive of all investments. It should, however, be remembered that a personal pension cannot be surrendered or assigned and considerable loss of access to capital is one price which must be paid for this tax efficiency, and the pension annuity, when payable, will be treated in full as taxable income.

With the notable exception of the tax-free cash sum portion of the pension, there is, therefore, an element of tax deferral rather than of complete tax avoidance. It may be desired to maximise the guaranteed income in retirement rather than receive a lump sum. However, it would still be desirable to take the lump sum and instead purchase an ordinary annuity. Part of the income under a purchased annuity is treated as a tax-free return of capital, thus improving total income as against the fully taxable annuity paid under a personal pension.

Under TA 1988, s 640(3) it is permissible to allocate part of the allowable premium, but not exceeding 5% of net relevant earnings, to provide for the payment of a lump sum on death before normal retirement age. This parallels the death in service cover which may be provided under an occupational pension scheme and offers extremely cost-effective family protection. There is no restriction on whom the life assurance benefit may be paid to and by writing this under a discretionary or accumulation and maintenance trust the death benefit need not form part of the partner's estate for IHT purposes. This is also true of the return of accumulated funds which would be paid as a death benefit from the personal pension itself.

The pension and tax-free cash sum secured under the personal pension contract must commence between the ages of fifty and seventy-five, although there are provisions to take benefits earlier in cases of ill health or for certain occupations where earlier retirement is usual, for example, sports people. It is not necessary to actually retire in order to take benefits.

It is not always appreciated that the pension annuity need not be purchased from the company with whom the personal pension plan is held. Indeed, if the personal pension provider is any institution other than a life insurance company it will not be possible to do so. It is common for significant improvements in the pension annuity to be secured by exercising the "open market option" and transferring the accumulated pension fund to another insurer to purchase the annuity.

Further flexibility is provided by FA 1995, s 58 and Sch. 11 in that the purchase of the annuity may now be deferred up to the age of seventy-five with the pension income being drawn from the fund in the mean time. This is a very welcome provision in that annuity rates vary considerably, both with interest rates generally and according to the age of the purchaser. The best time to lock into an annuity can, therefore, be selected by the pension plan holder rather than being at the whim of the markets at the time of retirement. This additional freedom does bring with it considerable dangers for the unwary. Imagine, for example, the disastrous effects of continuing to draw a regular income from an investment fund during a bear market. The ongoing investment medium, therefore, requires careful selection and there can be no guarantees that the annuity ultimately purchased will be as large as it otherwise would have been. One further benefit of deferring annuity purchase is that the personal pension fund remains intact to be paid out to the pension's nominated beneficiaries, less a 35% tax charge, in the event of death before the age of seventy-five.

GROUP LIFE COVER

Reference has been made above to the purchase of term life assurance under a personal pension. It is understood that some insurers may be prepared to provide cover to partnerships on a group basis with resultant premium savings. Individual s 640 contracts would, of course, still be issued to each member within the group.

RETIREMENT ANNUITY POLICIES

Personal pension plans were introduced with effect from 1 July 1988. Previous to this partners were able to contribute to retirement annuity policies (RAPs) under TA 1988, ss 619–622 which operated under similar principles. New retirement annuity policies ceased to be available with the introduction of personal policies. It is, however, still possible to increment RAPs by both single premiums and by increasing regular premiums. Partners with existing incrementable RAPs should be aware of the following advantages which these have.
- The tax-free cash sum is calculated as three times the remaining annual pension after commutation. This may be greater than the 25% of fund available under the personal pension rules.
- There is no ceiling to the net relevant earnings which may be eligible for a retirement annuity contribution. The percentage limits are, however, lower as follows:

Age at 6 April 1995	Percentage of net relevant earnings
Up to age 50	17.5
51 to 55	20
56 to 60	22.5
Over 60	27.5

These contribution limits will be beneficial to those who have earnings significantly in excess of the ceiling for personal pensions.

Partners who will benefit from higher levels of tax relief under retirement annuities should avoid paying anything at all into personal pensions in the appropriate years. Any contribution whatsoever to a personal pension in a particular tax year will cause the personal pension rates to apply, together with the ceiling on eligible net relevant earnings, thus restricting the relief available. For those potentially in this position great care needs to be taken, particularly before taking out regular premium personal pension, e.g. to provide life cover. By paying only single premiums to personal pension plans this problem can be avoided and from year to year contributions can be paid to whichever type of arrangement will give the maximum relief.

Sometimes it will be desirable to have a greater spread of investment risk and the only way of achieving this will be to take out a new personal pension plan which will, in turn, restrict the total relief available for pension contributions. This can be avoided by paying into retirement annuities and personal pensions in alternate years. In the years in which only personal pensions are paid the balance of otherwise higher retirement annuity relief can be carried forward and utilised in the following years. In that following year no personal pension contribution would be paid, thus avoiding the ceiling on eligible earnings.

The pension bought under a retirement annuity contract cannot commence before the age of sixty. If an earlier pension is required this can be secured by making a transfer of funds to a personal pension with a consequent restriction on the tax-free lump sum available.

SELF-INVESTED PERSONAL PENSIONS

Most personal pension arrangements are self-contained packages with the structure, administration and investment all being handled in-house by the provider. Typically, the plan holder will have a number of investment funds to choose from, depending upon his reading of the investment markets and tolerance of investment risk. That apart, all investment choices are at the discretion of the fund managers. Inland Revenue Memorandum 101 does, however, permit a wide range of investments, namely:

- quoted and USM traded stocks and shares;
- stocks and shares quoted on a recognised overseas stock exchange;
- unit and investment trusts;
- insurance company managed and other unit-linked funds;
- deposit accounts;
- commercial property.

Certain restrictions are also placed, particularly regarding transactions with pension scheme members and those connected with them. Commercial property may, however, be held by a personal pension scheme and let on a commercial rent to a business with whom the pension scheme member is connected. The commercial premises may not be purchased from a connected person, e.g. partner, but there is no objection where the acquisition is from an unconnected third party.

For partnerships, the possibility of acquiring premises for their business use will undoubtedly be the major attraction of a self-invested arrangement, although it may also appeal to a partnership of investment professionals wishing to take charge of their own pension scheme investments.

Taking the example of the acquisition of commercial property, this may be held in one of two ways: first, by the combined personal pension schemes of the individual partners; or, secondly, by a private fund set up by the nominated insurance company, the pension scheme holders then buying units in that fund. The rents paid to the fund will be tax free but still allowable as a tax deduction against partnership profits and can be used to service any loans taken out to assist in the purchase. When the property is eventually disposed of any capital gain will also be tax free.

Clearly, there must be ample unused and ongoing personal pension reliefs available among the partners to finance the initial deposit and to fund future loan repayments.

The principle is very similar to that of a small self-administered occupational pension scheme. The major difference is that no direct loanback facility is available from the pension fund to the partner or partnership.

PARTNERSHIP FRIENDLY SOCIETIES

A commonly used alternative to the self-invested personal pension is the partnership friendly society. However, with a minimum of seven members being required this will not be appropriate for smaller partnerships.

A partnership friendly society is registered under the Friendly Societies Act 1974 and may issue personal pensions to its members. Once again, the most common motivation for the formation of such a society will be the purchase of commercial property for use by the partnership in its business. The fact that no external pension provider needs to be involved may also appeal to partnerships which like to take personal control of all aspects of their financial arrangements.

CONSULTANCY AGREEMENTS

It used to be popular to pay what were basically partnership pensions as consultancy agreements in order to have the income treated as earned income of the recipient. It is often no longer necessary to do this in view of the provisions of TA 1988, s 628 dealt with below under pensions from the firm.

If a consultancy agreement is entered into it is important that it should refer only to the work to be done as in the case of *Hale v Shea* (1964) 42 TC 260 it was held that where a partner gave up his share in a partnership in return for a proportion of the profits over the next fifteen years the amount so paid was correctly assessed under Schedule D, Case I as consultancy income. The services rendered were negligible in that case and any consultancy payment that is excessive for the value of the work done would be liable to be disallowed by the Revenue under TA 1988, s 74 as not wholly and exclusively for the purposes of the trade. If the consultant is validly working for the partnership he may be paid a reasonable remuneration which might be assessed under either Schedule D or Schedule E depending upon the terms of his agreement with the partnership. If the consultancy income is assessed under Schedule D the consultant may have to register for value added tax purposes if his turnover is likely to be in excess of £47,000, the current registration limit for that tax.

A consultancy assessed under Schedule E on an employer/employee relationship is likely to be more beneficial in many cases as it will enable the consultant to belong to an occupational pension scheme. It is not uncommon for a senior partner to retire as an equity partner and to continue work full-time as a consultant for a period in order to increase his pension under the occupational pension scheme rules with the approval of the Pension Schemes Office, see IR 12 para 3.5. It sometimes happens that an individual has a period as an employee with a firm before becoming an equity partner and it is possible at a later date for him to join an occupational pension scheme and include the service prior to becoming a partner as part of his overall service as an employee so that he will be eligible to join an occupational pension scheme to provide for a pension, and if the total service exceeds twenty years, this can be for a pension of two-thirds final salary at retirement.

Commercially, it can sometimes be desirable to retain a former partner as a consultant so that his name may be kept on the notepaper and his personal goodwill preserved for the benefit of the continuing partners.

PENSIONS FROM THE FIRM

A pension from the firm on retirement because of old age or ill health may be treated as a charge for basic and higher rates of tax on the earned income of the paying partners under TA 1988, s 683. In order for the pension to be regarded as earned income of the recipient under the provisions of TA 1988, s 628, it must be within the allowable limits, i e no more than 50% of the average profits of the retiring partner for the best three out of the last seven years prior to his retirement during which he had devoted substantially the whole of his time to acting as a partner. Such income may be index linked to the end of the calendar year before retirement – under TA 1988, s 628(2). The payment must be in accordance with the partnership agreement or some supplementary agreement. A firm may make increases in the pension paid to a former partner in order that it may keep pace with inflation. The increase is measured by means of the General Index of Retail Prices for the December preceding the year of assessment for which the revised pension is to be paid compared with the December in the year of assessment in which he ceased to be a member of the partnership. If he ceased to be a member of the partnership before 1974–75 he is deemed to have ceased to be a member in that year. A pension from the firm may be a percentage of the profits in which case it will hopefully keep pace with inflation, and it is permissible for the pension to continue for a widow or dependant.

A pension from the firm has a number of disadvantages. It is usually limited to a fairly short period of, say, ten years, not for any tax reason but because the continuing partners would be unwilling and indeed ill advised to enter into an unlimited commitment to continue paying a pension for the life of the retired partner or even as in some cases, the life of his widow. This means, however, that at the end of the fixed term, if the partner or his widow is still alive, there could be some embarrassment if the pension from the firm constituted a large proportion of the former partner's or his widow's income. It is, therefore, suggested that a pension from the firm might be a supplement to a properly funded pension through a retirement annuity or occupational pension scheme, but should not be the sole means of support after retirement. Such a pension is sometimes taken in lieu of a capital payment for goodwill and in accordance with paragraph 8 of the Inland Revenue SP/D12 as amended, such an annuity would not be regarded as a disposal of its capitalised equivalent in view of the provisions of TCGA 1992, s 37(3). The annuity (including one-ninth of any capital sum paid in addition) must not exceed the allowable amounts as set out in that paragraph, ie a maximum annuity of up to two-thirds of the average profits of the retired partner for the best three out of the last seven years prior to his retirement after ten years service as a partner. For a shorter period of service as a partner the allowable annuity is reduced (see Chapter 7).

A further disadvantage of a pension from the firm is that the validity of the pension depends to a large extent on the continued success of the firm which would be beyond the control of the pensioner once he had ceased to be a partner.

If several partners left the firm, either on death or retirement, within a relatively short space of time, the pension liability could be too high a burden on the continuing partners, leading to the enforced dissolution of the partnership or abatement of the pensions to the detriment of the former partners entitled thereto. If the liability became too high a burden, not only would the continuing partners resent the proportion of their income going to former partners, but it would prevent new partners coming into the firm and mergers which might be commercially desirable.

The problem to be avoided is a partner under-providing for his widow and dependants or for his pension, so that on death or retirement his surviving partners are left with a moral responsibility to look after his family, which should have been provided for by proper insurance.

OTHER ASPECTS OF PERSONAL PENSIONS

Loans

Some policies allow for a loan, either from a bank or an associate of the pension provider, to be taken on on an interest only basis. The intention would be that the lump sum commutation on the maturity of the policy would be used to repay the loan. Usually, some form of security is required and loans may be restricted to certain professions or as a multiple of the annual premium.

Costs

A personal pension may be a single or regular premium contract. A single premium contract will suffer a one-off charge and the balance will be invested. A regular premium contract provides a useful savings discipline but typically charges relating to the whole life of the contract may be deducted in the early years. If a regular premium contract such as this is kept up to maturity it is possible that the overall level of charges will be less than a number of single premium contracts of a like amount. However, if such a contract is not kept in force the impact on the fund can be penal. A number of pension providers are now developing contracts on which charges are taken on a level basis throughout the life of the plan rather than being front end loaded.

Investment funds

We have already touched upon the investments permitted by the Inland Revenue. Many personal pensions are, however, still invested on a with-profits basis where bonuses are declared at intervals on the policy which, once declared, remain attached to the policy so long as it persists to maturity. Alternatively, the premiums may be invested in a series of funds invested in equities, properties, gilt-edged securities or the like. Unit prices fluctuate in accordance with the markets and can decrease in value as well as increased. Switches can generally be made between funds without penalty. It is advisable to consider switching to more secure funds as one approaches the normal retirement date. This avoids the situation where a fall in stock-market values occurs close to retirement with a consequent reduction in the value of the fund available to buy the pension.

Inland Revenue investigation settlements

On 31 July 1991, the Revenue issued the following Press Release. This supersedes Statement of Practice SP 9/80 (which dealt only with retirement annuity relief).

> "**Investigation settlements: retirement annuities and personal pension relief (SP 9/91)**
>
> 1   When an assessment to tax becomes final and conclusive more than six years after the end of the year to which it relates, TA 1988, ss 625(3), 642(4) provide special rules for taking account of any unused personal pension or retirement annuity relief arising from the assessment. In particular the taxpayer may pay contributions to utilise that relief and elect that the relief shall be allowed for the year of assessment in which the contributions are paid. These must be in addition to the normal maximum for that year under either TA 1988, s 619(2) (for retirement annuities) or TA 1988, s 640 (for personal pensions). Both the payment of the contributions and the making of the election must take place within six months of the assessment becoming final.
>
> 2   Where incorrect returns and accounts are found to have been submitted, offers in settlement of liability to tax, interest and penalties are often accepted by the Board of Inland Revenue without assessment of all the tax. In such an investigation settlement the absence of assessments means that the conditions for obtaining unused relief under either TA 1988, s 625(3) or 624(4) are not satisfied.
>
> 3   Nevertheless, where a settlement is reached in circumstances where—
>
> > – assessments which would have given rise to unused relief are not made; or
> > – assessments have been made and appealed against but not formally determined,
> >   and the tax for the years of assessment concerned is included in the settlement;
>
> claims under TA 1988, s 625(3) or 642(4) will be accepted if—
>
> > *(a)* the settlement includes tax on relevant earnings for a year of assessment which ended more than six years before the date of the letter accepting the offer and which, if assessed, would give rise to unused relief; and
> > *(b)* within six months of the date of the letter accepting the offer the taxpayer both—
> >
> > > (i) pays a qualifying contribution or premium to cover all or part of the unused relief, and
> > > (ii) makes a formal election under either TA 1988, s 625(3)(*b*) or s 624(4)(*b*).
>
> 4   It should be noted that unused relief carried forward can only be utilised by the payment of contributions or premiums in excess of the maximum applying under

whichever is applicable of TA 1988, s 619 or 640. It is only this excess that must be paid within the six months period referred to in para. 3(*b*). Contributions or premiums up to the normal limits for the year of assessment may be paid within the normal time span for TA 1988, ss 619, 639 and 641."

Doctors and dentists

Pension provision for doctors and dentists is a complex area which is outside the scope of this book.

Transfers

A number of provisions, including TA 1988, s 638(2), the PSS (Transfer Payments) Regulations 1988, SS(P)A 1975, Sch. 1A Sch. 13, together with the Personal and Occupational Pension Schemes (Modification of Enactments) Regulations 1987, gives the member of a personal pension the right to transfer his fund value to another personal pension or to an occupational pension scheme. Similarly, a personal pension may receive a transfer from other schemes. This right does, however, need to be exercised only with extreme caution and after a full assessment of the costs and potential benefits of so doing.

Trusts

The advisability of placing death benefits under trust has been discussed earlier in this chapter. The question arises as to whether the premiums paid will in any way give rise to a transfer of value for inheritance tax purposes. The exemption under IHTA 1984, s 151 will cover benefits arising from a pension fund on death before retirement. Premiums paid to a separated pension plan providing only term assurance cover should be exempt within the annual gifts exemption (IHTA 1984, s 19) or as normal expenditure out of income (IHTA 1984, s 21). Placing the death before retirement benefits of an existing pension fund under trust may, however, still be deemed to be a transfer for inheritance tax purposes if the pension plan member was in a poor state of health at that time.

Waiver of premiums

Where regular contributions are paid it is common for insurance companies to offer cover which provides for the premiums due to be made up should the plan holder be unable to work long term due to illness or disability. A small additional premium is charged for this facility.

OCCUPATIONAL PENSION SCHEMES

Although a partner, as a self-employed individual assessed under Schedule D, is not eligible to join an occupational pension scheme he might be so eligible in his capacity as a director or employee of a service company or associated trading company, or as a consultant assessed to tax under Schedule E, or as a salaried partner assessed under Schedule E. A partner's wife employed by the firm or by the service company could also be eligible to join an occupational pension scheme.

Many partnerships will also have an occupational pension scheme for the benefit of senior staff. All schemes have to be approved under the provisions of TA 1988, s 590 et seq. A controlling director, i e one with more than 5% equity interest in the share capital, is also able to join an occupational pension scheme. It is possible to tailor a pension scheme for an individual employee (individual pension arrangements or IPA) whether or not there is a general scheme for any other members of the staff. An occupational pension scheme involves the employer paying a premium to the trustees of a pension fund, who will usually delegate day to day responsibility to an insurance company, who will invest the proceeds and use the amount in the fund to pay pensions to former employees in due course and to provide other benefits allowed by the Pension Schemes Office. The Pension Schemes Office of the Inland Revenue, Lynwood Road, Thames Ditton, Surrey KT7 0DP have considerable power to control and supervise occupational pension schemes, the legislation governing such schemes being broadly enabling legislation. The Pension Schemes Office publish their rules in booklet IR 12 as amended by subsequent Pension Schemes Office Memoranda which are published from time to time.

The occupational pension fund is a tax-free fund on investment income in that there is no UK income tax, corporation tax or capital gains tax liability on such income.

There is no limit on the contribution made to the fund by the employer in monetary or percentage terms as for a professional pension scheme but there is a limit on the benefits that may be funded for. The employee may contribute to the occupational fund up to 15% of the income from the employment and any such contributions will qualify for full tax relief and be treated as a deduction from his earned income for tax purposes. So far as the employer's contribution is concerned, if it is an ordinary annual contribution it will be allowed in the year of payment. If it is a special contribution the tax relief may be spread in accordance with the Inland Revenue Pension Schemes Office rules as published in IR 12, para 5.7. If the premium is less than £25,000, or the employer's total ordinary annual contributions to exempt approved schemes if greater, no spread is required. If the premium exceeds this it is spread over a number of years.

A number of different regimes govern the benefits which may be taken from an occupational pension scheme, depending upon the date of joining. Under the current regime pensionable earnings are subject to a ceiling of £82,200 (1996–97).

The limits on the benefits that may be funded for under an occupational pension scheme are two-thirds of the final salary as a pension after twenty years' service with a lower maximum pension for shorter periods of service. A widow's or widower's pension may be provided of four-ninths of the final salary, i e two-thirds of the member's pension. It is possible to provide for death in service life cover of up to four times final salary. If the employee died in service the lump sum would be paid to the trustees of the pension fund who in turn would pay this amount at their discretion to the estate of the deceased employee or to any individual such as the surviving spouse or to any children. It is common practice for the employee to indicate to the pension scheme trustees in writing how he would like them to exercise this discretion which is known as a "letter of wishes". A payment from a pension scheme to the employee's children, for example, would be entirely free of inheritance tax under IHTA 1984, s 151. It is, therefore, often desirable for an employee to request the trustees to pay the death in service life cover direct to his children free of inheritance tax and leave the bulk of his free estate direct to his widow, which would normally be exempt from inheritance tax under IHTA 1984, s 18. A lifetime director or 20% director at the age of seventy-five or more can only have death in service life cover paid direct to his estate or to his widow.

When the employee reaches normal pension age, whether in fact he retires or not, he can commute part of his pension for a tax-free lump sum under the current regime. The maximum lump sum is 2¼ times the pre-commutation pension payable under the scheme.

It is possible to provide for pension increases after retirement and to pre-fund for such increases on the assumption that they will be up to 5.3% per annum compound. Such pensions are usually known as escalating or dynamic pensions. It is only possible to guarantee post-retirement increase of up to 3% per annum compound. In practice, the Pension Schemes Office will allow post-retirement increases that keep pace with the increase in the General Index of Retail Prices since retirement, provided that the fund can support such increases, and it is permissible to make further post-retirement payments to the fund to enable such increases to be made.

There are two alternative definitions of final salary. It is possible to take a single year's salary plus the average of any variable remuneration such as bonuses or commission over a three-year period of any years ending in the five years immediately prior to retirement. If the remuneration is chosen for a year other than that ending with retirement, it is possible to increase the actual remuneration by the increase in the General Index of Retail Prices from the end of the year chosen to the end of the month prior to retirement to arrive at a dynamised final salary. The alternative definition of final salary is to take the average emoluments for any three consecutive years ending in the ten years immediately prior to retirement and, again, it is possible to adjust each year's income in accordance with the increase in retail prices. A 20% director, somebody who with his associates controls 20% or more of the equity share capital, must use the second of these two alternative definitions of final salary. It will be seen from the definition of final salary that where the remuneration has not kept pace with inflation, either because of lack of profitability, wage freezes of one description or another, pursuing a dividend policy to avoid National Insurance contributions or merely because the remuneration would be taxed at such a high level that it is not worth drawing, the dynamised final salary for pension purposes can exceed the actual salary at retirement and a pension based on two-thirds of this notional final salary may not be much less than, and could conceivably be more than, the salary at retirement date. It is not possible to use the index linked increase of final salary merely for the purposes of commuting the pension, but if the index linking is used for the pension it can be used for the commutation.

An occupational pension scheme will normally provide for retirement at the age of seventy at the latest. If the employee continues to work after that date the four times death in service life cover may be retained for him and paid to his children, for example, even if he did not die until, say, the age of eighty-five, provided that he was still working. The exception is if he is a 20% director in which case from the age of seventy-five the lump sum can only be paid to his estate or his widow (see IR 12, para 11.12). This should be compared with the position under the lifetime directorship arrangements outlined below.

The advantages of an occupational pension scheme, particularly as regards levels of funding, make it desirable in many cases to arrange for substantial Schedule E income for partners, for example, as remuneration from an associated trading company.

UNAPPROVED RETIREMENT BENEFIT SCHEMES

If the partner can arrange an employment he may be able to take advantage of an unapproved scheme. It was FA 1989 that removed the stigma of illegitimacy from unapproved retirement schemes. Prior to this date, the mention of "unapproved" in relation to pension schemes carried a connotation of either:

failure to gain exempt approved status; or

removal of previously awarded exempt approved status.

Therefore, as such, the initial reaction of practitioners was one of limited interest.

Consequently, it was not until the taxation treatment of unapproved schemes was codified by the Inland Revenue in August 1991 that more advisers began to explore the potential benefits of such unapproved arrangements.

The Inland Revenue's publication "Tax Treatment of 'Top-up' Pension Schemes" confirmed the status of unapproved schemes as legitimate retirement planning products and, also, dispelled any myths that they were short-term schemes exploiting legislative loopholes that would soon be blocked.

The unapproved arrangements fall into two categories, as follows.

1. Unfunded

This consists simply of a promise by the employer to pay a pension or lump sum at retirement. This may be attractive where the employer is a substantial organisation but is unlikely to be attractive to employees who fear the organisation may find itself unable to honour its undertakings in twenty years' time or more.

Therefore this arrangement is insecure and should the employer be taken over, or wound-up, the entire benefit could be lost.

2. Funded

This involves a commitment from the employer with the creation of a tangible fund into which the employer *pays* contributions on behalf of the member. These plans are commonly known as FURBs (Funded Unapproved Retirement Benefits Schemes).

Unapproved retirement benefit schemes are not available to the self-employed and will, therefore, only be of interest to partnerships in so far as remuneration is taken through a service company or for certain highly paid employees.

One feature of the development of unapproved pension schemes is that close attention is being paid by the Inland Revenue to the exact definition of "retirement benefits scheme". This is because the FA 1989 is effectively permitting the establishment of schemes that look quite unlike a traditional pension scheme.

A retirement benefits scheme is defined under ICTA 1988, s 601 as: "A scheme for the provision of benefits consisting of, or including, relevant benefits".

Therefore, no matter what form the scheme takes, it is only a retirement benefits scheme for the purposes of the legislation if it includes "relevant benefits" among the benefits it gives. Relevant benefits are defined in ICTA 1988, s 612. They include a pension, lump sum, gratuity or other similar benefit which is, or will be, given:

(i) when a person retires or dies;
(ii) in anticipation of retirement;
(iii) after a person has retired or died (if the reason for payment is in recognition of past service); or

(iv) as compensation for any change in the conditions of a continuing employment.

Accidental death and disability benefits (whether regular payments of lump sums) are *not* relevant benefits if they are payable solely because of an employee's death or disablement by accident while employed.

So, by definition, a FURBs is designed to provide relevant benefits for an individual by way of prior funding by the employer without seeking exempt approval. Therefore, how much can be paid into the scheme?

The contribution levels are not subject to any restriction. Unlike traditional pension schemes, there is no requirement for there to be a correlation between the individual's earnings and the payment into a FURBs. Also, the level of contributions are not affected by any funding requirements in respect of Inland Revenue maximum benefits as with approved schemes.

The taxation treatment should be noted carefully as it is very different from occupational or personal pension plans. It is assumed that all contributions will be made by the employer since there are no attractions for an employee to do so.

1. Employer contributions

These are allowable as a corporation tax deduction and are not subject to any "spreading" rules whatever their level. The contributions will be treated as forming part of an individual's income from employment and, as such, will be taxed under Schedule E as a benefit-in-kind under P11D procedures. No employer or employee National Insurance contributions share will arise.

2. The fund

The investment income from the fund itself will be taxed only at basic rate as will any capital gains. Employer sponsored schemes set up under trust should fall within IHTA 1984, s 161. As a result, any lump sum benefits paid out on death will be free of any IHT charge, so long as these are payable at the scheme administrator's discretion within a specified group of possible beneficiaries (excluding the estate of the employee).

3. Benefits paid on retirement

These will be tax-free provided they are all taken as *cash* and it would not, therefore, be beneficial to arrange the payment of any annuities from the fund.

This tax treatment may not appear as favourable as that offered by the exempt approved pension scheme but does, none-the-less, provide interesting planning opportunities in the following principle areas:
- employees whose pension provision is limited by the imposition of the earnings cap or by insufficient service;
- as an alternative means of paying bonuses free of liability for National Insurance contributions;
- employees considering retirement abroad;
- as a means of boosting pensionable earnings to justify the highest possible benefits from the main occupational pension scheme;
- those wishing to fund for an additional tax-free lump sum rather than for pension;
- those whose pensionable earnings are limited for whatever reason, including directors of investment companies.

LIFETIME DIRECTORS

A director with a lifetime appointment will by definition die in service and will be entitled to death cover of four times final salary. Up to the age of seventy-five this lump sum on death can be paid to children or other dependants free of inheritance tax but once the individual has reached the age of seventy-five the lump sum death in service life cover must be paid either to his estate or to his widow under the provisions of IR 12, para 11.6.

As well as providing four times the final salary life cover, a lifetime director's policy will usually provide for a widow's pension on the basis of four-ninths of her husband's final salary and, again, the final salary may be index linked if so desired. Such a contract takes the form of a whole life policy to provide a capital sum on the death of the director and the amount required is normally four times final salary for his lump sum payment and something in the order of five times final salary in addition to provide for the widow's pension. The precise multiple of final salary required for the life cover will depend on the respective ages of the director and his wife. Although the policy is written in the form of the whole life policy, it is written within a pension fund so that, unlike a normal whole life policy on which the insurance company bears tax up to 25% on reinvested income and is liable to capital gains tax, the policy for the lifetime director is entirely tax-free.

SELF-ADMINISTERED PENSION SCHEMES

Self-administered pension schemes have become very popular over the last ten years or so since the Pension Schemes Office relaxed the rules on small schemes, ie those with twelve or fewer members. The idea behind such a scheme is that the employing company pays a premium to the trustees of the pension scheme in the normal way but the trustees are, for example, the directors of the employing company or partners of the partnership where the employees are members of a service company. The investment policy of the pension fund is, therefore, under the control of the trustees rather than being managed by an insurance company in pooled funds. The result is considerable flexibility in investments and possibly a saving in the running costs compared with an insurance company's management charges.

A self-administered scheme must include among the trustees what is known as a pensioneer trustee, who is somebody approved by the Pension Schemes Office and in day to day contact with them. The main purpose of the pensioneer trustee is to ensure that the pension fund is not prematurely wound up and is used for the proper purpose of providing pensions. The fund must be run as a proper pension fund, hiring the services of consulting actuaries, arranging for a triennial revaluation and investing the premiums with a view to meeting the liabilities as they arise.

At the present time the Pension Schemes Office will usually allow a self-administered scheme to lend back up to half the fund to the employing company at a commercial rate of interest. The interest paid would be allowable for tax purposes in the hands of the paying company or partnership and would be tax-free in the self-administered scheme. No more than 25% of the fund may be lent to the company in the first two years of the scheme's existence. The fund could also be used to buy shares in the employing company with Revenue clearance under TA

1988, s 707 or to buy a property used for the purposes of the company or partnership which would pay a commercial rent for the use. The rent would be deductible as a trading expense and tax-free in the pension scheme. The Pension Schemes Office will withdraw the approval if it considers that the scheme is being used for tax avoidance purposes. In particular, an investment in the employing company's shares would be referred to the company's inspector of taxes to see whether there was any transaction in securities within the meaning of TA 1988, s 703 and only if the inspector approved would the pension fund be allowed to buy the shares. Similarly, the fund must be kept reasonably liquid in order to meet its liabilities and the investment of the entire fund in, for example, a property used by the partnership is unlikely to be approved by the Pension Schemes Office if the funds are likely to be needed to buy an annuity or pay a lump sum in the near future. The larger the fund the easier it is to spread the investments and use the fund to the benefit of the business. Transactions with a member or a person associated with him will not be approved and this rule may somewhat restrict the occasions on which it is possible to purchase the shares of the employing company.

A small self-administered pension scheme needs to reinsure death in service benefits offered to members because the fund, as a small fund, does not have sufficient spread of risk to be able to provide such benefits without seriously undermining the financial stability of the fund should a member die unexpectedly. Similarly, it will be necessary to purchase a pension for a member, by the age of seventy-five, from an established insurance company. Again, the reason is that in a small fund the pensioner might live beyond his normal life expectancy, so putting a severe strain on the financial resources of a small fund.

Part 20 of IR 12 provides detailed guidance regarding that which the Inland Revenue will consider acceptable in the dealings of a small self-administered scheme.

ALTERNATIVE PENSION PLANNING

It is unlikely that a professional partnership will wish to be involved in planning or encouraging pension provision other than through the tax favoured methods discussed in this chapter. However, individual partners may not feel that they wish to commit all their investments for retirement into vehicles which do not allow earlier access in an emergency. Others will object to the requirement to buy a lifetime annuity under traditional pension scheme arrangements. Such individuals may earmark certain personal investments as part of their retirement planning. These may range from stocks and shares to property, and even to antiques or fine wines, and may cover the whole spectrum of investment risk.

However, to retain some semblance of tax efficiency the investments which, in particular, may be considered are:
- tax exempt special saving accounts (TESSAs);
- personal equity plans (PEPs);
- National Savings certificates;
- investments which assist in utilising the annual exemption from capital gains tax (which also includes an exemption from growth purely due to inflation). Particularly favourable investments from this standpoint include growth unit and investments trusts, second-hand endowment policies, and the zero dividend preference shares of split capital investment trusts.

A good rule of thumb is to put as much into traditional pension plans as can reasonably be committed through good times and bad.

The balance of any planning can then be carried out through alternative investment vehicles, one of the most useful of which may be the personal equity plan (PEP). While no tax relief is available on the initial contribution to a PEP, the fund does none-the-less grow entirely tax-free. At retirement, the whole of the fund may be taken as tax-free cash or, alternatively, a tax-free "income" be drawn as required. It should be remembered that under a traditional pension plan only part of the fund may be taken as tax-free cash and the ongoing income is fully taxable thus, effectively, repaying some of the tax relief earned at outset.

Chapter 12
Financial control of partnerships

BUDGETS

It is important to record the plans for running a business and to express them in financial terms to ensure that these plans make commercial sense and achieve the required profit. Such a record is a budget, and if the budget does not make commercial sense, then it will have to be modified until it shows a situation where a satisfactory level of profit can be achieved.

Budgets normally cover all aspects of the profit and loss account and relate to a specific future period. Usually the budget period is one year but this can vary depending on circumstances. Each item in the Profit and Loss Account should, therefore, be taken in turn and the nature of the expense and the factors which determine the level of expense should be analysed. Budgeting is, therefore, more than finding out what the level of expense was last year and then making an allowance for inflation; it is a systematic review of each expense to determine what the level of expenditure should be, and to ensure that the business is getting value for money. In this way a realistic budget can be established. The method of arriving at the budget should be recorded, ideally on a specially prepared form. For example, if the cost of rent is being budgeted, the details of the actual lease or leases involved should be recorded on the form together with the annual rent and any ancillary charges such as service charges, which may have to be estimated, in order to arrive at the total annual cost. If a specially designed form is used, it should have a facility to record the nominal ledger account description or number, the person responsible for controlling the cost, and whether the expense will vary within specified fluctuations in turnover. An example of such a budget detail form is given in Table 1 (see p. 208).

On the other hand, the budget for salaries should record the names of each individual person, the annual rate of salary, any bonus or overtime payments, employer's national insurance and any other special payments made to the individual. Allowance should also be made where applicable for additional members of staff being employed during the course of the year, for salary increases if they are expected to take place during the year, and for the employment of temporary staff during holidays, etc. Similar principles should be applied to each item of expense.

The budget for fees or sales will depend on the extent of growth in the volume and range of services being provided and the charge being made for these services. Providing services usually involves supplying the time of qualified or experienced personnel or groups of personnel in varying proportions depending on the complexity of the assignment. In these cases projected fees will often depend on the number of chargeable staff employed, the number of hours they actually spend on chargeable work and the rate at which each hour is sold. In such cases the budget for fees should be arrived at by taking each member of staff, that is each person in the wages or salaries budget, and deciding whether the cost of their time should be charged directly to clients or whether the cost should be included in overheads and recovered by increasing the charging out rate of chargeable staff. Once it has been decided which staff are chargeable, they should be listed by grade or by department and the total hours should be recorded against each person or group of persons. For example, if a thirty-five-hour week is worked, then the annual hours are 35×52, ie 1,820 hours per annum. From this figure a number of deductions have to be made. First, holidays must be deducted and this should include not only annual holidays but also bank holidays and any extra days which are given, such as an extra day at Christmas. Secondly, allowance should be made for sickness. This varies according to industry, location and sex, but is unlikely to be less than 3%. Lastly, allowance should be made for time spent on training, attending conferences, administration duties and non-chargeable activities, such as public relations work. After making these deductions one will be left with the anticipated available chargeable hours for each person or group of persons. These hours will then be valued at the charging out rate to arrive at the anticipated value of productive time. An example of such a calculation is given in Table 2 (see p. 208).

The method of arriving at charging out rates is described on p. 203.

The value of time spent on work directly associated with clients has to be converted into fees. There are several reasons why a fee may not equate to the value of time spent in earning the particular fee. For example, it may be customary to charge clients on the basis of a schedule of charges or scale of fees. Alternatively, it may be difficult to achieve a realistic level of fees because of competition or because of the value of the service to the client. The percentage of the value of input which is recovered by fees being charged varies from business to business, but can be arrived at by examining past performance and adjusting the resulting figure by any known changes, or events, which are going to have an effect in the budget period. The value of productive input should be adjusted by this recovery percentage to arrive at the fees budget. Another factor which can sometimes affect the conversion of time costs into fees is the level of work-in-progress at the end of the year. Work-in-progress at the end of the year can be projected on the basis of a percentage of the annual input budget. Alternatively it could be based on the input for a particular period of time. The value of work in progress at the end of the period should be deducted from the total of the value of input for the year and the value of the opening work-in-progress in order to arrive at the fees or sales budget.

It is quite possible that there are other forms of income such as rent received or interest received, and these should also be budgeted. When each item in the Profit and Loss Account has been budgeted then the figures can be summarised in order to arrive at the budgeted profit. These figures can be summarised in various ways. For example, expenses can be grouped together according to the department or section to which they relate or they can be grouped together by type of expense or by the person controlling such expense. Normally, if a firm is large enough, expenses will be recorded by department and the person responsible for controlling each expense will be noted alongside. If the firm is not large enough to have separate departments, then the budget figures should be summarised in the same sequence as the figures appear in the annual accounts so that both sets of figures can be easily compared. An example of a budget consolidation form is given in Table 3 (see p. 209).

If expenses have been analysed between those that are fixed and those that vary within certain ranges of turnover, then it will be possible to draw a break-even chart which will show the level of fees or sales which has to be achieved in order to cover expenses with or without notional salaries. A break-even chart will also show what profit will be achieved at various levels of turnover. Such a chart can be drawn by recording expenses on the vertical scale and sales on the horizontal scale. A horizontal line is then drawn at the level of the fixed expenses and the total cost line can be drawn by plotting the budgeted expenses against the budgeted income and by drawing a line from this point to the budgeted level of fixed expenses on the vertical axis. The income line can be drawn diagonally and the break-even point is where this crosses the total cost line.

An example of a break-even chart is given in Table 4 (see p. 210).

An alternative way to obtain the break-even point is to calculate it by using the following formula:

$$\frac{\text{Fixed costs} \times \text{sales}}{\text{Sales} - \text{Variable Costs}}$$

So if fixed costs are £150,000 and variable costs are £500,000 when sales are £1,000,000, then the break-even point will be £300,000.

During the course of the period being budgeted it would be quite usual for partners to make decisions which will affect the level of income and expenses. For example, it may be decided to employ an extra secretary or spend an extra £5,000 on advertising. When this happens it is inconvenient to amend the original budget, but at the same time it is not helpful to show such expenses as a variance. Consequently, a budget revision form can be completed which will record details of the new expense, and as various revision forms are completed so the budgeted profit can be updated so that at any one time during the course of the year a partner not only knows the original budgeted profit but also the expected profit after taking into account budget revisions. An example of a budget revision form is given in Table 5 (see p. 211) and the resulting adjustment to profit is shown in Table 6 (see p. 211).

CASH FORECAST

It is very useful to be able to project the bank balance or overdraft for at least one year ahead. If surplus funds are available, this will enable the return to be maximised by enabling funds to be invested for a specific period. On the other hand, if overdraft facilities are required the preparation of a forecast will help to determine what facilities are required and will also be of some help in obtaining the required facilities. More banks are asking for cash forecasts before granting overdrafts and it helps to be prepared.

The first step in the preparation of a cash forecast is to take each budget figure in turn and convert it into payments or receipts. The first figure to be considered will be fees. In order to convert this figure into cash receipts the average period of credit taken by clients must be determined. This can be easily obtained by looking at a previous age analysis of debtors. When this pattern has been determined it can be applied to the previous month's sales to see if it produces a debtors figure similar to the one that actually exists. If it does, then it is an indication that the pattern is consistent. The next step is to apply these percentages to the projected fees in order to determine cash received for each month throughout the budget period, and at the same time to determine the anticipated debtors figure at the end of each month.

These calculations can be recorded on a separate page and the receipts for each month can be transferred to a summary page. An example of the calculations is shown in Table 7 (see p. 211), and Table 8 (see p. 212) shows fees receipts from clients and the expected level of debtors for each month.

In addition to fees there may be other receipts, such as interest received, rent received or the sale of fixed assets. If there is more than one receipt it will be helpful to record them individually on a separate page and then transfer the total to the summary page. Receipts can then be totalled on the summary page as shown in Table 9 (see p. 213).

Each expense must then be taken in turn and converted into payments. Certain expenses such as depreciation do not result in any cash flows and so they can be ignored for the purposes of a cash forecast. Other expenses may be paid out each month throughout the year, such as salaries; or they may be paid out quarterly, such as rent; or half yearly, such as rates; or annually, such as an audit fee or insurance premiums. It may be helpful to break down the expenses into classes or groups of similar expenses, record each group on a separate page, and then transfer the total of each page to the summary. It makes good sense to break down expenses in the same way as they have been broken down in the budget, and to record items in the same order as they appear in the budget. An example of how establishment expenses can be converted into payments is given in Table 10 (see p. 214) and the total of the establishment expenses is then transferred to the summary on Table 9 (see p. 213).

When all the expenses have been converted into payments, partners' drawings, value added tax and any capital expenditure should be recorded. Again the detail can be recorded on separate schedules and the total transferred to the summary. This summary of payments should then be totalled to arrive at the total payments for each month, which can be compared with the cash receipts for each month to show the expected inflow or outflow of cash. By recording the opening bank balance or overdraft and adjusting this by the inflow or outflow for each month the projected bank balance or overdraft will be shown. An example of such a cash forecast summary is given in Table 9 (see p. 213).

Having completed a cash forecast it is possible to draw up a projected balance sheet as at the end of the budget period. The increase or decrease in debtors can be determined by comparing fees rendered with receipts from clients. For example, if fees rendered are £280,000 and receipts from clients £260,000, then debtors have increased during the period by £20,000. If debtors at the beginning of the period are £45,000, then debtors at the end of the period will amount to £65,000 which means that on average a client takes eighty-five days to pay his bill, ie £65,000 ÷ £280,000 × 365 days. Similarly the change in the creditors' figure can be obtained by comparing expenses in the budget excluding depreciation with

Capital and drawings 201

cash paid out on expenses. The bank balance or overdraft can be taken from the cash forecast and the fixed asset accounts can be increased by any capital expenditure shown in the cash forecast and reduced by the depreciation charge in the budget. By having a projected balance sheet in addition to the budget there will be a complete model of the business.

In order to show the relationship between the budget and the projected balance sheet it is helpful to draw up a Projected Source and Application of Funds Statement. This statement commences with the profits shown in the budget plus depreciation. Deductions are then made for taxation, drawings, capital expenditure and the change in working capital. The changes in the various elements of working capital are then shown. An example of a Projected Source and Application of Fund Statement is given in Table 11 (see p. 214).

It is then important that the budget is compared with the actual income and expenditure and that payments and receipts are compared with the cash forecast. Any variances should be investigated in order to determine the cause, so that corrective action can be taken if required.

CAPITAL AND DRAWINGS

Partners will no doubt require to draw out some of the anticipated profits during the course of the year. It is, therefore, important that the maximum drawing figures are calculated in order to preserve capital accounts. Calculation of drawings should be based on the budget but it should not be assumed that the budgeted profit will necessarily be achieved. Consequently, for the purpose of calculating drawings, a profit figure should be used which is less than the budgeted profit, say between 60% and 80% of the budgeted profit. A percentage should be determined according to how confident the partners are of achieving the budgeted profit. Having arrived at this percentage the profits can then be apportioned among partners in the profit sharing ratio. From each partner's share deductions should be made for the individual partner's income tax liability, for retirement annuity premiums paid by the firm and any expenses which are paid by the firm on behalf of individual partners, such as National Insurance, season tickets, etc. In addition, if certain partners are under-capitalised or if the capital of the firm has been increased, then a deduction should also be made in order to build up capital accounts of partners to the required level. The profit share, less all the deductions, will give the annual drawings for a particular partner. This figure can be divided by twelve in order to arrive at the monthly drawings figure (see Table 12 on p. 215).

A firm needs capital to finance both its fixed assets and working capital. Fixed assets can include property, whether it be freehold or leasehold, equipment such as typewriters, word processors, accounting machines and computers, furniture and fittings such as desks, filing cabinets, carpets, etc. Working capital will include the value of work-in-progress, debtors and cash balances less the creditors and the bank overdraft.

The required capital can be provided either by each partner contributing a certain amount of fixed capital, by loans from partners or others, or by the bank in the form of loans or overdraft facilities. The actual proportion of capital provided from each source will depend on the individual circumstances. Larger firms who own properties will tend to obtain more finance from their bank than smaller firms who do not own any properties. With regard to overdraft facilities, it must be remembered that an overdraft is a short-term source of finance and should not be regarded as permanent capital. Ideally an overdraft should provide for the seasonal requirements of the firm.

Having decided on the required capital and the proportions which should be provided by the bank and by partners, it should be decided how the partners are going to contribute to the capital requirements of the firm and also negotiate with the bank to obtain the required facilities. If partners are going to contribute capital in the same ratio as their profit sharing ratio then there will be no need to calculate interest on capital accounts unless certain partners are under-capitalised. However, it is possible that certain partners are able to contribute additional sums of capital; these can be regarded as loans to the firm, and interest will be payable to partners on these loan accounts. It would seem fair and equitable if partners received a similar rate of interest on their loan accounts and possibly their capital accounts to that which the firm would pay their bank, that is 1.5% to 3% above the bank base rate. However, as mentioned previously, interest on a loan account would be treated as investment income and accordingly it may be advisable to compensate the "loan creditor" partner by way of an increased share of profits thereby ensuring that the increase would be taxed as earned income.

In order to obtain bank facilities the bank should be provided with a copy of the budget, cash forecast and if possible a projected balance sheet and source and application of funds statement. In addition the facilities and loans required should be shown, together with the security being offered. Loans should be built into the cash forecast so that the projected bank balance or overdraft shown on the forecast can be compared with the facilities applied for.

From the partner's point of view, it is helpful to minimise the amount of capital tied up in the firm. This can be achieved by reducing fixed assets or working capital. Fixed assets can be reduced by disposing of assets which are not required for running the business, by entering into sale and lease-back arrangements as far as the partnership properties are concerned, or by leasing motor cars or equipment instead of purchasing them outright. Working capital requirements can be mitigated by reducing work-in-progress, debtors or cash balances on the one hand, and by increasing creditors and bank overdraft on the other hand. Work-in-progress can be reduced by ensuring that all work is billed immediately it is completed, by obtaining payments on account and by reducing the time to complete an assignment. Debtors can be reduced by sending out statements quickly and by telephoning or writing to clients who are slow in settling their accounts. In order to facilitate the reduction in both work-in-progress and debtors it is important to set targets for partners and managers and to monitor their actual performance in comparison with these targets. These targets can be set on the basis of the annual fees budget; for example, if the annual fees budget amounts to £560,000 and if it is reasonable for work-in-progress at selling value to equal three months' fees and debtors to equal two months' fees, then the target work-in-progress at selling value should be £140,000 and debtors should amount to £93,332. These target figures can then be allocated among the partners. For example, if a partner is responsible for 30% of the firm's income, ie £168,000, then his target work-in-progress should be 30% of £140,000, ie £42,000, and his target debtors should be 30% of £93,332, ie £28,000.

CHARGING OUT RATES

When charging clients for work completed, it is important that a realistic fee is charged. The fee should cover the costs of providing the service plus a reasonable profit. The profit level should provide the partners with a higher level of income than they would achieve if they were working on their own or were working as employees. At the same time the fee must be competitive with fees charged by other similar firms and should provide value for money.

In order to help arrive at a fee for a particular job or assignment it is helpful to have charging out rates for individual employees or partners or groups of employees or partners. A fee can, therefore, be arrived at by taking the hours that have been spent or ought to have been spent on the assignment and valuing those hours at the charging out rates for the particular staff.

It has to be decided how charging out rates are calculated. The first stage is to record the salary cost of all the chargeable staff on the one hand, including notional salaries for partners who undertake chargeable work, and all other expenses together with the desired level of profit after deducting notional salaries, on the other hand. The expenses and profit should be expressed as a percentage of the chargeable salaries and the resulting percentage should then be applied to the salary cost of each chargeable person or group of persons to arrive at the total cost of that person on group of persons. When people are combined in groups care must be taken to ensure that only people of similar seniority or value are combined. The charging out rate can then be calculated by dividing the total cost of each person or group of persons by the anticipated chargeable hours for that person or group of persons. An example of how charging out rates are calculated is given in Table 13 (see p. 216).

Certain adjustments may have to be made to the rates calculated in this way. First, if administration duties and other non-chargeable duties are not being distributed evenly, an individual or group of persons who spends a large proportion of their time on these non-chargeable activities could have an unrealistically high rate. This situation can be overcome by taking a percentage of the salary costs as non-chargeable and including this proportion with the overheads, or by calculating the charging out rate by using average hours instead of actual anticipated hours for each person or persons. In calculating the average hours the calculation should be weighted by salary costs so that the desired value of input will still be achieved. Secondly, it is sometimes the case that a firm provides a variety of services and some of these services are more expensive than others. A particular service could be more expensive than others because it involves more filing and secretarial costs or it could result in more chargeable time being incurred. If this is the case, then the above formula will not produce satisfactory charging out rates because the customer or client who receives the more costly service will be subsidised at the expense of other customers. This situation can be overcome by dividing the firm into departments and carrying out the necessary calculation for each department rather than for the firm as a whole.

When these charging out rates have been calculated and the fees budget has been established, it is possible that the desired profit is not being achieved. This may be due to the fact that the recovery percentage is less than 100%, or it may be due to the fact that the value of work in progress has increased during the period, and that because the value of work is at a lower valuation basis than if this work had been charged out, the profit is being reduced. This situation can be corrected either by making an allowance for these factors when establishing the desired profit or by increasing all charging out rates by a percentage which is sufficient to achieve the desired result.

TIME RECORDING

Now that the firm has a budget and charging out rates have been calculated, it is important to determine to what extent the anticipated chargeable hours incorporated in the budget have been actually achieved. This information can be obtained if each chargeable partner and each member of the staff records the time he spends on chargeable work. These chargeable hours evaluated at the appropriate charging out rate will give the value of work or input and this can be compared with the budget.

However, if not only the chargeable hours but also the time spent on each job are recorded, then the cost of a particular job or assignment can be determined and compared with the cost and the fee charged and therefore the recovery percentage can be calculated, ie the extent to which costs are being converted into fees. In order to determine the cost of a particular job, a record will have to be kept of each job or assignment showing the time spent on it by each employee or partner. This record can be periodically totalled and the hours valued at the appropriate charging out rates to arrive at the total cost to date, ie the value of work-in-progress. When the fee is rendered all or part of the time spent on the assignment will be written off or eliminated. This time which is eliminated must be totalled so that comparison can be made with the fee. These records or time ledgers can be maintained in several ways. For example, manual ledgers could be maintained with one ledger account for each job or assignment, or carbonised systems may be used whereby each person who undertakes chargeable work records his time on a slip of paper and at the same time the entry is duplicated on a backing sheet. The slip of paper is filed on the job file and the backing sheet provides the total hours charged each day or week. When the job is billed the slips of paper will be totalled to arrive at the total cost. Alternatively, the time ledger may be kept on a computer. The system which is most appropriate for any particular firm will depend on its size, the number of chargeable staff and the number of jobs being undertaken at any one time, together with the amount of management information required.

Most firms will use a computer to maintain their time ledgers and there are many companies who have written suitable software for professional firms.

Whichever system is used, there should be a system for identifying each particular job, the partner and/or manager responsible for it and each member of staff. This is normally done by allocating numbers and/or letters to partners, clients and assignments. For example, a particular assignment could be defined as A001–10, being the tenth assignment for the first client whose name begins with the letter A, or alternatively it could be defined as 101/95, being the 101st job undertaken in the year 1995. In addition to recording the client, it will normally be necessary to record the partner responsible for each assignment, and possibly to record the manager or person responsible for undertaking the work. This can be done by allocating numbers or letters to partners and to managers or job controllers. These numbers or letters can be added on to the client or assignment number or can be recorded with the permanent information, ie the names of the client and description of the assignment. By doing this the assignment number should not become too long.

In addition to time spent on assignments, disbursements may also be incurred on behalf of the client and, therefore, there must be a facility to record these expenses as well as to record the time on each assignment. An example of the costs on a particular assignment is given in Table 14 (see p. 216).

Whichever system is used to maintain the time ledger, the following information should be provided.

(a) value of work done on each job or assignment;
(b) value of work-in-progress allocated among partners;
(c) a comparison of fees rendered with time costs written off;
(d) statistics for each partner and member of the staff showing chargeable hours and value of work, and an analysis of non-chargeable time between the usual categories such as holidays, sickness, training, etc.

Whichever system is used, a number of decisions will have to be made when setting up the system:

(a) how to identify a particular client;
(b) how to identify a particular member of staff or a partner;
(c) how to indicate which partner and/or manager is responsible for a particular client;
(d) what information has to be recorded when a job is being opened. This could include client name and address and a description of the assignment or job and possibly the partner and manager number.

There are two important items of management information which ought to be extracted from the time ledger system. First, the recovery variance, which can be obtained by comparing the fees rendered to clients with the value of time written off against these fees. Secondly, the input variance, which is obtained by comparing the value of chargeable work in the budget which the value of chargeable work actually achieved. However, a favourable input variance can be caused by different factors. It may be caused by employing additional staff, or by increasing somebody's charging out rate, or by the existing staff spending a higher proportion of their time on chargeable work. It would be helpful to determine which factor is causing this variance, and this can be achieved by revising the budget whenever there is a change in charging out rates or staff; for example, if an existing member of staff leaves, then his value of input for the rest of the year is deducted from the budget, and when he is replaced or a new member of staff arrives the budget is increased by the anticipated value of his work. In this way the true variance can be obtained by comparing the original budget plus or minus the budget revisions with the actual performance.

The rapid development of personal computers over the last few years has led to a plethora of financial software packages ranging from the simple spreadsheet to complex relational database applications. An injudicious choice of software can lead to havoc and thus the choice of computer software is now one of the most difficult and important decisions of the finance partner.

SOURCES OF CAPITAL

1. Partners

It is usually necessary for the partners themselves to provide at least a proportion of the capital needed to run the firm. This capital may take the form of a capital account where each partner contributes a fixed amount of capital which is determined by the partners in accordance with the partnership agreement or as otherwise mutually agreed. It is normal for there to be a requirement that a partner's capital be introduced to the firm on his admission to the partnership, although many firms allow a period of say, five years, during which the partner is allowed to build up his capital to the required amount. If a partner cannot from his own resources produce the capital required, it might be necessary for him to borrow the appropriate funds in order to contribute his share of capital.

Interest on money borrowed by a partner is eligible for tax relief provided that the money is used to buy a share in a partnership, ie to buy goodwill from the other partners, or to contribute money by way of capital or loan to the partnership, or in replacing such an eligible loan (TA 1988, s 362). Relief can be lost if the partner has withdrawn capital from the partnership (TA 1988, ss 362 and 363).

Partners will usually have current accounts with the partnership and these are usually built up through undrawn profits. It is normally desirable to ensure that money available for drawing by partners on demand is kept in the current account so that the funds not normally available for drawing are kept in the capital account. It will obviously be necessary to review the capital account from time to time, and if it is necessary to increase the required capital, transfers may be made from the partner's current accounts as required.

It is also quite common for a partner to lend money to the firm in addition to his capital or current account. It is normally preferable to avoid such loans and to increase temporarily the capital account of that partner. The reason for this is that loan interest payable to a partner would normally be taxed as unearned income under Schedule D, Case III, whereas interest paid on capital account or current account balances is treated as an appropriation of profits in the same way as salary, profit percentage or other allocation of profits and is thus taxed as earned income under Schedule D, Cases I or II.

2. Banks

Bank finance is probably the next most common form of finance available to the partnership and in most cases the partnership would arrange for a suitable overdraft to cover the working capital.

It is found in practice that for many professional partnerships the provision of working capital in the ratio of one-third by the partners and two-thirds by the bank is an acceptable proportion. The bank would normally require a joint and several guarantee from the partners in respect of such an overdraft.

3. Creditors

Creditors are undoubtedly a source of capital, not only creditors for supplies, but also for PAYE, VAT and income tax on the partnership profits. The degree to which creditors can be used to finance the partnership depends very much on the activities of the firm, and a professional practice is usually not in a strong position as the major expenses of such a firm are usually staff salaries followed by rent. Staff salaries have to be paid monthly and rent is normally payable in advance. It is usual, therefore, for a professional practice to find that debtors are considerably in excess of creditors at any given time.

The extent to which a partnership provides for taxation varies considerably from firm to firm. The most conservative basis is to provide for taxation for the year of assessment for which the accounting period forms the basis period. This means that if the accounts are made up to, say, 30 April 1995, tax up to and including 1996–97 would be provided for. In most cases however it is not practical to adopt such a conservative attitude and it is common to provide for tax for the year of assessment up to the accounting date. In other words, in the accounts to 30 April 1995 there would be provided the whole of the taxation for 1994–95 and one-twelfth of the liability for 1995–96. In times of inflation this is probably an unduly optimistic provision and providing for taxation on the basis of a notional cessation at the end of the accounting period can often be a useful compromise. In such a case the accounts to 30 April 1995 would provide for tax for the years up to 1995–96 on the assumption that there would be a cessation on 30 April 1995. The reason for providing for taxation is to enable the partners to draw their current accounts without overdrawing and without unduly restricting their drawing and accumulating unnecessary funds in the partnership.

Under self-assessment, from 1997–98, a partnership will no longer be charged tax as an entity, each individual partner will self-assess and be liable to pay his own tax. Many partnerships appear likely to continue to allow partners to draw net of a notional tax charge which would be retained within the firm until the tax was payable when it would be paid to the Revenue on behalf of each partner. Other firms will allow partners to draw gross and fund their own tax bills.

Loans for specific purposes are often arranged. If, for example, the partnership is buying freehold or long leasehold premises it might well arrange to borrow a substantial proportion of the necessary funds from a bank on a long-term basis or from an insurance company. An insurance company loan would normally be on the basis of an endowment policy or series of endowment policies on the lives of younger partners to mature when the loan is due for repayment after fifteen or twenty years.

The purchase of plant and machinery, including partners' cars, can be arranged through the normal bank overdraft facilities or specific bank loans for specific purposes. Alternatively such assets can be acquired on hire-purchase, although this tends to be expensive, or may be leased, which is also rather expensive but might be necessary for equipment requiring a lot of maintenance, such as internal telephones, photocopying equipment, computer equipment, etc.

If assets, such as partners' cars, are provided out of the general partnership funds, it is unlikely that any of the overdraft interest would be disallowed, even though the partners' cars may be used partly for private purposes. If a car is purchased by a partner personally, he has to remember to claim capital allowances on the car in the partnership return, under self-assessment, and if he borrows in order to purchase the car it is unlikely that he would obtain relief for the interest paid, except for the business proportion on a fixed loan of up to three years under TA 1988, s 359.

It can be useful on occasions for a partnership to encourage clients who do not obtain tax relief on fees to deposit funds with the firm which could be placed on a clients' deposit account or building society account. The client would merely lose interest which would otherwise have been taxed at say 75%, and the partnership would receive interest. This idea can be developed further by the partnership arranging to hold the funds on a client's current account rather than a client's deposit account and arranging with the bank that overdraft interest is charged on only the excess, if any, of the overdrawn office account over the client's account. In this case not only is the interest liability reduced, but also no-one is in receipt of deposit interest taxable as investment income.

Table 1
Budget Detail Sheet

Item – Rent					
Account No.	Details				Annual Budget
		Rent	Services	Total	
401	Market Place	£1,500	£100	£1,600	
402	High Street	£10,500	£1,600	£12,100	
403	New Road*	£5,200	£200	£5,400	
				————	£19,100
	* includes six months at a rent of £4,400 per annum and six months at a rent of £6,000 per annum. The new lease, which commences on 25 June, is for 21 years with rent reviews every five years				

Table 2
Calculation of Productive Hours based on a 7-hour day

Total hours		1,820
Holidays		
Bank 8 days	56	
Annual 15 days	105	
Sickness say 10 days	say 70	
Non chargeable		
Training 5 days	35	
Administration 1 hour per day	222	
(see Note)		448
		1,332 hours

Value of input 1,332 × £100 per hour = £133,200
Note: 260 days less 38 days for holidays, sickness and training.

Table 3
Budget Consolidation Form

Description	Account No.	Detail sheet No.	Total budget
Staff Costs			£
Salaries	300	12	250,000
Temporary staff	310	13	80,000
Luncheon vouchers	320	14	4,000
Travelling	330	15	45,000
			£379,000
Establishment			
Rent, rates	500	16	100,000
Light and heat	510	17	25,000
Cleaning	520	18	18,000
			£143,000
Administrative			
Telephone	600	19	19,000
Postage	610	20	4,000
Printing and stationery	620	21	25,000
			£48,000

210 *Financial control of partnerships*

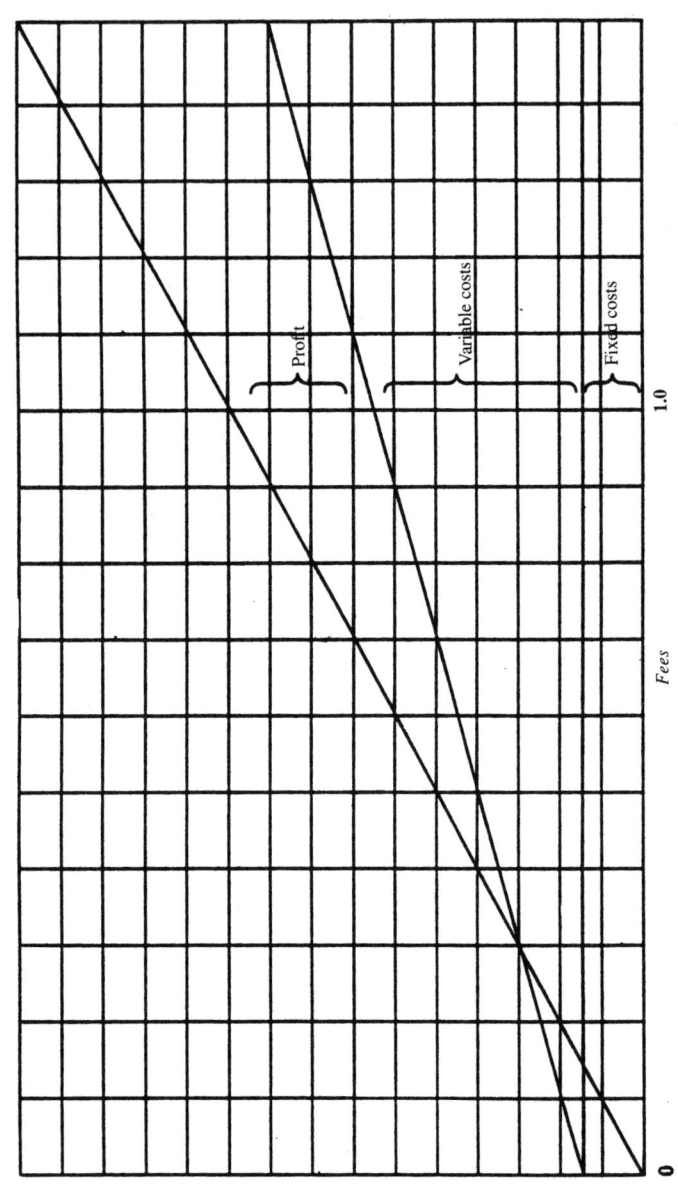

Table 4
Break-even Chart

Table 5
Budget Revision Form

Reference: Salaries – Secretaries. A/C 305	Revision No. 1 Date 5th May
Reason for change	Details of Change
Additional work undertaken in our High Street office means that we have to employ an additional secretary from 1 July.	Mrs Jones Salary £14,000 N.I. 1,000 ────── £15,000 ────── 6 months from 1st July = £7,500

Authorised by _____

Table 6
Calculation of Revised Budgeted Profit

Profit per Budget	£300,000
Revision No. 1	
1 Additional Secretary	–7,500
Revised Budgeted Profits	£292,500

Table 7
Calculation of Cash Receipts

		£
FEES		
(Note 1)	Month 1	160,000
	Month 2	200,000
	Month 3	240,000

CASH RECEIVED FROM CLIENTS		
	Current Month	25%
	First Month	50%
	Second Month	25%

Fees	Months		
	1	2	3
Cash Received	160,000	200,000	240,000
1	40,000		
2	80,000	50,000	
3	40,000	100,000	60,000
4		50,000	120,000
5			60,000

Note 1   Business commenced in Month 1

Table 8
Receipts from clients
£000

	Total	Month 1	Month 2	Month 3	Month 4	Month 5	Month 6
Fees	132.0	16.0	20.0	24.0	24.0	28.0	20.0
Receipts							
Current month	33.0	4.0	5.0	6.0	6.0	7.0	5.0
First month	56.0		8.0	10.0	12.0	12.0	14.0
Second month	21.0			4.0	5.0	6.0	6.0
	110.0	4.0	13.0	20.0	23.0	25.0	25.0
Opening balance	0.0	0.0	12.0	19.0	23.0	24.0	27.0
Fees	132.0	16.0	20.0	24.0	24.0	28.0	20.0
	132.0	16.0	32.0	43.0	47.0	52.0	47.0
Less: receipts	110.0	4.0	13.0	20.0	23.0	25.0	25.0
= Closing balance	22.0	12.0	19.0	23.0	24.0	27.0	22.0

Table 9
Cash Forecast Summary
£000

	Page	Total	Month 1	Month 2	Month 3	Month 4	Month 5	Month 6
Receipts								
From clients	1	110.0	4.0	13.0	20.0	23.0	25.0	25.0
Other receipts	2	4.0			2.0			2.0
		114.0	4.0	13.0	22.0	23.0	25.0	27.0
Payments								
Staff costs	3	46.7	5.5	8.0	8.0	8.4	8.4	8.4
Establishment expenses	4	20.3	6.0	1.0	1.1	10.0	1.1	1.1
Administration and finance	5	31.1	5.1	5.1	5.1	5.6	5.1	5.1
Drawings	6	21.0	3.5	3.5	3.5	3.5	3.5	3.5
V.A.T.	7	7.5			3.2			4.3
Capital expenditure	8	15.2	5.0			10.2		
		141.8	25.1	17.6	20.9	37.7	18.1	22.4
Net inflow (outflow)		(27.8)	(21.1)	(4.6)	1.1	(14.7)	6.9	4.6
Bank balance: Opening		(25.0)	25.0	3.9	(0.7)	0.4	(14.3)	(7.4)
Closing		(2.8)	3.9	(0.7)	0.4	14.3	(7.4)	(2.8)

214 *Financial control of partnerships*

Table 10
Cash Forecast Establishment Expenses
£000

	Month 1	Month 2	Month 3	Month 4	Month 5	Month 6
Rent	3.5			3.5		
Rates				4.4		
Electricity	.5			1.0		
Cleaning	.5	.5	.5	.5	.5	.5
Repairs	1.5	.5	.6	.6	.6	.6
	6.0	1.0	1.1	10.0	1.1	1.1

Table 11
Projected Source and Application of Funds
Statement for the Year Ending . . . .

	£000
Source of funds	
Profit	110
Depreciation	10
Additional bank loan	20
	£140
Application of funds	
Drawings	80
Capital expenditure	50
	130
Net increase in working capital	10
	£140
Changes in working capital	
Increase in debtors	22.0
Increase in work-in-progress	26.0
Decrease in bank balance	(27.8)
Increase in creditors	(10.2)
	£10.0

Table 12
ABC & Co. Partners' Drawing Schedule – Year to 30.4.94

	Total 100%	A 0.1432	B 0.1479	C 0.1336	D 0.1288	E 0.0955	F 0.0955	G 0.0955	H 0.08	I 0.08
BUDGETED PROFITS £1,100,000 × 75%	825,000.00									
Less: wives' salaries 8 × £4,500	36,000.00									
	789,000.00									
Prior share	4,500.00									4,500.00
Balance of profit in PSR	784,500.00	112,340.40	116,027.55	104,809.20	101,043.60	74,919.75	74,919.75	74,919.75	62,760.00	62,760.00
	789,000.00	112,340.40	116,027.55	104,809.20	101,043.60	74,919.75	74,919.75	74,919.75	67,260.00	62,760.00
LESS PAYMENTS OUT OF PROFITS										
Taxation										
1993/94 (one-half)	102,595.85	16,586.20	16,521.75	15,477.05	14,003.25	7,719.65	8,719.55	7,924.60	9,027.25	6,616.55
1994/95 (one-half)	113,625.45	18,348.75	18,341.75	17,120.75	15,587.00	8,695.55	9,659.60	8,864.50	9,836.00	7,207.55
SUBTOTAL	216,221.30	34,934.95	34,863.50	32,597.80	29,950.25	16,379.20	18,379.15	16,789.10	18,863.25	13,824.10
Class 4 NIC										
1993/94 (one-half)	4,394.25	488.25	488.25	488.25	488.25	488.25	488.25	488.25	488.25	488.25
1994/95 (one-half)	5,213.34	579.26	579.26	579.26	579.26	579.26	579.26	579.26	579.26	579.26
SUBTOTAL	9,607.59	1,067.51	1,067.51	1,067.51	1,067.51	1,067.51	1,067.51	1,067.51	1,067.51	1,067.51
Class 2 NIC										
1993/94 (11/12ths)	2,380.95	264.55	264.55	264.55	264.55	264.55	264.55	264.55	264.55	264.55
1994/95 (1/12th)	220.32	24.48	24.48	24.48	24.48	24.48	24.48	24.48	24.48	24.48
SUBTOTAL	2,601.27	289.03	289.03	289.03	289.03	289.03	289.03	289.03	289.03	289.03
Retirement Annuity										
Premiums (say) (1993/94)	37,465.00	5,335.00	5,510.00	4,975.00	4,795.00	3,555.00	3,555.00	3,555.00	3,205.00	2,980.00
Capital Retention	4,400.00								2,400.00	2,000.00
SUBTOTAL	41,865.00	5,335.00	5,510.00	4,975.00	4,795.00	3,555.00	3,555.00	3,555.00	5,605.00	4,980.00
Total payments out of profits	270,295.16	41,626.49	41,730.04	38,929.34	35,741.79	21,290.74	23,290.69	21,700.64	25,824.79	20,160.64
Total profits less payments	518,704.84	70,713.91	74,297.51	65,879.86	65,301.81	53,629.01	51,629.06	53,219.11	41,435.21	42,599.36
Add study allowance	12,570.00	1,520.00	1,535.00	1,200.00	1,660.00	2,680.00	1,675.00	1,080.00	85.00	1,135.00
Grand total	531,274.84	72,233.91	75,832.51	67,079.86	66,961.81	56,309.01	53,304.06	54,299.11	41,520.21	43,734.36
MONTHLY DRAWINGS	42,750.00	6,000.00	5,000.00	5,500.00	5,500.00	4,750.00	4,500.00	4,500.00	3,500.00	3,500.00

Table 13
Calculation of Charging Out Rates

Salaries of chargeable staff		430,000
Partners – notional salaries		300,000
		£730,000 (a)
Expenses excluding salaries of chargeable staff		
Expenses	750,000	
Less: salaries of chargeable staff	430,000	
		320,000
Add: profit loading		
Profit	400,000	
Less notional salaries	300,000	
		100,000
		£420,000 (b)

Calculation of percentage

$$\frac{(b)\ 420,000}{(a)\ 730,000} \times 100 = 57.5\%$$

Calculation of Charging out rates	Salaries Cost	Expenses 57.5%	Total	Hours	Rate per hour
Junior staff	180,000	103,750	283,750	10,000	28.375 say £29
Senior staff	250,000	143,750	393,750	7,000	56.25 say £56
Partners	300,000	172,500	472,500	3,940	119.92 say £120
	730,000	420,000	1,150,000		

Table 14
ABC Limited

			£
January	Jones	4 hours @ £29 =	116.00
	Smith	8 hours @ £56 =	448.00
February	Smith	10 hours @ £120 =	1,200.00
	Stamp duty		120.00
March	Printing		200.00
	Telephone		25.00
Total			£2,109.00

Chapter 13

Partnership insurance

PROFESSIONAL INDEMNITY INSURANCE

Clearly it is every professional man's aim that no claim shall be made against him by any client, former client or third party. However, in modern conditions, many partnerships often grow to a size where the partner's personal knowledge of each client is diminished. There is also a growing tendency for clients to sue their professional advisers.

Because of the nature of partnerships, involving unlimited liability, and usually with a high level of expertise expected, some insurance against claims for mistake or negligence is essential. Cover must be arranged at least against the following:

(a) Negligent act, error or omission.
(b) Breach of contract.
(c) Breach of delegated authority.
(d) Breach of trust committed in good faith.
(e) Libel or slander.
(f) Unintentional failure to account for clients' money.
(g) Dishonest or fraudulent act of any present or past partner, director or employee. (Note only the innocent partners will be indemnified, not the person committing the dishonesty.)
(h) Loss of documents which would cost a substantial sum to replace, including clients' documents held for safe keeping and the firm's own files.
(i) In the case of a firm acting as Registrar for share dealings, claims arising from forged documents.

It is important to ensure that the policy covers all activities in which the firm is likely to participate. For example, the standard Lloyd's policy for firms of Chartered Accountants includes appointment as director, receiver, liquidator, executor, trustee, company secretary or arbitrator, provided that fees arising from such activities are paid into the firm. As usual it is vital to read the policy carefully, or be able to rely on a known expert broker. Small points should be watched – again using the Institute of Chartered Accountants standard policy as an example, cover is given against claims arising from company formations "with legal assistance" and against investment advice provided that in the case of public companies, the advice is backed up in writing by a stockbroker. Such standard phrases can sometimes be amended to suit the policy-holder, but they have to be spotted first.

When taking out indemnity insurance, it is vital to be careful that all details given are strictly accurate. Like all insurance, the policy will be void unless the truth is strictly told. Make sure that all partners are named, not only those of the main firm, but also those of associated firms whether in the United Kingdom or overseas.

The level of cover to be taken must be for each firm to decide in the light of its own circumstances, having regard to the sort of business it handles and the likelihood of claims. The level of cover sometimes suggested for chartered accountants is often one to two years gross fees, or twenty times the largest fee, whichever is higher. Many firms appear to take cover of between 2 and 2.5 times fees, but if high risk work is undertaken, this may not be sufficient. The best general advice is to find a competent broker who also acts for other similar firms, and thus has a chance to acquire a broad range of information about claims and the general level of cover taken by similar firms. It is important to ensure that cover is stated for any one claim, and not as an annual total.

Cost of Professional Indemnity Insurance can vary enormously depending on the reputation of the firm, its past claims record and the skill of the broker, particularly in the case of Lloyd's policies. However, the first tranche of cover is likely to be the most expensive – the next somewhat cheaper, and the next cheaper still. The way such "slices" are arranged can also vary the price. Increasing the excess on the policy can save considerably on premium cost.

There are one or two drawbacks in Professional Indemnity cover. Most, if not all, policies insist, at the risk of the contract being void, that the underwriter or insurance company is told immediately a claim is received. The underwriter is then usually empowered by the policy to decide whether or not to fight the claim on the insured's behalf. The usual natural reaction of a professional man is to fight for his reputation to the bitter end, but after an independent examination of the papers and evidence by solicitors appointed and paid by the underwriters, a decision, with which the insured cannot argue, may be made to accept the claim. This is yet another reason to use a broker in whom the insured has complete confidence, and preferably who has confidence in the insured, but it is also a very important reason for ensuring that the professional methods and, equally important, documentary evidence of those methods, are up to date, professionally well thought out and properly recorded. Ill-founded claims can be more easily disposed of if the firm's files produce clear contrary evidence.

Product Liability Insurance may be a necessary addition to or substitute for Professional Indemnity Insurance in certain professions especially now that consumer protection is such a widely publicised and exploited area.

CAPTIVE INSURANCE COMPANIES

In view of the enormous cost of professional indemnity insurance a number of firms have entered into mutual agreements with firms of similar size and reputation or set up their own captive insurance company. Such a company will usually be formed in a tax haven such as Bermuda, Cyprus, Guernsey or the Isle of Man in order to limit the tax on investment income to the minimum so that the maximum cover can be provided at the minimum cost. Normally the firm will insure the first tranche of the insured liability with the captive and reinsure the next layers in respect of claims over a certain amount. It is unlikely that a captive would be worthwhile if the insurance premium for the cover to be borne by the captive is less than about £50,000 per annum in view of the costs of setting up and running the captive. The idea would be to pay a premium at the same rate as that quoted by the market or fractionally below this rate. The premium would be paid to the captive and invested pending any claim. Obviously if a captive insurance com-pany is to be effective it is essential for it to be capitalised sufficiently to enable it to meet claims as and when they arise, and this is often done by making the capital partly paid so that at all stages the captive could meet its liabilities although it would be necessary to provide security for the uncalled capital. After a few years, if claims do not have to be made against the captive, it should be possible to arrange for reduced premiums taking into account the good claims record. If on the other hand claims are made against the firm which are covered by the insurance these should be recovered from the captive, which may even have to increase the rate of premium charged in the light of the claims experience.

The Revenue are known to dislike captive insurance companies as they regard them as an attempt to convert a provision for a liability that may or may not happen into an allowable expense. The Revenue line of attack is likely to be in the first instance under TA 1988, s 74 on the grounds that the expenditure is not wholly and exclusively incurred for the purpose of the trade or profession. In order to argue this point it will be necessary to show that the premium payable is for insurance cover with an independent entity, viz. the captive insurance company, which is capable of meeting its liabilities should a claim be made under the insurance policy. They may also argue, under the transfer pricing provisions of TA 1988, s 770, that notwithstanding the premium being no more than that which would have been charged by Lloyd's for similar insurance cover it is nonetheless excessive for the cover provided by the captive. This could again be countered by showing that the captive is able to meet its liability and the additional claims could be met by reinsurance or insurance elsewhere. A further line of attack might be on the captive itself if it were owned by the partnership or U.K. partners on the grounds that it is a transfer of assets abroad, which it would be, under which income was accumulated overseas, which it would be to the extent of the investment income was reinvested to provide the ability to pay the claims. The counter to this argument is that the transfer and the payment of the premium were bona fide commercial transactions and were not designed for the purpose of avoiding liability to taxation but were incurred to provide insurance cover at an affordable cost. Finally, the Revenue might argue under *Furniss v Dawson* [1984] STC 153 that the captive insurance company was inserted as an artificial step between the partnership and the provision made by the insurance company, purely for tax reasons. This argument again should be capable of being defeated if it can be shown that the insurance is available commercially only at greater cost. Obviously if the insurance company is not owned by the partners or their associates it is likely to strengthen the argument that it is a bona fide commercial arrangement.

EMPLOYER'S LIABILITY INSURANCE

This form of insurance is required by law in the U.K. – The Employers' Liability (Compulsory Insurance) Act 1969 and the General Regulations of 1971 prescribe that all employers must ensure against liability for personal injury and disease sustained by their employees arising out of or in the course of their employment in Great Britain. The insurance must be made under one or more approved policies with a recognised insurer and a certificate of insurance is issued. Copies of this must be displayed for the benefit of all employees at each place of work. The amount of cover that must be taken out must be at least £2 million in respect of any claim arising out of one occurrence, though in most cases policies give unlimited cover.

An employee is defined as "an individual who has entered into or works under a contract of service (employment) or apprenticeship with an employer whether by way of mutual labour, clerical work or otherwise, whether such contract is expressed or implied or in writing". The only employees who do not have to be insured are as follows:

(a) relations, e g husband, wife, father, mother, grandfather, grandmother, etc.;
(b) employees not normally resident in Great Britain who are working here for fewer than fourteen days; and
(c) domestic servants employed solely to assist in the running of a private household.

The cost of such insurance varies according to trade, payroll costs, and number and location of employees.

Cover is often included in a general, so called "comprehensive" policy available to firms and designed to meet a wide range of possibilities. However, the word "comprehensive" does not, in this context, mean "all embracing", but such a policy is merely a convenient way of collecting together various forms of insurance.

Apart from employers' liability, such policies often include the following:

(a) Damage to offices and contents by fire, burglary, theft, and natural perils, with the usual exclusion for war, etc.
(b) Public liability, that is injury to persons on the premises other than employees. Cover here is difficult to assess but brokers should know the level of damages being given by the Courts. Remember here that if, say, an American is injured on the firm's premises, he may well, through the U.S. Courts, get a much higher award than a U.K. citizen would.
(c) Risks arising from the use of machinery, including accidental damage.
(d) Loss of partners' and employees' personal possessions (although this is often excluded and would therefore have to be specially added if desired).
(e) Cash on premises, or in transit, including assault cover for injury to cash carriers.
(f) Special perils (e g burst pipes, flood, tempest, falling aircraft engines, etc.).
(g) Loss of documents (this may not be required if covered by professional indemnity policy).
(h) Additional rent in case of inability to use the premises because of damage. (Note – suitable temporary premises may cost considerably more than those which the firm is currently occupying.)
(i) Loss of fees or income arising from damage to premises, and other such "consequential loss".

With all insurance, it is important to ensure that levels of cover are reviewed at least annually and are sufficient. Many policies now have a built-in inflation factor, but must still be reviewed. There is no point in being over insured, but of course in the case of under insurance, even if the total insurance is sufficient for a particular item, the claim for any one event will be reduced in the same proportion as the insurance cover bears to the total value of all items; that is, it will be subject to average.

Insurance of buildings is another vital area, and here it is advisable to ensure that cover is sufficient to pay rebuilding costs, which may bear no relation to the current rent being paid, and in the case of freeholds, will almost certainly bear no relation to the original cost of the building when purchased. When estimating the rebuilding costs, a current building price per square foot must be estimated, to which must be added demolition costs to remove the old shell, and professional fees, together with a reasonable estimate for escalation caused by British weather and general intransigence. Rented property will usually be insured by the landlord and the premium passed on with rent demands, but leases very often place the legal burden on the tenant, and therefore the landlord is under little or no pressure to ensure that the cover is reasonable. Tenants must review the cost and, if necessary, request the landlord in writing to increase it.

OTHER MATTERS

Car insurance can be an area of difficulty. Firms must ensure that staff using cars on business are properly covered for business use. However, it is possible and advisable to obtain a fall back policy which the firm can rely on if even its best efforts to ensure that staff are covered fail. This would probably cost only a small amount per car likely to be used, depending on type of business.

Costs of all insurance may vary widely, and "no claims" discounts can play a major part, even with professional indemnity policies. It is important to shop around, or make sure that the broker does this on the insurer's behalf.

PARTNERSHIP LIFE ASSURANCE

One of the main problems of a professional partnership is the provision of sufficient cash to repay the capital accounts of an outgoing partner on his death or retirement. Partnership life assurance can often help in these circumstances, although the abolition of life assurance premium relief by TA 1988, Schs 14 and 15 has reduced the attraction of such schemes.

It is important to bear in mind the basic aims of such assurance, which are:
  (a)   to provide liquid capital in the right hands at the right time;
  (b)   to ensure an equitable division of cost among the partners;
  (c)   to avoid liability to inheritance tax in cases involving discretionary or other trust policies, it appears that the Revenue will, after 14 September 1976, apply the rigours of IHTA 1984, ss 64 and 65 notwithstanding the commerciality and reciprocity of the arrangement, whenever possible the terms of a proposed policy should be cleared beforehand. For further details see the statement by the Life Offices Association of September 1976 set out below;
  (d)   to avoid liability to capital gains tax. Normally the exemption under TCGA 1992, s 210 will apply; but note the exceptions listed below;
  (e)   to ensure that any arrangements are flexible and will allow for resignation of partners or the addition of new partners.

There are various means of trying to achieve these ideals, which are set out under 1 to 7 below (headings 1 to 7 should be read in conjunction with the table on pp. 226–227).

1. Trust policies

Each partner insures his own life for the benefit of other partners. A separate policy is needed in favour of each partner and these policies mature at the life assured's retirement date enabling the continuing partners to repay his capital. Trust policies for a large partnership usually involve a multiplicity of policies which can be inconvenient.

A marked disparity of partners' ages would result in considerable disparity in the life assurance premiums payable and could possibly give rise to inheritance tax assessments on part of the premium payments if it were held that the excess of the eldest partner's premiums over the next eldest were a gift and not part of the overall commercial agreement. It is usually possible to overcome this by means of partnership salaries or other prior changes.

It was at one time quite popular to combine partnership trust policies in a small partnership with a buy and sell agreement. The idea would be that if there were say, two partners, each partner would insure his own life in trust for his fellow partner. If he died, the insurance proceeds would provide sufficient funds to enable his former partner to buy out his interest in the partnership and provide his widow or dependants with cash. In order to prevent the surviving partner receiving the proceeds, and then refusing to buy out the former partner's estate, there would be a buy and sell agreement under which the estate was required to sell and the surviving partner required to buy the interest in the partnership. The trouble with such a buy and sell agreement is that in the Inland Revenue's view such an agreement is a binding contract for sale within IHTA 1984, s 113 and as a result inheritance tax business relief will not be due on the partnership interest of the deceased partner (see SP 12/80).

The same effect as a buy and sell agreement can, however, be achieved by means of a double option agreement which the Inland Revenue have confirmed would not prevent the deceased partner's interest in the partnership qualifying for business relief. Under a double option agreement the surviving partner has the option to purchase the deceased partner's interest in the partnership by serving a notice in writing within say three months from the date of death and the deceased partner's personal representatives have an option to sell the deceased partner's interest in the partnership to the surviving partner on serving a notice in writing within say six months from the date of death. The price will normally be the fair value computed by the accountants to the partnership. Such a double option is enforceable by either party and therefore provides exactly the same protection as a buy and sell agreement without giving rise to any loss of business relief.

2. Joint life policies

The partners effect one policy based on all their lives for the sum required on the death of any one of them, and each pays his fair share of the premium. On the first death the policy proceeds are payable to the surviving partner or partners.

This type of arrangement is only suitable for partnerships of two or three individuals where the partnership holdings and ages are approximately equal, and has the advantage of being cheaper than the two life policies. There will, however, be no cover on the life of the survivor if he wishes to enter another partnership.

3. Life of another policy

Each partner effects a policy on the life of his other partners to provide for his share of the outgoing partner's capital account.

The policies on the lives of the surviving partners would be part of the deceased partner's estate for inheritance tax. The value would be based on market value (or premiums paid if greater) as at the date of death.

If there is a wide disparity of ages it may be difficult for a young partner to pay the premiums required on the lives of the senior partners.

4. Variable partner trust policies

Under this arrangement each partner effects a single policy on his own life on a discretionary trust in favour of his partners for the time being in profit sharing ratios. The power of appointment of the policy proceeds will be vested in the trustees who will be the life assured's partners and will normally appoint among themselves in profit sharing ratio or other equitable manner and use the proceeds to repay the deceased or retiring partners. The premiums would be a first charge on the profits. There could, however, be a periodic charge for inheritance tax as a discretionary trust and a charge on distribution payments. The present Revenue attitude appears to be that IHTA 1984, s 10 does not exclude IHTA 1984, ss 64 and 65 and that a trust liability exists which makes such a plan unattractive for inheritance tax, as per Life Offices Association press release 15 September 1976. The policy can be affected on a non-discretionary trust for other partners in profit sharing ratios or otherwise, and these may be the best policies for large partnerships.

5. Split joint life assurance

(a) In order to obtain life assurance relief on the premiums for a joint life assurance it used to be necessary to split the policy into two or more contingent assurances if on two lives, one payable on the death of Smith during the life of Jones and the other payable on the death of Jones during the lifetime of Smith. The first policy is effected by and paid by Smith and the other by Jones and then cross-assigned to or written in trust for the other party.

(b) In the interests of equity Smith and Jones would like to keep the premium payments equal. If there is a considerable difference in their age or health, the premiums would be anything but equal and it would be necessary for the younger partner to take out additional cover to provide the balance on his partner's death on a life of another basis.

6. Own life policies cross assigned

Each partner takes out a policy on his own life for the amount required, pays the premium himself and assigns the policy in favour of his partners.

The disadvantages of this arrangement include the fact that the profit element of the policy will be subject to capital gains tax on the recipients under TCGA 1992, s 210.

7. Individual's own policies

In view of the various disadvantages of life assurance schemes for partners, it may be appropriate to consider a more drastic approach.

As with goodwill, each partner provides that his capital account passes by survivorship to his partners for the time being on his death or retirement.

To replace his anticipated capital, each partner takes out an endowment policy on his own life in his own favour or in favour of his dependants. The premiums payable by all the partners are treated as a first charge on the profits so that each partner is paid out sufficient for him to pay the premium and thereafter the profits are distributed in the usual profit sharing ratio.

There are no complications on partners leaving and joining the partnership, as each partner has his own policy and no one else is interested in that policy.

It is submitted that as part of a commercial arrangement there are no inheritance tax liabilities caused by an arrangement to pass partnership assets by survivorship, although the question is not free from doubt. Under the estate duty rules the Revenue contended that the shares of each partner (other than in goodwill) had to be adequate consideration for such an arrangement and it seems that similar provisions apply to inheritance tax.

Each partner has his own policy on his own life which would be his only asset connected with the partnership for inheritance tax. It is not desirable to adopt this arrangement for any partner with less than seven and one-half years to go to retirement because of the size of the premiums required and the fact that a policy of less than ten years would not attract tax relief as it would be a non-qualifying policy. A non-qualifying policy may also become liable for a charge to higher rate tax on any gain arising from the policy. An endowment policy taken out for ten years and therefore qualifying may be made paid up after seven and one-half years without any tax charge. Alternatively a flexible whole life policy could be used and surrendered with bonuses at the retirement date. The participating partners' capital accounts would become part of a capital fund for the partnership belonging to the partners for the time being. Such an arrangement is obviously only feasible for a stable professional partnership which is likely to continue irrespective of the partners for the time being. In the case of an older partner, he may be left out of the arrangement, the younger partners effecting policies on his life.

A more tax efficient variation on this theme is to avoid endowment insurance policies completely. Each partner during the course of his life as a partner is entitled to withdraw a certain amount of his capital account annually in addition to his normal income drawings. The amount to be drawn is arrived at by finding the net premiums that would be required to provide the capital account balance which will now be subject to an automatic accruer in favour of the other partners at the normal retirement age. If any partner wishes to receive such a capital sum at retirement he merely pays the amount withdrawn into such a policy which will therefore provide the appropriate sum at his retirement or on earlier death as explained above. However, the partner might prefer to use the money so drawn, not for the payment of a premium on an endowment policy, but to pay an additional amount to a retirement annuity policy, if he is not already paying the maximum premium, which in many cases will not only give a larger lump sum on retirement by way of commutation but will also provide a pension as explained in Chapter 12. The reason why the personal pension policy is likely to be so much greater value is that for the same net cash sum spent a much greater premium can be paid because of the tax relief and the greater premium is invested in a tax free fund.

It is not essential that an arrangement such as this be confined to the whole of the capital account balance and it might be desirable, for example, merely to provide that £20,000 of each partner's capital account will be subject to an automatic accruer and the balance be repaid at retirement or death in the normal way. In that case each partner in the scheme would have £20,000 written off his capital account and transferred to a general reserve which would belong to the partners for the time being and in due course would reduce the capital required to be brought in by new partners and build up permanent capital within the partnership which is a further advantage of this particular scheme. In the following example, it will be seen that assuming that all existing partners survive to age sixty-five, capital of £100,000 is repaid at a total cost of £57,051, saving £49,949 which would remain in general reserves. The advantage of such a scheme is that the partnership is effectively repaying each partner's capital account during his period of partnership and each partner has an additional sum which it will normally be provided must be spent by him on providing for his withdrawal from his partnership of for his subsequent retirement in the manner which is most tax effective for his own particular circumstances. In a scheme such as this, partnership term assurance would be unnecessary as each partner would provide for his own death before retirement under, for example, TA 1988, s 637, as appropriate to his circumstances.

The drawings and profit sharing arrangements would not be affected by the scheme except that interest on capital would be lower, unless it was decided to calculate interest on capital on the amount transferred to general reserve, which could easily be computed if so desired. It is possible that the partnership would continue and that the surplus on general reserve would continue to grow over the years and would provide part of the working capital of the firm without the necessity of partners restricting drawings or having to introduce additional capital from their own resources. Incoming partners would have to introduce capital of, say, £20,000 over, say, five years, after which they would join the scheme; their capital would be transferred to general reserves and they would have an annual withdrawal from capital over the remainder of their active life as a partner.

The only eventuality the scheme does not really cater for is a partner withdrawing from the partnership before his normal retirement age other than on death, and no doubt in such circumstances the fact that he would not recover all the capital introduced would form part of negotiations for fair terms for the withdrawal. There is no need to limit the arrangements to repay the capital of £20,000 and if a partner's capital increases as a result of the necessity to inject more working capital into the firm, or by leaving undrawn profits a further tranche of the capital account could be transferred to reserve in the same way.

A further advantage of providing that part of the capital passes by automatic accruer to the continuing partners is that the value of the deceased partner's estate is reduced by the amount of the capital to which he is no longer entitled. This in turn would obviously reduce the inheritance tax liability, although the lump sum on any death before retirement under TA 1988, s 637 would be subject to inheritance tax, with no business relief, if received by the estate and not left direct to a third party such as the children.

General

Whether the actual policies are endowment, whole life or term depends on whether the actual retirement dates are known with precision, and whether the retirement cover can be afforded. Term assurance would only cover death before the usual retirement date. A mixture of policies may be required.

The effect of the various policies is summarised in the table on pp. 226–227.

In conclusion, therefore, it is noted that financing retirement by life assurance can have various advantages. For example, it is possible to charge such policies as security, eg for a house purchase. Reciprocal arrangements can be made as described above, which should constitute commercial arrangements between the partners, and therefore hopefully avoid a capital transfer tax charge (but note the probable application of IHTA 1984 chapter III – see below). Moreover the payments received under such policies are normally exempt from capital gains tax under TCGA 1992, s 210.

Upon the maturity of a life policy, the holder may then invest in an annuity and

Summary of taxation effect of some possible

		Inheritance tax on policy on life of deceased
1.	Own life – simple trust for benefit of other partner(s)	IHT on premiums but not *if equal* or within exemption limits
2.	Joint lives assurance in ordinary form	Possibly free if premiums charged actuarially according to age
3.	Life of another	None
4. (i)	Own life – special trust policy – (Trustees with discretionary powers)	Probably on full sum assured as "capital" distribution
(ii)	Non-discretionary	None
5.	Join Lives Assurance split:	
(i)	cross-assigned	IHT on premiums but not if equal or within exemption limits
(ii)	Life of another	None
(iii)	In trust	IHT on premiums but not if equal or within exemption limits
6.	Own life – cross assigned	Ditto
7.	Partnership deed amended for automatic accrual. Own life policies under MWPA or trust	Should be free as normal expenditure.

means of effecting partnership assurance

Inheritance tax on policy on life of survivor	Freedom from capital gains tax	Flexibility	Equity of premium payments among partners
IHT on premiums paid or market value	Yes	Some difficulty with new partner or one leaving	Own life premiums. Special arrangements may be necessary
N/A	Yes	Considerable difficulty with new partner or one leaving	Easily arranged
IHT on premiums paid or market value	Yes	Some difficulty with new partner or one leaving	Yes
None	Yes	No difficulties with new partner or one leaving	Own life premiums. Special arrangements may be necessary
None	Yes	Ditto	Ditto
None	No	Considerable difficulty with new partner or one leaving	Easily arranged
None	Yes	Ditto	Yes
None	Yes	Ditto	Yes
IHT on premiums paid or market value	No	Some difficulty with new partner or one leaving	Own life premiums. Special arrangements may be necessary
None	Yes	No difficulties with new partner or one leaving	Ditto

depending on his age at that time, a large proportion of this annuity, constituting the capitalised value, will be tax free, under the provisions of TA 1988, s 656(1). Retirement annuities on the other hand are fully taxable upon the recipient except to the extent that the limited commutation rights are exercised.

Life Office Association Press Release 15 September 1976:

> "Partnership assurance schemes are often arranged on the basis of each partner effecting a policy on his own life in trust for the other partners. Usually, the premiums for these policies are not 'gifts' because the policies are effected as part of a business transaction between all the partners and the premiums fall within (IHTA 1984, s 10).
>
> The trusts of these policies may take different forms but in many cases they constitute settlements, within the definition of (IHTA 1984, s 43(2)), for the purposes of inheritance tax. The imposition of this tax on existing partnership policies which are settlements, particularly those which are 'discretionary', could therefore have untoward consequences which the partners concerned could not have expected when these assurance schemes were entered into.
>
> Accordingly, following discussions between the Inland Revenue and the Life Officers' Association, the Revenue have offered a concession for all partnership assurance policies effected prior to 15 September 1976, on trusts which are governed by English law and which constitute settlements for IHT purposes. The Revenue are prepared to treat such policies as if their trusts did not constitute settlements ('discretionary' or otherwise) so that those policies will avoid any of the IHTA 1984, chapter III) charges to IHT.
>
> It should be noted that the concession is not available to partnership policies effected after 14 September 1976 nor to existing partnership policies if the trusts of these policies are varied in any way after that date. (The exercise of the power of appointment under a discretionary trust policy would not be regarded as a variation for this purpose.) Furthermore, the concession will apply only to those arrangements where payment of the premiums falls within (IHTA 1984, s 10). The reason for the restriction to policies which satisfy this condition is to confine the concession to cases where the payment of premiums can be regarded as a normal business transaction. This should, however, cover the great majority of policies already in existence.
>
> The Scottish Estate Duty Office have confirmed that the concession will also be available to partnership assurance policies on trusts which are governed by Scots laws but any such policies which directly or indirectly involved a partnership itself as a separate persona will have to be specifically considered."

It is now more common for such policies to be written under "business trusts". These are interest in possession trusts in favour of the current partners with a flexible power of appointment in favour of other beneficiaries, e g future partners. There would be a potentially exempt transfer if an appointment was made away from a current beneficiary. The premium paid would normally be deemed to be part of a bona fide commercial arrangement and therefore not "PETS" in themselves.

ACCIDENT INSURANCE

Many partnership will insure the partners and key employees against accidental death prior to normal retirement age, and this is particularly valuable where the partners do a material amount of travelling. The policy would usually be written for the benefit of the surviving partners. It seems that following the ruling in *Gray & Co Ltd v Murphy* (1940) 23 TC 225 and *Keir and Cawder Ltd v IRC* (1958) 38 TC 234 that the insurance proceeds of an accident insurance policy would be treated as a trading receipt of the partnership and the premiums would be an allowable deduction for tax purposes.

However, the Revenue in practice will not tax the proceeds if a partner is accidentally killed provided that no claim has been made for tax relief on the premiums.

Partners may also wish to provide accident cover for the benefit of their own families and there may be reductions in rates by having a group scheme for all partners, even though the premium would not qualify for tax relief.

The proceeds of key man accident insurance on an employee's life can be paid free of inheritance tax to his dependants in accordance with the Inland Revenue Press Release of 6 January 1976 where there was an arm's length employer employee relationship.

MEDICAL INSURANCE

If a partnership paid medical expenses for partners the expenses would not normally be a trading expense following such cases as *Norman v Golder* (1944) 26 T.C 293; *Murgatroyd v Evans-Jackson* (1966) 43 TC 581 and *Prince v Mapp* (1969) 46 TC 169. It would therefore follow that medical insurance such as subscriptions to BUPA would not qualify as an allowable expense for tax purposes. There might nonetheless be advantages in the partnership setting up a group scheme for the benefit of the partners and their families as this might qualify for a substantial discount compared with each partner providing for his own medical insurance.

If the partnership extends the group scheme to members of the staff, the premium would normally be treated as a business expense of the partnership under TA 1988, s 74, but would be taxed on a P11D or as a benefit in kind (TA 1988, s 157).

PERMANENT HEALTH INSURANCE

Permanent health insurance for the partners in a professional partnership would often be arranged on a group basis in order to get the benefits of a discount for group membership. In return for the premiums an income would be paid to a partner incapacitated from working by reason of illness or accident. Such insurance is normally essential for a partner to enable him to meet his commitments if he were to be so incapacitated and it is often desirable to ensure that partners are covered by paying the premium though the firm. As the insurance covers a personal expense the premiums would be disallowed for tax purposes under TA 1988, s 74(*b*) and would not qualify for life assurance relief, whether paid by the firm or by individual partners.

Most permanent health insurance policies provide for a period of incapacity due to accident or illness which is not covered and this period may be anything between one month and twelve months, and obviously the longer the period of non-payment before the insurance payments are made the cheaper the premium. It would be normally sensible to arrange a delay before the payments would commence of between six and twelve months in most professional partnerships on the assumption that the remaining partners could afford to continue payment to the incapacitated partner during this period.

Once payments start to be made they will be tax free under Extra-statutory Concession A26 (1980) until the benefit has continued for at least twelve months prior to the commencement of the year of assessment, and thereafter will be taxable as an annual payment on the recipient in the same way as any other investment income.

Personal health insurance provided for members of the partnership staff would be an allowable expense in the partnership and would only be taxable as a benefit in kind on P11D employees or directors, ie those who are directors of a service company or remunerated at a rate in excess of £8,500 per annum.

CRITICAL ILLNESS COVER

In the event that a partner contracts a serious illness or is permanently disabled, the consequences for the other partners may be as serious as on death. The partner concerned may wish to retire or work less strenuously. It is now possible to effect cover against such an event and this is known as critical illness or dread disease cover. The policy will pay out on diagnosis of one of a specified range of illnesses or disabilities. Such plans can be set up under similar trust arrangements as for life assurance and can even be contained in the same policy.

Appendix I

The preceding year basis

Partnerships in existence at 5 April 1994 are subject to the preceding year basis of assessment for all years up to and including 1995–96. Partnerships which have a change of partner without a continuance election before 6 April 1997 are subject to the old rules up to the date of the change and the new current year basis thereafter. The preceding year basis is discussed more fully below.

Partnership assessments under Schedule D, Cases I and II are calculated under TA 1988, s 60 on the preceding year basis of assessment with special rules for the opening and closing years of trade. Once the assessable profit has been ascertained it is apportioned among the partners in the way in which they share profits *in the year of assessment* even though the profit sharing arrangements in the basis period (i e, usually the accounting period ending in the fiscal year preceding the year of assessment) were dissimilar (*Gaunt v IRC* (1926) 10 TC 683; *Lewis v IRC* (1913) 7 TC 219; *Rutherford v IRC* (1933) 18 TC 174).

EXAMPLE AI.01

	£	£
Year ended 31 December 1994		
Profit per accounts		150,000
Add back: Depreciation	10,000	
Entertaining expenses disallowed under TA 1988, s 577	5,000	
		15,000
Assessable 1995–96		£165,000

Profit-sharing proportions

	A	B	C
Year ended 31 December 1994	½	¼	¼
1995	⅓	⅓	⅓
1996	¼	¼	½

Share of profit per accounts for the year ended 31 December 1994 is:

Total	A	B	C
	(½)	(¼)	(¼)
£150,000	£75,000	£37,500	£37,500

EXAMPLE AI.01 (continued)

But, for tax purposes, the share of the 1995–96 assessment is:

	Total £	A £	B £	C £
6.4.95 – 31.12.95 (say ¾)*	123,750	(⅓) 41,250	(⅓) 41,250	(⅓) 41,250
1.1.96 – 5.4.96 (say ¼)*	41,250	(¼) 10,313	(¼) 10,312	(½) 20,625
	£165,000	£51,563	£51,562	£61,875

*The profit sharing proportions have changed during the year of assessment (6 April – 5 April) 1995–96 and therefore the assessment must be divided between the parts of that year and then allocated to the partners in accordance with the relevant profit-sharing proportion.

Equity partners' salaries are an appropriation of profits not an allowable expense.

EXAMPLE AI.02

Year ended 31 December 1994	£	£
Profit per accounts after partners' salaries		100,000
Add back: partners' salaries	50,000	
depreciation	10,000	
entertaining expenses	5,000	
		65,000
Assessable 1995–96		£165,000

Profit-sharing proportions

	A £	B £	C £
Year ended 31 December 1994			
Salary	20,000	15,000	15,000
Share of profits	½	¼	¼
Year ended 31 December 1995			
Salary	20,000	20,000	10,000
Share of profits	⅓	⅓	⅓
Year ended 31 December 1996			
Salary	22,000	20,000	18,000
Share of profits	¼	¼	½

Share of profit per accounts for the year ended 31 December 1994 is:

	Total £	A £	B £	C £
Salary	50,000	20,000	15,000	15,000
Share of profits	100,000	50,000	25,000	25,000
	£150,000	£70,000	£40,000	£40,000

EXAMPLE AI.02 *(continued)*

But, for tax purposes, the share of the 1995–96 assessment is:

	Total £	A £	B £	C £
6.4.95 – 31.12.95 (say ¾)				
Salary	37,500	15,000	15,000	7,500
Share of profit*		⅓	⅓	⅓
	84,375	28,125	28,125	28,125
1.1.96 – 5.4.96 (say ¼)				
Salary	15,000	5,500	5,000	4,500
Share of profit**		¼	¼	¼
	28,125	7,031	7,031	14,063
	£165,000	£55,656	£55,156	£54,188

* £165,000 *less* salaries £52,500 = 112,500 × ¾ = 84,375
**£165,000 *less* salaries £52,500 = 112,500 × ¼ = 28,125

The profits for a partnership accounting year ending on 31 March 1994 fall within the fiscal year 1993–94 and would therefore form the basis of assessment for 1994–95. If the partnership accounting year ended on 30 April 1994, however, that would fall within the fiscal year 1994–95 and form the basis of assessment for 1995–96. As tax for these years is payable under Schedule D, Case I or II in two equal instalments on 1 January in the year of assessment and on the following 1 July it will be appreciated that an accounting date ending early in the fiscal year would give the maximum time interval between earning profits and paying the tax thereon. This is particularly valuable in times of high inflation and can give a very significant cash flow advantage. Although in theory the optimum accounting date is 6 April in each year, 30 April is very often found to be a more practical date for the preparation of accounts. Under the current year basis of assessment from 1997–98 an accounting date ending early in the fiscal year, such as 30 April, continues to have cash flow advantages as described in Chapter 2.

COMMENCEMENT

In the opening years of a partnership under the preceding year basis of assessment, ie for a business which commenced prior to 5 April 1994, there were *special* rules for assessment to tax for trading profits with any advantage going to the taxpayer in order to ease the financial burden on him in the usually difficult first years of trading. An assessment for each of the first three years was, in accordance with TA 1988, s 61 and 62;
  (a) on the profits from the date of commencement to the following 5 April for the first year of assessment (payable thirty days after issue of assessment),
  (b) and from the date of commencement to the anniversary thereof for the second year of assessment (payable thirty days after issue of assessment), and
  (c) the third year of assessment was based on the profits for the first twelve months as for the second year of assessment or on the basis of an accounting year ending in the preceding year of assessment if accounts have been prepared for such a period (payable thirty days after issue of the assessment or in two equal instalments on 1 January in year of assessment and following 1 July, if the assessment has been raised in time). Thereafter, under TA 1988, s 60, the profits would be assessed on the preceding year basis.

In order to take proper advantage of the benefits available from the bases of assessment in the opening years of business, due attention should be paid to when profits are earned and expense incurred – including capital expenditure, which may give rise to a capital allowance (see page 251).

EXAMPLE AI.03

Senior, Middle and Junior decide to trade in partnership sharing profits equally, profits for the first year to 5 October 1992 were £36,000. The assessments were:

	Senior £	Middle £	Junior £	Total £
1991–92 Actual[1]	6,000	6,000	6,000	18,000
1992–93 First 12 months[2]	12,000	12,000	12,000	36,000
1993–94 Preceding year	12,000	12,000	12,000	36,000
Total taxable income	£30,000	£30,000	£30,000	£90,000

Had the admission of Junior into the firm been delayed until 6 October 1992 with an election for continuation made under TA 1988, s 113(2) and Junior given a salary as an employee for the first year of £12,000 the position would have been:
Revised profits £24,000 (£36,000 less salary £12,000).

	Senior £	Middle £	Junior £	Total £
1991–92 Actual[1]	6,000	6,000	–	12,000
1992–93 First 12 months[2]				
– Period 1[3]	6,000	6,000	–	12,000
– Period 2[3]	4,000	4,000	4,000	12,000
1993–94 Preceding year	8,000	8,000	8,000	24,000
1991–92 Schedule E[4]	–	–	6,000	6,000
1992–93 Schedule E[4]	–	–	6,000	6,000
Total taxable income	£24,000	£24,000	£24,000	£72,000

[1] The 1991–92 assessment is based on the actual profits from date of commencement to the following 5 April (ie to 5 April 1992). These profits in practice would be a proportion (by time) of the profits of the first accounting period, in this case 6 months' (6 October 1991 to 5 April 1992) of the full year's profits.
[2] The 1992–93 assessment is based on the actual profits earned in the first twelve months (ie, the full year from 6 October 1991 to 5 October 1992).
[3] A quirk of the tax legislation required profits earned in the *basis period* (in this case, the first twelve months as explained in footnote 2) to be assessed, on the individual partners in the *year of assessment*, on the basis of the partner's fractional share of profit in that *year* and not otherwise. In the year of assessment 1992–93 (6 April 1992 to 5 April 1993) the partners shared profits as to Senior: ½ and Middle: ½, for the period of six months from 6 April 1992 to 5 October 1992 (Period 1), when Junior was admitted to partnership, and as to Senior: ⅓, Middle: ½ and Junior: ⅓ for the second six months to 5 April 1993 (Period 2). Thus, the profits for the full twelve months must first be apportioned between the two periods in order to be allocated in the appropriate profit-sharing fractions.
[4] Assessments under Schedule E in respect of a salary are on a current year basis so that the 1991–92 assessment was on the salary earned from 6 October 1991 to 5 April 1992 and the 1992–93 assessment was on the salary earned between 6 April 1992 and 5 October 1992, when Junior was admitted to the partnership and the Schedule E liability ceased and Schedule D liability commenced. Again, both these periods were of six months duration and the annual salary of £12,000 is assumed to have been earned as to £1,000 per month.

The choice of the first accounting period can influence the taxable profits.

EXAMPLE AI.04

Mann and Co. commenced business on 1 January 1993 and decide to have an accounting date of 30 April. Profits for the four months to 30 April 1993 were £4,000 and for the twelve months to 30 April 1994 £24,000.

(I)
If accounts were drawn up for the sixteen months ended 30 April 1994 (showing a profit of £28,000) the first four years assessments will be:

	£
1992–93 (period from commencement to following 5 April) $3/16 \times £28,000$	5,250
1993–94 (first 12 months) $12/16 \times £28,000$	21,000
1994–95 (preceding year) $12/16 \times £28,000$	21,000
1995–96 (preceding year) $12/16 \times £28,000$	21,000
	£68,250

(II)
If however accounts were drawn up to 30 April 1993 (showing a £4,000 profit) and annually thereafter (the first showing a profit of £24,000) the assessments become:

	£
1992–93 (period from commencement to following 5 April) $3/4 \times £4,000$	3,000
1993–94 (first 12 months) £4,000 + $8/12 \times £24,000$	20,000
1994–95 (preceding year) £4,000 + $8/12 \times £24,000$	20,000
1995–96 (preceding year) £24,000 to y/e 30.4.94	24,000
	£67,000

Although in practice the Revenue adopted the "first twelve-month" basis for the third and subsequent years of assessment, in certain circumstances, such as where there was no twelve-month account ending in the previous year, TA 1988, s 60(4) gave the Revenue power to choose any twelve-month period ending in the preceding year. In Example A.04 this power would apply in respect of 1995–96 in the first calculation (allowing a possible substitution of £23,000 for £21,000) and in respect of 1994–95 and 1995–96 in the second calculation (allowing a possible substitution of up to £23,000 for £20,000 in the former year, but no effective substitution in the latter year without a knowledge of subsequent profits). But in practice the Revenue would only exercise this option in extreme cases where the profits fluctuated substantially, and even if they did use their option their decision could be appealed against under TA 1988, s 60(6) or (7).

EXAMPLE AI.05

Planner & Co. commenced trading on 1 July 1992 and prepared accounts for ten months ended 30 April 1993 and for the year ended 30 April 1996 showing profits of £1,000 and £36,000 respectively.

Under normal practice the assessments would be:

	£
1992–93 (period from commencement to following 5 April) Actual $9/10 \times £1,000$	900
1993–94 (first 12 months) $£1,000 + 2/12 \times £36,000$	7,000
1994–95 (preceding year) $£1,000 + 2/12 \times £36,000$	7,000
1995–96 (preceding year) y/e 30.4.94	36,000
	£50,900

However if the Revenue used TA 1988, s 60(4) to choose for 1994–95 a period of twelve months ending in 1993–94 they might possibly adopt the twelve months ended 31 March 1994 and the profits assessable would be $1/10 \times £1,000 + 11/12 \times £36,000 = £33,100$, as opposed to the first twelve month figure of £7,000.

This problem could be overcome if the business had commenced on 1 May 1992 and the first accounts of 30 April 1993 had shown profits of £1,000 with 30 April 1994 showing £36,000.

The assessments would then be:

	£
1992–93 (period from commencement to following 5 April) Actual $11/12 \times £1,000$	917
1993–94 (first 12 months)	1,000
1994–95 (preceding year y/e 30.4.93)	1,000
1995–96 (preceding year y/e 30.4.94)	36,000
	£38,917

By ensuring that two twelve-month accounting periods followed one another from the date of commencement the 1994–95 and 1995–96 assessments are saved from being "tinkered" with by the Revenue under s 60(4) powers.

TAXPAYER'S OPTION

The taxpayer had an option under TA 1988, s 62 to have the second and third years of assessment based on the actual profits for those years instead of by reference to profits of earlier basis periods. The alternative assessment was arrived at by apportioning the adjusted profits for tax purposes over the appropriate fiscal years on a time basis. The election under TA 1988, s 62 had to be made within seven years of the end of the second year of assessment and could be withdrawn within six years of the end of the third year of assessment.

TA 1988, s 67 provided for apportionment to be on the basis of months and fractions of months but in practice is more usual to make the calculation on a daily basis, as is now a statutory requirement as a result of FA 1995, s 121.

EXAMPLE AI.06

Partners A, B and C commenced trading on 1 January 1992 and make up accounts to 30 April sharing profits ⅓ : ⅓ : ⅓. The profit sharing ratio changed to 30:30:40 on 1 May 1992 to 10:40:50 on 1 May 1993 and to 10:45:45 on 1 May 1994.

	Total £	A £	B £	C £
Accounts to 30.4.92				
Profit	30,000			
Profit share		⅓ 10,000	⅓ 10,000	⅓ 10,000
Disallowed expenses	6,000			
	£36,000			
Assessable 1991–92 (period from commencement to following 5 April)				
$\frac{95 \text{ (days)}}{120} \times 36,000$	£28,500	⅓ £9,500	⅓ £9,500	⅓ £9,500
Accounts to 30.4.93				
Profit	150,000			
Profit share		30% 45,000	30% 45,000	40% 60,000
Disallowed expenses	25,000			
	£175,000			
Assessable 1992–93 (First 12 months)				
1.1.92 to 30.4.92	36,000			
1.5.92 to 31.12.92				
$175,000 \times \frac{245}{365}$	117,465			
	£153,465			
Divisible				
6.4.92 to 30.4.92				
$\frac{25 \times 153,465}{365}$	10,511	⅓ 3,504	⅓ 3,504	⅓ 3,503
1.5.92 to 5.4.93				
$\frac{340 \times 153,465}{365}$	142,954	30% 42,886	30% 42,886	40% 57,182
	£153,465	£46,390	£46,390	£60,685

238 *Appendix I*

EXAMPLE AI.06 *(continued)*

Assessable 1993–94 (Preceding year)	£153,465			
Divisible				
6.4.93 to 30.4.93				
$\frac{25}{365} \times 153{,}465$		30%	30%	40%
	10,511	3,153	3,153	4,205
1.5.93 to 5.4.94				
$\frac{340}{365} \times 153{,}465$		10%	40%	50%
	142,954	14,295	57,182	71,477
	£153,465	£17,448	£60,335	£75,682
Accounts to 30.4.94				
Profit	110,000			
Profit share		10%	40%	50%
		11,000	44,000	55,000
Disallowed expenses	10,000			
	£120,000			
Assessable 1994–95 (Preceding year)				
Year ended 30.4.93	£175,000			
Divisible				
6.4.94 to 30.4.94				
$\frac{25}{365} \times 175{,}000$		10%	40%	50%
	11,986	1,199	4,794	5,993
1.5.94 to 5.4.95				
$\frac{340}{365} \times 175{,}000$		10%	45%	45%
	163,014	16,301	73,356	73,357
	£175,000	£17,500	£78,150	£79,350
TA 1970, s 117 option exercised				
Assessable 1992–93				
6.4.92 to 30.4.92				
$\frac{25}{120} \times 36{,}000$		⅓	⅓	⅓
	7,500	2,500	2,500	2,500
1.5.92 to 5.4.93				
$\frac{340}{365} \times 175{,}000$		30%	30%	40%
	163,014	48,904	48,904	65,206
	£170,514	£51,404	£51,404	£67,706
Assessable 1993–94				
6.4.93 to 30.4.93				
$\frac{25}{365} \times 175{,}000$		30%	30%	40%
	11,986	3,596	3,596	4,794
1.5.93 to 5.4.94				
$\frac{340}{365} \times 120{,}000$		10%	40%	50%
	111,781	11,178	44,712	55,891
	£123,767	£14,774	£48,308	£60,685

EXAMPLE AI.06 *(continued)*

Total 1992–93 and 1993–94	294,281	66,178	99,712	128,391
Normal basis 1992–93 and 1993–94	306,930	63,838	106,725	136,367
Saving (loss) on election	£12,649	£(2,340)	£7,013	£7,976

In these circumstances, it is possible that the election should be made, although in marginal cases it is wise to calculate the effect of a shift in taxable profits in terms of tax payable; increased assessments may attract higher rates of tax whilst reduced assessments may only be saving basic rate tax, and there may also be the effect of capital allowances and charges on income to take into account. An election under TA 1988, s 62 can be an informal request in a computation by the partnership or its agent. It does not have to be signed by all partners.

In this example, A, who loses out, may request B and C, who gain, to indemnify him for the additional tax payable as a result of the election; but he is not in a position to prevent it being made. The requirement for an equitable adjustment in such circumstances can be written into the partnership agreement.

CESSATION

If the business which commenced prior to 6 April 1994 is discontinued for tax purposes either on an actual cessation of trade prior to 6 April 1997 or on a change in partners prior to 6 April 1997 (or on a Revenue direction, under FA 1994, Sch. 20, para. 3(1), in the absence of an election under TA 1988, s 113(2), the final year's assessments will be on the adjusted profits from the 6 April in the year of discontinuance to the actual date of discontinuance. Under TA 1988, s 63 the Inland Revenue will substitute for the penultimate and ante-penultimate years of assessment the actual profits apportioned on a time basis over those two years of assessment for the assessable profits otherwise taxable on the preceding year basis provided that this would *increase* the aggregate profits assessed. The Revenue calculate whether or not to raise such additional assessments in terms of assessable income not in terms of tax, and they have to ignore capital allowance when deciding whether or not to exercise their option. As with the commencement provisions, the length of the final accounting period can influence the profits assessed.

EXAMPLE AI.07

Jennifer Paul & Co. ceased to trade on 30 September 1995 and had the following profits adjusted for tax purposes:

	£
Year ended 30.4.92	35,000
Year ended 30.4.93	30,000
Year ended 30.4.94	40,000
Year ended 30.4.95	50,000
Period ended 30.9.95	15,000

EXAMPLE AI.07 *(continued)*

Normal assessments would be:

	£
1995–96	
1.5.95 to 30.9.95	15,000
6.4.95 to 30.4.95	
$\frac{25}{365} \times £50,000$	3,425
	£18,425
1994-95	
Year ended 30.4.95	£30,000
1993–94	
Year ended 30.4.92	£35,000
Combined assessments 1993–94 and 1994–95	£65,000

If the Revenue adjust the assessments to an actual basis these would be as follows:

	£
1994–95	
1.5.94 to 5.4.95	
$\frac{340}{365} \times £50,000$	46,575
6.4.94 to 30.4.94	
$\frac{25}{365} \times £40,000$	2,740
	£49,315
1993–94	
1.5.93 to 5.4.94	
$\frac{340}{365} \times £40,000$	37,260
6.4.93 to 30.4.93	
$\frac{25}{365} \times £30,000$	2,055
	£39,315
Combined assessments 1993–94 and 1994–95	£88,630

As this figure is greater than £65,000, the assessments would be adjusted, by means of amended assessments if the original assessments had not been finally determined. This in turn means that there could be interest payable on unpaid tax as the reckonable dates would not be altered by the amended assessments. However, if the original assessment had been finally determined there would be additional assessments raised by the Revenue of £4,315 for 1993–94 and £19,315 for 1994–95 which would have their own reckonable dates and could give a further opportunity for retirement annuity payments.

Appendix I 241

The commencement rules for a change in partners after 19 March 1985 were modified by FA 1985, s 47 now incorporated in TA 1988, ss 61 and 62. The principal reason for the change was the exploitation of the previous provisions by some partnerships which had sought to engineer partnership changes and concentrate profit into a short period. This was usually known as the low, high, high, low arrangement and can be illustrated in an extreme form on the basis of a commencement on the 7 April in one year followed by a cessation on the 8 April, four years later.

EXAMPLE AI.08

Samuel Smith & Co. commenced trading on 7 April 1986 and had the following profits adjusted for tax purposes:

	£
Year ended 6.4.87	500
Year ended 6.4.88	48,500
Year ended 6.4.89	45,000
Year ended 6.4.90	800
Year ended 6.4.91	600

A new partner was introduced on 8 April 1990 which, in the absence of an election to continue under TA 1988, s 113(2), produced an automatic cessation at that date for tax purposes.

The assessments up to the date of introduction of the new partner were:

	£	£
1986–87		
7.4.86 to 5.4.87		
$\dfrac{364}{365} \times £500$		499
1987–88		
Year ended 6.4.87		500
1988–89		
Year ended 6.4.87		500
1989–90		
Year ended 6.4.88		48,000
1990–91		
6.4.90		
$\dfrac{1}{365} \times £800$	2	
7.4.90		
$\dfrac{1}{365} \times £600$	2	4
Total assessments		£49,503

If the Revenue were to adjust the assessments to an actual basis under TA 1988, s 63 the assessments for 1988–89 and 1989–90 would be:

1988–89
7.4.88 to 5.4.89
$\dfrac{364}{365} \times £45,000$ 44,877

6.4.88
$\dfrac{1}{365} \times £48,000$ 132

£45,009

EXAMPLE AI.08 (continued)

	£
1989–90	
7.4.89 to 5.4.90	
$\frac{364}{365} \times £800$	798
6.4.89	
$\frac{1}{365} \times £45,000$	123
	£921

The assessment for both years totals £45,930 which is less than the original assessments of £48,500 so the Revenue adjustment would not be made.

The assessments total £49,503 on adjusted profits of £94,304.

It is most unlikely that a professional partnership would have a profit flow of this order but an extreme example has been used to show the principle of the type of advantages that could be obtained where there was fluctuating profits.
The advantage could still be obtained if the profit flow was low, high, low, high.

PARTNERSHIP CHANGES AFTER 19 MARCH 1985

In respect of partnership changes after 19 March 1985 the normal commencement rules only applied on a sole trader taking another person into partnership and on a dissolution of a partnership following which a partner continued as a sole trader.

In other case where there was no election for continuation the result was that the first four years of assessment were assessed on an actual basis with the taxpayer having an option to have the fifth and sixth years of assessment similarly treated.

EXAMPLE AI.09

Sicon & Co. introduced a new partner into the firm on 1 January 1986, on which date the senior partner retired, and did not elect for continuation. The profits were as follows:

	£
Year ended 31 December 1982	48,000
Year ended 31 December 1983	50,000
Year ended 31 December 1984	60,000
Year ended 31 December 1985	40,000
Year ended 31 December 1986	70,000
Year ended 31 December 1987	80,000
Year ended 31 December 1988	90,000
Year ended 31 December 1989	65,000
Year ended 31 December 1990	75,000
Year ended 31 December 1991	55,000

EXAMPLE AI.09 (*continued*)

The assessments were:		£
OLD FIRM		
1983–84		
Year ended 31 December 1982		48,000
1984–85		
Year ended 31 December 1983		50,000
Penultimate and ante penultimate years, original		£98,000
1985–86		
$9/12 \times$ year ended 31 December 1985		£30,000

Revenue option on cessation

1983–84		
$9/12 \times$ year ended 31 December 1983	37,500	
$3/12 \times$ year ended 31 December 1984	15,000	52,500
1984–85		
$9/12 \times$ year ended 31 December 1984	45,000	
$3/12 \times$ year ended 31 December 1985	10,000	55,000
Penultimate and ante penultimate years – revised		£107,500

NEW FIRM

1985–86		
$3/12 \times$ year ended 31 December 1986		17,500
1986–87		
$9/12 \times$ year ended 31 December 1986	52,500	
$3/12 \times$ year ended 31 December 1987	20,000	72,500
1987–88		
$9/12 \times$ year ended 31 December 1987	60,000	
$3/12 \times$ year ended 31 December 1988	22,500	82,500
1988–89		
$9/12 \times$ year ended 31 December 1988	67,500	
$3/12 \times$ year ended 31 December 1989	16,250	83,750
1989–90		
year ended 31 December 1988		90,000
1990–91		
year ended 31 December 1989		65,000
1991–92		
year ended 31 December 1990		75,000

EXAMPLE AI.09 (*continued*)

Taxpayer's option		£
1989–90		
$9/12$ × year ended 31 December 1989	48,750	
$3/12$ × year ended 31 December 1990	18,750	67,500
1990–91		
$9/12$ × year ended 31 December 1990	56,250	
$3/12$ × year ended 31 December 1991	13,750	70,000

Assessments:

Old firm 1983/84	52,500	
Old firm 1984/85	55,000	} 137,500
Old firm 1985/86	30,000	
New firm 1985/86	17,500	
New firm 1986/87	72,500	
New firm 1987/88	82,500	
New firm 1988/89	83,750	
New firm 1989/90	67,500	
New firm 1990/91	70,000	
New firm 1991/92 year ended 31 December 1990	75,000	
	£606,250	

If an election for continuation had been made the assessments would have been:

Old firm 1983/84 year ended 31 December 1982	48,000	
Old firm 1984/85 year ended 31 December 1983	50,000	} 143,000
Old firm 1985/86 $9/12$ year ended 31 December 1984	45,000	
New firm 1985/86 $3/12$ year ended 31 December 1984	15,000	
New firm 1986/87 year ended 31 December 1985	40,000	
New firm 1987/88 year ended 31 December 1986	70,000	
New firm 1988/89 year ended 31 December 1987	80,000	
New firm 1989/90 year ended 31 December 1988	90,000	
New firm 1990/91 year ended 31 December 1989	65,000	
New firm 1991/92 year ended 31 December 1990	75,000	
	£578,000	

An election for continuation would actually have been beneficial in this case. However the assessments on the old firm were reduced by the cessation which clearly benefited the retiring partner. The election would have to have been made by 31 December 1987, long before the effect of an actual basis could be calculated under the recommencement rules.

In most cases it is likely to pay to elect for continuation unless there is a real likelihood of a substantial drop in profits for a considerable period, for example if two or more partners leave and are not replaced.

It should also be noted that if the taxpayer does not exercise his option for the actual basis for the fifth and sixth years of assessment under TA 1988, s 62(4), then the profits for the year ended 31 December 1988 are assessed twice and those for 1989 one and one-quarter times. If the option is exercised profits for 1990 are assessed twice and for 1991 one and one-quarter times. This could be an important factor in the timing of major allowable revenue expenditure.

It is imperative to establish correctly the exact status of a partner joining or leaving a firm. It is only upon a change of a full partner that a cessation of the business occurs.

CHANGE OF ACCOUNTING DATE

The preceding year basis of assessment can only be applied where the partnership consistently makes up accounts the same date in each year. It is permissible to make up accounts on a fifty-two or fifty-three week accounting period provided that the year end remains within four days either side of a particular date, although the Revenue will permit longer extensions in the case of stockbrokers.

As was explained earlier, if no accounts for a suitable period are available, the Revenue shall decide what period of twelve months ending on a date within the year preceding the year of assessment shall be deemed to be the "year" the profits or gains of which are to be taken to be the profits or gains of the "year preceding the year of assessment" under TA 1988, s 60(4). The Revenue have published an averaging procedure for a change of accounting date. On such a date the profits of the twelve month period ending on the new accounting date form the basis of assessment on the normal preceding year basis. If the new accounting date is later than the old accounting date, some profits will fall out of assessment and if it is earlier some profits will be assessed twice. In such cases the Revenue apply an averaging procedure as explained below. The Revenue procedure has been approved in *IRC v Helical Bar Ltd* (1927) 48 TC 221.

Averaging procedure

First, it is necessary to adjust the profits for the year to the new accounting date, making any necessary apportionments on a time basis. It is then necessary to compute the adjusted profits for the previous twelve months (the corresponding period). The assessments originally based on the profits included in these computations should be examined. If the earliest of those years of assessment cannot be based on the original accounting date on the normal preceding year basis, it is necessary to go back a further year and introduce another corresponding period. The total period of the accounts affected is compared with the total period of the fiscal years affected and the profits are expanded or contracted proportionately to arrive at the total notional adjusted profits. From this is deducted the assessments which are final leaving an adjusted figure for the intermediate period. If the intermediate period figure falls between the corresponding period figure and the original unadjusted assessment for that fiscal year, the intermediate figure will be substituted provided that the difference is at least 10% of the average profits or £1,000, whichever is lower.

This change of accounting date computation can best be illustrated by an example and further details will be found in the Revenue leaflet IR 26, reproduced below.

This averaging basis is not used by the Revenue where it would produce an unfair result, for example, where the intermediate figure does not fall between the original and corresponding figures or where the profits of the business are seasonal or where some of the periods involved were loss-making, or during the opening or closing years of a business.

EXAMPLE AI.10

On 30 April 1993 Pater Noster & Co. changed their accounting date. The results were:

		£
30 April 1993	– 4 months	10,000
31 December 1992	– 12 months	28,000
31 December 1991	– 12 months	24,000
	28 months	£62,000

Accounts will be made up to 30 April in future.

Assessment 1994–95	£
Year ended 30.4.93	
4 months to 30.4.93	10,000
$^8/_{12} \times £28,000$ (y/e 31.12.92)	18,667
	£28,667

Assessment 1993–94 (corresponding period)	
Year ended 30.4.92	
$^4/_{12} \times £28,000$ (y/e 31.12.92)	9,333
$^8/_{12} \times £24,000$ (y/e 31.12.91)	16,000
	£25,333

Original assessment 1993–94	
Year ended 31.12.92	£28,000

Original assessment 1992–93	
Year ended 31.12.91	£24,000

Fiscal years originally based on these profits 1992–93, 1993–94 and 1994–95
3 years = 36 months
Average profits.

	£	£
$\frac{36 \text{ months}}{28 \text{ months}} \times £62,000$		79,714
Less: assessed 1994–95	28,667	
1992–93	24,000	52,667
Intermediate period		£27,047

This £27,047 falls between the original assessment (£28,000) and the corresponding period assessment (£25,333), but is within £1,000 of the original assessment. As the difference is also less than 10% of the average profits for the current (1994–95 £28,667) and preceding years' assessments (1993–94 £28,000) ie £2,833, the average basis for 1993–94 is not used and the original assessment of £28,000 remains.

The capital allowances basis periods will be calculated in accordance with CAA 1990, s 160, only if the taxpayer so requires. By unpublished concession, the Revenue only adjust the capital allowances basis periods if the taxpayer so insists (capital allowances are dealt with at pp. 82 and 251).

Revenue leaflet IR 26 is reproduced below.

"1. This leaflet sets out briefly the practice of the Board of Inland Revenue in cases where a trader permanently changes his accounting date.

Statutory provisions

2. The relevant statutory provisions are contained in TA 1988, s 60. The effect on these provisions is briefly as follows:
   (i) In the normal case where there is only one account ending in the year preceding the year of assessment and that account is for a period of one year, the assessment is to be based on the profit of that account (section 60(3)).
   (ii) In other cases, the Board of Inland Revenue are to decide what period of 12 months ending on a date in the preceding Income Tax year is to be the basis year (section 60(4)). There is no appeal against that decision.
   (iii) Where the Board have determined the basis year for any Income Tax year under (ii), they may direct that the assessment for the preceding Income Tax year is to be adjusted to the profits of the corresponding period, i e the year ending on the same date in the previous year (section 60(5)); an appeal against the Board's decision to make or not to make any such direction lies to the General or Special Commissioners, who are empowered to grant 'such relief, if any, as is just'.

Board's normal practice

3. Under section 60(4) the Board normally decide that the assessment is to be based on the profits of the period of 12 months ending on the new accounts date in the preceding Income Tax year, ie the date to which the trader proposes to make up his accounts in future.

4. The question then arises whether there is to be any adjustment of the assessment for the preceding Income Tax year under section 60(5) to the profits of the 'corresponding' period. Such an adjustment may increase or decrease the liability, according to the trend of profits.

5. The considerations which the Board have in mind in determining this question are as follows:

Where there is a permanent change of accounting date then, whether or not revision under section 60(5) is ordered, one of two things must, in the ordinary course, happen:
   (*a*) If the new date is later in the Income Tax year than the old, the profits of some period will not come into assessment at all.
   (*b*) If the new date is earlier in the Income Tax year than the old, the profits of some period will come into assessment twice.

If the profits of the period omitted were relatively low, or the profits of the period coming in twice were relatively high, the Revenue would gain: conversely, if the profits of the period omitted were relatively high, or the profits of the period coming in twice were relatively low, the taxpayer would gain. The Board attempt to secure that the profits to be assessed twice, or to be omitted from assessment, as the case may be, are 'average' profits. As a rule this object can be secured neither by straightforward revision nor by non-revision, but only by taking for the year to which section 60(5) applies some figure intermediate between the revised and unrevised figures, and it is the Board's normal practice to propose, subject to the concurrence of the Commissioners of Income Tax having jurisdiction in the particular case the adoption of such an intermediate figure. That intermediate figure is computed by reference to consideration of:
   (i) the profits of all the accounting periods of which any part enters into either the basis year (or, in some cases, years) under section 60(4) or the 'corresponding period' under section 60(5) (referred to subsequently as the 'relevant accounting periods'), and

(ii) the number of years for which the assessments are based in whole or in part on any of the profits of the 'relevant accounting periods' (referred to subsequently as the 'relevant years').

The profits of the 'relevant accounting periods' are expanded or reduced on a time basis so as to give a proportionate figure (referred to subsequently as the 'aggregate profit') for the 'relevant years', and the assessment for the year to which section 60(5) applies is adjusted, up or down as the case may be, so that the total of the assessments for all the 'relevant years' is precisely equal to the 'aggregate profit'.

[The working of this practice can best be illustrated by an example – see Example A.11.]

Right of appeal

6. It is open to the taxpayer, if he does not accept the Board's proposal, to appeal to the General or Special Commissioners against any direction by the Board that may be made under section 60(5) or against a decision not to issue a direction, and the Commissioners are empowered on appeal to give such relief, if any, as is just. The Board's proposal represents the solution which they consider would be likely to commend itself to the Commissioners and where it is accepted there is in effect an agreed recommendation as to which is thought to be just.

Special cases

7. The practice outlined above is suitable for the majority of cases. There are, however, certain classes of case which are incapable of solution along those lines for which modifications are necessary, e g:

(*a*) cases where the 'aggregate profit' is not intermediate between the sum of the assessments for the 'relevant years' without revision under section 60(5) and the sum of the assessments for those years after revision under that section;
(*b*) cases where there is a marked seasonal fluctuation in the rate of profit (e g as in the case of the seaside hotel);
(*c*) cases where in some or all of the periods concerned losses were incurred;
(*d*) cases where any one of the years concerned is affected by the commencement or cessation provisions.

The modifications that are introduced to deal with these special types of case cannot be described in detail within the limits of this leaflet, but the general method followed throughout is that of equating the average rate of assessments over the years affected to the average rate of profits in the accounting periods that form the basis of those assessments. In cases falling within head (3) it may be necessary in order to secure this result to depart from the general rule mentioned in paragraph 3 and to determine a basis year under section 60(4) which, when regard is had to the profits of that year and existing assessments, will enable effect to be given to the 'average' adjustment. Again in cases falling within head (4) it may be necessary to modify the 'average' adjustment so that the assessments reflect a true annual rate of profit and not a rate that is inflated or depressed by seasonal results.

Small differences

8. Where the 'average' computation brings out an 'aggregate profit' which exceeeds, or falls short of the sum of the unrevised assessment for the preceding year and the assessments for the other 'relevant years' by a relatively small amount, it is not the Board's normal practice to take any action by way of 'average' adjustment. For this purpose, the Board would normally regard as relatively small a difference that was less than ten per cent of the average of the current and preceding years' assessments and also less than £1,000 [see Example AI. 12]".

EXAMPLE AI.11: Normal practice (IR26, paras. 3–5)

The accounts of a business have been made up annually to 30 September for years up to and including 30 September 1981. The next account is for the nine months to 30 June 1982, and it is intended that subsequent accounts will be made up annually to 30 June.

The trading profits are as follows:	£
12 months to 30 September 1980	36,000
12 months to 30 September 1981	18,000
9 months to 30 June 1982	12,000
33	£66,000

The 1982–83 assessment has been made on £18,000, the profit of the year to 30 September 1981.

The 1983–84 assessment based on the year to 30 June 1982, under s 60(4) will be:

	£
($^3/_{12}$) × £18,000	4,500
9 months to 30 June 1982	12,000
	£16,500

The following review is made to see whether the 1982–83 assessment of £18,000 should be revised.

(i) "Aggregate profit"

The profit for the "relevant accounting periods" is £66,000 for the thirty-three months to 30 June 1982.
The relevant years are 1981–82, 1982–83 and 1983–84 a period of thirty-six months. The aggregate profit is therefore the profit for thirty-six months at the rate of £66,000 for thirty-three months, i e ($^{36}/_{33}$) × £66,000 = £72,000

(ii) Sum of assessments for "relevant years" without revision under section 60(5):

"Relevant years"	Assessments
	£
1981–82	36,000
1982–83	18,000
1983–84	16,500
Sum of assessment for "relevant years"	£70,500

Since the difference between (i) £72,000 and (ii) £70,500 is greater than £1,000 (see paragraph 8) the calculation proceeds as follows:

(iii) Sum of assessments for "relevant years" after revision under section 60(5):

"Relevant years"		Assessments
		£
1981–82		36,000
1982–83 ($^3/_{12}$) × £36,000 = £9,000		
($^9/_{12}$) × £9,000 = £13,500		22,500
1983–84		16,500
Sum of assessment for "relevant years"		£75,000

250 *Appendix I*

EXAMPLE AI.11 *(continued)*

The figure at (i) £72,000 is intermediate between (ii) £70,500 and (iii) £75,000. The assessment for 1982–83 is therefore revised to such an amount that the total of the assessments for relevant years equals the figure at (i) as follows:

	£	£
Figure at (i)		72,000
Assessed 1981–82	36,000	
Assessed 1983–84	16,500	
		52,500
Balance to be assessed for 1982–83		£19,500

The assessment for 1982–83 is therefore revised to £19,500 by means of a further assessment of £1,500 (£19,500–£18,000).

EXAMPLE AI.12: Small difference (IR 26, para. 8)

The accounts of a business have been made up annually to 31 March for years up to and including 31 March 1981. The next account is for the 18 months to 30 September 1982, and it is intended that subsequent accounts will be made up annually to 30 September.

The trading profits are as follows:	£
12 months to 31 March 1980	2,400
12 months to 31 March 1981	3,000
18 months to 30 September 1982	6,000
42	£11,400

The 1981–82 assessment has been made on £3,000, the profit of the year to 31 March 1981.

The basis of assessment for each of the years 1982–83 and 1983–84 requires to be determined under s 60(4). In accordance with paragraph 3 the years to 30 September 1981, and 30 September 1982, will be taken as the basis years and the assessments will be:

		£
1982–83	$(6/12) \times £3,000 =$	1,500
	$(6/8) \times £6,000 =$	2,000
		3,500
1983–84	$(12/18) \times £6,000 =$	4,000

The following review is made to see whether the 1981–82 assessment of £3,000 should be revised.

(i) "Aggregate profit"
  The profit for the relevant accounting periods is £11,400 for the forty-two months to 30 September 1982.
  The relevant years are 1980–81, 1981–82, 1982–83 and 1983–84 a period of forty-eight months.
  The aggregate profit is therefore the profit for 48 months at the rate of £11,400 for 42 months, ie $(48/42) \times £11,400 = £13,028$

(ii) Sum of assessments for relevant years without revision under s 60(5):

EXAMPLE AI.12 *(continued)*

"Relevant years"	Assessments
	£
1980–81	2,400
1981–82	3,000
1982–83	3,500
1983–84	4,000
Sum of assessment for "relevant years"	£12,900

The difference between (i) £13,028 and (ii) £12,900 is £128. This is less than £1,000 and 10% of mean of £3,500 for 1982–83 and £3,000 for 1981–82 ie 10% of ½ of (£3,500 + £3,000) = £325.

The case accordingly falls within paragraph 8 and no action is therefore necessary under s 60(5).

CAPITAL ALLOWANCES

Under CAA 1990, s 160 the basis period for capital allowances under the preceding year basis of assessment is the same as the basis period for income tax except that in the opening and closing years of assessment special rules apply.

Where two basis periods overlap, the period common to both falls in the first basis period only. If there is a gap between basis periods, for example, on the change of accounting date, the interval falls in the second basis period, except if that is the basis period for the year of permanent discontinuance in which case the interval is added to the first basis period.

A full year's writing-down allowance is given for each basis period, except for the opening period and the period of cessation if they are for periods of less than one year, in which case a proportionate part of the writing-down allowance is given. This applies whether or not the capital allowances basis period is, under these rules, a greater or lesser period than twelve months.

EXAMPLE AI.13

Actual commencement 29 December 1987; cessation 17 August 1995. Accounts made up to 30 April each year.

	Capital allowance basis period	*Income tax basis period*
1987–8?	29.12.87–5.4.88	29.12.87–5.4.88
1988–89	6.4.88–28.12.88	29.12.87–28.12.88
1989–90	no basis period	29.12.87–28.12.88*
1990–91	29.12.88–30.4.89	1.5.88–30.4.89
1991–92	1.5.89–30.4.90	1.5.89–30.4.90
1992–93	1.5.90–30.4.91	1.5.90–30.4.91
1993–94	1.5.91–30.4.92	1.5.91–30.4.92
1994–95	1.5.92–5.4.93	1.5.92–30.4.93
1995–96	6.4.93–17.8.94	6.4.93–17.8.94

*Probable Revenue selection

Had an election been made for the actual basis of assessment for the two years following commencement under TA 1988, s 62 and the Revenue applied the actual basis on discontinuance under TA 1988, s 63 the capital allowances basis periods would have been as follows (changed basis periods are italicised).

EXAMPLE AI.13 *(continued)*

	Capital allowances basis period	*Income tax basis period*
1987–88	29.12.87–5.4.88	29.12.87–5.4.88
1988–89	6.4.88–5.4.89	6.4.88–5.4.89
1989–90	6.4.89–5.4.90	6.4.89–5.4.90
1990–91	No basis period	1.5.88–30.4.90
1991–92	6.4.90–30.4.90	1.5.89–30.4.90
1992–93	1.5.90–30.4.91	1.5.90–30.4.91
1993–94	1.5.91–5.4.94	6.4.93–5.4.94
1994–95	6.4.94–5.4.95	6.4.94–5.4.95
1995–96	6.4.95–17.8.95	6.4.95–17.8.95

In both cases a full year's writing-down allowance under CAA 1990, s 24 or CAA 1990, s 3 will be made for all years other than 1987–88 and 1995–96 which will be time apportioned. Initial and first year allowances together with balancing allowances and charges will fall into the appropriate basis periods in which the expenditure was incurred or disposal occurred.

On a change of partners after 19 March 1985 giving rise to a cessation the income tax basis periods would be on actual for the first four years or six years at the taxpayer's option.

EXAMPLE AI.14

In example AI.14 the cessation on 17 August 1987 arose on a change of partners.

	Capital allowances basis period	*Income tax basis period*
1987–88	18.8.87–5.4.88	18.8.87–5.4.88
1988–89	6.4.88–5.4.89	6.4.88–5.4.89
1989–90	6.4.89–5.4.90	6.4.89–5.4.90
1990–91	6.4.90–5.4.91	6.4.90–5.4.91
1991–92	no basis period	1.5.89–30.4.90
1992–93	6.4.91–30.4.91	1.5.90–30.4.91
1993–94	1.5.91–30.4.92	1.5.91–30.4.92

Had the taxpayer elected for the actual basis for 1991–92 and 1992–93 the basis periods would be:

	Capital allowances basis period	*Income tax basis period*
1987–88	18.8.87–5.4.88	18.8.87–5.4.88
1988–89	6.4.88–5.4.89	6.4.88–5.4.89
1989–90	6.4.89–5.4.90	6.4.89–5.4.90
1990–91	6.4.90–5.4.91	6.4.90–5.4.91
1991–92	6.4.91–5.4.92	6.4.91–5.4.92
1992–93	6.4.92–5.4.93	6.4.92–5.4.93
1993–94	no basis period	1.5.91–30.4.92
1994–95	6.4.93–30.4.93	1.5.92–30.4.93

The basis period for capital allowances other than those given against income tax under Schedule D, Cases I and II is the year of assessment in which the expenditure was incurred, for example on a computer used for the purposes of the business bought by a salaried partner assessed under Schedule E. If the computer was bought on 31 July 1995 the allowances would first be claimed for 1995–96.

CAA 1990, s 140(3) provides that it is necessary to claim capital allowances in the income tax returns, not merely within the normal six year time limit under TMA 1970, s 42. This in turn means that if an assessment has been confirmed by the Commissioners it is deemed to be an assessment on the adjusted profits after deducting capital allowances. Otherwise it would be possible to reduce a confirmed assessment by a late claim for capital allowances. It is only those allowances given by way of discharge or repayment of tax, such as certain agricultural building allowances, that are subject to a claim within the normal six year time limit under TMA 1970, s 42. (CAA 1990, s 141).

If there is a cessation, including a deemed cessation on a partnership change, CAA 1990, s 152 provides that assets qualifying for capital allowances are deemed to be disposed of and re-acquired at market value, except that no initial allowances if any are due to the acquirer. Nor would there be any first year allowance in respect of plant due to the acquirer in view of CAA 1990, s 75. However CAA 1990, s 157 introduces CAA 1990, s 158 of that Act and under CAA 1990, s 158(i) it is possible to make a joint election for the transferee to take over the transferor's written-down values for capital allowances purposes. This election would normally be made in the case of a change in partners if there was no election for continuation under TA 1988, s 113(2).

CAA 1990, s 154 provides that where a contribution is made to another trader in respect of capital expenditure to be incurred by him the contributor is usually entitled to capital allowances as if he had himself incurred the capital expenditure.

Apart from the basis periods the capital allowances rules for a partnership are the same for any other business. From a tax planning point of view it is necessary to decide whether or not to claim first year or writing down allowances, for example, if the allowances, would give rise to a loss where there is no other income but a small profit would be covered by personal allowances.

It is also necesary to consider whether to claim for assets to be classed as short life assets under CAA 1990, s 37. A short life asset is treated on an individual basis with a balancing allowance or charge on disposal, unless the asset is retained beyond the fourth anniversary of the end of the basis period in which it is acquired.

EXAMPLE AI.15

Knight & Co. bought a word processor for £10,000 on 1 July 1993 and a computer for £25,000 in May 1994. They make short life elections in respect of both. The word processor is sold in March 1997. The computer however, continues to be used beyond 1998.
Knight & Co. make up their accounts to 30 June each year. The capital allowances computation in respect of the short life assets is as follows:

	Word processor £	Computer £	Allowances £
1995–96 (basis period 1.7.93–30.6.94)			
additions	10,000	25,000	
writing down allowance @ 25%	(2,500)	(6,250)	8,750
qualifying expenditure c/f	7,500	18,750	
1996–97 (basis period 1.7.94–30.6.96)			
writing down allowance @ 25%	(1,875)	(4,687)	6,562
qualifying expenditure c/f	5,625	14,063	

254 Appendix I

EXAMPLE AI.15 *(continued)*

	Word processor £	Computer £	Allowances £
1997–98 (basis period 1.7.96–30.6.97) writing down allowance @ 25%	(1,406)	(3,516)	4,922
qualifying expenditure c/f	4,219	10,547	
1998–99 (basis period 1.7.97–30.6.98) disposal value	(3,000)		
	1,219		
balancing allowance	(1,219)		1,219
	£Nil		
writing down allowance @ 25%		(2,637)	2,367
			£3,856
qualifying expenditure c/f		7,910	
1999–2000 (basis period 1.7.98–30.6.99		(1,952)	1,952
qualifying expenditure transferred to general pool		£5,958	

PARTNERSHIP LOSSES

If partnership results produce an adjusted loss for tax purposes for an accounting period, ending in 1996–97 on earlier years of assessment, that loss will usually be apportioned among the partners in the fiscal year in which the accounting period ends and apportioned amongst them in the manner in which they share losses during that fiscal year unless the strict basis is applied. A loss in the first three years of assessment and, if the strict basis was applied thereafter, was apportioned to the fiscal year on a time basis and then divided among the partners in the manner in which they share losses from the appropriate accounting periods. The loss relief could not exceed the total adjusted loss, *IRC v Scott Adamson* (1932) 17 TC 679; *Westward Television Ltd v Hart* (1968) 45 TC 1.

EXAMPLE AI.16

S.L.G. & Co. made up accounts to 30 April 1995 which showed a loss as adjusted for tax purposes of £20,000, borne equally between S. and G. The previous year produced a profit of £45,000 and (1993) £36,000.

Appendix I 255

EXAMPLE AI.16 (*continued*)

	£
Assessment 1995–96	
Adjusted profit year ended 30.4.94	45,000
Less: loss year ended 30.4.95	(20,000)
Revised assessment 1995–96	£25,000

Alternatively:

1995–96

	£
Adjusted profit year ended 30.4.94	45,000
Less: loss year ended 30.4.95	
$\dfrac{25}{365} \times £20{,}000$	(1,370)
Revised assessment	£43,630

1994–95

	£
Adjusted profit year ended 30.4.93	36,000
Less: loss year ended 30.4.95	
$\dfrac{340}{365} \times £20{,}000$	(18,630)
Revised assessment	£17,370

Once each partner's share of a loss has been ascertained he can use it in accordance with his own personal circumstances. In other words he can set the loss against his total income for the year of the loss or to the extent it remains unrelieved for the immediately following fiscal year under the provisions of TA 1988, s 380. Relief, in any year, is given first for any unrelieved loss from the earlier year, then for the current year's loss, if any. However, relief for an unrelieved loss brought forward will only be given if the trade or profession continues to be carried on by him

EXAMPLE AI.17

Diplo, Docus & Co. made up their accounts to 30 April each year. In the year ended 30 April 1996, there was an adjusted loss of £10,000.

Profit sharing ratios	*Diplo*	*Docus*
Year ended 30.4.94	1/2	1/2
Year ended 30.4.95	2/5	3/5
Year ended 30.4.96	1/3	2/3
Year ended 30.4.97	2/7	5/7

EXAMPLE AI.17 *(continued)*

Loss apportioned
Normal basis – loss treated as 1996–97

		£	£
		(¹/₃)	(²/₃)
¹/₁₂ × £10,000 =	£833	278	555
		(²/₇)	(⁵/₇)
¹¹/₁₂ × £10,000 =	£ 9,167	2,619	6,548
	£10,000	£2,897	£7,103

Strict basis – loss treated as ¹/₁₂ in 1996–97, ¹¹/₁₂ in 1995–96

1996–97		£	£
		(¹/₃)	(²/₃)
¹/₁₂ × £10,000 =	£833	278	555
1995–96		(¹/₃)	(²/₃)
¹¹/₁₂ × £10,000 =	£ 9,167	3,056	6,111
	£10,000	£3,334	£6,666

On the normal basis the loss would first be set against the partnership profits for the year ended 30 April 1995 (1996–97) and any other income for 1996–87 and thereafter against other income for 1997–98. On the strict basis a large part of the loss is set first against the partnership income for the year ended 30 April 1994 and other income for 1995–96 and thereafter against 1996–97; the remainder of the loss would be set first against income for 1996–97 and thereafter against income for 1997–98.

If there is an overall adjusted profit of the partnership, but, because of prior charges, such as salaries to equity partners and interest on capital, certain partners suffer an accounting loss, they are not entitled to loss relief, but the profit sharing partners have the adjusted partnership profit apportioned amongst them in accordance with their share of profit in the year of assessment.

EXAMPLE AI.18

Andrew and Simon shared profits as follows:

	Andrew	Simon
	£	£
Salary	1,000	9,000
Interest of capital	500	750
Balance	²/₃	¹/₃

The adjusted profits for the year ended 30 April 1994 were £3,500.

	Total	Andrew	Simon
	£	£	£
Salary	10,000	1,000	9,000
Interest on capital	1,250	500	750
Balance	(7,750)	(5,167)	(2,583)
	£3,500	£(3,667)	£7,167
Assessment 1995–96	£3,500	Nil	£3,500

Such treatment could call for an equitable adjustment among the partners through the tax equalisation accounts. If, in Example A.18 it was agreed between the partners that Simon should pay tax on the income he actually received, ie £7,167, tax could be calculated on this income and the excess over tax on £3,500 actually charged would be debited to Simon and credited to Andrew. In this way Andrew would be compensated for the loss of £3,667 he suffered but for which he could claim no tax relief. Alternatively it would be possible to calculate the tax saving which Andrew would have been able to make had his actual loss of £3,667 been allowable for tax. The tax saving would have been debited to Simon and credited to Andrew. It would also be possible to agree a compromise figure. If, for example, Simon's additional tax was £1,500 and Andrew's tax loss was £1,000 it could be agreed to debit Simon and credit Andrew with £1,250 through a tax equalisation account.

The introduction of independent taxation in 1990–91 meant that a loss can no longer be set against a spouse's income, although there is a limited transferability of personal allowances under TA 1988, ss 257 BA and BB. A claim for relief under TA 1988, s 380 must be submitted within two years of the end of the year of assessment for which the loss year is the basis period.

Where accounts to 30 April 1994 show an adjusted loss, the loss may be relieved under TA 1988, s 380(1) in 1994–95 (claim before 6 April 1997) or under TA 1988, s 380(2) in 1995–96 (claim before 6 April 1998).

A partnership is deemed to cease on a change of partners under TA 1988, s 113(1) is treated as the same trade for loss relief, thus enabling losses to be carried forward.

Under TA 1988, s 383 a taxpayer may claim to augment a trading loss by capital allowances for the year of assessment for which the year of the loss is the basis period. Such allowances may be used to convert a trading profit into a loss for which a claim under TA 1988, s 380 may be made. However, capital allowances must first be used to cover any balancing charges for the year of assessment and only the surplus may be added to losses for the purpose of set-off against other income or carry foward against future profits from the same trade.

Loss relief under TA 1988, s 380 is restricted by TA 1988, s 384 to losses from a trade or profession carried on commercially with a view to profit.

Under TA 1988, s 385 a Schedule D, Case I and II loss which has not been fully relieved against other income under TA 1988, s 380 may be carried forward against future income from the same trade. It is possible to include as income of the trade interest or dividends taxed at source if they would, were they not so taxed, be taken into account as trading receipts of, for example, a banking partnership. A partnership discontinuance under TA 1988, s 113 does not prevent losses being carried forward against profits of the new partnership so far as the continuing partners are concerned. So far as the outgoing partner is concerned, however, his share of losses which cannot be set against other income under TA 1988, s 380 cannot be carried forward as there will be no future income from the same trade.

Unused capital allowances can be added to the loss carried forward. A claim under TA 1988, s 385 must be made within six years from the end of the year of assessment in which the loss arose, but a claim actually to set the losses carried forward against future profits from the trade need only be made within six years of the end of the year of assessment for which the claim is made.

Limited partnership losses

Where losses are incurred or interest or charges paid in a chargeable period beginning after 19 March 1985 relief may be restricted under TA 1988, s 117. This applies where a person is carrying on a trade as a limited partner under the Limited Partnership Act 1907 or is a general partner whose liability is limited and who is not entitled to take part in the management of the business. Losses and relief for interest and charges are not available against general income but may be carried forward against future profits of the trade under TA 1988, ss 385 or 387. These anti avoidance provisions were introduced following *Reed v Young* [1985] STC 25.

Terminal losses

A loss incurred in the last twelve months of trading prior to discontinuance is known as a terminal loss and it can be carried back and set against profits of the same trade for the years of cessation on the three preceding years of assessment.

The losses are set against the latest year's assessment first and a terminal loss claim can be used to relieve the proportion of a loss not available for relief under TA 1988, s 380. Dividends and interest received under deduction of tax may be included as trading income if they would, were they not so taxed, be treated as such income. A terminal loss claim has to leave in charge to tax sufficient income to cover annual payments, except in the case of charges incurred for the purposes of the trade for which relief would have been available as an addition to losses carried forward under TA 1988, s 387 had the tax been accounted for to the Revenue under TA 1988 ss 349 and 350, which is usually necessary where there is insufficient taxable income to cover annual payments. Capital allowances for the year of assessment in which the cessation took place may be added to a terminal loss as may the appropriate proportion of the capital allowances for the preceding period in order to arrive at the total of the final twelve months losses and capital allowances.

Terminal loss relief can be given to a partner against each individual partner's share of the previous year's assessment. A terminal loss relief claim on a partnership cessation is only available for outgoing partners and not to those partners continuing in the new business, even though the hold business is deemed to have ceased under TA 1988, s 113.

A transfer to a company could be useful in order to give partners the option of terminal loss relief or carry forward against future income from a company under TA 1988, s 386.

There are two Inland Revenue Extra-statutory Concessions relating to loss relief and partnerships and these provide as follows:

> **"A7. Business or other source of income passing on the death of a husband or wife**
>
> The death of a trader and the consequent passing of his business to his successor is an occasion for the application of the discontinuance provisions of the Income Tax Acts. Where, however, a business passes on death to the trader's husband or wife who has been living with her or him, the discontinuance provisions are not enforced unless claimed. But, in any case, losses and capital allowances for which the deceased had not obtained relief are not permitted to be carried forward.
>
> This concession also applies where a business has been carried on by a husband and wife in partnership and one succeeds to the whole of the business on the death of the other, but no election for continuance treatment is made under Section 113(2) Income and Corporation Taxes Act 1988. In such a case, losses and capital allowances which may be carried forward are restricted to the share appropriate to the surviving partner."

Similarly, the death of a husband or wife normally gives rise to a "cessation" adjustment in the assessment of income arising under Case III, IV or V of Schedule D. Where, however, a source of income so assessable passes in its entirety from the deceased to the surviving spouse, cessation and commencement adjustments will not be made unless requested by the personal representatives or the survivor.

> "**A8. Loss relief for capital allowances unused on the cessation of a business**
>
> Section 383 Income and Corporation Taxes Act 1988 enables capital allowances to be taken into account in arriving at the amount of loss on which relief is given, under Section 380 Income and Corporation Taxes Act 1988, against the tax on the trader's aggregate income. When there is a trading profit, loss relief is given on the excess of the capital allowances over the trading profit of the same basis period, and normally the capital allowances up to the amount of the trading profits are relieved by being set against those trading profits (resulting in a nil assessment). Where, however, there are capital allowances brought forward from earlier years, these must be allowed in the assessment in priority to the current allowances, and the current allowances, so far as they cannot be set against the assessment, must in turn be carried forward. In a year of cessation no such carry forward of these unused current allowances is possible. Relief may be due for them under s 388 (terminal losses), but so far as it is not, relief will be lost. Where there would otherwise be a loss of relief, it is the practice in the calculation of the loss, for the purpose of s 380, to treat the profits of the final year as reduced by the amount of capital allowances brought forward, thus increasing the amount of the capital allowances for the final year where are available for loss relief."

A partnership with income taxed under Schedule D, Case VI may have a loss in respect of such income and such loss may only be set against any other Case VI income for the same fiscal year or carried forward and set against Case VI income for succeeding years under TA 1988, s 392. The loss relief does not extend to a loss on a premium on a lease or lease at an undervalue taxed under Case VI or Schedule A in accordance with TA 1988, ss 34, 35 or 36. A claim to carry forward loss relief must be made within six years of the end of the year of assessment in which the loss arose, but the claim to set against other Case VI profits need only be made within six years of the end of the year of assessment for which relief is being claimed. Losses have to be used against the first available profit.

Losses in opening years of business

Relief may also be claimed under TA 1988, s 381, if a loss (as computed for tax purposes) is incurred in any of the first four years of assessment during which the trade, profession or vocation is carried on. That loss may be relieved against the claimant's total income chargeable to tax for the last three years of assessment preceding the year in which the loss is sustained. The loss is set against the earliest year first and whilst it can have the effect of negating earlier years' personal allowances, this can be balanced by the receipt of a non-taxable repayment supplement. An additional benefit of making a claim under these provisions is the cash flow advantage of the early receipt of a tax refund.

EXAMPLE AI.19

Victor, who had been employed for many years decided to resign and start his own business. He commenced on 6 April 1993 and drew up his accounts to 5 April 1994 and annually thereafter. His financial position is as follows:

EXAMPLE AI.19 *(continued)*

	1990–91	1991–92	1992–93	1993–94	1994–95	1995–96
Salary	£4,000	£5,000	£5,000	–	–	–
Profits (losses)	–	–	–	(£6,000)	(£3,000)	£10,000
Personal allowances	£1,000	£1,000	£1,500	£1,600	£2,000	£2,000
Basic rate % (say)	25	25	25	25	25	25
Tax paid	£750	£1,000	£1,000			

If TA 1988, s 381 was not involved the position would be:

		Assessment	
1993–94	£6,000 loss carry forward	Nil	Actual
1994–95	£9,000 loss carry forward	Nil	First 12 months
1995–96	£9,000 loss carry forward	Nil	Preceding year basis
1996–97	transitional year (say)	£11,000	
	less: losses brought forward	(£9,000)	
		£2,000	

If a TA 1988, s 381 claim is made the situation becomes:

	1990–91	1991–92	1992–93	1993–94	1994–95	1995–96
Salary	£4,000	£5,000	£5,500	–	–	–
s 381 claim 1994–95	(£4,000)	(£2,000)				
s 381 claim 1995–96		(£3,000)				
Schedule D	–	–	–	–	–	11,000
Personal allowances	–	–	(£1,500)			(£2,000)
Revised assessable	Nil	Nil	£4,000	Nil	Nil	£9,000
Tax payable/repayable	(£750)	(£1,000)	£1,000			£2,250

Assuming tax refunds are received on 6 October 1994 and 1995 the repayment supplements will be:

1991–92 £375 paid 1.1.91 × say 8% × 2½ years = £ 75
         £375 paid 1.7.91 × say 8% × 1½ years = £ 45
                                                 ─────
                                                 £120
                                                 ═════

Receivable 6 October 1994

1992–93 £500 paid 1.1.92 × say 8% × 2½ years = £100
         £500 paid 1.7.92 × say 8% × 1½ years = £ 60
                                                 ─────
                                                 £160
                                                 ═════

Acccordingly the cash flow on tax account for the period 6 April 1993 to 1 July 1997 is as follows:

EXMAPLE AI.19 *(continued)*

	s 381 claimed	s 381 not claimed
1990–91	£ 750	£ 750
1991–92	£ 1,000	£1,000
1992–93	£ 1,000	£1,000
1993–94	– (1)	–
1994–95	(£ 870) (2)	–
1995–96	(£1,160) (3)	–
1996–97	£2,250 (4)	
Net payment	£2,970	£2,750

Notes:

		£
(1)	1990–91 repayable	750
	Repayment supplement	120
		870
(2)	1991–92	1,000
	Repayment supplement	160
		1,160

Note that the repayment supplement is insufficient to cover the loss of personal allowances on carrying back the loss, but the example does not take interest into account on the repayment when received until tax is paid out in 1996–97.

Transfer to company

On a transfer of a business to a company, losses can to a limited extent be carried forward under the provisions of TA 1988, s 386. Provided that the business is transferred to a company in exchange for shares, unused losses from the business can be carried forward and set against income from the company in the form of dividends, directors' remuneration etc. For this relief to apply the transfer of the business has to be soley or mainly in exchange for shares, although in practice the Revenue will still give the relief if up to 20% of the shares are subsequently disposed of. The relief is not however available for unused capital allowances. An election may, in pratice, be made to carry forward capital allowances on plant at the written down value on a joint election made by the transferor and transferee under the provisions of CAA 1990, s 77 in respect of plant and machinery and CAA 1990 s 158 in respect of other assets eligible for capital allowances. The Revenue do not regard the legislation as covering a succession by a company to a business carried on by a partnership but in practice will usually give the required relief on an election signed by the company and all partners. In the absence of such an election the assets would be deemed to have been disposed of and reacquired at market value under CAA 1990, s 157(4) which would probably have given rise to a balancing charge on the partnership transferring the assets to the company.

Interest incurred for trading purposes may be added to a loss carried forward or to a terminal loss under TA 1988, s 390.

CHARGES ON INCOME

Certain expenses, known as annual payments, such as patent royalties, are paid under deduction of tax at the basic rate and it is necessary to charge the payer tax equivalent to the amount withheld. This is usually done by excluding the payment from relief for tax at the basic rate so that it becomes "held in charge to tax" under TA 1988, s 348. Annual payments are dealt with on an actual, not a preceding year basis and each partner has allocated to him his share of such partnership charges in accordance with the profit sharing ratios in the fiscal year in which the annual payment is made.

EXAMPLE AI.20

XYZ & Co. had an accounts profit for the year ended 30 April 1994 of £45,000 after providing for royalties payable of £10,000

	£
Profit per accounts	45,000
Add back: royalties	10,000
Adjusted profit and basic rate paid on	£55,000
Royalties actually paid in 1995–96	12,000
Less: basic rate tax withheld @ 25%	3,000
Cash paid to licensor	£9,000

Annual payments actually paid in the tax year are an allowable deduction from total income for higher rate tax purposes for each partner individually.
Higher rate tax charged 1995–96

	£
Adjusted profit	55,000
Less: royalties paid	12,000
	£43,000
Higher rate tax thereon (say)	£7,480

By paying basic rate tax on £55,000 when the higher rate taxable profit was only £43,000, the taxpayer has effectively accounted not only for his own tax liability but also for the tax withheld on the royalty of £3,000 which is thereby paid over to the Inland Revenue.

If, however, the basic rate liability for any partner were less than his share of the annual payment, it is necessary to pay over to the Inland Revenue under TA 1988, ss 349 and 350 the excess tax deducted.

EXAMPLE AI.21

If in example A.20 XYZ & Co. had an accounts loss of £6,000 for the year ended 30 April 1994, after providing for royalties payable of £10,000, the position becomes:

	£
Loss per accounts	6,000
Less: royalties	10,000
Adjusted profit	£4,000
Basic rate tax payable thereon	
1995–96 (say)	£1,000
Royalties actually paid in 1995–96	12,000
Less: basic rate tax withheld	3,000
cash paid to licensor	£9,000
excess charges assuming no partner has other taxable income £12,000–£4,000	£8,000
Tax thereon of basic rate payable @ 25% to Inland Revenue under TA 1988, s 359	£2,000

The Inland Revenue therefore picks up £1,000 on the basic rate assessment and £2,000 under TA 1988, ss 349 and 350 which equals the £3,000 withheld from the royalty payment. The higher rate position is:

	£
Adjusted profit	4,000
Less: charges	4,000
	Nil

This means that £8,000 of the royalty paid, which was incurred for trading purposes, remains unrelieved. Relief is given by TA 1988, s 387 to each partner which treats his share of the excess charges of £8,000 as trading losses which may be carried forward and set against his share of future profits from the same trade.

PAYMENT OF TAX

Income tax under Schedule D, Case I or II is payable up to and including 1995–96 in two equal instalments on 1 January in the year of assessment for which the tax is payable and on 1 July following the end of the year of assessment for which the tax is payable, under TA 1988, s 5.

Income tax under Schedule D, Cases III, IV, V and VI is due on 1 January in the year of assessment for which the tax is payable. Capital gains tax is payable on 1 December following the end of the fiscal year in which the gain was made. The due dates of payment of tax are modified for 1996–97 and future years.

Where an appeal is lodged against an assessment under Schedule D, the appeal notice must be lodged within thirty days of the date of issue of the assessment, state the grounds of the appeal, the amount of tax which the taxpayer considers should be postponed and the reasons for this belief. If no application is made for postponement the tax is due as if no appeal had been lodged. If, as would usually be the case, an application is made to postpone part of the tax under TMA 1970, s 55 that not in dispute becomes due and payable thirty days after the agreement of the amount postponed, unless this is before the normal due date as specified in TA 1988, s 5. The taxpayer may make application for postponement outside of the thirty day limit if circumstances have so changed such that he has grounds for believing that he is overcharged to tax by the assessment (TMA 1970, s 55(3A)).

If the taxpayer and the Revenue cannot reach agreement as to the amount to be postponed, the Commissioners will determine the amount of tax not in dispute, without considering the merits of the dispute which will be considered by the Commissioners at a later time. In such cases the tax not in dispute is due thirty days after the date of the Commissioner's determination unless this is before the normal date. Either party can apply to the Commissioners for a further determination if they consider circumstances have changed so that the previous determination was insufficient or excessive.

Interest on overdue tax runs from the reckonable date until the date of payment under TMA 1970, s 86 subject to extra statutory concession A17 on death. The reckonable date can be the normal due date, the actual due date or the table date as set out in TMA 1970, s 86. If the tax charged by an assessment is increased as a result of the determination of an appeal the reckonable date for the additional tax is as for the original tax charge (TMA 1970, s 86(3)(*aa*)).

The actual due date is when the tax is payable and can never be earlier than the normal date but may be later, for example, as a result of an appeal. The table dates are approximately six months later than the normal due dates for an assessment issued on time. If the actual due date is earlier than the table date interest will run from the actual due date.

If the actual due date is later than the table date interest will run from the later of the normal due date or the table date. The normal due date would normally be earlier than the table date but if, for example, an assessment were raised late the normal due date would be thirty days after the date of assessment which could well be later than the table date. The reckonable date from which interest will run could be a considerable time before the actual due date of payment of tax. If, for example, an appeal is lodged against an assessment issued in the normal course of events a claim is made for postponement of the whole or part of the tax payable and a contentious point is argued at length it might be several years before the point is finally determined by the Commissioners, but any interest would run from the table date being later than the normal due date for an assessment issued on time.

It should be noted that if an appeal is won before the Commissioners but is subsequently lost before the Courts, interest will not run from the table date, but, under TMA 1970, s 86(3)(*b*), from thirty days after the Court's determination. This is because sub-section 3(*a*) provides that the table date only applies where TMA 1970, s 55 applies and if the case is won before the Commissioners but lost before the Courts, the tax is payable under TMA 1970, s 56, not s 55. There is a *de minimis* exemption enabling the Revenue to waive interest of less than £30.

A repayment supplement may be made under TA 1988, s 824(1), on tax overpaid (minimum £25) by an individual and repaid after 31 July 1975 if the repayment is delayed more than one year after the end of the year of assessment. The supplement is calculated from the "relevant time" to the end of the tax month (ending on the 5th) in which the repayment is made, and is tax free.

The "relevant time" is one year after the year of assessment for which the tax was due or the end of the year of assessment in which the tax was paid whichever is later.

Appendix II

Partnership changes under the preceding year basis

AUTOMATIC CESSATION AND CONTINUATION ELECTION ON CHANGES BEFORE 6 APRIL 1997

Where there is a change in the partners carrying on a trade, profession or vocation which commenced before 6 April 1994 there is an automatic cessation for tax purposes unless there is at least one common partner before and after the change in which case an election may be made within two years of the date of the change for the partnership to be treated as continuing for tax purposes. An election can be made where a sole practitioner takes in a partner or where one partner leaves a two partner firm and the business continues to be carried on by a sole practitioner (TA 1988, s 113).

In the majority of cases when profits are rising, at least in monetary terms, it will pay to elect for continuation particularly since a cessation on a change of partners after 19 March 1985 would result in the first four years of assessment being taxed on an actual basis under TA 1988, ss 61 and 62. A cessation without a continuation election after 5 April 1994 would result in the current year basis of assessment applying to the deemed new business, as explained in Chapter 2. If the partnership has previously been assessed on a cash basis it will almost certainly pay to elect for continuation in order to avoid a compulsory assessment of the next three accounting years' profits on an earnings basis. It is usual in the partnership agreement to provide that any outgoing partner or his personal representative must join in an election under this section if so required by the continuing partners. It is usual to elect for continuation very soon after the change and submit the notice to the Inland Revenue with the proviso that the taxpayers reserve the right to withdraw the notice at any time within the statutory two-year period. Such a provisional election notice is accepted by the Revenue in accordance with their Press Release of 17 January 1973 which reads as follows:

"Partnership – change in membership
Where there is a change in the persons carrying on a trade, profession or vocation involving:
(a)   a change in the membership of a partnership;
(b)   a sole trader entering into partnership with one or more partners; or
(c)   a partnership being dissolved and the business being carried on by one partner as a sole trader;
the parties may elect under TA 1988, s 113(2) to have the profits of the business taxed as though it continued. In the absence of such an election the business has to be treated as ceasing and a new business as set up and commencing. The time limit for making this election was extended from 1 year to 2 years by FA 1971, s 17 and this has lengthened the period during which there may be uncertainty as to the basis of assessment for the years immediately before and immediately after the change.

Where an election is to be made it would save work in both accountant's and tax offices if it could be made early enough to prevent the Inspector having first to make assessments applying the cessation and commencing provisions and then to revert later to the continuing basis of assessment. The Board would welcome co-operation from accountants in achieving this end.

It is recognised that in some cases the decision whether or not to make an election is delayed in order to estimate more accurately the trend of profits after the partnership change. The Board think it might be helpful, and lead to an earlier election in such cases, if it were more widely known that it is the practice of inspectors to accept a revocation of an election under TA 1988, s 113(2) *provided* that the notice of revocation, signed by all the interested parties, is given before the expiry of the 2 year time limit for making the election."

Equitable adjustment

If, as frequently happens, an election for continuation is beneficial for some partners but detrimental to others, there may be an equitable adjustment among the partners whereby the net overall saving arising from the election calculated in terms of tax is apportioned among the partners in their average sharing ratios, and those partners who obtain an additional advantage reimburse those who show a loss or lesser advantage from the election. Sometimes such an equitable adjustment is written into the partnership agreement and at the very least an outgoing partner would usually require an indemnity before agreeing to sign a continuation election under TA 1988, s 113(2) so that his tax is no more than it would have been had there been a cessation. Equitable adjustments will not normally be necessary under the current year basis.

See Example AII.01 on p. 269.

CONTINUATION ELECTION FOLLOWED BY CESSATION

If there is an election for continuation followed by a subsequent cessation within two years of the end of the fiscal year in which the first change occurred where there is no election for continuation on the second cessation the penultimate and anti-penultimate year's adjustment which the Revenue may make under TA 1988, s 63 may be taken back through the earlier change and could therefore affect the tax liability of the partners who retired at the earlier change. Any indemnity given to such partners should, therefore, take into account the effect of any further change which could affect their share of the assessable profits. Personal representatives of a deceased partner have to sign the election in respect of his interests.

ENGINEERING A CESSATION

It should be noted that a change of partners introduces an automatic cessation under TA 1988, s 113(1) and in the unlikely event that a cessation is required for tax purposes the introduction of a new partner with a modest profit share would bring about the required cessation. Under TA1 988, s 114(3)(*b*) the introduction or retirement of a corporate partner does not give rise to an automatic cessation.

If profits fluctuate materially it can give rise to a situation where a continuation election is desirable, but an incoming partner could be subject to a share of a tax assessment in excess of the share of profit that he has actually enjoyed in the first year or two, and in such circumstances an equitable adjustment is desirable.

EXAMPLE AII.01

Ramrod & Co. had the following tax payable prior to a cessation in 1995–96 on partner D joining the firm; the partners agreed to make an appropriate equitable adjustment if necessary.

	Total	A	B	C	D
	£	£	£	£	£
Continuation election					
1993–94 PY basis	21,000	6,000	7,000	8,000	
1994–95 PY basis	24,000	7,000	8,000	9,000	
1995–96 PY basis	31,000	8,000	9,000	10,000	4,000
1996–97 transitional	31,000	7,000	8,000	9,000	7,000
1997–98 CY basis	35,000	8,000	9,000	10,000	8,000
	142,000	36,000	41,000	46,000	19,000
If firm ceased					
1993–94 actual basis	25,500	7,500	8,500	9,500	
1994–95 actual basis	28,500	8,500	9,500	10,500	
1995–96 actual CY basis	30,000	8,000	9,000	10,000	3,000
1996–97 CY basis	34,000	8,000	9,000	10,000	7,000
1997–98 CY basis	35,000	8,000	9,000	10,000	8,000
	153,000	40,000	45,000	50,000	18,000
Gained from continuation election	11,000	4,000	4,000	4,000	(1,000)
Apportion gain equally and indemnify D against any increase in assessments.	11,000	2,750	2,750	2,750	2,750
Equitable adjustment debited		1,250	1,250	1,250	
to partner's current accounts credited					3,750

RETIREMENT WINDFALL

If the profits are increasing, and a continuation election is submitted, a retiring partner is likely to receive a share of profits in excess of the profits actually assessed. This will compensate him for the profits originally assessed more than twice under the commencement provisions or for the tax paid on profits which he did not receive because he had joined the partnership under a continuation election. However, in view of inflation it is likely that the saving on leaving the partnership will be materially greater than the multiple assessment on joining as he is likely ultimately to pay tax on a lower figure than his actual share of profits during his career as a partner. This tax free windfall on retirement can be very useful in supplementing the capital at retirement available to invest for retirement. The saving in assessable profits by the outgoing partner may be partly balanced by assessments on the new partner in excess of their profit share, which will be compensated for, in due course, by their own windfall on retirement, in the form of overlap relief under the current year basis.

EXAMPLE AII.02

Racket & Co. has been in existence for many years having an accounting date of 6 April. The senior partner, A, has a profit share of 30% and retires on 6 April 1995 when D is introduced and an election is made for continuation

Profits

Y/e:	Total	A £	B £	C £	D £	Profit Share
6.4.92	110,000	33,000	55,000	22,000	–	⎫
6.4.93	130,000	39,000	65,000	26,000	–	⎬ 30:50:20: Nil
6.4.94	150,000	45,000	75,000	30,000	–	
6.4.95	170,000	51,000	85,000	34,000	–	⎭
6.4.96	200,000	–	100,000	50,000	50,000	⎱ Nil: 50:25:25
6.4.97	240,000	–	120,000	60,000	60,000	⎰
		168,000	500,000	222,000	110,000	

Assessments

	Total	A	B	C	D	
1993–94	110,000	33,000	55,000	22,000	–	⎱ 30:50:20: Nil
1994–95	130,000	39,000	65,000	26,000	–	⎰
1995–96	150,000	–	75,000	37,500	37,500	⎫
1996–97	185,000	–	92,500	46,250	46,250	⎬ Nil: 50:25:25
1997–98	240,000	–	120,000	60,000	60,000	⎭
		72,000	407,500	191,750	143,750	
Saving		96,000	92,500	30,250		
(Loss)					(33,750)	

A's saving has in part been transferred to the new partner D.

CAPITAL ALLOWANCES ON CONTINUATION

A continuation election under TA 1988 s 113(2) does not apply to capital allowances and under the provisions of CAA 1990, s 152, all assets on which capital allowances are claimed are deemed to have been disposed of and immediately re-acquired at market value on the partnership change irrespective of the continuation election. No initial allowance, however, is due to the partnership after the change (CAA 1990, s 152(1)) and neither will a first year allowance on plant and machinery be available in view of CAA 1990, s 75. However, it is possible to obtain the effects of continuation by an election under CAA 1990, s 77 in the case of plant and machinery and CAA 1990, s 158 in respect of other assets eligible for capital allowances. The new business will be deemed to take over the plant and machinery at the written-down value for capital allowances purposes. In practice, if the tax computations show the capital allowances being taken over at written-down value where there is a continuation election in force a separate election in respect of capital allowances is not normally required, although it might be worthwhile incorporating such an election in the continuation election to be on the safe side.

MERGERS PRIOR TO 6 APRIL 1997

On a merger there is technically a cessation of two or more existing firms and the creation of a new firm so a continuation election would not be available (*George Humphries & Co v Cook* (1934) 19 TC 121). However, in practice the Revenue will accept a continuation election for both firms so that the assessment on the combined firm after the merger will be based on the aggregate profits of the two or more constituent firms prior to the merger. The Revenue will usually also accept a continuation election for one firm and a cessation for the other provided that the profits of the merged firm are split and the commencement provisions applied to the portion not covered by the continuation election, see SP 9/1986.

The Revenue will often accept a calculated division of the profits of the merged firm based on, for example, the proportionate profits of the merging firms prior to the merger. The continuation of one firm and cessation of the other can also be engineered by introducing a new partner into the firm due to cease and not making a continuation election on that introduction. This would take place just prior to the merger and on the merger itself a continuation election would be made by both firms. As the Revenue will usually accept the effect of this arrangement by agreement it is not normally necessary to seek artificially to create the situation. Such artificial creation would in any event be subject to Revenue attack on the grounds that the merged firm carries on a different trade enabling them to refuse a continuation election at all.

The Revenue will not accept the continuation of one firm and the cessation of the other firm without also applying the commencement provisions to that part of the business of the combined firm which ceased and recommenced, arrived at by apportionment on a just and reasonable basis, for example, by reference to turnover, or if there were still two separate firms, unless the business carried on by the firm ceasing is insignificant in relation to the total. For example, on the introduction of a partner who has a small part-time practice the Revenue may well allow cessation provisions to be applied and accept a continuation election for the large practice, even where the clients of the part-time practitioner have been brought into the large partnership. A similar situation can sometimes arise where a firm splits up so that some partners continue with some of the existing clients, in which case there is a cessation, and a commencement of their new business. Other partners may then leave the practice taking with them a proportion of the clients and join up with an existing practice. In such cases the Revenue might accept the continuation of the firm taking on the additional partners without segregating the profits arising from the clients absorbed on the introduction of the new partners, provided that the profits arising from such clients were but a small proportion of the total profits of the combined firm.

The split treatment could continue for up to five years following the merger, depending on the circumstances of the merger. It may also be necessary if one of the businesses is already on the current year basis, having commenced, or deemed

Demergers

A continuation election is not possible where, on a partner leaving, the business is split into substantive parts, for example where two partners decide to go their separate ways, each taking part of the practice with them and becoming sole traders: *C Connelly & Co v Wilbey* (1992) STC 783; *Rolls-Royce Motors Ltd v Bamford* (1976) STC 162.

CHANGE OF ACCOUNTING DATE

If there is a continuation basis election and the two firms do not have a common accounting date it will be necessary for there to be a change of accounting date calculation for one, or both, of the firms. The new accounting date for the combined firm should be considered and again the 30 April will often prove a convenient date. The earlier the accounting date in the fiscal year the longer a period of credit between earning the profits and paying the tax thereon. A continuation election will effectively enable losses and capital allowances to be carried forward if necessary, although it is likely that some of the partners will have claimed for loss relief against other income which will reduce the losses to be carried forward.

The optimum date for any change of accounting date, or indeed the merger itself, will depend on the level of the past and anticipated future profits which will no doubt have to be estimated in order to prepare the required calculations. In making such computations it is important to complete the calculation in terms of tax and not merely in terms of assessable profits, because the partners may be subject to tax at significantly different levels in different years.

EXAMPLE AII.03

Fred Nerk & Co. have the following taxable profits and projections:

	£	£	
Year ended 31.12.92		144,071	Actual
Year ended 31.12.93		148,744	Actual
Year ended 31.12.94	170,000		Estimated
Period ended 30.4.95	65,000		Estimated
16 months to 30.4.96		235,000	
		£527,815	

The partners have decided to have a new accounting date of 30 April and a decision is required as to whether to produce some accounts for the year ended 31 December 1994 and then 30 April 1995, or a long account to 30 April 1995. In view of the Revenue's practice of not requiring a revision of capital allowance basis periods, this factor has been ignored in the calculations. Adopting the principles set out in Chapter 1, the following results are obtained:

EXAMPLE AII.03 (*continued*)

	Y/e 31.12.94 P/e 30.4.95 £		16 months to 30.4.95 £	
1993–94	144,071		144,071	
1994–95	148,744		148,744	(3)
1995–96	166,308	(1)	157,913	(4)
1996–97	178,333	(2)	176,250	(5)
	£637,456		£626,978	

There would appear to be a prima facie case for adopting the sixteen month account to 30 April 1995 although to be certain the total tax payable should be calculated under each alternative, for 1995–96 and 1996–97 to be sure of the choice.

Notes:
(1) *Calculation of averaged adjusted profits 1995–96*
Profits of 28 months to 30.4.95 = £383,744
Averaged over 3 years of assessment = 36 months
Therefore $^{36}/_{28}$ × £383,744 = £493,385
Less: assessed 1994–95   148,744
              1996–97   178,333

                                327,077

                                £166,308

Calculation of corresponding adjusted profits 1995–96
Profits for y/e 30.4.94 $^4/_{12}$ × £170,000   56,667
                         $^8/_{12}$ × £148,744   99,163

                                £155,830

Original assessment 1995–96
Profits for y/e 31.12.94   £170,000

Averaged adjusted profits (1) satisfy the intermediacy test and averaged adjusted profits differ from original adjusted profits by £1,000. Therefore, original assessment will be altered to average adjusted profits.

(2) 1996–97 (£65,000 + $^8/_{12}$ × £170,000) £178,333

(3) *Calculation of averaged adjusted profits 1994–95*
Profits of 40 months to 30.4.95 = £527,815
Averaged over 4 years of assessment = 48 months
Therefore $^{48}/_{40}$ × £527,815 = £633,378
Less: assessed 1993–94   144,071
              1994–95   157,913
              1996–97   176,250

                                478,234

                                £155,144

EXAMPLE AII.03 *(continued)*

Calculation of corresponding adjusted profits 1994–95

Profits for y/e 30.4.93 ie $4/12 \times £148,744 =$		49,581
$8/12 \times £144,071 =$		96,047
		£145,628

Original assessment 1994–95
Profits for y/e 31.12.93 £148,744

Averaged adjusted profit fails the intermediacy test and therefore the original assessment stands.

(4) *1995–96* ($4/16 \times £235,000 + 8/12 \times £148,744$) £157,913

(5) *1996–97* ($12/16 \times £235,000$) £176,250

It will be noted that the change of accounting date calculations ignore the transitional rules for 1996/97. Any figure or basis period produced for 1996/97 on the averaging calculation will be ignored and the transitional basis period for 1996/97 will commence immediately after whatever basis period is used for 1995/96 in the normal way.

DIFFERENT BASES

A further complication on mergers can arise where the firms have prepared accounts on a different basis so that, for example, one of the merged firms has previously prepared accounts on a cash basis whereas the other has worked on the full earnings basis. The Revenue will insist that the accounts of the combined firm are prepared on the earnings basis and this in turn will give rise to post cessation receipts of the firm converting from the cash basis to the earnings basis. A measure of top-slicing relief used to be given by extra statutory concession A18, but this was abolished on 15 March 1988. In some cases it may be possible to run two firms on different bases in parallel with common partners rather than merge them into a single firm.

Index

Accident insurance, 228–9
Accountants
  service and trading companies, rules on, 157
Accounting changes
  anti-avoidance provisions, 43–4
Accounting date changes
  current year basis of assessment, 11–12
    accounting period of less than twelve months, 12–13
    accounting period of more than twelve months, 13–16
    deemed changes, 14
    partnerships, 18
    second or third year, changes in, 16–18
    statutory provisions, 12
  mergers, 273–5
  preceding year basis of assessment, 245
Accounts
  partnership agreements, 138, 146
Actuaries
  service and trading companies, rules on, 157
Allowable expenditure
  annuities, 61
  apportionment between business and private use, 61
  appropriations of profit, 65
  bad debts, 62
  capital expenditure, 65–7
  compensation for loss of office, 62
  counselling services for employees, 65
  court decisions, basis of, 61–2
  dual purpose, 61
  employment of future partners, 63
  entertaining expenses, 65
  gifts, 65
  interest, 63–4
    loans from partners, 65
  land, annual equivalent of premiums on, 65
  lease premiums, 64
  legal expenses, 64

Allowable expenditure — *contd*
  ordinary principles of commercial accountancy, 61–2
  patent expenses, 65
  pension scheme contributions, 63
  pre-loading expenses, 65
  premiums on leases, 64
  principle, 61
  provisions, 62, 64
  redundancy payments, 62
  rent, 64
    partners, to, 65
  repairs, 64
  royalties, 61
  salaries, 62–3
  staff, entertaining of, 65
  technical education payments, 63
  travelling expenses, 65
  wages, 62–3
Annuities
  capital gains tax, 105–6
  charges on income, 61
  inheritance tax, 90, 91
  life policy proceeds used to purchase, 225–8
  partnership agreements, 140, 148
  payments by sole proprietors, 71
  personal pension lump sums, 182
Anti-avoidance. *See* TRANSITIONAL PROVISIONS: ANTI-AVOIDANCE
Apportionment between business and private use
  capital allowances, 61
  home used partly for business purposes, 69
Appropriations of profit. *See* PROFIT SHARING
Architects
  service and trading companies, rules on, 157
Assessment to tax, 1
Asset sharing ratio
  capital gains tax, 96, 100–1

Assets
  disposal, 98–9
  divided in kind among partners
    capital gains tax, 99–100
  transfer abroad, 128–30
  transferred to trading companies, 168
Auditing
  companies, carried out through, 157
Automatic accruer
  capital, 224
  inheritance tax, 90–1
Automatic cessation, 267–8
Averaging procedure
  preceding year basis of assessment, 245–51

Bad debts, 62
Balance sheets, projected, 200–1
Balancing charges. *See* CAPITAL ALLOWANCES
Bank facilities, 202
  source of capital, 206
Bank interest
  service companies, 167
Bank overdrafts
  service companies, 166
Barristers
  service and trading companies, rules on, 157
Benefit tests
  anti-avoidance provisions, 39
Bills delivered basis, 73
Boden clauses, 90
Break-even charts, 199, 210
Budgets. *See* FINANCIAL CONTROL: BUDGETS
Buildings
  capital allowances, 67
Business asset relief
  trading companies, 173
Business names
  partnership agreements, 135, 143
  requirements, 2
Business practice changes
  anti-avoidance provisions, 43–4
Business property relief
  service companies, 162
Business relief
  inheritance tax, 92–4
Business trusts, 228
Businesses transferred to companies
  capital gains tax, 109–10
  preceding year basis of assessment, 261
  trading companies
    business asset relief, 173
    capital gains tax

Businesses transferred to companies — *contd*
  trading companies — *contd*
    avoidance, 172–3
    deferral, 168–9
    roll-over relief, 168
    chargeable gains, 169
    consideration wholly in shares, 169
    examples, 171–3
    specimen agreement, 169–71
    stamp duty, 169, 173
    tax implications, ICAEW guidance note, 173–9
Buy and sell agreements
  partnership trust policies, 222

Capital
  financial control, 201–2, 205–7
  partnership agreements, 136, 144
  sources, 205–7
Capital allowances
  balancing charges
    trading receipts, 23
  basis period rules, 25
  buildings, 67
  cars, 66
  connected persons, transfers from, 66
  continuation elections, 270–1
  current year basis, 5, 23–6
  first year allowance, 66
    service companies, 165
  enterprise zones, commercial and industrial buildings allowance, 60
  immediate write-off, 60–1
  initial allowances
    trading expenses, 23
  losses, 19
  plant, 66–7
  preceding year basis of assessment, 251–4
  qualifying expenditure, 65
  Schedule A, 53
  scientific research allowance, 60
  service companies
    cars, 164
    fixtures and fittings, 165
  sole proprietors, 70
  writing down allowances
    cars, 66
    computation, 25–6
    trading expenses, 23
Capital expenditure, 65–7
Capital gains tax
  fees, purchase of blocks of, 71
  funded unapproved retirement benefit schemes, 192
  own life policies cross assigned, 223

Capital gains tax — *contd*
  partnerships, 96–7
    asset sharing ratio, 96
    connected persons, 96
    goodwill written off, 116–23
    hold-over, 109
    ill-health retirement, 111
    indexation allowance, 115–16
    loss claims, 116–17
    profit sharing ratio, 96
    rebasing, 116
    reinvestment relief, 114–15
    retirement relief, 111
      gains qualifying for relief, 112–14
      reinvestment relief, 114
    Revenue statement of practice
      adjustments through accounts, 102–3
      annuities provided by partnerships, 105–6
      assets divided in kind among partners, 99–100
      deferred charges, 101
      disposal of assets, 98–9
      elections under TGCA 1992, 107
      indexation, 101–2
      mergers, 106–7
      nature of asset liable to tax, 97–8
      partnership sharing ratio changes, 100–102
      payment outside accounts, 103–4
      rebasing, 101
      shares acquired in stages, 107
      transfer between persons not at arm's length, 104–5
      transitional arrangements, 107–8
    roll-over relief, 108–9
    transfer of business to company, 109–10
    wasting assets, 108–9
  payment date, 263
  service companies
    property considerations, 164, 165
    share considerations, 162–3
  trading companies
    avoidance, 172–3
    deferral, 168–9
    roll-over relief, 168
Capital taxes. *See* CAPITAL GAINS TAX; INHERITANCE TAX
Captive insurance companies, 218–19
Carry-back election
  post-cessation receipts, 77
Cars
  capital allowances, 66
  expenses, service companies, 167
  fuel, service companies, 164
  insurance, 221

Cars — *contd*
  partnership agreements, 139, 147
  private usage, 66
  service companies
    partners' 163–4
    setting up and operational considerations, 165
Cash basis, 73
  change in basis, 73–4
  double tax charge, 74
  factoring debtors, 74–5
  first three years, 73–4
  mergers, 275
  partnership changes, 267
  post-cessation receipts
    assessment, 76
    carry-back election, 77
    insurance recoveries, 76
    mergers, 275
    notional discontinuance, 76, 77
    sale of business, 77
    Schedule D, Case VI, 75, 76
    stock transfers, 75
    transitional provisions for older taxpayers, 77
    work-in-progress transfers, 75–6
  Revenue policy, 73–4
  sole proprietors, 71
Cash forecasts. *See* FINANCIAL CONTROL: CASH FORECASTS
Cessation, 18
  1998/99, in, 33–4
  change of residence, 126
  corporate partners, 180
  deemed, 28, 126
  mergers, 271
  partnership changes. *See* PARTNERSHIP CHANGES: PRECEDING YEAR BASIS
  preceding year basis of assessment, 239–42
  prior to 6 April 1998, 31–32
  service companies, effects, 160
  terminal loss relief, 22–3
  transitional provisions, 26
CGT. *See* CAPITAL GAINS TAX
Chargeable gains
  trading companies, 169
Charges on income
  preceding year basis of assessment, 262–3
Charging out rates, 202–3, 216
Chartered surveyors
  service and trading companies, rules on, 159
Clients accounts, 60
  partnership agreements, 138, 146

Commencement
  inheritance tax, 90
  mergers, 271–2
  preceding year basis of assessment, 233–6
    change in partners, 241–2
    taxpayer's option, 236–9
Commercial property
  pension schemes, 184–5
Commission
  service companies, 166
Commutation
  occupational pension schemes, 190
Companies. *See* BUSINESSES TRANSFERRED TO COMPANIES; SERVICE COMPANIES; TRADING COMPANIES
Company directors. *See* DIRECTORS
Compensation
  paid
    loss of office, 62
  received, 57–8
Computer systems
  service companies, 168
Connected persons
  anti-avoidance provisions, 38–9, 44–5
  capital gains tax, 96
  inheritance tax, 89
  transfers from, capital allowances, 66
Constructive remittances, 127
Consultancy agreements
  retirement provisions, 185–6
Consultants
  fees, service companies, 167
  occupational pension schemes, 186, 189
Continuation elections, 267–8
  capital allowances, 270–1
  equitable adjustments, 268
  followed by cessation, 268
  indemnities to outgoing partners, 268
  mergers, 271
  partnership agreements, 267, 140–1, 148–9
  preceding year basis of assessment, 242–5
Conventional basis. *See* CASH BASIS
Corporate partners
  foreign partnerships, 127
  members of partnerships, 179–80
  retirement, 268
Corporation tax
  corporate partners, 179–80
  service companies
    marginal relief, 161
    payment, 163
    rates, 160–1
Counselling services for employees, 65

Court decisions
  allowable expenditure, 61–2
Covenants in restraint of trade
  partnership agreements, 141, 149
Creditors
  sources of capital, 206–7
Critical illness insurance, 230
Current assets
  service companies, 165
Current liabilities
  service companies, 166
Current year basis of assessment, 1, 5–6
  accounting date changes, 11–12
    accounting period of less than twelve months, 12–13
    accounting period of more than twelve months, 13–16
    deemed, 14
    partnerships, 18
    second or third year, in, 16–18
    statutory provisions, 12
  capital allowances, 5, 23–6
  cessation, 18
    1998/99, in, 33–4
    deemed, 28
    prior to 6 April 1998, 31–32
    service companies, effects on, 160
    terminal loss relief, 22–3
    transitional provisions, 26
  commencement years, 6–7
  fourth and subsequent years of assessment, 11
  legislation, drafting, 5
  losses, 19
    capital allowances, 19
    carried forward, 19–20
    carry-back, 19, 20
    early years of trade, 20–2
    overlap profits excess on cessation, 18
    second deemed trades, 38
    set-off, 19
    terminal, 22
  overlap periods
    accounting date changes, 12–13
    cessation, 18
    commencement years, 8, 11
  overlap profits
    accounting date changes, 12–13
    cessation, 18
    commencement years, 8, 11
    excess on cessation resulting in loss, 18
  overlap relief, 13, 18, 26
    partners, 34
    transitional, 30
  partnerships' other income
    accounting date changes, 34

Current year basis of assessment — *contd*
  partnerships' other income — *contd*
    commencement, 36–8
    investment income, 34
    overlap on commencement, 34
    overlap relief
      cessation, 34
      set against total income, 38
    overseas income, 34, 54–6
    property income, 34, 51–4
    second deemed trade, 34
    losses, 38
    sundry income, 34, 54–6
    transitional averaging, 34–6
  second year of assessment
    accounting date twelve months or more from commencement, 8–9
    accounting period of less than twelve months, 9–10
    fiscal year accounting 7–8
    no accounting date, 10–11
  third year of assessment, 11
  transitional provisions, 26
    anti-avoidance, 38–42
      accounting changes, 43–4
      benefit tests, 39
      business practice changes, 43–4
      connected party transactions, 38–9
      connected persons, 44–5
      de minimis tests, 39
      interest privatisation, 50–1
      motive tests, 39
      overseas income, 50
      relevant changes, 43–4
      relevant transactions, 44–5
      self-cancelling transactions, 38–9, 44
      transitional overlap, 45–50
    overlap, 29–31
    Schedule A income, 51–4
    transitional averaging, 27–9, 38–42

De minimis tests
  anti-avoidance provisions, 39
Death
  inheritance tax, 91–2
Death in service life cover, 182, 190
Deemed cessation, 28, 126
Deferred charges
  capital gains tax, 101
Demergers, 273
Dentists
  retirement provisions, 188
  service and trading companies, rules on, 157
Depreciation
  service companies, 167

Directors
  fees, 58
    service companies, 166
  lifetime, retirement provisions, 193
  retirement relief, 111
  service companies, occupational pension schemes, 189
  trading companies, occupational pension schemes, 189
Discontinuance. *See* CESSATION
Dissolution
  inheritance tax, 91
  partnership agreements, 141
Doctors
  retirement provisions, 188
  service and trading companies, rules on, 158
Donations
  service companies, 167
Double option agreements
  partnership trust policies, 222
Double tax charge
  change in accounting basis, 74
Double taxation treaties, 125
Drawings
  financial control, 201, 215
  partnership agreements, 137, 145–6
Dual purpose expenditure, 61
Dual residents, 125
Duration
  partnership agreements, 135, 142–3
Duties of partners
  partnership agreements, 138, 147

Earned income, 3–4
Earnings basis, 73
  mergers, 275
Employer's liability insurance, 219–21
Employment
  future partners, 63
  overseas, 130–1
  partners' spouses by service companies, 163
Engineers
  service and trading companies, rules on, 158
Enterprise zones
  commercial and industrial buildings allowance, 60
Entertaining expenses, 65
  service companies, 167
Equitable adjustment
  preceding year basis of assessment, 257
Equity partners, 2–3

Estate agents
   service and trading companies, rules on, 158
***Ex gratia* receipts**, 58
Expenditure
   service companies, 166–7
Expenses
   service companies, 163
   work done abroad, 131
Factoring debtors
   change to cash basis, on, 74–5
Fees
   budgets, 197–8
   cash forecasts, 199–200
   charging out rates, 202–3
   purchase of blocks of, 71
   service companies, 166
Final salary, definitions, 190
Financial control
   bank facilities, 202, 206
   budgets, 197
      break-even charts, 199, 210
      consolidation forms, 198–9, 209
      detail sheet, 208
      fees, 197–8
      productive hours calculation, 208
      revision forms, 199, 211
      salaries, 197
      sales, 197–8
   capital, 201–2
      sources
         bank facilities, 206
         creditors, 206–7
         loans for specific purposes, 207
         partners, 205–6
   cash forecasts, 199
      establishment expenses, 214
      expenses, 200
      fees, 199–200
      projected balance sheets, 200–1
      Projected Source and Application of Funds Statements, 201, 214
      receipts, 211–12
      summaries, 213
   charging out rates, 202–3, 216
   drawings, 201
      schedules, 215
   fees, 197–200, 202–3
   taxation provisions, 206–7
   time recording, 204–5
First year allowance. *See* CAPITAL ALLOWANCES
Fiscal year basis
   Schedule A, 52
Fixed assets
   service companies, 165

Fixtures and fittings
   service companies, 165
Foreign partnerships, 127
Friendly societies, partnership, 185
Funded unapproved retirement benefit schemes (FURBS), 191–3
Furnished lettings
   removed from Schedule D, Case VI to Schedule A, 52
   taxable income, 59, 60

General expenses
   service companies, 167
Gifts
   income forgone by, 58
   made, 65
      inheritance tax, 92
Goodwill
   definition, 117
   inheritance tax, 90
   partnership agreements, 136, 144–5
   purchase of, 71
   written off, capital gains tax, 116–23
Group life cover, 183

Hold-over
   capital gains tax, 109
Home used partly for business purposes, 69

Ill-health retirement
   capital gains tax, 111
Income
   service companies, 166
Incorporation. *See* BUSINESSES TRANSFERRED TO COMPANIES
Indemnities
   outgoing partners, to, 268
Indexation
   capital gains tax, 101–2, 115–16
Individual pension arrangements (IPA), 189
Inheritance tax
   connected persons, 89
   individuals' own life policies, 224
   partnership trust policies, 222
   partnerships, 89
      annuities, 90, 91
      automatic accruer, 90–1
      Boden clauses, 90
      business relief, 92–4
      commencement, 90
      death, 91–2
      dissolution, 91
      exemptions and reliefs, 92–4
      gifts made, 92

Inheritance tax — *contd*
  partnerships — *contd*
    goodwill, 90
    new partners, introduction of, 90
    partners' property used by firm, 92
    retirement, 91
    super profits valuation basis, 94–6
    time and attention clauses, 90
    total capitalisation valuation basis, 94–6
    transfer of interests, 90–1
    valuation of interests, 94
  payment by instalments, 94
  service companies, 162
  trusts, death benefits written in, 188
  variable partner trust life policies, 223
Initial allowances. *See* CAPITAL ALLOWANCES
Inland Revenue investigation settlements, 188
Insurance
  accident, 228–9
  captive insurance companies, 218–19
  car, 221
  critical illness, 230
  employer's liability, 219–21
  key person, 228–9
  medical, 229
  permanent health, 229–30
  product liability, 218
  service companies, 167
  See also LIFE ASSURANCE; PROFESSIONAL INDEMNITY INSURANCE
Insurance brokers
  service and trading companies, rules on, 158
Insurance provisions
  partnership agreements, 140, 148
Insurance recoveries
  post-cessation receipts, 76
Interest
  overdue tax, on, 264
  paid, 63–4
    loans from partners, 65
    partnership agreements, 136, 144
    privatisation
      anti-avoidance provisions, 50–1
  received, 54
    clients' deposits, 59–60
    deposits, 59
    offshore banks, 59
    UK banks, 59
Investment income, 34, 54–6
  overlap relief, 38

Investments
  sale of, 57
IPA (individual pension arrangements), 189

Joint life policies, 222
  split, 223
Joint ownership of property, 2
Joint ventures
  taxed as partnerships, 1

Key person insurance, 228–9

Land
  annual equivalent of premiums on, 65
  sale of, 57
Leases
  partnership agreements, 136, 143–4
  premiums on, 64
  service companies, 165
Legacies
  partnership agreements, 137
Legal expenses, 64
Letters of wishes, 190
Life assurance, 221
  individuals' own policies, 223–5
  joint life policies, 222
    split, 223
  life of another policies, 222
  own life policies cross assigned, 223
  taxation effects summary, 226–7
  trust policies, 221–2
  type of policies, 225
  variable partner trust policies, 223
Lifetime directors
  retirement provisions, 193
Limited partners, 3
  partnership agreements, 142
Limited partnerships
  losses, 258
Loans
  personal pension plans, from, 187
  sources of capital, 207
Loss claims
  capital gains tax, 116–17
Loss relief
  partners changing residence, 127
Losses, 19
  capital allowances, 19
  carried forward, 19–20
  carry-back, 19, 20
  early years of trade, 20–2
    sole proprietors, 70
  overlap profits excess on cessation, 18
  preceding year basis of assessment, 254–7
    limited partnerships, 258

Losses — *contd*
preceding year basis of assessment — *contd*
opening years, in, 259–61
terminal, 258–9
transfers to companies, 261
Schedule A, 53
second deemed trades, 38
set-off, 19
sharing, 2
terminal, 22

Marginal relief
service companies, 161
Medical insurance, 229
Mergers
accounting date changes, 85–7
capital gains tax, 106–7
cash basis, 275
cessation, 271
commencement provisions, 271
continuation elections, 271
differences in accounting basis, 275
earning basis, 275
post cessation receipts, 275
prior to 6 April 1997, 271–2
Motive tests
anti-avoidance provisions, 39
Motor cars. *See* CARS
Motor expenses
service companies, 167
See also CARS

National Savings certificates
retirement provisions, 195
Negative covenants
partnership agreements, 138–9
Non–residents
interest payable to, 63
partners, 6, 127
trading in UK, 125–6
Notional discontinuance
post cessation receipts, 76, 77

Occupational pension schemes
commutation, 190
consultants, 186, 189
death in service life cover, 190
final salary, definitions, 190
employees' contributions, 189
employers' contributions, 189
increases after retirement, 190
individual pension arrangements (IPA), 189
letters of wishes, 190
limits on benefits, 189

Occupational pension schemes — *contd*
partners ineligible, 189
retirement age, 191
service companies, 163
directors or employees, 189
spouses of partners, 163, 189
trading companies, 168
directors or employees, 189
widows' or widowers' pensions, 189–90
Ordinary principles of commercial accountancy
court decisions, basis of, 61–2
Outgoing partners
partnership agreements, 140, 148
Overlap
transitional provisions, 29–31
Overlap periods
accounting date changes, 12–13
cessation, 18
commencement years, 8, 11
Overlap profits
accounting date changes, 12–13
cessation, 18
commencement years, 8, 11
excess on cessation resulting in loss, 18
Overlap relief, 13, 18, 26
partners, 34
partnership investment income, 38
retirement windfalls, 81
transitional, 30
Overseas activities
change of residence, 126–7
constructive remittances, 127
corporate partners, 127
double taxation treaties, 125
employment, 130–1
expenses in connection with work done abroad, 131
foreign partnerships, 127
loss relief, 127
non-resident partners, 127
non-residents trading in UK, 125–6
remittances, 127–8
transfer of assets abroad, 128–30
UK partnerships with foreign element, 125–6
Overseas income
anti-avoidance provisions, 50

Partners
individual treatment, 6
interest on loans from, 65
interest paid personally by, 63–4
new, inheritance tax, 90
non-resident, 6, 127
property used by firm, inheritance tax, 92

Partners — *contd*
rent paid to, 65
service companies shareholdings, 162–3
sources of capital, 205–6
tax liabilities, responsible for payment, 6
taxable income allocated among, 5
See also CORPORATE PARTNERS
Partnership admission, 152–5
Partnership agreements, 1–2
accountants, 138, 146
accounts, 138, 146
annuities, 140, 148
bankers, 138, 146–7
business, 135, 142
capital, 136, 144
cars, 139, 147
clients accounts, 138, 146
continuation elections, 79, 140–1, 148–9
covenants in restraint of trade, 141, 149
dissolution, 141
drawings, 137, 145–6
duration, 135, 142–3
duties of partners, 138, 147
goodwill, 136, 144–5
insurance provisions, 140, 148
interest, 136, 144
leases, 136, 143–4
legacies, 137
limited partners, 142
model agreement, 135–41
 commentary, 142–9
name, 135, 143
negative covenants, 138–9
outgoing partners, 140, 148
parties, 135, 142
partnership admission, 152–5
partnership retirement, 155
pensions, 140, 148
place of business, 136, 143–4
profit sharing, 136, 145, 149–50
 points system, 150–2
salaries, 137, 146
spouses of partners as partners, 142
tenancy agreements, 136, 143–4
trustees as partners, 142
Partnership changes
preceding year basis
 after 19 March 1985, 242–5
 capital allowances on continuation, 270–1
 cash basis, 267
 cessation
  automatic, 267–8
  continuation elections followed by, 268
  corporate partner retirement, 268

Partnership changes — *contd*
preceding year basis — *contd*
 engineering, 268–9
 equitable adjustments, 269
 mergers, 271
 retirement windfalls, 269–70
commencement provisions
 mergers, 271–2
continuation elections, 242–5, 267–8
 capital allowances, 270–1
 equitable adjustments, 268
 followed by cessation, 268
 indemnities to outgoing partners, 268
 mergers, 271–2
corporate partner retirement, 268
demergers, 273
mergers prior to 6 April 1997, 271–2
 accounting basis differences, 275
 accounting date changes, 273–5
 post–cessation receipts, 275
provisional continuation elections, 267–8
sole practitioners taking in partners, 267
Partnership friendly societies, 185
Partnership retirement, 155
Partnership returns, 5, 56
Partnership sharing ratio changes
capital gains tax, 100–102
Partnership statements, 5, 56
Partnerships
accounting date changes, 18
agreements. *See* PARTNERSHIP AGREEMENTS
assessment to tax, 1
capital gains tax. *See* CAPITAL GAINS TAX
changes. *See* PARTNERSHIP CHANGES
corporate partners in, 179–80
definition, 1, 89
earned income, 3–4
equity partners, 2–3
existence for tax purposes, 1–2
incorporation. *See* BUSINESSES TRANSFERRED TO COMPANIES; TRADING COMPANIES
inheritance tax. *See* INHERITANCE TAX
joint ventures taxed as, 1
limited partners, 3
losses
 sharing, 2
nature, 1–4
non-resident partners, 6
other income
 accounting date changes, 34
 commencement, 36–8
 investment income, 34

Partnerships — *contd*
  other income — *contd*
    overlap on commencement, 34
    overlap relief
      cessation, 34
      set against total income, 38
    overseas income, 34, 54–6
    property income, 34, 51–4
    second deemed trade, 34
      losses, 38
    sundry income, 34, 54–6
    transitional averaging, 34–6
  overseas activities. *See* OVERSEAS ACTIVITIES
  partners' meetings, 2
  profits
    sharing, 2
  salaried partners, 2–3
  Scottish. *See* SCOTLAND: PARTNERSHIPS
  service companies shareholdings, 161–2
Patent agents
  service and trading companies, rules on, 159
Patent expenses, 65
Pension scheme contributions, 63
Pensioneer trustees, 194
Pensions
  partnership agreements, 140, 148
  See also RETIREMENT: PROVISION FOR
Permanent health insurance, 229–30
Personal equity plans (PEP)
  retirement provisions, 195
Personal pension plans (PPP), 181–3
  capital withdrawals paid into, 224
  contribution effects on retirement annuity policies, 184
  costs, 187
  Inland Revenue investigation settlements, 188
  investment funds, 188
  loans, 187
  transfers, 188
  waiver of premiums, 188–9
Petty cash
  service companies, 167
Place of business
  partnership agreements, 136, 143–4
Plant
  nature for capital allowances purposes, 66–7
Post-cessation receipts
  cash basis. *See* CASH BASIS: POST-CESSATION RECEIPTS
  mergers, 275
PPP. *See* PERSONAL PENSION PLANS
Pre-loading expenses, 65

Preceding year basis of assessment, 1, 231
  accounting date changes, 245
    averaging procedure, 245–51
    Revenue leaflet IR26, 247–8
  capital allowances, 251–4
  cessation, 239–42
    service companies, effects on, 160
  charges on income, 262–3
  commencement, 233–6
    change in partners, 241–2
    taxpayer's option, 236–9
  equitable adjustment, 257
  interest on overdue tax, 264
  losses, 19, 254–7
    limited partnerships, 258
    opening years, in, 259–61
    terminal, 258–9
    transfers to companies, 261
  partnership changes. *See* PARTNERSHIP CHANGES: PRECEDING YEAR BASIS
  payment of tax, 263–5
  profit apportionment, 231–3
  transitional provisions, 26
Premiums on leases, 64
Product liability insurance, 218
Professional indemnity insurance, 217–18
  captive insurance companies, 218–19
  estate agents, 158
  service companies, 163, 167
Professional rules
  service and trading companies, on, 157–9
Profit and loss account items
  service companies, 166–7
Profit sharing, 2, 65
  partnership agreements, 136, 145, 149–50
    points system, 150–2
  preceding year basis of assessment, 231–3
  ratio
    capital gains tax, 96, 100–1
Projected balance sheets, 200–1
Projected Source and Application of Funds Statements, 201, 214
Property
  joint ownership, 2
  self-invested personal pensions, 184–5
  service companies. *See* SERVICE COMPANIES: PROPERTY
Property expenses
  service companies, 166
Provisional continuation elections, 267–8
Provisions, 62, 64

Quantity surveyors
service and trading companies, rules on, 159

RAP (retirement annuity policies), 183–4
Rebasing
capital gains tax, 101, 116
Redundancy payments, 62
Reinvestment relief
capital gains tax, 114–15
Remittance basis, 127–8
change of residence, 126–7
constructive remittances, 127
Rent, 64
partners, to, 65
service companies, 164
sub-let premises, from, 59
Repairs, 64
Residence
change of, 126–7
Retirement
inheritance tax, 91
partner not replaced, 155
provision for
  alternative to pension schemes, 194–5
  commercial property, 184–5
  consultancy agreements, 185–6
  death in service cover, 182
  dentists, 188
  doctors, 188
  group life cover, 183
  lifetime directors, 193
  National Savings certificates, 195
  occupational pension schemes. *See* OCCUPTIONAL PENSION SCHEMES
  partnership friendly societies, 185
  pensions from the firm, 186–7
  personal equity plans (PEP), 195
  personal pension plans. *See* PERSONAL PENSION PLANS
  retirement annuity policies (RAP), 183–4
  self-administered pension schemes, 193–4
  self-invested personal pensions, 184–5
  tax exempt special savings schemes (TESSA), 195
  trust, death in service cover written in, 182, 188
  unapproved retirement benefit schemes
    background, 191
    funded (FURBS), 191–2
    benefits, 192–3

Retirement — *contd*
provision for — *contd*
    employer contributions, 192
    fund, 192
    taxation, 192–3
    unfunded, 191
relief, capital gains tax, 110, 114
windfalls, 269–70
Retirement annuity policies (RAP), 183–4
Revenue statement of practice
capital gains tax. *See* CAPITAL GAINS TAX: PARTNERSHIPS
Roll-over relief
capital gains tax, 108–9
trading companies, 168
Royalties, 61

Salaried partners, 2–3
Salaries, 62–3
budgets, 197
partnership agreements, 137, 146
Sale of business
post cessation receipts, 77
Sales
budgets, 197–8
Sales at less than market value
income forgone by, 58–9
Sales ledger systems
service companies, 168
Schedule A
capital allowances, 53
fiscal year basis, 52
furnished lettings
  removal from Schedule D, Case VI, 52
  taxable income, 59
losses, 53
partnership property income, 34, 51–2
transitional rules, 52–4
Schedule D
Cases I and II, 1
Case III
  clients' deposit interest, 59
  deposit interest, 59
  partnership investment income, 34, 54–6
Case IV
  partnership investment income, 34, 54–6
Case V
  constructive remittances, 127
  foreign partnerships, 127
  offshore deposit interest, 59
  overseas income, transitional provisions, 50

Schedule D — *contd*
  Case V — *contd*
    partnership investment income, 34, 54–6
    partnership overseas income, 34
    remittance basis, 127
  Case VI
    furnished lettings
      removal to Schedule A, 52
      taxable income, 60
    partnership income, 34
    post cessation receipts, 75, 76
    payment of tax, 263

Schedule E
  cars, benefit in kind, 164
  consultancy agreements, 186
  overseas employments, 130–1
  service company directors and employees, 163

Scientific research allowance, 60

Scotland
  partnerships
    nature, 1, 89
    VAT registration, 133, 143

Self-administered pension schemes, 193–4

Self-assessment, 5, 207

Self-cancelling transactions
  anti-avoidance provisions, 38–9, 44

Self-invested personal pensions, 184–5

Semi-cash accounting, 73

Service companies
  bank overdrafts, 165
  car fuel, 164
  cars
    partners', 163–4
    setting up and operational considerations, 165
  cessation, 160
  charges, 160, 164
  computer systems, 167–8
  current assets, 165
  current liabilities, 165
  employment of partners' spouses, 163
  expenses, 163–4
  fixed assets, 165
  fixtures and fittings, 165
  functions, 159
  occupational pension schemes, 163
  operation and setting up, 165–8
  professional indemnity insurance, 163, 167
  professional rules
    accountants, 157
    actuaries, 157
    architects, 157

Service companies — *contd*
  professional rules — *contd*
    barristers, 157
    chartered surveyors, 159
    dentists, 157
    doctors, 158
    engineers, 158
    estate agents, 158
    insurance brokers, 158
    patent agents, 159
    quantity surveyors, 159
    solicitors, 159
  profit and loss account items
    bank interest, 167
    car expenses, 167
    commission, 166
    consultants' fees, 167
    depreciation, 167
    directors' fees, 166
    entertaining, 167
    expenditure, 166–7
    fees, 166
    general expenses, 166–7
    income, 166
    insurance, 167
    motor expenses, 167
    petty cash, 167
    property expenses, 166
    staff expenditure, 166
    subscriptions and donations, 166
    travelling expenses, 167
    widows of former partners, payments to, 167
  property
    capital gains tax considerations, 164, 165
    leases, 165
    ownership, 164, 165
    rent, 164
    service charge, 164
    setting up and operational considerations, 165
  remuneration, 163
  sales ledger systems, 168
  setting up and operation, 165–8
  shares
    capital gains tax considerations, 162–3
    inheritance tax considerations, 162
    partners, held by, 162–3
    partners' spouses, held by, 161
    partnership, held by, 161–2
    revaluation, 162
  structure, 168
  tax
    payment, 163

Service companies — *contd*
  tax — *contd*
    rates, 160–1
    setting up and operational
      considerations, 166
    unlimited company, as, 168
    value added tax
      service charges to partnership, on, 164
    work-in-progress, 168
Shared expenses, 71
Shares
  service companies, in. *See* SERVICE COMPANIES: SHARES
Shipbrokers
  trading companies, rules on, 159
Sole proprietors
  annuity payments, 71
  blocks of fees, purchase of, 71
  capital allowances, 70
  cash basis, 71
  continuing former partnerships, 242, 267
  goodwill, purchase of, 71
  home used partly for business purposes, 69
  losses on commencement, 70
  shared expenses, 71
  specialist assistance, 71
  starting up, 69
  taking in partners, 79, 242
  wife's salary, 69–70
  work-in-progress, purchase of, 71
Solicitors
  clients' accounts, 60
  service and trading companies, rules on, 159
Source and Application of Funds Statements, Projected, 201, 214
Specialist assistance, 71
Split joint life policies, 223
Spouses of partners
  occupational pension schemes, 163, 189
  partners, as, 142
  service companies shareholdings, 161
Staff
  entertaining of, 65
Staff expenditure
  service companies, 166
Stamp duty, 134
  transfer of businesses to trading companies, 169, 173
Stock. *See* TRADING STOCK
Subscriptions
  service companies, 167
Super profits valuation basis, 94–6

Surveyors
  service and trading companies, rules on, 159
Tax
  deferral, 60–1
  funded unapproved retirement benefit schemes, 192–3
  partnership insurance effects summary, 226–7
  payment dates, 263–5
  provisions, 206–7
  service companies
    payment, 163
    rates, 160–1
    setting up and operational considerations, 166
  shelter, 60–1
  transfer of businesses trading companies, ICAEW guidance note, 173–9
  See also CAPITAL GAINS TAX; CORPORATION TAX; INHERITANCE TAX; SCHEDULE A; SCHEDULE D; SCHEDULE E
Tax exempt special savings schemes (TESSA), 195
Taxable income
  allowable expenditure. *See* ALLOWABLE EXPENDITURE
  compensation, 57–8
  directors' fees, 58
  ex gratia receipts, 58
  furnished lettings, 59, 60
  gifts, income forgone by, 58
  interest
    clients' deposits, 59–60
    deposits, 59
    offshore banks, 59
    UK banks, 59
  investments, sale of, 57
  land, sale of, 57
  rent from sub-let premises, 59
  sales at less than market value, income forgone by, 58
  tax deferral, 60–1
  tax shelter, 60–1
Technical education payments, 63
Tenancy agreements
  partnership agreements, 136, 143–4
Terminal losses, 22
  preceding year basis of assessment, 258–9
TESSA (tax exempt special savings schemes), 195
Time and attention clauses, 90
Time recording, 204–5

Total capitalisation valuation basis, 94–6
Trading companies
  assets transferred to, 168
  associated activities, for, 168
  businesses transferred to. *See* BUSINESSES TRANSFERRED TO COMPANIES: TRADING COMPANIES
  occupational pension funds, 168
  professional rules
    accountants' auditing work, 157
    actuaries, 157
    architects, 157
    chartered surveyors, 159
    doctors, 158
    engineers, 158
    estate agents, 158
    insurance brokers, 159
    patent agents, 159
    quantity surveyors, 159
    shipbrokers, 159
Trading stock
  definition, 44
  transfers at cessation, 75
Transfer of business to company. *See* BUSINESSES TRANSFERRED TO COMPANIES
Transfer of interests
  inheritance tax, 90–1
Transitional averaging, 27–9, 38–42
Transitional overlap, 29–31
  anti-avoidance provisions, 45–50
Transitional overlap relief, 30
Transitional provisions, 26
  anti-avoidance, 38–42
    accounting changes, 43–4
    benefit tests, 39
    business practice changes, 43–4
    connected party transactions, 38–9
    connected persons, 44–5
    de minimis tests, 39
    interest privatisation, 50–1
    motive tests, 39
    overseas income, 50
    relevant changes, 43–4
    relevant transactions, 44–5
    self-cancelling transactions, 38–9, 44
    transitional overlap, 45–50
  overlap, 29–31

Transitional provisions — *contd*
  Schedule A income, 51–4
  transitional averaging, 27–9, 38–42
Travelling expenses, 65
  service companies, 167
Trust life policies, 221–2
Trustees as partners, 142
Trusts
  death in service cover written in, 182, 188

Unapproved retirement benefit schemes
  background, 191
  funded (FURBS), 191–2
    benefits, 192–3
    employer contributions, 192
    fund, 192
    taxation, 192–3
  unfunded, 191
Unfunded unapproved retirement benefit schemes, 191
Unlimited companies
  service companies as, 168

Valuation of interests
  inheritance tax, 94
Value added tax, 133–4, 143
  consultancies, 186
  service companies' charges to partnerships, 164
Variable partner trust life policies, 223

Wages, 62–3
Waiver of premiums
  personal pension plans, 188–9
Wasting assets
  capital gains tax, 108–9
Widows of former partners, payments to
  service companies, 167
Widows' or widowers' pensions
  occupational pension schemes, 189–90
Wife's salary, 69–70
Work-in-progress
  definition, 44
  purchase of, 71
  service companies, 168
  transfers, post-cessation receipts, 75–6
Writing down allowances. *See* CAPITAL ALLOWANCES